CW00971370

# REMEMBER THE LADIES

*Overleaf:*

ABIGAIL ADAMS: *In March, 1776, she wrote to her husband, John: "Remember the Ladies, and be more generous and favorable to them than your ancestors. Do not put such unlimited power into the hands of the Husbands. Remember all Men would be tyrants if they could. If particular care and attention is not paid to the Ladies, we are determined to foment a Rebellion, and will not hold ourselves bound by any Laws in which we have no voice, or Representation." And John Adams's response? "As to your extraordinary code of laws," he wrote, "I cannot but laugh."*

LIBRARY OF CONGRESS

# REMEMBER THE LADIES

## A Woman's Book of Days

Kirstin Olsen

THE MAIN STREET PRESS • PITTSTOWN, NEW JERSEY

*For Erica,*
*my sister by birth*
*and by conviction*

*and*

*for Eric,*
*who wanted me*
*to dedicate it*
*to Spiny Norman.*

First edition

Copyright © 1988 by Kirstin Olsen

All rights reserved. No part of this book may be reproduced in any form except by a newspaper or magazine reviewer who wishes to quote brief passages in connection with a review.

Published by The Main Street Press
William Case House
Pittstown, New Jersey 08867

Published simultaneously in Canada by
McGraw-Hill Ryerson Ltd.
330 Progress Avenue
Scarborough, Ontario M1P 2Z5

Designed by Ronald R. Misiur

Printed in the United States of America

Library of Congress Cataloging-in-Publication Data

Olsen, Kirstin.
    Remember the ladies: a woman's book of days.

    Bibliography: p.
    1. Women—Biography. 2. Birthday books.
I. Title.
CT3202.O45 1988      920.72      88-13413
ISBN 1-55562-070-1

# CONTENTS

# INTRODUCTION

FEMINISM, LIKE SEXISM, has been with us for a long time. If this book has piqued your interest, you probably already know this. Like all ideologies, both are kept alive by faithful partisans. None of the battles feminists have waged are over; they can still be won or lost through diligence or negligence.

*Remember the Ladies* was conceived to illustrate a point that women through the ages have fought to have recognized—that, like men, they can learn, lead, achieve, and accomplish. This book is a celebration of the lives of almost four hundred specific women—many obscure, some well-known—and it is a tribute to the truth that women are people whose capabilities for good or ill are limitless. You will find plenty of saints, philanthropists, and other equally laudable women in these pages, but I confess to a particular affection for bandits, scoundrels, and women of ill repute, so they too are here in abundance.

By organizing *Remember the Ladies* as a book of days—a day-by-day calendar commemorating dates of birth and death—a reader can find, perhaps, a new heroine for each day of the year, or discover such heretofore unknown colorful women as the pirate Anne Bonny or the "queen of the demimonde," Lulu White.

I can offer no apologies or excuses for the subjective process of selecting the women included in *Remember the Ladies,* but I *am* sorry if I've left out any of your favorites. It's impossible to be entirely fair when trying to choose only a few hundred examples of half the human race—especially when most of them had to be considerate enough to die or be born on specific dates.

For some dates there were many choices; for others there were none. Compounding the problem of choosing subjects for this book was the fact that many women lived before the time when dates of birth and death were regularly recorded. What's more, some women chose to obscure their dates of birth, while others sank into historical oblivion simply because of their sex and vanished from conventional texts. I felt it impossible to exclude these fascinating, powerful women because we do not know their dates of birth. Such women have therefore been assigned arbitrarily to dates on which no one else of greater significance had been born or died. The lack of verification for the missing dates has been noted in every case.

The elusive nature of the facts about so many of the women remembered in these pages underscores a theme common to most of the stories presented here. Despite the disparity in time, place, class, race, and circumstance, these women share many of the same problems.

For example, although this is precisely what it claims to be—a *women's* book of days—you'll find men's shadows on every page. To begin with, there is the issue of names. A good friend of mine once complained that trying to find old friends is nearly impossible. Even if she knows in what city they live, if she doesn't know their *married* names, she's lost. Even today, when so many women keep their birth names at marriage or choose alternatives to marriage, many others consider it a matter of course to adopt a married surname—even when it causes them great inconvenience.

When I undertook the research for this book, the problem of names surfaced constantly. For example, to gather information about a woman like Annie Winifred Ellerman, the companion of American poet Hilda Doolittle, I had to look under the names Annie Winifred Ellerman (her birth name), Winifred Ellerman (the name by which she was known in youth), Winifred McAlmon (her married name), Winifred MacPherson (her second married name), and Bryher (her pseudonym), often only to find she wasn't included in whatever book I happened to be perusing because she wasn't considered important enough. To illustrate this confusion of identities which most women still accept as part of life, I have listed the birth names of the women in this book whenever possible.

Men appear in this book in many other ways as well. It is nearly impossible to read a biography of a notable woman, however brief, without coming across a reference to marriage, even if the woman in question remained single all her life. In most eras, whether or not a woman married, and who she married, were far from trivial concerns. This is how her options were determined, and such designations defined how she would be treated by everyone she met. On the other hand, biographies of men, especially short profiles in reference works, frequently ignore the question of marriage altogether. Marriage, unless it had unusual consequences, was for men much like hiring a housekeeper. No biographer with limited space would waste time saying that Disraeli or Lincoln hired a cook unless the cook involved him in a scandal, helped substantially with her employer's career, had some drastic effect on her employer's finances, or was the object of her employer's passionate affection. Similarly, wives are only included for such reasons, while husbands loom large in biographies of women. After all, *anything* a married woman did had to be done in spite of her husband's opinions or with his express permission. Men rarely suffered from similar contraints.

So men—fathers, husbands, brothers, and authority figures of all kinds—are ever-present in this book. If they were not, many of these women's actions would seem incomprehensible.

It is my sincere hope that each of you who reads this book, whether you begin with your own birthday and skip randomly through the pages, or you start at January 1 and read the book throughout, will find something new—women whose lives you'd never known about, a bit more about some you already know—and in so doing will understand how the collective history of individual women is an inspiration for each of us.

Kirstin Olsen
May 1988

SPECIAL THANKS should go to a number of people who were instrumental in shaping this book. I am indebted to Martin Greif and Beth Kalet of The Main Street Press for their patience, advice, and encouragement; to Erica and Joe, for help with research; to Sam Daniel of the Library of Congress, for his generous assistance; to Moana, for typing at the last minute; to Brian O., Brian E., Nancy, Dan, Dave, Linda, Holly, Staci, Lisa, and Leo, for listening to endless stories and helping to choose the best ones; to Laura, Geraldine, and Goodyear, for opening my eyes; and to Eric, for everything.

# REMEMBER
# THE LADIES

ALICE PAUL: *Picketing the White House for woman suffrage during World War I, she dismayed many who thought that in wartime other concerns should be put aside. Paul disagreed: "Suffrage comes before war."*

LIBRARY OF CONGRESS

## 1

**MARIA EDGEWORTH,** *born in Black Bourton, Oxfordshire, England, 1767.* Ah, yes, the bad old days—when men were men, women were girls, and girls never wrote books. Well, almost never. Maria Edgeworth managed that most difficult of feats in the early days, when women were just beginning to make themselves a real presence in the literary world. She managed to have a successful career as an author, without being stigmatized as an immoral woman. Writing was dangerous business. It involved the handling of words and ideas, and a woman who played with such toys was bound to become tainted. Few well-educated women could overcome the suspicion with which they were viewed, especially if they wrote, and above all if they did not let their works remain absolutely anonymous.

Edgeworth avoided these pitfalls. She was almost universally admired rather than condemned for her productions, which included translations, treatises on education, novels, plays for children, and a defense of education for women. To be sure, there were some critics. Some readers felt, for example, that translation was a thoroughly suspect occupation for a woman, and novels had such a bad reputation at the time as the corrupters of young girls' minds that Edgeworth published her first novel, *Castle Rackrent,* anonymously. But she made a good living from her writing. In her old age she was made an honorary member of the Royal Irish Academy. It is said that Sir Walter Scott modeled his work on hers. When she died, a London obituary praised her as "a woman of singular intellectual acquirements."

Such acceptance, of course, came at a price. Edgeworth had to go to extraordinary lengths to prove she was pure of heart, and she had to make sacrifices which would not have been asked of a man. She was the second of twenty-one children, and as soon as she was finished with school she was enlisted to educate her younger siblings. She also helped to run her father's estate and ministered to him all his life. She even gave him the credit—or perhaps the blame—for her career. She insisted that she began writing "to please my father" and "to please him I continued." Edgeworth never showed much interest in marriage; when, in 1802, a Swedish officer named Edelcrantz proposed to her, she refused on the grounds that she had to care for her father. But she was not escaping the lordship of a husband, merely clinging to the lordship of her father. When he died in 1817, she grieved deeply and published almost nothing afterward—except, of course, *his* memoirs.

## 2

**HARRIOT KEZIA HUNT,** *dies at 69 in Boston, Massachusetts, 1875.* Just because women were kept out of the medical profession for many years doesn't mean that they didn't practice medicine. Harriot Hunt is the most famous of the female "irregular" practicioners, who couldn't or wouldn't get a medical degree but who offered remedies of a sort. Men as well as women performed these sorts of services, and in a time when the medical profession was loosely organized and when medical schools often provided minimal information, an irregular practicioner might be as handy and as skillful as a "real" doctor.

Hunt was a former schoolteacher who had become interested in healing when her sister Sarah fell ill. Together the two women studied anatomy and physiology in order to effect a cure, and when that was accomplished they opened a medical practice. Within a few years, Sarah married and left the business, but Harriot remained, trying to expand her education by reading extensively and by applying repeatedly to Harvard's medical school. After several direct appeals to the school's dean, Oliver Wendell Holmes, she was finally admitted in 1850. However, she never got to attend her first class. Appalled at the "sacrifice of her modesty," Harvard students rioted, and she was forced to withdraw.

Harriot Hunt received an honorary M.D. from the Female Medical College of Pennsylvania in 1853, but after her experience with Harvard she never seemed to miss society's seal of approval. She gave lectures on medicine and hygiene (often for no charge), urged the entry of women into the medical profession as the surest way to preserve the modesty of female patients, and advocated higher education for women and payment for housework and child-rearing. A rebel in almost every facet of her life, she was a staunch feminist and abolitionist, and, for twenty years, she registered a formal "taxation without representation" protest when she paid her taxes. In her clinical work, she rejected the established practice of dosing patients heavily with harsh medications, substituting mild remedies, proper diet and exercise, rest, and good hygiene in place of drugs. Not surprisingly, she was especially adept at handling cases of psychosomatic illness, and she helped many patients to change their health by changing their lives.

# 3

**LUCRETIA MOTT,** *born Lucretia Coffin in Nantucket, Massachusetts, 1793.* In 1850, Congress passed the Fugitive Slave Law, mandating that an escaped slave was no longer safe upon reaching a free state and imposing penalties for those who helped runaways. In outrage, a Philadelphia Quaker named Lucretia Mott made her home a stop on the Underground Railroad.

It was not her first act of defiance, nor was it her last. In 1838 her anti-slavery work was so unpopular that an angry mob stormed her house. In 1840, she attended the World's Anti-Slavery Convention in London, but she, along with every other woman there, was rejected as a delegate. Angry but not discouraged, she spent her time during the convention befriending another rejected delegate, young Elizabeth Cady Stanton. The two women discovered they had much in common and pledged to work together on behalf of their sex. Eight years later, they organized the world's first women's rights convention.

Mott was always ready to defend her beliefs, particularly if they met with disfavor. Even after the Civil War, when most abolitionists con-

LUCRETIA MOTT: *Her face is a little forbidding, but not her heart.*

sidered their work at an end, she campaigned for the rights of freed slaves. Eventually she even grew bold enough to attack clergymen who opposed women's rights. "The pulpit has been prostituted," she charged, "the Bible has been ill-used." Never resting, she spent her life working for religious toleration and equal rights for all.

# 4

**EKATERINA DASHKOVA,** *dies at 66 in Moscow, Russia, 1810.* When Dashkova died, she had two hundred servants and three thousand serfs, yet she was entirely alone. She had been abandoned, forgotten, or ignored by almost everyone who had known her, and almost no one attended her funeral. Yet for many years she had been one of the most powerful women in Russia, second only to Empress Catherine II herself.

She was born Ekaterina Romonovna Vorontsova in 1743, and she

could have opted for the lavish, easy, monotonous life of a great lady. Her family was powerful and distinguished; her older sister, Elizabeth, was the mistress of the future tsar; she herself had married well, to guards officer Prince Mikhail Dashkov, at the perfectly respectable age of sixteen. But Dashkova had two interests that were inconsistent with the life of a leisured Russian noblewoman: power and knowledge. She satisfied the latter by reading voraciously, learning Latin and French, and ac-

quiring a nine-hundred-volume library by the time of her marriage. She satisfied the former by cultivating a friendship with the future tsarina, Catherine.

It was a mutually beneficial relationship. Dashkova found Catherine overwhelming and inspiring; as she wrote later, the future tsar's wife "forthwith captured my heart and mind and inspired me with enthusiastic devotion." On Catherine's side, the interest was entirely political. She had little personal interest in this young intellectual who refused, in a time of suffocating face powder and bright circles of rouge, to wear makeup. However, Dashkova was a member of a powerful family. Through her older relatives, she had contacts with the Empress Elizabeth, aunt of the future tsar. Through her sister Elizabeth, she had contact with Catherine's increasingly estranged husband. And through her husband, Prince Dashkov, she had contacts in the guards. Catherine used Dashkova as a sort of early-warning signal of impending trouble.

Dashkova's help turned out to be of some value when, in 1762, Catherine deposed her husband, Tsar Peter III, and took control of the Russian government. Now that Dashkova had served Catherine's purpose, however, Dashkova's foibles and hunger for power were less acceptable, and the friendship between the two women cooled—a situation hastened by Catherine's discovery that her lover Ivan Rimsky-Korsakov was sleeping with Dashkova. Dashkova spent a few years abroad, where she was a social success. British author Horace Walpole called her "extraordinarily frank and easy . . . very quick and very animated." Denis Diderot, the French writer and encyclopedist, thought her "by no means pretty," but noted that "the general effect of her features is one of character; she is serious-minded, has an easy command of our language, does not say all that she knows and thinks, but what she does say has the ring of truth about it and she says it simply and definitely."

LIBRARY OF CONGRESS

In 1771, she returned to Russia; Catherine's disapproval had faded, and she presented Dashkova with seventy thousand rubles, which Dashkova then lent to her father at hefty interest. She managed to stay in the Empress's good graces for many years, and in 1783 she was made the director of the new Russian Academy of Sciences and the first president of the Russian Academy. Unfortunately, these distinctions proved to be the cause of her final downfall. In 1794 she permitted the publication of a play which Catherine felt was too critical of the government. Dashkova's house was searched and ransacked, and all copies of the play were burned. Dashkova was scolded and banished to the country, and in 1796, when Catherine died, Dashkova was stripped of all her offices by the new tsar. She spent the remaining years of her life cultivating passionate friendships with young women, writing her memoirs, and doing a little bit of everything. As one of her young friends wrote: "She helps the masons to build walls, she assists with her own hands in making the roads, she feeds the cows, she composes music, she sings and plays, she writes for the press, she shells the corn, she talks out loud in church and corrects the priest if he is not devout, she talks out loud in her little theatre . . . she is a doctor, an apothecary, a farrier, a carpenter, a magistrate, a lawyer."

# 6

**IDA TARBELL,** *dies at 86 in Bridgeport, Connecticut, 1944.* Ida Tarbell, in her heyday, was a nationally known writer, an assistant editor of *McClure's Magazine,* and a biographer of Napoleon, Lincoln, and Madame Roland. She was the original "muckraker," a term invented by Theodore Roosevelt for a journalist who got to the scene of the crime before he did. She was also the nemesis of big, bad John D. Rockefeller.

Big, bad John D. Rockefeller, according to Tarbell, was nothing more than a "cunning, ruthless Shylock" who drove old ladies out of business and built a massive oil

# 5

**OLYMPIA BROWN,** *born in Prarie Ronde, Michigan, 1835.* Suffragist, abolitionist, pacifist, and early American Civil Liberties Union member, Brown was the first woman in the United States to study theology with men and the first to be ordained by full denominational authority as a minister. She was first inspired to seek a career in the ministry when, as a student at Antioch College, she heard a speech made by abolitionist Frances Gage. "It was the first time I had heard a woman preach," she said later, "and the sense of victory lifted me up."

OLYMPIA BROWN: *She would not have been amused by Samuel Johnson's quip that "a woman preaching is like a dog's walking on his hind legs. It is not done well: but you are surprised to find it done at all."*

LIBRARY OF CONGRESS

trust by bleeding the little people. He did, as a matter of fact, drive a lot of little entrepreneurs out of business, although Tarbell tended to exaggerate. Her highly successful articles in *McClure's* accused him of robbing a widow, sabotaging a rival refinery, infiltrating rival firms, and deriving "special and unjust privileges from the railroads." Rockefeller, in turn, nicknamed her "Miss Tarbarrel" and had a newspaper that he owned print the headline, "Hysterical Woman Versus Historical Facts." The fuss ended with a 1911 Supreme Court decision against Rockefeller. And generations of Rockefeller family philanthropy still haven't quite removed that taint.

Ironically, the aggressive, ambitious, eloquent Tarbell claimed to hate women like herself. She wrote two popular books on feminism, *The Ways of Woman* and *The Business of Being a Woman,* which is not to say that she wrote two feminist books. Far from it. In these texts, she discourages women from working—single women, of course, since she never dreams of a married woman having an outside

LIBRARY OF CONGRESS

IDA TARBELL: *She brought down the great John D. Rockefeller and spent her last years gardening. "The proof that I am able to do anything so worthwhile as raise a potato never fails to thrill me."*

job. To the girls of America, she says that there is no hope of "doing the same things a man does," since "a woman's temperament and intellectual operations" are radically different from a man's.

The home, she says, is woman's place, and a woman's purpose is the care "of man and child"; she should not hope to be a citizen but "to prepare the citizen." Tarbell attacks everything from the suffragists to coeducation and professes to be horrified that "women are casting off all forms of restraints" and that "women of character, position, and sense" are dressing "in mannish suits and boots calmly smoking cigarettes while they talk, and talk well, about things which women are not supposed to be interested." All this from a woman who never married, who worked almost entirely with men, "doing the same things a man does," and who was so little interested in children and domesticity that at fourteen she prayed to be spared from marriage. "I must be free," she prayed, "and to be free I must be a spinster."

# 7

**ZORA NEALE HURSTON,** *born in Eatonville, Florida, probably in 1901.* Living in Eatonville, America's first incorporated all-black town, gave Hurston a self-confidence and a racial pride that might have been suppressed elsewhere. Encouraged by her mother, she decided early to "wrassle me up a future, or die trying." Her positive rearing was abruptly ended by her mother's death, when Hurston was nine. At thirteen, she was sent to school in Jacksonville and became aware of prejudice for the first time: "I was not Zora of Orange County any more," she wrote later. "I was a little colored girl."

So at fourteen she ran away, joining a Gilbert and Sullivan troupe as

a wardrobe girl, entering school in Baltimore with only a dress and a change of underwear to her name, and working as a manicurist and a maid to put herself through college. By the late 1920s, she had made her way to New York on a scholarship to Barnard College, studied anthropology with Franz Boas, became Barnard's first black graduate, published some essays and stories, and met many of the black writers at the heart of the Harlem Renaissance. By the mid-1930s, she had taught, worked as a drama coach, published a novel and a play, was recognized for her talent and her beauty, and had married and divorced. She had sold hot dogs in Washington, D.C., so she could record the speech patterns of

blacks, and had worked in Florida, Alabama, Louisiana, Haiti, and Jamaica, studying with hoodoo doctors, watching hoodoo ceremonies, collecting stories, songs, games, prayers, and sermons, and publishing her findings in an anthropological gem, *Mules and Men.*

And in 1937 she wrote *Their Eyes Were Watching God,* a joyous, sensual book that Alice Walker calls "one of the greatest novels America had produced—though, being America, it did not realize this."

And at about that point, the story turns ugly. Hurston's pride, dignity, and personal style had a way of offending people. She offended her condescending white patron by refusing to grovel. She offended liberals with her conser-

LIBRARY OF CONGRESS

ZORA NEALE HURSTON: *She called her hometown "the city of five lakes, three croquet courts, three hundred brown skins, three hundred good swimmers, plenty guavas, two schools, and no jailhouse."*

vative sympathies and conservatives with her taste for pants and boots. She offended integrationists by claiming that integration demeaned black institutions. She offended the Harlem literati by dubbing them the "niggerati." And her sensuality, her willingness to accept fellowships from whites, and the brightly colored scarves she wore on her head

offended just about everybody else.

By 1959, Hurston had been reviled, disowned, and forgotten. She had married again and divorced again; her writing had lost its power. She had been arrested for "impairing the morals of a minor," and her arrest got far more publicity than her acquittal. She had been reduced once again to working as a maid, since publishers now rejected her work. Broke and ashamed to ask for help from her family, she was evicted from her home, and a stroke landed her in the local welfare home, where she died in 1960. She was buried in an unmarked grave.

**JACKIE MITCHELL,** *dies at about 64 in Chattanooga, Tennessee, 1987.* Andy Warhol once said that "in the future, everyone will be famous for fifteen minutes." Well, fifteen minutes was about all Jackie Mitchell got, but what a glorious fifteen minutes they were. In 1931, she became the first woman to play professional baseball. Known to her teammates as "Jack," the seventeen-year-old pitcher was hired on March 25 by the AA Chattanooga Lookouts of the Southern Association. *The New York Times* reported: "Jack will work out regularly with the Lookouts and has been named to start an exhibition game with the New York Yankees here next week. She said her greatest ambition was to strike out Babe Ruth."

A few days later, the Memphis Chicks tried to trade two men for her, but Lookouts manager Joe Engel wouldn't trade her. "Joe once traded a shortstop for a turkey," the papers reported, "but parting with his only girl lefthander is another matter." Other clubs were also tempted to bid for her, since, as one reporter put it, "Her advertising value is worth two Chambers of Commerce."

On the big day, April 2, four thousand people showed up to watch the Lookouts take on the Yankees. Mitchell struck out Ruth. She struck out Lou Gehrig. Then she walked the next batter and was taken out of the game. Some claimed that Ruth and Gehrig weren't really trying, but Ruth was visibly angry at missing the ball, and Mitchell said, "Why, hell yes, they were trying, damn right. Hell, better hitters than them couldn't hit me." Two days later, the *New York Times* said: "Perhaps Miss Jackie hasn't quite enough on the ball yet to bewilder Ruth and Gehrig in a serious game. But there are no such sluggers in the Southern Association, and she may win laurels this season which cannot be ascribed to mere gallantry. The prospect grows gloomier for misogynists." And that was all. Mitchell's moment of fame was over, although she would play professional ball until 1937. Fortunately, she didn't start playing

CHATTANOOGA REGIONAL HISTORY MUSEUM

the game to become famous; as she said in 1931, "All I want is to stay in baseball long enough to get money to buy a roadster."

JACKIE MITCHELL: *On the day of her professional baseball debut, she struck out Babe Ruth and Lou Gehrig.*

# 8 _____

**AGNODICE,** *born in Greece in the fourth century, B.C., exact date unnown.* Agnodice has something in common with a number of women in this book; no one knows her date of birth or her date of death. Agnodice had very little written about her because she was born so long ago, and the ancient Greeks wrote about women only when it was absolutely necessary. In fact, we wouldn't have known anything at all about her if she hadn't masqueraded as a man.

Agnodice wanted to be a doctor, and women in ancient Athens were forbidden to study or practice medicine upon penalty of death. So she dressed herself in men's clothing, cut her hair, and studied with Herophilos, a famous physician. A talented student, she became the first woman to be a professional gynecologist (although hardly the

first woman to offer medical treatment to other women). She was so successful in her work that she quickly rivaled the established doctors, and in their jealousy they denounced her as "one that does corrupt men's wives." The penalty for raping one's patients was also death, and Agnodice revealed her sex in order to clear herself. She was instantly championed by her female patients, all of whom declared that if Agnodice were executed for practicing medicine, "they would all die with her." Not only was our heroine acquitted, but also she was allowed to continue her medical work and to wear men's clothing if she liked. In addition, Athenian law was altered to allow women to study medicine, but they were only allowed to treat members of their own sex.

# 9 _____

**SIMONE DE BEAUVOIR,** *born in Paris, 1908.* Simone de Beauvoir was a walking contradiction in terms. She was from the middle class and marked by its prejudices and values, yet she hated the middle class. She lost her faith, yet her personal beliefs were largely secularized versions of Catholic mores. She called fidelity "a mutilation" and refused to marry Jean-Paul Sartre, her lifelong companion, yet she was often passionately jealous and possessive. She detested the forces which kept women powerless and dependent on men, yet wrote: "I would fall in love the day that a man would subjugate me by his intelligence, his knowledge, his authority." In fact, what drew her to Sartre initially was that in their examination in philosophy at the Sorbonne, she placed second and he placed first. So it seems appropriate that her 1953 masterpiece, *The Second Sex,* is a tangled web of biology, psychoanalysis, literary criticism, mythology, history, anthropology, and existentialist philosophy that both defends women and betrays a certain amount of contempt for them. And yet it does contain some delightful passages, like: "When a little girl climbs trees it is, according to Adler, just to show her equality with boys; it does not occur to him that she likes to climb trees."

*The Second Sex* is one of those classics that very few people actually *love,* that's just a little too confusing and a good deal too long, but that you're supposed to have read. So for those of you who don't want to wade through the whole thing (at least not without a preview), here are a fews tidbits:

• Indeed no one is more arrogant toward women, more aggressive or scornful, than the man who is anxious about his virility.

• Man is defined as a human being and woman as a female— whenever she behaves as a human being she is said to imitate the male.

• We sometimes say "the sex" to designate woman; she is the flesh, its delights and dangers. The truth that for woman man is sex and carnality has never been proclaimed because there is no one to proclaim it. Representation of the world, like the world itself, is the work of men; they describe it from their own point of view, which they confuse with absolute truth.

# 10

COCO CHANEL, *dies at 87 in Paris, France, 1971.* The woman Yves St. Laurent called "the godmother of us all" got her start in a milliner's shop in Deauville after being orphaned at an early age. In 1912, she opened her own store, and by 1920, she was the hottest name in fashion. She specialized in clothes that were simple and comfortable—the chemise dress, the collarless cardigan jacket, cardigan sweaters, and bias-cut dresses. She shortened skirts, dispensed with corsets, and introduced neck scarves, spaghetti straps, artificial fabrics, and the use of heavy costume jewelry and long strands of cultured pearls. In 1922, she became as well known for her perfume as for her clothing when she introduced Chanel No. 5, named for her lucky number.

Chanel quickly became the wealthiest couturier in France, but in the late 1930s she was induced to retire by continuing competition from rival designer Elsa Schiaparelli. She did not return to fashion design until 1954, when she made a triumphant comeback in response to what she believed was too much male control of the industry. When she died, Coco Chanel was not only a world-famous fashion designer and the creator of a staggeringly popular perfume but the owner of successful textile and jewelry businesses as well.

# 11

ALICE PAUL, *born in Moorestown, New Jersey, 1885.* She called herself "the timid type" and was convinced she was a poor speaker, but events proved otherwise. An extremely well-educated social worker, she was studying at the London School of Economics when she became involved with the English suffrage movement. In 1908 and 1909, she was repeatedly imprisoned for demonstrating on behalf of woman suffrage. When she staged hunger strikes to protest her arrests, she was forcibly fed by means of a hard rubber tube forced down her throat through one nostril.

In 1910, she returned to the United States, determined to make use of the tactics she'd learned in England, but she soon found that older suffrage leaders were afraid of offending anyone. They gave her a minor appointment, hoping to get rid of her. She was to lobby for the passage of a bill that had been floating around Congress for years. Nicknamed the Susan B. Anthony bill, granting women the right to vote, it always had the genteel and ineffectual support of a few congressmen, and never went anywhere. No one actually expected Paul to make any progress, and she was told from the start that she would receive no money for expenses.

But no one had counted on Paul's resourcefulness or her taste for grand gestures. The day before Woodrow Wilson's 1913 inauguration, she staged a huge suffrage parade. Somewhere between five and ten thousand marchers came from across the country at their own expense, and about half a million people showed up to watch. Next, she established the Congressional Union, an organization which raised funds for the suffrage battle. When President Wilson refused to talk to feminist groups, she began daily picketing of the White House. (She and her colleagues continued this picketing even during U.S. involvement in World War I, when they were

physically assaulted by patriotic bystanders.)

By 1916, the more conservative suffragists were tired of Alice Paul. They managed, by some clever rule-bending and rule-making, to kick her out of their organization and to disown her. Undaunted, she renamed the Congressional Union the National Woman's Party and redoubled her efforts. "I was full of enthusiasm," she said, "and I didn't want any lukewarm person around." In October, 1917, she was arrested outside the White House and sentenced to seven months in a filthy Washington jail. The local authorities, trying (unsuccessfully) to discredit her, placed her in solitary confinement in the prison's psychiatric ward. She went on a hunger strike for about three weeks, was forcibly fed, and was suddenly released with little explanation. In January of 1918, President Wilson, bending at least in part to pressure from Alice Paul, declared that woman suffrage was urgently needed as a "war measure." Within two years, American women got the vote they'd been demanding since 1848.

A few months later, Paul held a meeting of the National Woman's Party. A decision had to be made. Either the group could decide that its work was over and disband, or it could seek new frontiers of equality. It chose the latter. Paul hired a group of lawyers to draft an Equal Rights Amendment, then decided she didn't like their version and drew up her own. She went back to college and got three law degrees "because I thought I could be more useful to the campaign if I knew more about the law." Three years before her death in 1977, she was still fighting for equality, still calling herself "timid," and still determined to win her battles. "You can't have peace," she said, "in a world in which some women or some men or some nations are at different stages of development. There is *so* much work to be done."

# 12

**MARIE BASHKIRTSEFF,** *born in Poltava, Russia, 1859.* Bashkirtseff was only twenty-five when she died. She was an artist by profession, but it is not for her painting that she is remembered. It is for the diary she left behind, which describes the loves, fears, and ambitions of eleven years. Not always truthful, it is always absorbing; Bashkirtseff was a flamboyant, passionate girl with strong opinions. She writes of her wish to be married and have children; if she had a daughter, she says, she would wish the child to be "beautiful and stupid, and with some principles, so as not to be lost." She writes of art, which makes her "so happy, so free, so proud!" She writes of love: "Let us love dogs, let us love only dogs! Men and cats are unworthy creatures."

Mostly, however, she writes of herself—her infatuations, her beauty, and her desire to be a singer or an actress and so "enjoy the happiness of being celebrated, and admired." In fact, although a diary should be about oneself, hers is so vain that at times it's easy to sympathize with the reviewer who called her "a horrid little pig." She repeats for us her childhood prayer "that I may never have the smallpox; that I may grow up pretty; that I may have a beautiful voice; that I may be happily married." She says that she hates seeing people in love because she wants all the happiness for herself, and she says, "I love to be alone before a looking-glass, and to admire my hands, so fine and white, and faintly rosy in the palms." However, even Bashkirtseff's vanity and arrogance are fascinating. Four months before her death from tuberculosis, she writes that she once longed to visit Italy, but "if I went to Italy, I should no longer be in Paris, and my desire was to be everywhere at once . . . If I had been born a man, I would have conquered Europe."

# 13

**ERNESTINE ROSE,** *born Ernestine Louise Siismondi Potowski in Piotrkow, Russian Poland, 1810.* The daughter of a Polish rabbi, Rose was born into a situation without room for compromise. On the one hand was acceptance by her society, but it could only be purchased by conformity and submission. On the other hand lay the apparent freedom of the outside world, but to grasp it she must rebel against everything she knew, against authority, tradition, and her own family. For many years, she tried to find some middle ground between these two alternatives. She tried to fulfill her family duties while insisting on being taught the Talmud in Hebrew, but eventually the strain grew too great. She asked too many questions and had too little respect for authority to fit in, and the final break came when her father arranged a marriage for her and she refused to honor a contract which she had not signed.

So she left her home and traveled to Prussia, Holland, France, Scotland, and, finally, England. There she married an Englishman who shared her rebellious disposition, and with him she sailed for the United States in 1836. Before her final retirement to England in the 1870s, she would become associated with almost every radical movement of the day. She agitated for married women's property rights, woman suffrage, abolition, and higher education for women, traveling up and down the east coast and as far west as Ohio and Michigan. Everywhere she went, she was attacked by her political opponents; Southern slaveholders threatened to tar and feather her, and almost everyone was horrified by her atheism and her refusal to believe in an afterlife. On one of her lecture tours she had tremendous difficulty finding a place to speak. She was in Washington, D.C., and she was refused permission to speak in the Capitol because it was a Sunday and she had no religious affiliation (a fine example of the separation of church and state), and the Smithsonian would not lend her a hall because it would supposedly tarnish the Institution's dignified reputation if a woman were allowed to speak there.

But it was not these indignities that truly wounded her. It was the attacks she suffered from her own colleagues that hurt. As her friend Susan B. Anthony said, Rose was more radical than the radicals, and (unfortunately for her peace of mind) she was, as an outsider, the first to notice hypocrisies that the American activists harbored in their ranks. "No one can tell the hours of anguish I have suffered," she told Anthony one evening when they were on a speaking tour, "as one after another I have seen those whom I had trusted betray falsity of motive." And then Ernestine Rose, who had stood unflinchingly before hostile audiences and violent mobs, who had revolted against her

LIBRARY OF CONGRESS

ERNESTINE ROSE: *An eternal rebel, she went from studying the Talmud in Poland to fighting for women's property rights and the abolition of slavery in the United States.*

father's tyranny, wept. "I expect never to be understood while I live," she sobbed while Anthony tried to comfort her. "No one knows how I have suffered from not being understood."

# 14

**ANAÏS NIN,** *dies at 73, 1977.* Anaïs Nin was a novelist and a diarist who had a deep appreciation of the richness of words, but her real work of art was as much her life as her writing. Almost everything she wrote was autobiographical or nearly so, and her skill lay in being able to record a life lived passionately and fully. She was born in Paris in 1903, the daughter of a Spanish pianist and composer and his wife, a French-Danish singer. Her compulsion to write was the result of two personal tragedies. The first happened when she was nine years old; after an illness, doctors told her (incorrectly) that she would never walk again. It was what she called a "traumatic genesis," and she began writing.

The second "traumatic genesis" occurred at eleven, when her mother and father separated. Nin went to the U.S. with her mother, and her father went to live with another woman. A few year later, Nin began to keep the diaries which she would maintain all her life; they were, in her own words, "written to persuade my absent father to return." In time, however, they became simply an artistic extension of her feelings—anxiety, eroticism, love, anger, and amusement. The diaries record events, of course. She had a life that would have been interesting in its own right; she worked as a fashion model and dancer, studied psychoanalysis and practiced it in Europe, knew famous intellectuals and writers, and became the personal friend and philosophical enemy of writer Henry Miller. But it is the language of the diaries that carries her life into the realm of art, and her record of her experiences is worth reading.

# 15

**SOFIA KOVALEVSKAIA,** *born Sofia Vasilevna Korvin-Krukovskaia in Moscow, Russia, 1850.* By the time she was eighteen years old, Kovalevskaia had studied physics, geometry, algebra, trigonometry, calculus, and biology. This was an exceptional accomplishment for any nineteenth-century woman, especially one from Russia, but it was well that she got an early start. She would die at the age of forty-one, from influenza and pneumonia.

Her eighteenth year was an important one for Kovalevskaia since it was in 1868 that she got the chance to continue her education. There were no such opportunities for women within Russia, but a Russian woman could travel abroad to study if she got permission from her father or husband. Kovalevskaia chose not to go to her father. She chose, instead, to marry.

Her decision was influenced by her recent conversion to radicalism, especially to nihilism, which held among other principles that the sexes were equal and that women as well as men should educate themselves and serve society. In radical circles, it was a common practice to make marriages of convenience so as to travel abroad and escape parental supervision. These marriages were seldom consummated, and after the ceremony, bride and groom often never saw each other again. Kovalevskaia made such a marriage to paleontologist Vladimir Kovalevsky, but she

LIBRARY OF CONGRESS

SOFIA KOVALEVSKAIA: *August Strindberg considered a female professor of mathematics "a monstrosity." He was not alone.*

was to pay for her "freedom" with fifteen years of misery. Her husband was irresponsible, unreliable, a swindler, and mentally unstable, but he refused to leave her alone, and until his suicide in 1883 he was a constant burden.

To compensate for this, however, Kovalevskaia had new interests. She got an introduction to University of Göttingen professor Karl Weierstrass, who assigned her some difficult problems just to get rid of her. When she returned with the correct answers, he was impressed, and they began a lifelong friendship. He tutored her, and she did brilliant work, but recognition was long in coming. When she was studying in Heidelberg, she had to get special permission from each of her professors to be allowed to attend lectures. After her graduation from Göttingen *summa cum laude*, she was unable to get a teaching job in Russia because of her sex.

She turned to writing for a time, producing an autobiography and an autobiographical novel, *The Sisters Rajevsky*. Then, in 1883, she took a job as a lecturer in mathematics at the University of Stockholm. Some Swedes greeted her graciously; others did not. Playwright August Strindberg welcomed her with the statement, "A female professor of mathematics is a pernicious and unpleasant phenomenon—even, one might say, a monstrosity." Nonetheless, she became widely known for the Caucy-Kovalevsky Theorem of differential equations and for her essay *On the Rotation of a Solid Body About a Fixed Point,* which won the French Academy's Prix Bordin. So impressive was her entry, the prize money was increased from three thousand to five thousand francs. She was made a tenured professor in 1889, and in the same year, Russia's Imperial Academy of Sciences changed its rules to allow her election to its ranks. She had been honored by France, Sweden, and Russia. She was admired throughout Europe. She was a celebrity who received huge quantities of fan mail and hate mail. Despite all this, just two years before her death, she was banned from teaching in her native land—because she was a woman.

# 16

**DOROTHY EADY,** *born Dorothy Louise Eady in London, England, 1904.* When she was three years old, Eady had an experience that most people would have considered strange enough for one lifetime. She fell down a flight of stairs and was pronounced dead. She was carried to her room and left there while her family grieved and began to make funeral arrangements. But when they went back to wash her body, they found little Dorothy playing happily and eager to tell them what she'd "dreamed." She had dreamed of a temple, and it was a dream that would change her forever and convince her that she was not Dorothy Eady at all.

Her childhood got stranger and stranger. When she was four she was taken to the British Museum, and she was thoroughly bored until she got to the Egyptian displays. Suddenly she began kissing the feet of the mummies, and when her mother tried to take her home, she growled, "Leave me . . . *these* are my people." She finally had to be dragged from the museum. At six she became convinced that she had once been able to read hieroglyphics and that, if she only tried hard enough, she could do so again. At seven she saw a picture of a ruined temple at Abydos and called it her home, only to be reproved for lying by her father. She was kicked out of her Sunday school when she called Jesus and Mary cheap imitations of Osiris and Isis, and she was expelled from a girls' school for refusing to sing a hymn that went, "curse the swart Egyptians." She habitually skipped school to haunt the British Museum, and when her parents threatened to send her to a convent school in Belgium, she counter-threatened to run away to Egypt if they did.

Almost everyone thought Eady was out of her mind. The rest thought she was at least a little peculiar. Only when she was ten did she meet someone who encouraged her interests. He was Sir E. A. Wallis Budge, Keeper of Egyptian and Assyrian Antiquities at the British Museum, and he taught her hieroglyphics. When he expressed surprise at the quickness with which she learned, she explained that she was not *learning,* she was *remembering.*

Her eccentricities, as her parents would have called them, only intensified as she grew older. At the age of twelve, she began praying to Isis, and in the fall of 1918 she had a terrifying dream. A mummy's face—the face of Pharaoh Sety I—appeared before her. He ripped her nightgown all the way from top to bottom and then disappeared. In the morning she found her nightgown ripped just as she'd dreamed; she told her mother she had done it herself, "But I *knew* that I hadn't." She began to have recurring nightmares in which she was watched or tortured.

For many years Eady waited for a chance to go to Egypt, and then, quite unexpectedly, it came. She had worked in England on behalf of the Egyptian independence movement, and through this work she met a Cairo police officer, Imam Abdel Meguid. He asked the twenty-nine-year-old Eady to marry him, and she agreed. She changed her name to Bulbul (Arabic for "nightingale") and became Bulbul Abdel Meguid. The marriage was a dismal failure practically from the start; Abdel Meguid wanted a good cook, a docile helpmate, and a scrupulous housekeeper, and Eady failed on all three counts. But her relationship with

Egypt as a whole was blissful. When she first landed in Port Said, she kissed the ground and swore she'd never leave. She never did.

The birth of a son, Sety, did nothing to help her marriage, and in 1936 she and Abdel Meguid were divorced. Abdel Meguid took Sety away from her when he was five, and Eady did nothing to stop him. She always remembered her ex-husband as a "very patient and very decent man." She rarely saw Sety afterward, although according to tradition she was known for the rest of her life as Omm Sety, an honorific meaning "the mother of Sety."

Eady got a job at thirty dollars a month as an artist for the Egyptian Department of Antiquities, learned all she could about Egyptology, continued to support the independence movement, and kept her sense of humor. Once, when she was walking down a disreputable street, some Egyptian women shouted at her, "Go home, English whore!" Without missing a beat, she replied, "And leave all the customers to you?"

Meanwhile, she experienced some very bizarre nocturnal visions. She later claimed that during this period she was educated in the events of her past life by a spirit. He told her that she had been a virgin priestess of Isis named Bentreshyt who, at fifteen, had fallen in love with and been seduced by Pharaoh Sety I. When she became pregnant, she had been tortured and questioned and had killed herself rather than bring shame upon her illustrious lover. Once she had been educated in these facts, Eady said, she visited Sety in out-of-body experiences in the land of the dead, and eventually he began to visit her and to make love to her. He told her that they would be allowed to marry in the land of the dead, but only if she passed a severe test while living—she must return to the temple at Abydos, the home of Bentreshyt, and live there as a virgin for the rest of her life.

Omm Sety made her first pilgrimage to Abydos in 1952, and she soon arranged to be transferred there. She remained there until her death in 1981, living for most of those years in a two-room house with a donkey, two

geese, a rabbit, dogs, snakes, and cats. She regarded the temple as an active place of worship and never wore shoes inside; in fact, sometimes she didn't wear anything—she always felt more comfortable in the nude. She prayed in the temple and celebrated its ancient festivals, and in time she acquired a local reputation as something between a witch and a priestess, who could cure impotence, halt the spread of disease, and control snakes. Most who encountered her did not believe her story of rein-

carnation, but almost everyone who met her respected her. Besides, even if her stories seemed strange, they were definitely interesting, and she had such a pleasant way of telling them; in 1979, for example, she summarized her recollections of her past life for *The New York Times:* "I can't remember any ordinary life, so I must have been stuck in the temple. I have a vague memory of the processions. I can remember an awful old killjoy of a priest."

# 17

LOLA MONTEZ: *On the occasion of her American tour, one reporter wrote: "How am I to describe Lola's breasts when I cannot find words to describe even her teeth?"*

**LOLA MONTEZ,** *dies at about 42 in New York City, 1861.* Montez was known to her audiences as "the Andalusian," but she was far from Spanish. She was the daughter of a Birtish army officer, and she was born Maria Dolores Eliza Rosanna Gilbert in Limerick, Ireland. At nine-

teen, threatened with an arranged marriage to an elderly judge, she eloped with a younger man, Lieutenant Thomas James. She divorced James within a few years, but the marriage had by that time served its purpose; it had gotten her far away from home—as far away as India.

She studied dancing and appeared in London as "Lola Montez, the Spanish dancer," but she experienced little success and was soon recognized by an acquaintance as plain old Eliza Gilbert from Ireland, so she took her act to the Continent. In 1847 she arrived in Munich, determined to play in a particular theatre. She managed an audience with King Ludwig I of Bavaria himself and demanded to be allowed to dance there. During the audience, she noticed that he was staring at her breasts, wondering if they were real or somewhat augmented by padding. Seizing a pair of nearby scissors, she snipped open the front of her dress to prove that they were real. King Ludwig was in love.

He made Montez Countess of Lansfield and Baroness Rosenthal. He gave her wealth. He let her sign her bills, "The King's Mistress." It was the literal realization of one of Montez's own sayings: "To be beautiful! What power and what good fortune!" Snubbed by the Bavarian nobility and ignored by the theatregoing public, she threw herself into politics. She fought the power of the Jesuits and worked for liberal reforms. But the Jesuits fought back and formed a strong coalition of groups who resented Montez and her protector, King Ludwig. The King was forced to strip her of her titles, banish her, and proclaim that she had "ceased to possess the rights of a Bavarian subject." She left, but the King was unable to regain the ground he had lost during her ascendancy, and the Jesuits forced him to abdicate.

Montez returned to Great Britain, much more famous than when she left, and she continued her dancing career. In 1849 she married another lieutenant, George Heald. Shortly thereafter she abandoned him and went on a tour of the United States, where she was met with great enthusiam—and lust. The breasts that had lured King Ludwig became her chief assets in the U.S., but soon even Americans tired of her spectacular profile and meager talents. She became something of a character, touring in second-rate and then third-rate theatres, attacking her

enemies with a bullwhip, turning to the lecture circuit when no one came to see her dance, and taking lovers everywhere she went. She married a Californian, Patrick P. Hall, although she never bothered to divorce Heald; she divorced Hall soon afterward. She wandered back

to New York, where she underwent a religious conversion and spent her last years doing charitable work. She died alone and in poverty and was buried, not as Lola Montez, the Spanish dancer, but as Mrs. Eliza Gilbert.

**CATHERINE BOOTH,** *born in Ashebourne, Derbyshire, 1829.* It's not every woman who regularly gets to be the target of paint, mud, stones, dead cats, kicks, blows, and live coals, and there are few, perhaps, who could handle such abuse with equanimity. Catherine Booth, who founded the Salvation Army with her husband William, was such a woman. It was she who ensured women's active participation in the Salvation Army, and William undoubtedly had his wife in mind when he said, "The best men in my army are the women."

Both Booths were moved by the plight of the poor, and it was to the poor that they addressed their evangelical crusade. They turned converted criminals into a "Hallelujah Band," spoke on street corners, and generally aroused the anger of the privileged classes and the established church. Catherine, however, was especially concerned with women and children, and she spoke strongly for social purity and an end to prostitution. She also contributed indirectly to the cause by bearing eight children, all of whom were active in the Salvation Army.

But it was as an orator that she was most useful. Quiet, earnest, and intelligent, she drew large crowds and made many converts. Ironically, it was only on impulse that she began speaking in public at all. She was never afraid to voice her opinions—early in their marriage, she read William the riot act for praising a sermon on woman as the weaker sex—but in public she generally let him do the talking. Then, one Sunday, as he was preaching, she felt the urge to

preach as well. She realized, she said, that it was the devil who had urged her to be afraid and remain silent. She stood and walked up to the pulpit. Both William and his congregation feared she was ill, and William asked her what was wrong. When she said that she wished to say a few words, he was so shocked that he could just manage to sit down and gasp, "My dear wife wishes to speak." To his surprise, she moved the audience to tears, and he made sure thereafter that she always got a chance to preach.

# 18 _____

**VALENTINA GRIZODUBOVA,** *born Valentina Stepanovna Grizodubova in Kharkov, Russia, 1910.* Grizodubova's father was an impoverished mechanic named S. V. Grizodubov who, in 1908, built his own plane. It was one of the first planes in Russia, and he became a prominent pilot and aircraft designer. His daughter, who often flew with him, became a pilot at the age of nineteen and quickly became famous for her stamina and skill. She was assigned to the prestigious Maxim Gorky Squadron, which flew to all parts of the Soviet Union on educational missions.

In 1938 her fame suddenly spread to the world at large when she and two other women broke the women's world long-distance flying record. Although they had been forced to crash-land in a swamp, their nonstop trip from Moscow to the Far East was a success. They had flown four thousand miles, 3,687 of those miles in one direction. Grizodubova was made a Hero of the Soviet Union and received the Order of Lenin. She then received a series of awards and decorations. In 1939 she was made head of women's aviation for the Soviet Union. She set more records, ran an airline, and received the Order of the Red Banner of Labor, the Order of the Patriotic War (first class), and the Order of the Red Star. During World War II she was given command of the 101st Long-Range Air Group (later the 31st Guards Bomber Group), a bomber squadron composed of three hundred male pilots and technicians.

# 20

**JOY ADAMSON,** *born Friederike Victoria Gessner in Troppau (now Opava), Czechoslovakia, 1910.* Joy Adamson is most famous for her literary endeavors. *Born Free,* her book about a lion cub she trained to return to the wild, was an instant success, as were its sequels, *Living*

# 19

**JANIS JOPLIN,** *born in Port Arthur, Texas, 1943.* "I was always outrageous," she said in 1970, explaining why she left Texas. She was more than that. She was a tangle-haired, passionate, charismatic, energetic, sexual, hard-drinking, drug-taking, blues-singing, loud, tough performer. She was the first woman to leave behind the demure image of the "girl bands" and to become a full-fledged rock and roll star. But stardom was the bright side of her dark life. She survived a series of unhappy and ruinous relationships only to succumb to her drug addiction. Despite several attempts to dry out, Joplin died of a heroin overdose in 1970. "I just made love to ten thousand people," she said after a concert, "but now I'm going home alone."

JANIS JOPLIN: *She lived hard and fast, and her death underscored the violence of the drug culture.*

*Free* and *Forever Free*. She also achieved lesser fame in other ways. Raised in Vienna, she studied piano, singing, art history, dressmaking, shorthand, metalwork, typing, bookbinding, woodwork, archaeology, drawing, psychoanalysis, and medicine. She achieved her first real success in any of these fields while she was living in Kenya with her second husband, Peter Bally. She received a commission from the Kenyan government to do anthropological paintings of members of twenty-two African tribes before these tribes vanished forever. Six hundred of these paintings now belong to the National Museum of Kenya, and some of them were published in book form as *Peoples of Kenya*. Adamson's early botanical paintings, of which she did at least seven hundred, have also been widely praised.

Adamson also achieved a certain notoriety in a more grisly fashion, and she never got to appreciate it. In 1980, she was staying at her compound, "Shaba," in northern Kenya, where she was engaged in research on the behavior of leopards. Her third husband, George Adamson, was a British game warden; they had been living apart since the 1960s, but they still communicated by radio at regular intervals. On January 4, Joy's body was found near her compound, apparently mauled by a lion. The press had a field day. The great lion-trainer and lion-lover Joy Adamson had ironically been killed by a lion. However, the newspapers did report that the authorities were waiting for the autopsy before making a final determination as to the cause of death. Their caution turned out to be well founded. The autopsy revealed that Adamson had died, not from the attentions of a hungry lion, but from head wounds. Three men, all former employees of hers, were held for questioning, and one of them, twenty-three-year-old herdsman Paul Nakware Ekai, was charged with her murder on February 2.

# 21

**NOVELLA,** *born in Bologna, Italy, in the fourth century.* Novella is another woman from the past whose exact birth and death dates are unknown. She died young in 1333, but she lived long enough to establish a solid reputation in Bologna's legal community and to become the victim of one of Italy's stranger examples of sexism. She was the daughter of a Bolognese professor of law, and she was also his brightest pupil. On occasion, when he could not be present to teach his classes, he would appoint Novella to take his place, but the university authorities were appalled at the thought of a woman in such a prominent position. They were convinced that the young male students, when confronted with Novella's beauty, would go mad with desire and be unable to concentrate on their studies. Yet no one was as qualified as she to substitute for her father. In the end, a bizarre compromise was reached; Novella was allowed to teach in her father's stead, but her dangerously feminine appearance was kept hidden by a curtain placed in front of her while she lectured. Thus protected from their teacher's allure, the students thankfully survived with their sanity unimpaired.

LIBRARY OF CONGRESS

VICTORIA: *Even the peevish matriarch who lent her name to both an age and a frame of mind was once a child.*

# 22

**VICTORIA of England,** *dies at 81 on the Isle of Wight, 1901.* The fat, dour old prude that comes to mind when someone mentions Queen Victoria is a tough person to love. After all, she's the one who said, "We are not amused," called feminism a "mad, wicked folly," refused to outlaw lesbianism because she couldn't even imagine that it existed, and fostered an age of such repression that piano legs were considered too sexy to be left uncovered. A more human image is that of the young princess, barely eighteen years old, being awakened in the middle of the night to be told that she was now the Queen of England. Or there's the still relatively young and handsome woman of forty-two stupefied with grief at the death of her beloved husband, Albert, and sleeping, until her own death forty years later, "with his night-shirt in her arms and a cast of his hand within reach." Or there's the mother of nine, England's living symbol of blessed maternity, saying of pregnancy, "I own it tried me sorely; one feels so pinned down— one's wings clipped," and telling her pregnant daughter Vicki: "What you say of the pride of giving life to an immortal soul is very fine, dear, but I own I cannot enter into that; I think much more of our being like a cow or a dog at such moments; when our poor nature becomes so very animal."

# 23

**ANNE WHITNEY,** *dies at 93 in Boston, Massachusetts, 1915.* Educated at home and at private schools, Whitney ran a school in Salem, Massachusetts, for two years and wrote a collection of poems in 1859, but she found her true calling four years earlier in 1855 when she began to sculpt busts of her relatives. Captivated, she went to New

ANNE WHITNEY: *When the mind works together with the hand, the chisel can be mightier than the sword.*

LIBRARY OF CONGRESS

York and Philadelphia to study art, then studied anatomy at a Brooklyn hospital. By 1860 she had her first exhibition at the National Academy of Design, and her career was under way.

A devoted abolitionist and feminist, Whitney had an instinctive sympathy for underdogs. Her subjects were often blacks (as in *Africa,* completed in 1865), and women (as in *Lady Godiva,* 1864). She also empathized with the poor, and her statue of a beggar woman, entitled *Roma,* caused such an uproar in the Papal Court that it had to be moved out of Italy altogether; it finally found a home in

France. Whitney's subjects also included contemporary abolitionists, intellectuals, and feminists, including Lucy Stone, Harriet Beecher Stowe, Frances Wilkard, Harriet Martineau, Mary Livermore, and William Lloyd Garrison. She received a number of public commissions as well, although on occasion she also lost them. For instance, she was hired to create a monument to Charles Sumner for the city of Boston; however, when the city discovered that she was a woman, the commission was revoked. She completed the statue anyway; it now stands outside Harvard Law School.

# 24

**EDITH WHARTON,** *born Edith Newbold Jones in New York City, 1862.* Shortly before her marriage, Edith Jones asked her mother where babies came from. Her mother, after some embarrassment, said that surely Edith had noticed that Greek statues of men and women were somewhat different, and refused to say anything more.

That is one side of Edith Wharton's life—the family so genteel and wealthy that it refused to mention sex, to provide its daughter with any formal education, or even to furnish her with paper so that she could write poetry. The other side of her life—her own passion and rebelliousness—provided her with the solutions to these problems.

She was trapped in a disastrous and sexless marriage, but she had intensely erotic affairs and finally, despite pressure from most of the people she knew, she divorced her husband. She was not allowed to go to school, but she read voraciously and taught herself four languages. She was denied paper, so she hoarded bits of brown wrapping paper and wrote anyway; as an adult she won two Pulitzer Prizes. Wharton's work included twenty novels, ten collections of short stories, and works on interior design, houses, travel, and the theory of writing. In addition, she found time to entertain Paul Valéry, André Gide, Aldous Huxley, A. E. Housman, Henry James, and Henry Cabot Lodge at her home in France. She refused to go back to the United States during World War I and threw herself into relief work, taking supplies to the front, rescuing war orphans, and finding work and shelter for refugees, for all of which she received the Legion of Honor. She delivered very definite opinions about the works of other artists, calling Joyce's *Ulysses,* for example, "a welter of pornography . . . and uninformed and unimportant drivel." Toward the end of her life, she was the highest-paid novelist in America, sometimes criticized for her dry, old-fashioned style, but famous for her portraits of the cramped, superficial lives of upper-class women. Her talent for tragedy she ascribed to a wise choice of subjects. "In any really good subject," she wrote, "one has only to probe deep enough to come to tears."

# 25

**VIRGINIA WOOLF,** *born Adeline Virginia Stephen in London, England, 1882.* Woolf's family was demented in a very Victorian way. Her father, Sir Leslie Stephen, was a puritanical scholar who ruled his family as a Biblical patriarch might have done. Her beautiful mother and her stepsister Stella exhausted themselves and died young in the service of the men. Her half-brother George Duckworth, eleven years her senior, sexually assaulted her and her sister Vanessa for years.

Given this sort of environment, it's hardly surprising that Woolf was a little unstable, and even less surprising that she hated everything her family represented. She rebelled against her world from the time she was a child, becoming a tomboy and periodically falling into mental illness. Then, in 1904, Sir Leslie died, and Woolf's world changed drastically. She was still haunted by voices that urged her to harm herself, but she was closer to being free. She and Vanessa moved into a house in Bloomsbury, where on Thursday evenings they met with their brother Thoby's Cambridge friends and discussed "Weighty Things." In 1906, Vanessa married one of the Bloomsbury group, Clive Bell, and Thoby died of typhoid. Woolf felt very much alone. She spent a few years flirting with various men, including Lytton Strachey and Clive Bell, and she finally married Leonard Woolf, who became her nurse, companion, protector, and literary assistant.

With his help, she resisted her suicidal impulses long enough to produce some of the greatest works of twentieth-century English literature. Among them were several extraordinary novels, such as *The Waves, Mrs. Dalloway, Between the Acts,* and *To the Lighthouse; Orlando,* a bizarre epic based on her affair with Vita Sackville-West; and a long essay called *A Room of One's Own,* which is considered one of the greatest feminist works of all time. But World War II put great strain on her, and her husband couldn't be with her every minute. On March 28, 1941, she filled her pockets with stones and drowned herself in the River Ouse, convinced that she was going insane again and would not have the strength to recover.

# 26

**BESSIE COLEMAN,** *born in Atlanta, Texas, 1896.* Coleman came from a poor family and couldn't finish college because she ran out of money, but unlike many people who have been deprived for many years, she wasn't obsessed with material wealth. Even after she established a successful restaurant in Chicago, and was finally able to live comfortably, she wasn't satisfied. She knew she had found her real purpose in life the moment she saw a stunt pilot's demonstration.

She went from teacher to teacher, asking for flight lessons, but no one would train her because she was black. So she saved her money, went to France, and got her license there, becoming the first black woman pilot in the world. Returning to the United States in 1921, she opened a flight school and worked against discrimination in aviation, saying that "the air is the only place free from prejudice." Unfortunately, all pilots, are equally susceptible to bad luck and engine failure, and in 1926, while rehearsing a stunt for a Florida air show, Bessie's plane malfunctioned, and she plunged two thousand feet to her death.

# 27

**ELLEN TERRY,** *born in Coventry, England, 1847.* On a London stage in the mid-nineteenth century, a little girl was playing Puck in *A Midsummer Night's Dream* when something went wrong. She was delivering the play's final speech when a trap door closed on her foot, breaking her toe. Trembling with pain, she finished her speech with her foot stuck in the door. The theatre manager doubled her salary on the spot.

She was one of nine children born to a family of strolling players and, as a baby, had slept wrapped in shawls in a drawer in her mother's dressing room. She'd never been to school (a fact which filled her with shame all her life), but she knew the rules of the theatre intimately.

What she didn't know until later was that good little Victorian girls didn't run wild, dress as boys, express anger, or do just as they liked. She began to learn that lesson when she hit adolescence. Audiences began to murmur when she reached her teens and was still showing her legs on stage. And Terry began to get stage fright, feeling, she wrote, "as if a centipede, all of whose feet [had] been carefully iced, [had] begun to run about in the roots of [my] hair."

At sixteen, she gave up the fight, ran away, and married a painter, George Frederic Watts. He soon decided that she was too boisterous for him, and she seemed to have found him impotent. At any rate, she soon eloped to the country with an architect and stage designer, Edward William Godwin. They lived together six years and had two children, Edy and Gordon. What is not surprising at this point is that she was suddenly considered a strange, wicked creature or that her respectable sister Kate gave her the cold shoulder. What is surprising is that in 1874 she made a triumphant return to the stage, eventually becoming the *grande dame* of the English theatre, loved by all and praised for her "voice of plum-

colored velvet," her dignity, her beauty, and her sweetness.

However, it isn't quite a fairy-tale ending. She had a long and financially successful partnership with actor Henry Irving, but he twisted scripts to flatter himself and refused to let her play the comic or evil roles she wanted, restricting her to ingenues. She had more and more trouble remembering her lines.

An appearance in a play by her friend George Bernard Shaw was a failure, despite Virginia Woolf's impression that "she filled the stage and all the other actors were put out, as electric lights are put out in the sun." She sank slowly into blindness and insanity. When she died, her children fought a battle in print over the interpretation of her life, Edy remembering her as a feminist heroine, Gordon as the "loving, vulnerable, and little mother whom only he had known, whose helpless sweetness was violated." Moreover, burial in Westminster Abbey, which had honored the body of Henry Irving, was sanctimoniously refused to her.

# 28

**SIDONIE GABRIELLE COLETTE,** *born in Saint-Sauveur-en-Puisaye, Burgundy, France, 1873.* Passionate, talented, beautiful, and seemingly without fear, Colette once gave her daughter this advice: "You will do foolish things, but do them with enthusiam."

Colette herself certainly did many things which were called foolish and which might have destroyed another woman, but in her case they seemed only to magnify her legend. A country girl with extraordinarily long hair and mysterious green eyes, as a child she dreamed of being a sailor and promptly read every book she was forbidden to read. At twenty she married Henry Gautier-Villars, known to all as Willy, an unscrupulous, lecherous, impoverished gentleman who made a living by signing his name to books written by a stable of ghostwriters. His family was ashamed of him and horrified by Colette, by her "language," and by "the horrifying amount of butter and jam she ate."

Colette spent the first few years of her marriage playing at being submissive. As she wrote later, "there are two kinds of love; the love that is never satisfied and makes you hateful to everyone, and the love that is satisfied and turns you into an idiot." When her husband discovered her talent for writing, they began a bizarre partnership. Every day, he would lock her in a room for four hours, forcing her to work. Then he edited what she gave him and added risqué passages. The result, *Claudine At School* and its sequels, were all published in his name and were all immensely successful.

Gautier-Villars proved to be a marketing genius. He licensed Claudine products, started rumors about himself and Colette, and encouraged her taste for beautiful women. In 1902, long before even the most daring trend-setters bobbed their hair, he convinced her to cut off her five-foot braids.

But Colette got tired of being manipulated, tired of her husband's infidelity, and tired of writing, which she disliked. She wanted to dance or to act. So she left her husband, began telling people that *she* had written the Claudine books, and moved in with her lover, Mathilde de Mornay, the Marquise de Belbeuf. The Marquise, known as Missy, took care of Colette while she took acting lessons and shocked everyone.

COLETTE: *The famous braids that Willy ordered cut.*

In fact, Colette's supreme talent was not for writing or acting, although she did both well. It was for shocking eveyone, being rude and vulgar, doing the unexpected, breaking taboos—and ending up with applause rather than ostracism. She did almost everything she was expected not to do, from riding astride instead of sidesaddle to bursting from a giant cake clad only in whipped cream. She played the heroine and Missy the hero in an erotic play that caused a riot and police intervention. She appeared in a play called *La Chair* in 1907 with her left breast bared, prompting a reviewer to sum up the play's merits in the words: "damn it all, / Colette really does have fine tits / Anyone who likes breasts will love them."

She had no respect for conventions; when Proust told her ad-miringly that her soul was full of voluptuousness and bitterness, she retorted, "Monsieur, you are raving. My soul is full of red beans and bacon." She was twice divorced, flaunted her sexuality in old age, and began an affair with her step-son when she was forty-seven and he was seventeen. Her second hus-band left her at least in part because his colleagues were afraid Colette would seduce their wives. She had no love for children and refused to sentimentalize mother-hood. During her one pregnancy, at forty, she referred to herself as "a swollen she-rat." She was not nearly as fond of her own wonderful, sen-sual books as she was of good food.

Her outrageous behavior made her a celebrity; and her celebrity made her a living legend. When she died in 1954, she was refused a Catholic burial because of her three marriages and two divorces, but thousands attended her funeral.

# 29

**GERMAINE GREER,** *born in Melbourne, Australia, 1939.* If you ever want to stir up a party, haul out your copy of Germaine Greer's latest book, *The Madwoman's Underclothes.* Read an essay, any essay, aloud. Unless all the people at the party happen by some odd, unlikely twist of fate to be Ger-maine Greer fans, you will spark in mere moments a conversation full of outrage, shock, revelation, joy, embarrassment, admiration, and, best of all, *thought.* So few people actually *think* anymore that a Greer reading can be a blessing beyond words.

Greer has done things and been places that most of us have trouble imagining. She's been to Ethiopia, Brazil, and Southeast Asia. She spent three months living with Southern Italian peasants and three months in India researching fertili-ty. She's been a columnist for the London *Sunday Times* and a writer for underground publications like *Oz.* And, in 1970, she achieved in-stant notoriety with *the Female Eunuch,* a feminist treatise which made proclamations like "Women fail to undestand how much men hate them" and "Freud is the father of psychoanalysis. It has no mother."

*The Madwoman's Underclothes* is full of the echoes of these ex-periences. Read it and you'll learn how Greer spent three weeks in jail for saying "fuck" in a public meet-ing. You'll read about the politics of reproduction in articles covering everything from appreciating your own body to the question of con-traception in third-world countries. And if you can stand a chilling, ac-curate, demystifying appraisal of rape, I know of none better than

Greer's essay, "Seduction Is a Four-Letter Word," which has one simple message for men: *"if you do not like us, cannot listen to our part of the conversation, if we are only meat to you, then leave us alone."*

# 30

**MATILDA,** *dies at 64 in Notre Dame des Prés, France, 1167.* The first woman to rule England was never actually crowned queen. She was Matilda, also known as Maud, Mold, Aethelic, Aaliz, and Adela, and she was the daughter of Henry I, King of England. She married Henry V, the Holy Roman Emperor, a man thirty years her senior. Over the course of their childless eleven-year marriage, he came to respect her judgment highly, and her subjects loved her and called her "the good Matilda." Nonetheless, when Henry died in 1125, she became a woman without a position. She had no sons and no husband to protect her, and she was sent back to England to become a pawn again in the marriage game.

It didn't take long to find another potential ally to marry her. This time it was fifteen-year-old Geoffrey of Anjou, whose lands bordered on English possessions in Normandy. In 1129, two years after her marriage, Matilda had a son named Henry, and her father forced his nobles to accept her and her infant son as his heirs. But when her father died in 1135 from eating too many eels, they chose as his successor not Matilda but Stephen, a grandson of William the Conqueror. Matilda and Geoffrey were considered "aliens" and therefore ineligible for the throne.

Incensed, Matilda appealed to the Pope, who rejected her claims. Perhaps the Pope underestimated her. Perhaps he had not heard the assessments of those who knew her, who said "she had the nature of a man in the frame of a woman" and called her "a woman who had nothing of the woman in her." She gathered strength and waited for Stephen to make a mistake, a deed of which he was eminently capable.

Matilda invaded England in 1139, and for two years the country was ravaged by civil war, famine, arson, and vicious taxation by the nobles. At last, in 1141, Matilda captured an imprisoned Stephen and took the titles Lady and Queen of England. But she was never actually crowned. According to one source, she "behaved like an empress when she was not quite a queen," and many of her supporters abandoned her and freed Stephen. In 1147, she fled back to Normandy and her husband, leaving her son Henry to continue the fight.

Henry eventually succeeded, but Matilda remained in Normandy and became especially reclusive after her husband's death. She spent most of her time doing charitable work, but she helped Henry whenever she could, offering advice and acting as a mediator on occasion. On her deathbed, she took vows as a nun; her will left most of her wealth to churches, religious establishments, and hospitals. A sum was left for distribution to the poor, and another was set aside to build a bridge across the Seine at Rouen. Her epitaph, which she composed, is as follows: "Here lies Henry's daughter, wife, and mother; great by birth, greater by marriage, greatest by motherhood."

# 31

**TALLULAH BANKHEAD,** *born in Huntsville, Alabama, 1903.* The problem with Tallulah Bankhead is that you can't see her best work anymore, since she was infinitely better on the stage than in the movies. Part of the problem was that Paramount tried to remake her into a Marlene Dietrich clone, and part of it was that she simply wasn't cast in very good movies. (Alfred Hitchcock's *Lifeboat* is a notable exception.) By the time television rose to prominence, her blonde beauty was gone and only the rich baritone drawl was left. Her last

TALLULAH BANKHEAD: *"I can say 'shit,' darling. I'm a lady."*

performance was as the Dragon Lady in ABC's Batman."

But a glimpse at her life reveals a little of what she must have been like in the flesh. She adored the South, the Democratic party, and her father, Speaker of the House of Representatives William Brockman Bankhead. Her wit, her vitality, and her desire to please her audiences charmed everyone except the victims of her bitchier remarks. For example, a mother was complaining about her poorly behaved son and sighed, "We don't know what to make of him." Said Bankhead, "How about a nice rug?"

Usually, however, her wit was directed at herself. "I am as pure as the driven slush," she bragged, and she is said to have invented the line, "only good girls keep diaries. Bad girls don't have the time." Upon meeting producer Irving Thalberg, she drawled, "Dahling, how does one get laid in this dreadful place?" And once, in a moment of reflection, she announced: "The only thing I regret about my past life is the length of it. If I had my past life over again I'd make all the same mistakes—only sooner."

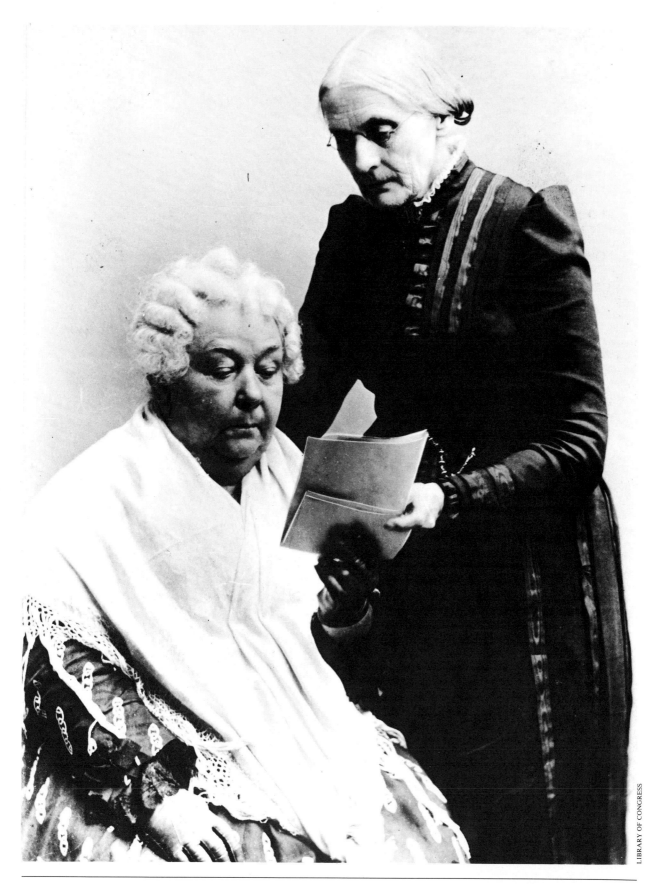

SUSAN B. ANTHONY (right), with Elizabeth Cady Stanton: *"It is the disheartening part of my life that so very few women will work for the emancipation of their own half of the race."*

LIBRARY OF CONGRESS

# 1

**HEDDA HOPPER,** *dies at 80 in Los Angeles, California, 1966.* From childhood, Hedda Hopper (who was born Elda Furry in Pennsylvania) had two qualities that would serve her well. She was tough, and she was stragestruck. She *had* to be tough; she was one of nine children.

She quit school after the eighth grade and ran away to join the theatre. She was forcibly returned to her home, but didn't stay there long. As soon as she could get away, she joined the chorus of the Aborn Light Opera Company and made her stage debut in 1907. Her New York debut came a year later in *The Pied Piper* at the Majestic Theatre, and it was there that she met her husband, actor William DeWolf Hopper. He was twenty-seven years older than she and had been married four times, but that didn't frighten her. They were married in 1913, and their one son, William Junior, was born two years later.

At first Hopper tried to be a nice, submissive little wife. She trotted after her husband when he was on tour and tended to his career and their son. However, she still took parts on stage and in movies now and then, and when she changed her name to Hedda on the advice of a numerologist, she found herself in demand for film roles. By 1920, she was making $1,000 a week, the same salary as her husband. He was outraged by her success, and she was equally infuriated by his affairs. They were divorced in 1922.

In 1923 Hopper signed a $250-a-week contract with MGM, making "B" movies in such rapid succession that she became known as the "Queen of the Quickies." But her career never really took off.

It was in 1937 that she found her real calling. The press was looking for a rival to gossip columnist Louella Parsons. Hopper was sug-

gested since she had plenty of contacts in the entertainment industry but wasn't a large enough star to throw her weight around. Her column began syndication in thirteen papers, and at first she tried to print relatively tame news that wouldn't offend anyone. Readers were bored. So she started writing scandal, and suddenly she was a hit. As she said later, "The minute I started to trot out the juicy stuff my phone began to ring."

In the process of achieving extraordinary power and popularity, Hopper and her rival Parsons destroyed a number of careers and wounded many others. Hollywood personalities hated the two women—one actress sent Hopper a live skunk in a hatbox—but they were afraid of the columnists's abilities to make or break stars. Hopper thought her power was rather amusing and dubbed her Beverly Hills mansion "the house that fear built." She also had no qualms about dabbling in politics. Staunchly conservative, she attacked F.D.R. and Adlai Stevenson, convinced Richard Nixon to run for Congress, and backed Barry Goldwater, Joseph McCarthy, J. Edgar Hoover, General Douglas MacArthur, and Ronald Reagan "after he got over being foolishly liberal." She favored the blacklisting of artists "with communist connections" and dubbed MGM "Metro-

HEDDA HOPPER: *Dressed to kill.*

Goldwyn-Moscow." A number of newspapers dropped her column in response to these views, but she remained influential, and there was little that her victims could do about her often arbitrary judgments. Once actress Merle Oberon asked Hopper why she wrote such awful things about her. Hopper simply patted Oberon's arm kindly and said, "Bitchery, dear. Sheer bitchery."

# 2

**NELL GWYN,** *born Eleanor Gwyn in London, England, 1650.* Gwyn got a bad start in life. Her mother was an ex-prostitute; her father was nowhere to be found. By the age of ten Gwyn was working as a barmaid, dodging insults, pickpockets, and men's roving hands. At thirteen

she graduated to selling oranges at the new King's Theatre in Drury Lane, and a year later, probably *via* the bedroom of the leading actor, she landed on the stage. She immediately became a public favorite, less for her universally acknowledged comic talent than for her

NELL GWYN: *From barmaid to royal mistress.*

pretty face and shapely legs. She showed off the latter as frequently as possible by playing male, or "breeches," parts.

Eventually "pretty, witty Nell" caught the eye of King Charles II, which was exactly what she wanted. Charles was notorious for his mistresses, and he spent much of his time lavishing titles and wealth on them and on his fourteen illegitimate children, although the treasury strained under the pressure. For nearly twenty years, Gwyn worked to get similar treatment for herself and her two sons by Charles, but there was a difference between Gwyn and the other mis-

tresses. They were noblewomen, and she was not. So it took threats of going back on the stage, pleas, scenes, tears, and elaborate ploys to get her older son named Baron of Heddington, Earl of Burford, and Duke of St. Albans. According to one story, what finally did it was her saying to the boy in Charles's presence, "Come hither, you little bastard." When Charles protested at such language, she said slyly that "she had no better name to call him by."

For Gwyn herself there were no titles; that would have been going too far. But the people, who hated the king's mistresses and his toler-

ant attitude toward Catholicism, loved good old working-class Protestant Nell. And she never pretended to be anything but what she was; she called whoring her profession.

A classic story about Gwyn's blunt honesty concerns the rivalry between the King's two chief mistresses—Gwyn and the Catholic Duchess of Portsmouth. The Duchess served as a focal point for public animosity, and one day, when Gwyn was riding through the streets of London, her carriage was mistaken for the duchess's. Stones were hurled and insults flew thick and fast until Gwyn poked her head out of the carriage and called, in her best Drury Lane-trained voice: "Pray, good people, be civil. I am the *Protestant* whore."

# 3

**GERTRUDE STEIN,** *born in Allegheny, Pennsylvania, 1874.* Her name has come to symbolize a strange and magnificent era, when most of the artistic talent in the Western world convened in Paris to challenge old ideas. The greats of the time were all there—Hemingway, Joyce, Fitzgerald, Gide, Valery, and Pound—but above and apart from them all sat Stein, reigning over the expatriate circles like a fleshy deity. Some thought she looked like a Jewish buddha. Sherwood Anderson called her "a strong woman with legs like stone pillars." Ezra Pound called her "an old tub of guts." Others were kinder. Sylvia Beach, who ran the notable Paris bookstore called Shakespeare & Company, said that Stein had "a delectable voice, mannish but velvety."

There were a few people, of course, who adored Gertrude Stein, especially her lover, Alice Toklas, but most of those who knew her nourished a deep dislike of her, of her books, or of both. Few people, at least in Paris, gave a damn about her lifestyle; it was her monstrous ego that disturbed them. Fortunately for Stein, the same egotism that drove people away from her convinced her that she was indeed a goddess in her own time, a living muse, and a woman of infinite genius. Her childhood had been spent in Vienna, Paris, and San Francisco. She had attended Radcliffe, where she studied with William James, and then went on to Johns Hopkins to study medicine. She might have graduated, but a complicated love affair with two other women led to her withdrawal in 1902. Still, she had no reason to doubt her intellectual capacity, so she had gone to Paris to join her brother Leo and start what she was sure would be the greatest literary and artistic salon in that city.

And, to the distress of her critics, she was right. Picasso, Matisse, and Braque graced her home with their conversation and their paintings. (In 1969, her art collection was valued at six million dollars.) And as the years passed, the literary figures of the day began to come, one by one, to pay homage to her. The only holdout was James Joyce, whose rivalry with Stein became legendary and split the artists of Paris into two camps.

In about 1910, Stein and her brother began to grow apart. This estrangement began when her brother called Picasso's work "god-almighty rubbish." It ended when Stein realized that "it was I who was the genius, there was no reason for it but I was, and he was not."

Although Stein's early books, particularly *Three Lives*, demonstrate a brilliant mastery of traditional English prose, she elected to write in a deliberately experimental style. Like the music of her contemporary, Arnold Schönberg, her dense and repetitive style confused and bewildered some and infuriated others. Stein was almost universally attacked. One critic summarized her work as follows: "Gertrude Stein's prose song is a cold, black suet pudding. . . . Cut it at any point, it is the same thing; the same heavy, sticky opaque mass . . . it is mournful and monstrous, composed of dead and inanimate material." Such attacks merely convinced her that she was ahead of her time. "Einstein was the creative philosophic mind of the century," she insisted, "and I have been the creative literary mind of the century." On another occasion, when she was asked why she didn't write the way she talked, she replied, "Why don't you read the way I write?"

Stein, unlike many of her fellow expatriates, remained in France through both world wars. She had little reason to return to the U.S.; her only visit back had been in 1935 to promote one of her books, *The Autobiography of Alice B. Toklas,* and she had been consistently harrassed—by cartoonists, who attacked her clothes, her body, and her eccentricities; and by critics, who attacked the book. Nevertheless, in 1946, just after the war, she made plans to return to America. She never had the chance to leave. On July 27, 1946, she succumbed to cancer. As she lay dying, she asked those assembled around her, "What is the answer?" No one spoke. After a long pause, she tried again. "What is the question?"

# 4

**BETTY FRIEDAN,** *born Betty Naomi Goldstein in Peoria, Illinois, 1921.* In June 1947 a graduate of Smith College married a man named Carl Friedan and became a housewife. By 1957 she had come to the conclusion that "there was something wrong with *me* because I didn't have an orgasm waxing the kitchen floor." And in 1963, she published *The Feminine Mystique,* a wonderful, sad, funny, revolutionary book that sparked the modern women's movement. In 1966, she founded the National Organization for Women (NOW), the most powerful lobbying group for women's rights in the United States. In 1970, she led the National Women's Strike for Equality. Throughout the '70s, she wrote, spoke, organized, advised, and was honored for her efforts on behalf of women. And in 1981, she wrote *The Second Stage,* an assessment of the new needs of the women's movement, which was almost as controversial as its predecessor. Not a bad track record for one person. Not bad at all.

# 5

**BELLE STARR,** *born Myra Belle Shirley in Carthage, Missouri, 1848.* Men didn't last very long around Belle Starr, but it wasn't really her fault. She just seemed to end up in the middle of violence all her life. Her father's house served as a hideout for a number of outlaws, including the Younger brothers and Jesse James. Her brother, Edward, who rode with Quantrill's gang, was killed by Union troops in 1863. By 1867 her other brother was dead as well. She worked in saloons and continued to house fugitives from the law. The extent of her hospitality can be witnessed in the birth of her daughter, Pearl Younger, in 1869.

Starr eloped with outlaw Jim Reed, and the happy pair ran off to Los Angeles, where they had a son,

Edward Reed. Then they headed for Texas, and within a year, Jim Reed had been shot to death. Starr refused to identify the body just to keep the deputy who shot him from collecting the bounty.

Apparently deciding (with a little help from her neighbors) that Texas was not her lucky state, she moved to Oklahoma, married Cherokee Indian Sam Starr, and set up a lucrative business in stolen horseflesh. She was charged four times with organizing gangs of horse thieves, but it wasn't until 1883 that she actually went to jail, and then only for nine months. She eloped with another man, but he drowned, and not long afterward, Sam Starr was shot to death. Her last lover, a young Cherokee name Jim July, seems to have survived unscathed. In 1889, Starr died—you guessed it—of gunshot wounds. No one was ever arrested for her murder, despite the fact that there were numerous suspects, the most likely of them her son, Edward Reed.

# 6 ———————————

**ANNE of England,** *born in St. James's Palace, London, England, 1665.* The last of the Stuarts to rule England, Anne had an unenviable life. When she was six, her mother died, and Anne's childhood was little more than a lonely series of illnesses. At eighteen she was married to Prince George of Denmark, with whom she diligently tried to produce an heir. Seventeen pregnancies in seventeen years resulted in only five live births, and four of those five babies died in infancy. When her last son died of smallpox at age eleven, Anne signed a document which granted the throne to the family of Hanover upon her death.

In 1702, she became Queen. She was prematurely aged, and crippled with gout. She had no education in governing and knew little of either history or geography; she could sew, say her prayers, play cards, sing, dance, draw, and speak

French. Her husband was dull, bored with government, and a heavy drinker who died in 1708. All in all, they were not a couple to capture the hearts and minds of their century. Still, Anne accomplished a great deal by emphasizing her "English heart," and she was soon known to her subjects as "Good Queen Anne." Her reign marked a number of beginnings and endings, including the rise of the two-party system in Parliament and the last royal veto of an act of Parliament.

# 7 ———————————

**LAURA INGALLS WILDER,** *born Laura Elizabeth Ingalls in Pepin, Wisconsin, 1867.* Until she was in her sixties, Laura Ingalls Wilder's life was not unusual for her time. Her family moved from state to state, living in Wisconsin, Missouri, Kansas, Minnesota, Iowa, and South Dakota, carving farms from the wilderness or searching for work for Laura's father. Sporadically educated, she helped her sisters and parents with various chores and eventually contributed to the family income by teaching school and sewing shirts at twenty-five cents a day. And in 1885, she married Almanzo James Wilder, a farmer ten years her senior. They had two children, one of whom died in infancy, and they dealt with their share of misfortunes—crop failures, fire, and illness—before establishing a profitable farm in Missouri.

But in the early 1930s, her life changed. Her daughter, Rose, encouraged her to combine her talent for writing with her memories of a frontier childhood, and in 1932 Wilder published *Little House in the Big Woods*. There was praise for her simple, elegant, unsentimental style, and sequels followed. By 1943, she'd written eight books, only one of which failed to win a Newbery Award for children's books. By 1977, twenty million copies of her books had been sold,

and they had spawned a television series and translations in fourteen foreign languages and Braille. Their heroine, a very slightly fictionalized version of Wilder herself, is strong, likeable, and spirited, and at one point makes a cautious declaration of her strength that sounds eerily like the "I'm not a feminist, but . . ." statements of today. In the description of her wedding, Wilder reports that she refused to say "obey." Her husband was quite surprised and asked, "Are you for woman's rights?" "No," she responded. "I do not want to vote. But I can not make a promise that I will not keep."

# 8 ———————————

**KATE CHOPIN,** *born Katherine O'Flaherty in St. Louis, Missouri, 1851.* In 1899, a perfectly respectable-looking, intelligent, charming mother of six, plump, white-haired, and still quite attractive, was being skinned alive by some well-meaning reviewers who were convinced that she meant to corrupt the morals of youth and destroy civilization as they know it. She *did* mean to destroy civilization—or selected parts of it, at least.

The book causing all the fuss was *The Awakening*, Kate Chopin's second novel. Writing had been her favorite hobby ever since, at seventeen, she had learned to smoke Turkish cigarettes and to hate being "one of the acknowledged belles of St. Louis." However, for twenty years, during her marriage and early widowhood, she'd set it aside, devoting her time to her family and to reading voraciously. By 1890, when her first novel appeared, she was a confirmed radical and agnostic. In 1894 and 1897, she published collections of short stories that made her moderately famous; critics, seeing precisely what they wished, called them "mild yarns about genteel Creole life," ignoring the undertones of protest and rebellion in almost every tale. Taking the side of the underdog and the inarticulate, her stories challenged marriage, misogyny, racism, and the Victorian myth of female asexuality. However, *The Awakening* was a different matter entirely. This time the message was unmistakable—the heroine, Edna Pontellier, is a married woman who dares to fall in love with another man. She demands independence, leaves her husband, and, because there is no place for her in her society, kills herself. The public was appalled.

Critics called *The Awakening* "sad and mad and bad," "an essentially vulgar story," and "not a healthy book." It "leaves one sick of human nature," wrote one reviewer, and another added, "the purport of the story can hardly be described in language fit for publication." Even Willa Cather, who called the style "exquisite and sensitive," found the plot "trite and sordid." Libraries in St. Louis banned it, and Chopin became a social pariah. To make matters worse, the royalties over the first three years amount to only $145, and her next collection of stories was rejected by her publisher. She tried to apologize, saying it was not her fault but Edna's for "making such a mess of things and working out her own damnation as she did," but it was futile. Little wonder that, although she lived for five more years, she never wrote another novel.

# 9

**AMY LOWELL,** *born in Brookline, Massachusetts, 1874.* Imagine, if you will, a very fat woman from one of the most illustrious families in Massachusetts, wearing frilly clothes, smoking cigars, sleeping in the daytime, writing poetry at night, keeping all the mirrors in her house covered, and submitting her guests to the tender mercies of her pack of untrained dogs. You will then understand why Amy Lowell's eccentricities were often more widely discussed than her poetry, which was excellent and which established here as the new American leader of the Imagist movement begun in England by Ezra Pound. Imagism rebelled against old-fashioned romanticism, using new subjects and abandoning tightly structured verses. Lowell mastered these techniques so thoroughly that Pound jokingly renamed his movement "Amygism," and thus she realized a dream she had nurtured since adolescence. In her journal, she had lamented at fifteen, "I am ugly, fat, conspicuous & dull," but she had consoled herself with a wish: "I should like best of anything to be literary." And so in her poem "The Sisters," it is with more than a touch of pride that she accepts her own oddities, announcing, "Taking us by and large, we're a queer lot / We women who write poetry."

# 10

**ELIZA LYNN LINTON,** *born Eliza Lynn at Crosthwaite vicarage in Cumberland, England, 1822.* It would be an understatement of massive proportions to say that Eliza Linton had strong opinions. An opponent of higher education for women, she hated those of her sex who were "bold in bearing" and "masculine in mind," loving those who were instead "tender, loving, retiring [and] domestic." She called feminists "the Shrieking Sisterhood" and feminism "a pitiable mistake and a grand national disaster." In 1868, she castigated "The Girl of the Period" as "hard, unloving, mercenary, ambitious, without domestic faculty and devoid of healthy natural instincts." "Men are afraid of her; and with reason," she insisted. "They may amuse themselves with her for an evening, but they do not readily take her for life."

Her sentiments were hardly uncommon in her own time, and we can hear their echoes even today. But ironically, she made her views well-known and influential by breaking the very rules she laid down for others. She was a successful novelist and England's first salaried woman journalist, an aggressive, angry writer who was considered an unfeminine rebel by her own family. She had no children and separated from her irresponsible husband when he spent her money and interfered with her ability to write. Although she had many close female friends, she claimed to hate women "as a race" and wrote her autobiography as *The Autobiography of Christopher Kirkwood*, changing herself into a male protagonist. Furthermore, with all her spite for educated women, feminism, and feminists, she had a much-loved protegee named Beatrice Harraden, a university graduate and feminist writer whom Linton called "my little B.A."

# 11

**SYLVIA PLATH,** *dies at 30 in London, England, 1963.* Sylvia Plath was a living paradox: an instinctively creative woman who spent most of her life trying to destroy herself. She began her literary career in high school, publishing poetry in the *Christian Science Monitor* and submitting forty-five stories to *Seventeen* before one was finally accepted. In her journal she called herself "the girl who wanted to be God" and wrote, "I am afraid of getting older. I am afraid of getting married. . . . I want to be free."

She was born in the wrong era. As she grew to womanhood and began attending Smith College, the "feminine mystique" that Betty Friedan would later describe was in full bloom. The women who had taken defense jobs during World War II had been told to go home; the men were back, and women were now unnecessary. A woman's place was in the home, her duties to be pleasantly submissive to her husband and to bear as many children as possible. Her greatest fears were supposed to be loneliness and waxy yellow buildup.

At Smith, Plath continued to be an excellent student and a popular one. Everything seemed to be going her way. She even won a month in New York City as a guest editor for *Mademoiselle,* but her experiences there only made her feel desperately insecure. She suffered a nervous breakdown and was subjected to electroshock treatments, but they didn't help. She tried to kill herself and almost succeeded.

After being institutionalized briefly and dyeing her hair blonde, Plath returned to Smith, where she had a number of affairs. In 1955, she graduated *summa cum laude* with a special award for her thesis on Dostoevsky. Once again, all seemed to be right with the world, and she headed for England on a Fulbright scholarship. There she met poet Ted Hughes and fell in love with him, dreaming of a poetic partnership in which they would train each other—and in which he, of course, would be her superior. "The girl who wanted to be God" was looking for a better, a bigger god to run her life. Not to do so would have made her seem unwomanly.

In 1956, she married Hughes, and they did indeed form a literary partnership of sorts. However, Plath thought that Hughes's work was more important than hers and spent a great deal of time typing his manuscripts and working as his literary agent, with the predicable result that he became better known more quickly than she. Nonetheless, her poetry improved, and she

managed to complete her degree at Cambridge without another suicide attempt.

In 1960, Plath published her first collection of poems, *The Colossus,* which was well received by critics. In the same year, after a long period of trying and feeling inadequate as a woman, she finally had a child. It is clear in her writing from the first years of her marriage that she thought of her husband as a poet first and a man second, while she herself was primarily a woman, who must finish the housework, take care of her husband, and produce babies before she could turn to the "pleasant extra" of writing.

The year 1962 was the most important, perhaps, in her entire life. It was certainly one of the most active. She wrote short stories and worked on a novel, *The Bell Jar,* based on her 1953 nervous breakdown. In January her second child was born, and she wrote a verse play, *Three Women.* Then, in July, she discovered that her husband was having an affair. They separated and began divorce proceedings, and Plath suddenly felt reborn. "I shall be a rich, active woman," she wrote joyously, "not a servant-shadow as I have been." She began eight months of extraordinary productivity, writing in this period almost all of the passionate,

mythological, violent, autobiographical poetry for which she is known. She knew how good these poems were and wrote to her mother, "I am a writer . . . I am a genius of a writer . . . I am writing the best poems of my life; they will make my name." She started work on a new novel with a hopeful ending, and in December, she moved into a London house once occupied by Yeats.

Once again, everything seemed to be wonderful for her, which meant that something awful was just around the corner. London's worst winter in more than a century set in. Light and heat were frequently cut off, the pipes froze, and she had no telephone. On February 11, she set mugs of milk by her children's cribs, went into the kitchen, stuffed towels into the cracks around the door, and turned on the gas, killing herself. The poems she had written were published as *Ariel* in 1965, establishing her reputation as one of the great writers of her time. They were not published in the order she had intended. She had wanted to end the collection with "Wintering," a hopeful poem, but the published arrangement, which places the darkest, most violent poems near the end, unfortunately makes her appear desperate.

# 12

**ALICE ROOSEVELT LONG-WORTH,** *born Alice Lee Roosevelt, New York City, 1884.* If you think Amy Carter got a lot of attention, you should have seen the fuss the press made over Theodore Roosevelt's daughter. Her family called her "Baby Lee," and T. R. called her "Mousiekins" on occasion, but reporters called her "Princess Alice." Even she admitted to "a proclivity toward malice" and later said, "I was a very disagreeable young person—very disagreeable." She was also beautiful, with golden curls, blue eyes, and a proud,

haughty face. A color was named for her. A song was written about her. She smoked in public. She was one of the first women in America to drive a car, and she drove with reckless abandon. A friend asked T. R., "Can't you control your daughter?" And T. R. answered, "I can either run the country or control Alice, not both." At twenty-two she married Nicholas Longworth, later Speaker of the House; they honeymooned in Cuba and climbed San Juan Hill together. He died in 1931, but she continued to be a prominent figure in Washington, and the stories about her sharp tongue and sense of mischief were legion.

She held legendary dinner parties with guests chosen for conflict rather than compatibility. She was unfailingly loyal to her friends and unflinchingly vicious to her enemies. She had a pillow in her library that read, "If you can't say something good about someone, sit right here by me." She did a mean imitation of her cousin Eleanor, never drank, and loved prize fights. One evening, as her chauffeur was driving her to a fight, he was sideswiped by a driver who yelled, "You black bastard." Longworth leaned from the car and shouted

back, "Shut up, you white son of a bitch." She refused to trim the poison ivy that grew by her door, insisting that she liked it. She became famous for her low, wide-brimmed hats, which bothered Lyndon Johnson. "Mrs. Longworth, it's hard to kiss you under that brim," he once said. "That's why I wear it," she snapped back.

But perhaps the best Longworth story is the one in which Senator Joseph McCarthy made the fatal error of calling her by her first name. She stared at him coldly and replied, "The policeman and the trash man may call me Alice; you—can—not."

# 13

**SAROJINI NAIDU,** *born Sarojini Chattopadhyaya in Hyderabad, India, 1879.* Sarojini Naidu is hardly to be seen in Richard Attenborough's virtually all-male film, *Gandhi,* yet she was so important within the Indian independence movement that Gandhi once suggested her as the first prime minister of free India. Even if she had not been a prominent political figure, she would have been a fascinating woman. Born to a highly respected Brahmin family, she was encouraged by her father to become a great mathematician or scientist, but she wanted to be a poet. She entered the University of Madras at the age of twelve, where she did brilliant work and earned a scholarship to study in England. She attended King's College in London and Girton College at Cambridge, charmed English society, worked for woman suffrage, and met Thomas Hardy, Oscar Wilde, Henry James, and Aubrey Beardsley. She rebelled against tradition and alienated her family by marrying out of caste, and she became one of India's most celebrated poets, bridging two cultures by writing in English about Indian life.

Add to these accomplishments her work with the independence movement, and we have before us a woman of conviction, poetic skill, intelligence, and charisma. She was imprisoned almost as many times as Gandhi and led his Anti-Salt Law campaign after he was jailed. She headed a Bombay salon at which people of all religions and colors were welcome. She served as president of the Indian National Congress and worked for a time "when the finest Untouchables will be ruling me, a Brahmin." To the Indians she announced herself as "the emblem of our Mother India"; to the British she cried, "Come and imprison me." To both she said, "I was born a rebel, have lived a rebel, and expect to die a rebel unless I free India."

LIBRARY OF CONGRESS

ALICE ROOSEVELT LONGWORTH: *She had wealth, beauty, and power, and a legendary viper's tongue.*

# 14

**MARGARET E. KNIGHT,** *born in York, Maine, 1838.* As a child, "the only things" Mattie Knight wished for "were a jack knife, a gimlet and pieces of wood." At twelve she created her first invention while watching her brothers work in a cotton mill—a device to keep the potentially dangerous steel-tipped shuttles from falling out of place.

In 1870 she patented a machine for making square-bottomed paper bags. In all, she held about twenty-seven patents for inventions which included a dress and skirt shield, a clasp for holding robes, a spit, six machines for shoemaking, a window frame and sash, a numbering machine, and various devices relating to rotary engines.

# 15

**ACCA LAURENTIA,** *dies in Rome, date unknown.* According to tradition, Rome was founded by two brothers, Romulus and Remus, who were miraculously saved as infants after they were abandoned. They were suckled by a she-wolf and later taken from the wolf and raised by a shepherd named Faustulus. However, the word for "she-wolf" in Latin, *lupa,* can also mean "prostitute," and it just so happens that the wife of Faustulus, Acca Laurentia, was locally known as Lupa for her bodily generosity. In fact, her home was known as the Wolf's Den or Lupercal.

So it may not have been a wolf who suckled Romulus and Remus; it may have been a prostitute, and a legend was constructed around later Romans' desire to "cleanse" the truth. That there was some whitewashing going on is obvious. During the early days of Rome Laurentia's death was commemorated by a festival called the Lupercalia held annually on February 15, which was noted for outbursts of public sexuality. As the years passed, it was considered undignified to celebrate a holiday so closely associated with a prostitute, so although sexual excesses during the Lupercalia continued, the ostensible purpose of the festival was changed into a tribute to Faunus, or Pan. The manipulation of Rome's origins hardly seems fair, especially as Laurentia probably gave her foster sons more than their lives. She apparently invested her earnings from her profession in real estate, and when she died she seems to have left them a lovely little piece of land with a scenic view of seven hills—the future site of Rome.

# 16

**TITUBA,** *born in the West Indies, in the seventeenth century, exact date unknown.* The infamous Salem witch trials of colonial Massachusetts resulted in the arrest of 150 people, and the deaths of over twenty. Once the frenzy started, those accused in turn accused anyone they could think of, and the few people who were sane enough to realize the madness of it all were executed for disagreeing with their fellow citizens. The whole thing started deceptively simply in the home of Reverend Samuel Parris, who had a slave named Tituba. In the evenings Tituba used to entertain some girls from the neighborhood whom one of the accused in the trials would later dub the "witch bitches." The youngest of the girls was Reverend Parris's nine-year-old daughter Elizabeth; the oldest was Mary Warren, a twenty-year-old servant.

Tituba regaled these girls with tales of the West Indies, and these tales led to descriptions of voodoo rituals, fortune-telling, and spirits. She also seems to have shown them or performed for them a few simple charms, like the "witch cake," used to cure disease. Excited by these stories and bits of magic, the girls began to react strangely with fits and episodes of disobedience and blasphemy. When the fits were ascribed to witchcraft, the girls quickly accused a series of helpless people, Tituba among them; later they progressed to attacking "respectable" townspeople as well.

Poor Tituba did not fare well, although she was not executed. She was sentenced to death in 1692 but not immediately hanged. She was instead held in jail for thirteen months, until May 1693, when another jury failed to reach a decision on her fate and freed her. But she could not leave jail. Prison inmates at the time were required to pay for their own maintenance, and Tituba had no money. The court finally sold her to pay for her expense.

# 17

**MARIAN ANDERSON,** *born in Philadelphia, Pennsylvania, 1902.* At the age of six, Anderson began singing in the local Baptist church. By the time she graduated from high school, she knew her rich contralto voice was something special, and she went to New York to train it. There, in 1925, despite the considerable disadvantage of being black, she defeated nearly three hundred competitors in a contest, and within five years she was touring Europe. Her New York debut didn't come until 1936, but it was a great success, and her popularity rose steadily.

In 1939, she was scheduled to perform in Washington, D.C., but trouble arose. The Daughters of the American Revolution refused to let her sing at Constitution Hall, claiming that the problem was one of scheduling, not of Anderson's race, but no one believed it for a

LIBRARY OF CONGRESS

MARIAN ANDERSON: *A contralto of great dignity and presence.*

minute. Outraged, First Lady Eleanor Roosevelt resigned from the D.A.R. and arranged for Anderson to perform at the Lincoln Memorial to an estimated crowd of 75,000.

By the time of her retirement in 1965, Marian Anderson had been the first black singer to appear at the Metropolitan Opera, had sung at the White House, worked for civil rights, served as a delegate to the United Nations, and had written her autobiography, *My Lord, What a Morning.* In 1978 she was awarded a special gold medal by Congress for her "unselfish devotion to the promotion of the arts" and her "untiring efforts on behalf of the brotherhood of man."

# 18

**MARY I of England,** *born in Greenwich Palace, Greenwich, England, 1516.* Poor Mary. The daughter of Henry VIII and Catherine of Aragon, she was caught up in the turmoil following Rome's refusal to allow a royal divorce so that Henry could re-marry and father the male heir he felt necessary for the continuity of his line. Rome's refusal left Henry with only one option if he wanted a male heir, and he took it. He severed his ties to Rome, declared himself Supreme Head of the Church of England, granted himself a divorce, and married his pregnant mistress, Anne Boleyn, a lady-in-waiting to the former queen. With her attempted ecape to Calais foiled, Mary was declared illegiti-mate and separated from her mother, never to see her again. Then, as a final insult, she was made a lady-in-waiting to the new queen's daughter Elizabeth. But the tide soon turned—Anne Boleyn was discarded and beheaded, and now Elizabeth was also declared il-legitimate. Mary was released from her duties and given her own household with her own servants, including a female jester named Jane the Fool. To her credit, Mary urged her father to treat Elizabeth kindly.

But not many people treated Mary kindly. After Henry's third wife bore him the long-awaited son, Edward, he declared that if Edward died without heirs, Mary would succeed him, and that if Mary died without heirs, the crown would pass to Elizabeth. However, as soon as Henry died, the boy king Edward was surrounded by Protestants eager to keep the Catholic Mary out of the succession. When Ed-ward died in 1553, Mary almost lost her chance at the throne, and she had a hard time keeping it at that.

To begin with, although she started her reign with a policy of religious tolerance, she became the focus of strong anti-Catholic senti-ment. Dead animals dressed as priests were left in conspicuous places, and her chaplain was attacked in St. Paul's Cathedral. In 1554, she made matters worse by marrying King Philip II of Spain. Rumors of Spanish invasions and duels in the streets flew widly, but she didn't care. She loved Philip and she was desperate for children. Unfortunately, Philip didn't love her and loved England even less. He stayed with her only long enough to realize that she was barren and that Parliament was not going to make him King of England.

Mary, never healthy, grew increasingly ill and nervous. Convinced that her childlessness, her lovelessness, and her misery were due to a lack of religious zeal, she began executing Protestants, acquir-

ing the nickname "Bloody Mary," not entirely deservedly, especially given the behavior of other rulers at the time. She died at forty-two, almost alone, since most of her supporters had gone rushing off to Elizabeth, each anxious to be the first to declare his undying loyalty to the crown.

MARY I: *"When I am dead and opened, you shall find 'Calais' lying in my heart."*

LIBRARY OF CONGRESS

# 19

**CARSON McCULLERS,** *born Lula Carson Smith in Columbus, Georgia, 1917.* Whoever popularized the stereotypical image of "The Writer" must have been thinking of Carson McCullers or someone like her. At sixteen she went to New York to make her fortune and worked at various low-paying jobs while she took creative writing courses and tried to find a publisher. When she did, fame was instantaneous; she was hailed as "the most remarkable novelist to come out of America for a generation."

However, she was mentally unstable. She put enormous emotional demands on those around her. She had a tempestuous, difficult relationship with her husband, Reeves McCullers, whom she married in 1937, divorced in 1941, remarried in 1945, left in 1948, rejoined in 1949, and left again shortly before his suicide. She drank heavily, had crippling bouts of insecurity and illness, and tried to kill herself. Self-destructive and brilliant, she was a living archetype, and although her later works were failures, her early, remarkable tales of isolation, freakishness, and grotesqueries should not be missed. *The Heart Is a Lonely Hunter* (1940) and *The Member of the Wedding* (1946) are her best-known, and perhaps her best-written works, but "The Ballad of the Sad Café" is a bizarre, tragic story that's also well worth reading.

# 20

**SUSAN BROWNELL ANTHONY,** *born in Adams, Massachusetts, 1820.* If we could move backward in time to about 1835 or 1840 to watch Susan B. Anthony in action, we might have trouble finding her. The newspapers wouldn't help us; the keepers of lecture halls would never have heard of her. Eventually, we might find her teaching school for $1.50 a week plus board or managing the family farm. She would be a rather handsome young Quaker, plainly dressed, looking like any of a number of handsome, plainly dressed Quaker women.

But if we could follow her for a while, silently and invisibly, we might see hints of things to come. We would see her rejecting two marriage proposals. We would see her bake biscuits for her brother-in-law and hear him say condescendingly, "I'd rather see a woman make biscuits like these than solve the knottiest problem in algebra." And we'd hear her firm reply, "There is no reason why she should not be able to do both." We'd see her attend a temperance meeting and try to speak, only to be told, "The sisters were not invited here to speak, but to listen and to learn." And we'd see her march out of the hall, leading a few brave women in her first public protest.

From that moment on, Anthony's life was one of action, and even invisible observers would have to move quickly to keep up. She championed the causes of temperance, abolition, women's rights, and labor, using all of her considerable skill to remake the world. She spoke, wrote, organized, circulated petitions, edited a newspaper, mourned for colleagues who married, took joy in the younger women who flocked to her and her cause, and generated support for women victimized by unfair laws. In 1871 alone she traveled thirteen thousand miles and made over 170 speeches. Arrested for trying to vote, she received a ridiculously unfair trial in which the judge directed the jury to find her guilty, and she refused to pay the fine he levied or to serve the jail sentence he imposed.

Throughout it all, she had an opinion on every issue and an answer for every critic. A Unitarian minister named Mayo told her, "You are not married. You have no business to be discussing marriage." "Well, Mr. Mayo," Anthony replied, "you are not a slave. Suppose you quit lecturing on slavery." That, in the proverbial nutshell, was Susan B. Anthony, whom Gertrude Stein, in her eponymous opera, called "the mother of us all."

# 21

**MARY EDWARDS WALKER,** *dies at 86 in Oswego, New York, 1919.* Mary Walker died as the result of a fall. She fell on the steps of the Capitol Building in Washington, D.C., which, like politicians, can be

LIBRARY OF CONGRESS

MARY EDWARDS WALKER: *Congress granted her permission to dress in male garb.*

particularly treacherous. Her mission had been in vain. She was trying to get her Congressional Medal of Honor back.

One of the first women doctors in America, Walker volunteered her

services to the Union during the Civil War. At first she could only find work as a nurse, but in 1863 she got an official appointment as an Army surgeon. Wearing her officer's uniform, she operated on the boys in blue and discovered the freedom that pants gave her. Off duty, she slipped behind Confederate lines to treat civilians. In 1864 she was captured in enemy territory and held for four months in a Richmond, Virginia, prison. Her freedom, achieved through the release of a Confederate surgeon, was probably the first exchange of male and female prisoners of equal rank.

After the war, Walker was awarded the Congressional Medal of Honor (presumably for her work behind enemy lines), becoming the only woman to receive the prestigious decoration. It was the source of her greatest pride, and she wore it for the rest of her life. Although her contemporaries doubted her sanity and taste (since she continued to dress in men's clothing), no one doubted the sincerity of her joy in the medal. It was therefore the greatest tragedy of her life when, in 1916, she was stricken from the rolls of the Medal of Honor recipients. She and 910 others who were not cited for specific acts of valor were purged from the list to preserve the medal's elite status. She spent the next three years trying to get the decision reversed, but she was not reinstated until 1977.

# 22

**EDNA ST. VINCENT MILLAY,** *born in Rockland, Maine, 1892.* A friend once described Millay as "very much a revolutionary in all her sympathies, and a wholehearted feminist." A man who had proposed to her called her "intoxicating." Supporters called her poetry elegant and skillfully written; opponents thought it old-fashioned. All of them were correct. Her poetry *was* old-fashioned; she wrote lyrical sonnets in an age of free verse. But it was also elegant and full of fire and rebellion, poetry of grace and technical skill in which she demanded free thought, free love, and equality.

A graduate of Vassar who moved to New York's Greenwich Village, then in its prime as America's artistic Bohemia, she had red hair, green eyes, a strong will, charisma, and a powerful love of sexual freedom. She was indeed intoxicating. As for the feminism, it takes only a

look at one sonnet written in 1923 to discover her views. The speaker's lover sees a book she is reading and cries, "What a big book for such a little head!" At first the speaker feels shock and betrayal; then she decides that she will play along with her lover's view of women, but that he will not like the results. "Give back my book and take my kiss instead," she says obligingly, but warns, "I never again shall tell you what I think. I shall be sweet and crafty, soft and sly." And one day, she predicts, she will leave him, because he would not let her be what she was.

# 23

**RUTH NICHOLS,** *born in New York City, 1901.* Nichols held thirty-five "firsts" for women in aviation. She was the first woman to earn an international hydroplane license, one of the first two women to get a transport license, and the first woman to fly a twin-engine executive jet. She set altitude, speed, and distance records throughout her life. She loved flying, loved "the power of [her] own hands managing this fierce and wonderful machine," the airplane.

It's almost frightening to think of what she might have accomplished had she not had such dreadful luck.

To begin with, her family tried everything it could, including bribery and browbeating, to make her "forget about a career and take her proper place in society." But Nichols secretly took flying lessons, and in 1928 she and her flying instructor made the first nonstop

RUTH NICHOLS: *In the days when a female aviator was an aviatrix and all Washington bureaucrats were men.*

LIBRARY OF CONGRESS

flight from New York to Miami. Suddenly she was famous, a turn of events that she found to be a mixed blessing. It got her a job with Fairchild Airplane and Engine Company, but she had to endure headlines like: "Flying Deb Pioneers New York-Miami Hop."

From then on, her life was a series of achievements snatched from the jaws of bad luck, of disappointments, and of "almosts." She entered the 1929 Women's Air Derby, the first cross-country air race for women, but she was eliminated in Columbus, Ohio, when a side wind blew her plane into a tractor. She tried to establish a national chain of Aviation Country Clubs, but the stock market crash destroyed her plans. In 1931, she set a women's altitude record of 28,743 feet despite fuel limitations and a primitive oxygen system. As she rose, the oxygen cooled to sixty degrees below zero, but she climbed higher and higher until her mouth was frozen and her fuel reserve was down to five gallons.

She was determined to be the first woman to fly solo across the Atlantic, but on her first attempt in June 1931, she crashed in New Brunswick, New Jersey, and was badly hurt. When she was partially recovered, and still wearing a back brace, she attempted a cross-country flight. She didn't make it, but she did fly from Oakland, California, to Louisville, Kentucky, setting a world women's distance record. Unfortunately for her transatlantic plans, her gas tank exploded, and her plane burned on the ground in Louisville. She fixed the plane, but she was stopped again by bad weather, so she made a record New York-to-Los Angeles run instead.

Next she decided to make a round-the-world flight, so she spent the following few years lecturing and trying to finance her plan. When it failed to materialize, she took a job as a copilot on commercial transport planes. In October of 1935, one of these planes missed the runway and exploded. She was thrown from the plane and seriously injured. Fifteen years later,

touring the world on behalf of UNICEF, she was a passenger on a plane that overshot an Irish airport and crashed into the sea. She wasn't hurt this time, but she spent the night in a lifeboat, and you'd think she would finally have given up on

airplanes. Far from it. In 1958, only two years before her death, she set two new records—a women's altitude record of 51,000 feet and a women's speed record of 1,000 miles per hour.

# 24

**GLADYS AYLWARD,** *born in Edmonton, England, 1902.* From the time she was a little girl, Gladys Aylward wanted to be a missionary in China. It was practically all she thought about, and at her first opportunity she began training with a group called the China Inland Mission. Unfortunately, after a short time, she was expelled from the program, not for lack of enthusiasm but for lack of ability.

Aylward was disappointed but not utterly crushed. If she couldn't go to China, she decided, perhaps there was work to be done in England, and she began doing social work in the slums of Bristol and Swansea. Then fate dealt her another blow; she almost died of double pneumonia. She returned to her home in Edmonton to recuperate and to look for a new purpose in life. She found it at a Methodist meeting. An assistant was needed for Mrs. Jeannie Lawson, a Scottish missionary in China. Anyone who could pay her own passage was welcome to take the post.

Aylward jumped at the chance. She took a job as a parlor maid and lived as cheaply as possible, saving all of her wages for the trip to the Orient. As soon as she could afford the least expensive ticket on the Trans-Siberian Railway, she left her job and her country, taking with her "a bedroll, a kettle, a saucepan, a suitcase of canned food, a little change and much religious fervor." By 1932 she was installed in Yancheng in northern China, where she quickly learned the local dialect and established an inn for mule drivers. There she and

Mrs. Lawson dispensed food and religion, making as many converts as they could.

Within a year, Mrs. Lawson died, and Aylward was left to run the Inn of the Sixth Happiness on her own. She earned the respect and friendship of the local villagers, who called her "Ai Weh-te"—both an approximation of "Aylward" and a phrase meaning "the virtuous one." Aylward told stories about Christianity, and her simple approach to religion was far more successful than the more sophisticated techniques she hadn't been able to master at the China Inland Mission. She became a Chinese citizen and was made the local foot inspector as part of the national campaign to end the mutilation of women's feet by binding.

Aylward's most famous accomplishment, however, had little to do with either religion or government reforms. In 1940, she escorted one hundred children, most of them between the ages of four and eight, on a twenty-seven-day march to escape the Japanese. As it had in the English slums, her selflessness nearly cost her her life; when she arrived at her destination she was suffering badly from typhus. She recovered, however, and spent the rest of her life lecturing, preaching, and working with lepers. Her march with the children was made famous by an Ingrid Bergman movie, *The Inn of the Sixth Happiness,* a film which Aylward detested because of Bergman's well-publicized private life. Aylward died in Taiwan in 1970.

# 25

**IDA NODDACK,** *born Ida Eva Tacke in Lackhausen/Wesel, Germany, 1896.* Marie Curie wasn't the only woman to make additions to the periodic table of the elements. Ida Noddack discovered two elements. Noddack worked with her husband, Walter, from the 1920s until his death in 1960 and alone thereafter. By the time she began her research, scientists already knew a great deal about elements found in nature. They knew, for example, that each element had a different number of positively-charged particles, or protons, in the nucleus of each atom. Up to a certain point, there seemed to be an element for every number—hydrogen had one proton, helium two, lithium three, and so on. But there were a few gaps in the lists. There should have been elements with forty-three and seventy-five protons each, but no one had ever found them.

So, motivated perhaps by the same instinct that makes people solve crossword puzzles, Noddack decided to fill in the gaps. In 1925 she discovered element 43 and named it masurium, after Masuria, where it was found. Since that time it has been renamed technetium. Later, she also isolated element 75, a rare metallic substance which is called rhenium after the River Rhine, near which Noddack was born. She is also credited with being one of the first scientists to suggest the possibility of nuclear fission, an idea which was met with disbelief at the time. Only in 1939, when American scientists confirmed the reported fission of the uranium atom in Germany, did Noddack receive the acknowledgment she deserved.

ETHEL LEGINSKA: *Two little letters transformed her into an instant Pole.*

# 26

**ETHEL LEGINSKA,** *dies at 83 in Los Angeles, California, 1970.* Ethel Leginska was actually Ethel Liggins of Hull, England. A child piano prodigy who studied in Frankfurt, Berlin, and Vienna, she changed her last name in the hope that it would help her career. Appropriately enough, she was nicknamed "the Paderewski of women pianists" by critics, who called her a "remarkably sound, intelligent, and finished player." She rapidly became famous in Europe and the U.S. because of

LIBRARY OF CONGRESS

her magnetic presence, her innovative style, and her ability to play demanding pieces with apparent ease. She was also somewhat notorious for her appearance; she bobbed her hair and on stage wore a black velvet jacket and skirt rather than an evening dress since it was "always the same and always comfortable, so that I can forget my appearance and concentrate on my art."

Her costume, unusual for the second decade of the twentieth century, was only one reason that she

shocked her audiences. They were also appalled at the fact that she spoke frequently on women's issues and advocated a system of child care for working women, a subject with which she was quite familiar until 1918, when she lost custody of her young son during her divorce proceedings. She offered to abandon her concert career and teach piano instead, but custody was awarded to her ex-husband.

Leginska made a career change in 1926, when she recovered from her third nervous breakdown. She

stopped performing and became a conductor and composer. Her compositions were highly regarded, and many of her pieces were performed by major orchestras during her lifetime. Her conducting career was similarly distinguished; despite claims that women couldn't handle the rigors of conducting, she led orchestras in Boston, Chicago, New York City, London, Munich, Paris, Havana, Dallas, and Berlin. She also organized three women's orchestras—for the cities of Boston, New York, and Chicago.

# 27 _____

**ALICE HAMILTON,** *born in New York City, 1869.* Taught by her mother that "personal liberty was the most precious thing in life" and that ambition was a virtue even in women, Alice Hamilton grew into a religious, curious tomboy with very definite goals. She wanted to be a doctor, but her family, primarily her father, objected. She enrolled in the Fort Wayne College of Medicine anyway, determined to improve her knowledge of science and to prove to her father that she was serious. Over the next several years, she became one of the best-educated physicians of her day. She studied at the University of Michigan's medical school, served internships at Minneapolis' Northwestern Hospital for Women and Children and at Boston's Northeastern Hospital for Women and Children, studied bacteriology in Ann Arbor, studied bacteriology and pathology in Germany, and put in a year at Johns Hopkins Medical School.

After serving as professor of pathology at Northwestern University, Hamilton expanded her education in a different way by becoming

ALICE HAMILTON: *Excellence in the public interest.*

LIBRARY OF CONGRESS

a resident at Chicago's Hull House. Eventually, she continued her work with bacteriology, studied at the Pasteur Institute in Paris, helped to stop a typhoid epidemic in Chicago, tried to end cocaine traffic in that city, and published a number of papers, but she felt "stranded" and aimless.

She had convinced herself that she'd "never be more than a fourth-rate scientist" when she chanced to read a book called *Dangerous Trades*. She realized how little care was taken in the United States to protect factory workers, and when she did more research on the subject she discovered that the U.S. had not one occupational safety law, few unions, and almost no company medical records. With great enthusiasm, she immersed herself in the study of industrial toxicology and became that specialty's great pioneer. Collecting case studies of industrial poisoning, she pushed for safety procedures in the lead, rubber, and munitions industries and proved that lead, nitrous fumes, and viscose rayon were causing side effects that included mental illness, loss of vision, paralysis, and death.

In 1919 Hamilton became the first woman professor at Harvard, when she took a job as assistant professor of industrial medicine at that university's prestigious medical school. But the honor associated with this position was greatly diminished by her rude treatment. She was never promoted beyond the rank of assistant professor, and was not allowed to enter the Harvard Club, march in the commencement procession, or claim her designated football tickets.

In a long and full life, Hamilton was active in a number of political causes, speaking on behalf of peace, state health insurance, birth control, and anarchists Sacco and Vanzetti—and against child labor, U.S. involvement in Vietnam, and the Cold War.

At the age of eighty-eight she said, "For me the satisfaction is that things are better now, and I had some part in it."

# 28

**MARY MASON LYON,** *born in Buckland, Massachusetts, 1797.* "It has sometimes seemed," wrote Mary Lyon, "as if there were a fire shut up in my bones." No wonder. The poor woman was trying to do the nearly impossible—to found the first women's college in the United States. Without compromising her purpose—the rigorous and thorough education of young women—she had to avoid offending the powerful and wealthy men capable of donating the necessary funds.

She knew she was playing a difficult game; "Many good men," she said, "will fear the effect on society of so much female influence." So she emphasized the fact that educated women would make superior wives and mothers, and she tried desperately to avoid taking credit for the project, saying, "It is

MARY LYON: *Founder of the first of the Seven Sisters.*

LIBRARY OF CONGRESS

desirable that the plans relating to the subject should not seem to originate with us, but with benevolent *gentlemen.*"

Lyon was, however, not willing to rely solely on the gentlemen. She scoured the countryside (raising eyebrows because she traveled without an escort), approaching women for donations which ranged from six cents to a few hundred dollars. More frequently, she was offered feathers for students' pillows or quilt scraps for students' sewing baskets, since few women had any money of their own to give. Nevertheless, in 1836, a charter was obtained, the cornerstone was laid, and Mary Lyon was elated. "The stones and brick and mortar speak a language which vibrates through my very soul." And in 1837, at a cost of $64 per student per year, Mount Holyoke began its task of making each young woman "a handmaid to the Gospel and an efficient auxiliary in the great task of renovating the world."

# 29

**"MOTHER" ANN LEE,** *born in Manchester, England, 1736.* At the death of her fourth successive child in infancy, a young mother, a blacksmith's wife and former textile mill worker, had a series of visions she believed to be divinely inspired. She saw herself die and be reborn, and she had a revelation of the perfect life, a life of plainness and celibacy. She began to preach her new gospel, but she met with persecution and imprisonment, so in 1774, after another vision, she went to America with eight disciples. She established a colony at Niskeyuna (now Watervliet), New York, operating on principles of communism and equality of all believers, regardless of race or sex. Her followers, known as the Shakers, believed that God had both a masculine and a feminine component and that Mother Ann was

Christ's second coming; worship consisted of singing, preaching, dancing, or sitting silently as the spirit moved. The Shakers were quite successful throughout the nineteenth century and founded a number of new communities, but only a handful of adherents remain today.

LIBRARY OF CONGRESS

CARRIE CHAPMAN CATT: *A champion of woman suffrage who, fearing "some increase in immorality through safety," shrank from birth control.*

# MARCH

## 1

**ASPASIA,** *born in Miletus, Greece, in the fifth century B.C., exact date unknown.* Athenian women in ancient times lived highly circumscribed lives; married early and confined to the women's quarters of their homes, they were rarely seen on the streets and were educated as little as possible. As long as they could spin, sew, keep house, bear children, and remain faithful to their husbands, they were good wives. No less and no more was tolerated from them.

The exceptions to this rule were the hetairai, or courtesans. Almost never Athenian by birth, they had no rights of citizenship and no secure legal status, but they had advantages that wives did not. They were not only allowed but expected to be able to discuss politics and philosophy. Hetairai could go where wives could not. They could speak on subjects forbidden to wives. And they were free agents sexually—they could flaunt their beauty as they chose, express their sexuality if they liked, and accept as clients anyone they wished.

Frequently, prominent men had favorite hetairai, and on occasion they married them. In any case, hetairai were always close to the centers of power. One of the most famous—and powerful—of them all was Aspasia, who was the mistress (and perhaps the wife) of Pericles. Some Athenians thought her breathtaking or at least unusually gifted; Plato credited her with teaching him about love, and Plutarch summarized her position as follows: "Pericles . . . was attracted to Aspasia mainly because of her potential wisdom. Socrates visited her from time to time with his disciples and some of his close friends brought their wives to listen to her conversation, even though she carried on a trade that was anything but honorable or even respectable, since it consisted of keeping a house of young courtesans."

Some resented Aspasia's business, but most of her enemies really resented her power. Pericles was deeply in love with her and respected her completely, taking her advice on all sorts of problems. When he discarded his wife and brought Aspasia to live with him in 445 B.C., the hetairai's critics grew more vociferous in their disapproval. Cratinus, a comedian, expressed the general feeling when he called her "that shameless bitch Aspasia," and Hermippus, another comedian, accused her in court of impiety and "procuring free-born Athenian women for Pericles." Only the eloquence and tears of Pericles won her acquittal, and they continued to live together until his death in 429. From the scant descriptions available, it appears that they had a remarkably equitable, affectionate, and happy relationship, especially for their times. That things were somewhat different then is illustrated by the wonder in Plutarch's tone as he relates a "legend": "The story goes that every day, when he went out to the market-place and returned, he greeted her with a kiss."

## 2

**ANNE FRANK,** *dies at 14 in the Bergen-Belsen concentration camp, Germany, 1945.* Anne's date of death is approximate; her mother and sister, Margot, both died before she did, and witnesses who knew her in Bergen-Belsen only knew that she died of typhus sometime at the beginning of March. Ironically, she died very shortly before her camp was liberated by Allied troops. But Anne is not known for her death. She is famous for her affirmation of life in the face of death and terror, for her eloquent expression of ordinary feelings in the midst of a world gone mad.

She was born on June 12, 1930, in Frankfurt, Germany, but she did not live there long. As soon as the Nazis came to power, her family fled Germany and moved to Amsterdam, and Anne's father, Otto Frank, started a business. As it turned out, the Franks did not flee far enough. In 1940, the Nazis invaded the Netherlands, and the persecution of the Jews began. The issuance of identification papers and gold stars, and the confiscation of bicycles were followed by the inevitable detentions and deportations, and the Franks, along with a few friends, went into hiding. Anne's diary records the persecutions and the pressures of hiding, along with her anger at her mother, her growing sexual awareness, her longing for privacy, her anxiety to be understood, and her ambition "to become a journalist someday and later on a famous writer."

In 1944 an informer denounced the Franks, and they were dragged from their hiding place and deported. All of the members of the group died during the war except Anne's father, who returned to the "Secret Annexe" after the war. Miep Gies, the Dutch woman who had sheltered the Franks, gave Otto Frank some papers she had found after the arrests; among them was Anne's diary. He had it published in 1947 (although he omitted many parts of it), and in the past forty years it has been translated into thirty languages and has been adapted for the stage, for films, and for television. The diary has become a symbol of what might have been and of what was destroyed by the Holocaust, and Anne has become an international heroine for her intelligence, her eloquence, her ordinary yet complex emotions, and her chilling, wrenching optimism: "Think of all the beauty still left around you and be happy."

# 3

**HYPATIA,** *born in Greece, in about 370, exact date unknown.* Hypatia was the daughter of Theon, a mathematician who gave her a rigorous education. She studied in Athens, established a mathematical reputation of her own, and then moved to Alexandria, where she quickly became famous for her knowledge. As one writer said, she was noted not only for her talents but also for "the singular modesty of her mind." She was also well known for her exquisite beauty.

But not everyone admired Hypatia. Some objected to the fact that she was equally willing to take pagans, Jews, and Christians as pupils. Some, like Cyril, Patriarch of Alexandria, thought her too quick to question religion and too dangerous to the young Christian Church. For the most part, Hypatia ignored such controversy. She concentrated on her studies, doing important work in algebra, giving public lectures, writing several books (none of which has survived) including a commentary on Ptolemy's *Almagest* and a commentary on Euclid, and inventing two astronomical instruments, a device for measuring the specific gravity of liquids, and a distillation machine.

Unfortunately, she could not immerse herself entirely in her work, nor could she achieve perfect isolation from her world. She was constantly hounded by church fathers for her secular humanism, and in March of 415 Cyril (who was later canonized) aroused a mob against her. As one author put it, "certain heady and rash cockbrains . . . watched this woman coming home from some place or other, they pulled her out of her chariot: they hauled her into the church called Caesarium: they stripped her stark naked: they razed the skin and rent the flesh of her body with sharp shells, until the breath departed out of her body: they quartered her body: they brought her quarters unto a place called Cinaron and burned them to ashes."

# 4

**MARIA BOCHKAREVA,** *born Maria Frolkova in Russia, in 1889.* Bochkareva never had an easy life. She was a peasant whose alcoholic, abusive father was a former serf. She began working at the age of eight, and at fifteen to escape her father she married Afansi Bochkarev. She found that she was no better off than before; Bochkarev was just as cruel as her father, and she ran away, working as a dishwasher, a laundry worker, and an asphalt contractor's foreman. She lived with a series of men and ended up with Yakov Bok, the son of a butcher, who beat her, drank heavily, and at one point tried to hang her.

It was at this point that Bochkareva heard voices telling her to "go to war to save the country." So, in 1914, she joined the Tomsk Reserve Battalion. She was its only female regular soldier, and she quickly became conspicuous for her bravery and "famous for rescuing wounded comrades in the face of machine-gun fire." In 1915 alone she was promoted to corporal, decorated twice, and wounded five times—the last time by a shell fragment in her spine which left her paralyzed for months.

In 1917 she visited St. Petersburg (now Leningrad) and suggested that she organize a "Women's Battalion of Death" to raise morale. Her project was approved and she made a recruiting speech that announced: "Our mother is perishing . . . I want to help save her. I want women whose hearts are pure crystal, whose souls are pure, whose impulses are lofty." She received fifteen hundred applications that night and five hundred the next day. Of these she chose three hundred and organized them into two battalions. Recruits cut off their hair and swore "to conquer or die." The Women's Battalion of Death went into battle in July 1917, and in its short history distinguished itself. Of the original three hundred soldiers, forty were wounded, twenty-nine were killed by the enemy, and one, who was found making love to a male soldier, was bayoneted to death by Bochkareva.

The Women's Battalion might have had a more illustrious history —and certainly a longer one—had the Bolsheviks not been so eager to end the war. After the revolution, Bochkareva's military fervor was out of style, and she was sentenced to death in 1918. She managed to escape to the United States, but there and in England she found that her expertise was not wanted, and she drifted away. A little later, she was stripped of her rank by the Soviets, and shortly afterward she vanished. The rest of her life is a mystery.

# 5

**ROSA LUXEMBERG,** *born in Zamosc, Poland, 1870.* The youngest of six children born to a Jewish merchant and his wife, Rosa was physically small and fragile. In spirit, however, she was courageous, confident, and rebellious, and from her teens she was keenly interested in politics. She joined a socialist organization and began an illegal discussion group that was discovered by the police. She fled to Zurich to escape prosecution, and there she studied economics, philosophy, law, and the development of European labor movements. To gain German citizenship, Luxemberg married a German anarchist, Gustav Lubecks, but no one country remained her base for long. In 1893 she established the Polish Social Democratic Party; in 1897 she was in France; in 1899 she was in Berlin, writing for *Vorwärts,* a socialist newspaper.

After a brief imprisonment in 1904, Luxemberg traveled to Poland again, using a false passport. In Warsaw she incited workers' rebellions. She returned to Germany to advocate large-scale demonstrations in a pamphlet called *The Mass Strike.* She wrote a great deal on economics, publishing her most famous work, *The Accumulation of Capital,* in 1914. Her hope for an international brotherhood of workers was shattered by World War I, and when her fellow socialists supported the war, she felt betrayed. She spent most of the war in prison, but this didn't put a stop to her political activities. With two others, she helped activists on the outside to form the German Communist Party. She was released from jail in 1918, and in January of 1919, members of her group began a riot. Luxemberg, now known as "Red Rosa," offered support in encouraging editorials, and, as a result, she and a co-worker were arrested. On their way to jail, the two prisoners were dragged from police custody by soldiers, questioned, beaten, shot, and thrown into a canal. The murderers were never punished for their actions.

LOUISA MAY ALCOTT: *She preferred to write lurid novels, but* Little Women *and its treacly sequels made her rich and famous.*

# 6

**LOUISA MAY ALCOTT,** *dies at 55 in Boston, Massachusetts. 1888.* If you've read *Little Women,* you already know a lot about Louisa May Alcott's life. She was, like Jo, the second of four daughters in a household largely run by their mother. She was, like Jo, a writer, a tomboy, and an actress from her earliest days, and she did have a great deal of trouble fitting into her world. Many of the incidents in *Little Women* are based on fact, and there was a real boy very much like Laurie, although he didn't marry the youngest Alcott sister, or any Alcott sister for that matter. However, that's where the resemblance ends. Patient, perfect Marmee is not at all like Abba Alcott, Louisa's mother, and the all-wise, all-seeing Mr. March is nothing like Bronson Alcott, Louisa's father.

Abba Alcott was a fairly ordinary woman who found herself married to a selfish, lazy, idealistic man. As a result, she had to become selfless, hard-working, and practical. The Marmee of *Little Women* says, "I

LOUISA MAY ALCOTT MEMORIAL MUSEUM

am angry every day of my life, Jo; but I have learned not to show it; and I still hope to learn not to feel it, though it may take me another forty years to do so." The real Marmee showed her anger. Her married life had consisted of poverty, hard work, debilitating pregnancies, and insensitivity from her husband. "A woman . . . lives neglected, dies forgotten," she said. She was furious that "girls are taught to seem, to appear—not to be and *do*," and she was always suspicious of men and their plans.

Bronson Alcott was even more unlike his fictional counterpart than Abba. The Mr. March of *Little Women* is a patriarch, true, but he's a distant, benevolent, rather benignly ineffectual patriach. Bronson Alcott, on the other hand, was a domineering autocrat with little compassion and a lot of strange ideas. Intolerant and impatient, he demanded absolute devotion from his daughters and wife. He lost his last steady job when Louisa was seven. He started a commune, worked his family like draft animals, renounced sex, and imposed a vegetarian diet so strict that he allowed his family to eat only coarse bread and apples. No one was allowed to wear cotton or wool, because he had political objections to both. He refused to use animal fertilizer on his crops because it was "disgusting in the extreme," with the predictable result that almost nothing grew. Furthermore, he believed that a fair complexion was a sign of God's grace, and he believed that Louisa, with her dark skin and hair, was destined for evil. For her tenth birthday he gave her nothing but a letter which urged her to be obedient and give up her "anger, discontent, impatience, evil appetites, greedy wants, complainings, ill-speakings, vileness, heedlessness, [and] rude behavior."

Since Mr. and Mrs. Alcott were so little like Mr. and Mrs. March, it shouldn't surprise anyone that Louisa was different from both Jo and from her public image as "The Children's Friend." At one time she was like Jo, anxious to cure her faults, which she considered "idle-ness, impatience, selfishness, wilfulness, independence, activity, vanity, pride and love of cats." These vices she wished to replace with virtues, namely "patience, obedience, industry, love, generosity, respect, silence, perseverance, [and] self-denial." Unlike Jo, however, Louisa decided at some point that self-assertion was better than dependence, and unlike Jo, she never married, concluding that "liberty is a better husband than love to many of us."

She determined not to be a seamstress, a laundress, or a lady's companion, as she had been in the past. Nor would she kill herself as she had once longed to do. (At seventeen, she had written, "I'm so tired. I don't want to live; only it's cowardly to die till you have done something.") Instead, she would write. "I will make a battering-ram of my head," she said, "and make a way through this rough-and-tumble world."

At first she had little luck. One publisher said bluntly, "Stick to your teaching, Miss Alcott. You can't write." She published a collection of sentimental stories called *Flower Fables* and a controversial novel called *Moods,* but it wasn't until she began writing sensational fiction that she began to make money. Such "blood and thunder" tales sold for high prices to cheap magazines and scandal sheets. Alcott's, published anonymously or under the pseudonym "A. M. Barnard," featured passion, intrigue, hashish and opium use, incest, imperfect heroines, insanity, and powerful sexuality. All her life she would prefer "the lurid style" to what she called "moral pap for the young," partially because it was more fun to write and partially because it was "better paid than moral & elaborate works."

It was better paid, until a publisher convinced her, against her better judgment, to write a book for girls. The book, *Little Women,* made Alcott $200,000 during her lifetime and has sold over two million copies. The sanitized version of her life story led to other pieces of well-paid "moral pap" like *Little Men, Eight Cousins, Rose in Bloom, Under the Lilacs,* and her last novel, *Jo's Boys.* Alcott became wealthy. She sent her youngest sister to Europe, paid her father's debts, dispensed charity, and ruined her own health by writing furiously while doing all of the family's sweeping, ironing, and cleaning as well. She never liked the books she wrote; they were all too sentimental and upright for her taste, but she did manage to sneak in a few radical causes here and there—dress reform, temperance, civil rights, and suffrage. In *Rose in Bloom,* the heroine insists that women have "minds and souls as well as hearts; ambition and talents, as well as beauty and accomplishments; and we want to live and learn as well as love and be loved. I'm sick of being told that is all a woman is fit for! I won't have anything to do with love till I prove that I am something beside a housekeeper and a babytender!"

# 7

**ARTEMISIA GENTILESCHI,** *born in Italy, in 1593.* Gentileschi was a painter of extraordinary talent, passion, and power, yet only recently has she received any real attention for her work. For the first three centuries after her career ended, her violent and vivid narrative paintings, her powerful female nudes, and deft portraits of her contemporaries and of women like Cleopatra and Mary Magdalene were all secondary to the fact that she was considered a "loose woman." Long after her death she was stigmatized by an ancient myth—that women invite rape.

She was the daughter of painter Orazio Gentileschi, who taught her all he knew. But after he had given her all he could, she still needed some help with perspective, so he paid for a tutor, Agostino Tassi. A chaperone was present at all of her lessons, but in spite of this precaution, in May of 1612 Gentileschi accused Tassi of repeatedly raping his daughter. Tassi already had a bad history; he had previously been convicted for conspiring to murder his wife. But for five months, it was the victim who was on trial. She was tormented with thumb screws to extort the "truth," and the general belief was that since the rape had occurred multiple times she *must* have allowed it and wanted it. Miraculously, however, Tassi was convicted, and in November Artemisia married a Florentine gentleman, Pietro Antonio di Vincenzo. She had a very successful career and even traveled to England at the request of King Charles I, but people continued to believe the rape her fault. Tassi spent eight months in prison and was then acquitted.

ANNE BONNY: *A bolder pirate than many men.*

LIBRARY OF CONGRESS

# 8

**ANNE BONNY,** *born in Cork, Ireland, 1700.* Forget everthing you've seen in the Hollywood swashbucklers. The bravest pirate of them all (though not the most successful) was Anne Bonny. She was the illegitimate daughter of an Irish lawyer and a serving maid who had moved to North Carolina to escape the local scandal surrounding their daughter's birth. She was raised in the colonies in comfortable surroundings, but she refused to blossom into the sweet young lady she was supposed to be. Instead, she seemed to grow more impulsive, energetic, and rebellious as she grew older.

Eventually, against her father's wishes, she eloped with a penniless, but presumably attractive, sailor named James Bonny and went to Providence Island to trade with the pirates who frequently docked there. On Providence she met the notorious Captain "Calico Jack" Rackham, who persuaded her to leave Bonny and join him in his raids. She agreed, dressed herself as a man, and had a magnificent time stealing from the rich and giving to herself. She took one brief respite from piracy to have a baby in Cuba, but soon she was up and fighting again, and, as one chronicler said, "no body was more forward or courageous than she."

At one point, she and Rackham raided a ship bound for the West Indies and captured a passenger, Mary Read, who opted to join their crew. Now things get really complicated. While Rackham and Bonny were having their affair, Bonny and Read were doing the same, and Read had an affair with at least one male crew member, probably Rackham. There was never time to sort it all out, since in 1721 their ship was attacked by the Jamaican government. The men, including Rackham, hid in fear belowdecks while Bonny and Read fought desperately above; at the trial the women "pleaded their bellies" and were spared the hanging that awaited their colleagues. Bonny had little pity for Rackham. On the day of his execution, she snarled at her former lover that "if he had fought like a man, he need not have been hang'd like a Dog." Bonny and

Read were apparently kept in prison until they gave birth, and Read died there, but Bonny disappeared. Did she too die in Jamaica? Did she join another pirate ship? No one knows.

# 9

**CARRIE CHAPMAN CATT,** *dies at 88 in New Rochelle, New York, 1947.* Born in Wisconsin, Carrie Clinton Lane was one of a new breed of woman. The previous generation had won certain privileges, and women like Carrie rushed to take advantage of these new opportunities, full of optimism and a new sense of entitlement. She, like many of her contemporaries, went to college. She studied law, and although she went into a "woman's" job, teaching, she brought ambition and determination to her work. By 1881 she was a high school principal, and within two more years she was one of America's first female superintendents of schools.

In 1885, Carrie Lane married a publisher named Chapman, who took her to San Francisco. Unfortunately, he died there in 1886, leaving her stranded. With the energy and decisiveness that would serve her all her life, she got a job as a reporter, and saved enough money to travel eastward. She stopped at Iowa, where she began to work for woman suffrage.

Carrie rose quickly in the suffrage ranks, largely because of her organizational skills and fund raising abilities. She reorganized the National American Woman Suffrage Association (NAWSA) with Susan B. Anthony's permission and conducted effective statewide campaigns. In 1890 she married again, this time choosing a Seattle engineer named George W. Catt. Catt was in favor of woman suffrage, and he signed a marriage contract giving her half of each year to devote exclusively to the cause.

From 1900 to 1920, she was especially busy. She was president of NAWSA from 1900 to 1904 and

from 1915 to 1920, established the International Woman Suffrage Alliance in Berlin in 1904, co-founded the Women's Peace Party with Jane Addams, and established the League of Women Voters in 1920. She was a charming, intellectual, relatively popular speaker, although her arguments were often distasteful. She believed that the ends justified the means—the means, in this case, being her attacks on militant feminists, racist arguments, exploitation of class prejudices, arguments based on the essential differences of the sexes, and abandonment her own pacifist beliefs to support World War I.

# 10

**HARRIET TUBMAN,** *dies at about 91 in Auburn, New York, 1913.* Of all the approximately three thousand workers on the Underground Railroad, Tubman is the best known. She deserves to be. Born as a slave in Maryland in 1821 and named Araminta Ross, she worked as a maid, nurse, field hand, cook, and woodcutter. At thirteen she was struck on the head by an overseer, and she suffered from the effects of the beating for the rest of her life. In 1849, fearing that she was about to be sold farther south, she escaped to Philadelphia; her husband, John Tubman, refused to go with her. He was afraid of the perils of escape—the inevitable manhunt conducted by slaveholders anxious to retrieve their "property," the fact that any black traveling on his or her own

# 11

**ZELDA FITZGERALD,** *dies at 47 in Asheville, North Carolina, 1948.* At midnight on March 10, 1948, a fire broke out in an Asheville, North Carolina, mental hospital. When the blaze was finally extinguished the next day, the remains of ten women were found in the wreckage. One of them, identified by a slipper found beneath her body, was Zelda Fitzgerald.

She was born Zelda Sayre in Montgomery, Alabama, the daughter of a State Supreme Court judge. At ten she was "a friendly and direct little girl" who liked reading, running, the theatre, Indians, and painting. A reporter doing articles on local children wrote, "If she were a litter mister instead of the little lady she is, it would be a safe prediction to forecast that she would emulate her father . . . or her great uncle, General John T. Morgan, who adorned the Senate . . . for so many years."

At eighteen she was a pretty,

was suspect and could be stopped and forced to produce proof of emancipation, and the scarcity of safe houses, or hiding places, run by abolitionists. Escape from a slave state was difficult and dangerous enough when it was only done once, but Harriet Tubman did it again—nineteen times—leading numerous slaves to freedom on each dangerous mission. Her efforts resulted in the freedom of more than three hundred slaves and an accumulation of $40,000 in rewards posted for her capture. During the Civil War, she worked as a cook, laundress, scout, nurse, and spy for the Union Army, but it took thirty years of petitioning for "the Moses of her people" to get a pension of twenty dollars a month for her services.

spoiled flirt with blonde hair, a talent for dancing and acting, and a reputation as the best kisser in town. She smoked, drank a little, and swore a little, saying "What the hell!" whenever she thought she could get away with it. In that year, 1919, she was in heaven; there was an army base near her home, and she flirted madly and successfully with the soldiers. Among others, a young writer-to-be named F. Scott Fitzgerald fell in love with her, and, after a stormy courtship, they were married.

They were "the prince and princess of their generation," seen at the best parties in Paris and New York, on Long Island and the Riviera. But by the end of the twenties, their lives had begun to deteriorate. Fitzgerald drank heavily; Zelda became obsessed with ballet and

practiced day and night, only to turn down an offer from the San Carlo Opera Ballet in Naples. She had an exhibit of her artwork in New York in 1933 and began two novels, one of which, *Save Me the Waltz,* was published in 1932. She also wrote six short stories (five published in *College Humor* under her name and Fitzgerald's and one which appeared in *The Saturday Evening Post* under Fitzgerald's name alone). Despite her successes, however, she grew more and more unstable. She had breakdowns in 1930 and 1932 and was institutionalized for a while in North Carolina. In 1940, she was released, but in November of 1947 she suffered another breakdown and returned to the hospital, where she died only a few months later.

# 12

**LADY HESTER LUCY STAN-HOPE,** *born in Chevening, Kent, England, 1776.* Lady Stanhope was one of England's odder characters. She began her unusual career in 1802 when her uncle, William Pitt, summoned her to London to act as his hostess. When he became Prime Minister, she found herself at the center of a world of power and wealth, and she loved it. In 1806, though, Pitt died. Parliament, in recognition of her services, awarded Lady Stanhope an annuity which would have kept her quite comfortable, but she missed the action of politics. So, four years later, she left England with a doctor and a lady's maid, never to return.

During the next few years, Lady Stanhope traveled to Gibraltar, Malta, Greece, Constantinople (now Istanbul), Egypt, Tripoli, and Syria, taking a younger man as a lover but refusing to marry him, getting involved in local intrigues, and being entertained by provincial governors, emirs, and pashas. Between Rhodes and Egypt, her ship sank, and she survived but lost all her luggage.

She interpreted the loss as an opportunity and adopted a male Arabian costume that she wore for the rest of her life "for its splendor and convenience." Eventually, she settled in an abandoned monastery, where she studied the occult, learned to smoke a Turkish pipe, dispensed charity, sheltered fugitives, created her own religion, and fantasized about becoming the Queen of the Jews. To herself she was the "Queen of the Desert"; locals considered her half prophetess and half madwoman; visiting Europeans found her a tedious, eternal talker who once lectured an English traveler for so long that he actually fainted; and Parliament began to think that she was an embarrassing way to spend several hundred pounds a year. Her pension was terminated, and she walled herself into her house in protest, dying in 1839 with no one of her own nationality near her. When visitors found her body soon afterward, they found little else. Her servants had looted her house and disappeared.

# 13

**MESSALINA,** *born in Rome, in the first century, exact date unknown.* This Roman Empress has been raked over the coals more times than almost any other woman in Western history except Eve. For centuries upon centuries her name was synonymous with depravity and vice of every kind. Messalina *was* in fact cruel, greedy, and rapacious. She took lovers in rapid succession and had them executed as she grew bored with them. She married one of her lovers, an unfortunate gentleman named Silius, in an attempt to dethrone her *real* husband, the Emperor Claudius.

But there's been a great deal said about Messalina's crimes throughout the years, and precious little said about her circumstances. She was born into a noble family and married to Claudius when he was forty-eight and she was only fourteen. When she was fifteen he became Emperor, and she found herself a young, attractive woman with the world at her feet and nothing to do but dress herself, perfume herself, take baths, take lovers, and seek power—or, more appropriately, influence.

She did no more than many powerful men of the early imperial days, and she had fewer outlets than they for ambition and rage. And in the end, she paid for her crimes with her life in the year 48. She tried to plead with Claudius and walked barefoot through the streets to find him, but his men had her executed before she could sway him. They handed her a dagger with which she was expected to kill herself, but her hands shook too badly to do it, and an officer was forced to dispatch her. The Senate ordered her name and image removed from all public and private monuments, but her name survived —as a curse and an insult.

# 14

**FANNIE LOU HAMER,** *dies at 69 in Ruleville, Mississippi, 1977.* "I've been called 'Mississippi's angriest woman' and I have a right to be angry," said Fannie Lou Hamer. She grew up in unbearable poverty and watched her mother struggle through year after year of hard work, her clothes "heavy with patches, just mended over and over." And as she grew older, Hamer realized that she was simply replacing her mother, that one day she too would be bent with work and clothed in patches. All she had was her dignity, another inheritance from her mother, who had told her, "you respect yourself as a black child, and when you get grown, you respect yourself as a black woman; and other people will respect you."

So as Hamer grew, she tried to show that she respected herself. She refused to allow whites to treat her like a child and talked back to them, whereupon "they would look at me real funny." But nothing really improved until 1962, when Hamer was fourty-four. In that year she was approached by Student Non-Violent Coordinating Committee (SNCC) workers who were running a voter registration drive. She realized then, for the first time, that black people could vote.

She and seventeen others banded together and registered to vote. When she got back to the plantation where she had worked for eighteen years, Hamer was told to withdraw her name from the list of voters or be fired. She said, "I didn't go down there to register for you, I went down there to register for myself." She was fired. Wisely, she chose to sleep with a friend that night; a mob shot sixteen times into her home.

With that incident as her farewell, Hamer left home and began working with the civil rights movement. A member of the National Organization for Women and the National Women's Political Caucus and a field secretary for SNCC, she refused to be intimidated or si-

lenced by threats, insults, or violence. Once, in 1963, she and coworker Annelle Ponder were arrested in Winona, Mississippi, and beaten. One man beat Hamer with a leather strap until he was exhausted. Then another took over with a blackjack. Her dress rode up above her waist; a third man pulled it down, then up again. The beating left Hamer scarred for life, and for a month afterward, she refused to let her family see her.

Hamer became most famous during the Democratic National Convention in Atlantic City, New Jersey, in 1964. She and others had

organized a black delegation as a protest against functional disenfranchisement of blacks. Calling themselves the Mississippi Freedom Democratic Party, they got quite a bit of attention, although cameras switched away from Hamer's speech when her appeal became too powerful. When she was asked why she had devoted her life to civil rights, Hamer replied that she was "just sick and tired of being sick and tired. We just got to stand up as Negroes for ourselves and our freedom, and if it don't do me any good, I do know the young people it will do good."

LIBRARY OF CONGRESS

MARY WILKINS FREEMAN: *A weaver of quiet tales.*

# 15

**MARY WILKINS FREEMAN,** *dies at 77 in Metuchen, New Jersey, 1930.* One of four children born to a deeply religious family, Freeman was the only one to survive to adulthood. She attended Mount Holyoke Female Seminary for a year, but she found her course of studies too intense and went back to live with her mother, who was working as a housekeeper. Freeman unfortunately fell in love with the son of her mother's employer, and while she worshipped him, he had no interest in her.

She seemed destined for a life of poverty and spinsterhood, but when she was twenty-nine a new option presented itself. She sold a story called "The Beggar King" to a children's magazine for a few dollars, and soon she was selling adult stories to the Boston *Sunday Budget* and *Harper's Bazaar.* Her works usually featured middle-aged or elderly heroines who lived in small towns and were isolated from mainstream life but were also strong and courageous. She enjoyed twenty years of popularity and happiness while she wrote her much-admired stories and lived with her longtime friend and emotional supporter, Mary Wales.

Her career was prematurely ended in 1902, when, after many delays and one break in the engagement, she married Dr. Charles Manning Freeman. It was a disastrous move. He supported her career, but he turned out to be an alcoholic and mentally unstable. Her work and health suffered as a result, and she had terrible nightmares and became addicted to sedatives. Not until 1922 did she obtain a legal separation, and by that time her stories were being called old-fashioned by the critics.

After her death, her reputation fell into decline and was not revived until recently. Late in her life she became, with Edith Wharton, one of the first two women elected to the National Institute of Arts and Letters.

# 16

**ROSA BONHEUR,** *born Rosalie Bonheur in Bordeaux, France, 1822.* "I have no patience with women who ask permission to think," she said in 1841. Bonheur never asked. She demanded, as she did when her father, a painter, tried to apprentice her to a seamstress. She rebelled and insisted that she receive the same education as her brothers—and she got it. She studied painting and visited slaughterhouses to study anatomy, and by the late 1840s she was recognized as one of the best living painters of animals. Her *Cows and Bulls of the Cantal, Ploughing in the Nivernais,* and *The Horse Fair* were magnificient celebrations of the earth and its cultivation and the physical power of draft animals. People flocked to see her paintings, bought reproductions, and whispered about her private life. Bonheur lived for most of her life with another woman, Nathalie Micas, who was almost certainly her lover, but that didn't shock her public nearly as much as her masculine features, her short hair, and the men's clothes she wore while she painted. Every six months,

ROSA BONHEUR: *"In the way of males, I like only the bulls I paint."*

LIBRARY OF CONGRESS

Bonheur had to renew her *Permission de Travestissement,* a police permit which authorized her to wear male attire "for reasons of health" except at "spectacles, balls, or other public meeting places." Bonheur took pride in her preference for women, but she always felt apologetic about wearing men's clothes and refused to be painted or photographed in them, insisting that she wore them "simply to facilitate [her] work."

In 1853, Bonheur and Micas bought the Château de By, near Fontainebleau. The grounds housed an impressive menagerie of models for Bonheur's paintings—dogs, horses, ponies, cattle, goats, monkeys, deer, elk, gazelles, a yak, and a lioness. Bonheur was a virtual recluse there, ignoring fame and honors. Although she was dismissed after her death as a mediocre artist, in her own time she was considered a great painter. She had certainly accomplished as much as many male artists who had received the Legion of Honor, but Emperor Napoleon III refused to award it to a woman. So in 1864, while the Emperor was away from France, the Empress Eugénie, acting as Regent, took the opportunity to visit Rosa Bonheur and deliver the decoration herself. Eugénie wasn't the only woman to be impressed by Bonheur's work; other admirers included Queen Victoria and Susan B. Anthony, who said, "Her work not only surpasses anything ever done by a woman, but is a bold and successful step beyond all other artists."

**CAROLINE HERSCHEL,** *born in Hanover, Germany, 1750.* Almost from her birth, Caroline Herschel was considered secondary to her brother, William, whom she idolized. All the family's resources went to help him, while her education consisted mainly of being taught to cook and clean. And when he went off to England to seek his fortune, she was sent along as his housekeeper. It was all she could imagine doing; she thought little of herself and did not even aspire to marriage. Her father, she said, had warned her "against all thoughts of marriage, saying as I was neither handsome nor rich, it was not likely that anyone would make me an offer."

Blithely accepting her family's assessment of her, and feeling a genuine love for her brother, Herschel did everything William told her to do. When he was interested in music, she allowed herself to be trained as a singer. She became quite good at it, but when his interests turned toward astronomy, she gave up singing to assist him in his new career. He began by building telescopes better than any which were then available; she helped him. Together they studied the skies, and their collaboration lasted for fifty years.

During those fifty years of what Herschel called "minding the heavens," both she and her brother achieved great things. William discovered the planet Uranus, and Caroline discovered fourteen nebulae and eight comets. Together they discovered 2,500 nebulae and star clusters, one thousand double stars, and a number of variable stars. They established that the sun had a gaseous outer layer, and they measured the periods of rotation of several heavenly bodies. The difference between the perceived value of their accomplishments, was that William was made Astronomer Royal at a salary of £200 a year, and Caroline was made his assistant at a salary of £50 a year.

This is not to say that Herschel didn't get any recognition. As a matter of fact, she got far more than she wanted. "I know too well," she insisted, "how dangerous it is for women to draw too much notice to themselves." She shrank from the honors she received, which included medals from the kings of Denmark and Prussia, election to the Royal Irish Academy, and election, with Mary Somerville in 1835, as one of the first two women members of the Royal Astronomical Society. The awards simply made her angry, and more eager to lay all of her achievements at her brother's door. "All I am," she said, "all I know, I owe to my brother." When he died in 1822, Herschel retired to Germany and spent the rest of her life protecting his reputation. To the time of her death in 1848, she claimed: "I did nothing for my brother but what a well-trained puppy-dog would have done: that is to say, I did what he commanded me. I was a mere tool which *he* had the trouble of sharpening."

CAROLINE HERSCHEL: *Content to be a distant planet to her brother's sun.*

LIBRARY OF CONGRESS

# 17 _____

**MALINCHE,** *born in the Coatzacoalcos Province, Mexico, in about 1504, exact date unknown.* What many people don't know about Cortez's defeat of Montezuma's Aztec empire is that the conquest would have been impossible without the loyalty and verbal skills of an Indian woman. She was named Malinali and was a princess, the daughter of the *cacique*. Her education prepared her for a life of wealth and power, but it was a life she was not destined to lead. Her father died when she was still young, and after her mother remarried, Malinali was considered an inconvenience and given to a tribe called the Xicalangos, who in turn sold her as a slave to the Tabascans.

Her life became one of ceaseless drudgery, and at first it was made doubly uncomfortable by a language barrier. Her native language was Nahuatl, but the Tabascans spoke Mayan, and it took Malinali a while to learn to communicate with her captors. As if life weren't bad enough already, she faced another threat. The Aztecs appeased their gods with human sacrifices, and Malinali was threatened with this fate if she didn't behave. All in all, there was little to endear her masters to her.

There was even less in March, 1519, when Cortez and his Spanish troops landed and terrified the twelve thousand Tabascan warriors with their guns, their European swords, and especially their horses. The Tabascans, eager to appease the powerful Spaniards, presented them with lavish gifts, including twenty women to serve as corn grinders and concubines. One of these women was Malinali.

Cortez gave Malinali to one of his captains, but she soon won the respect of all his officers for her beauty, her dignity, and her conversion to Catholicism. They called her Doña Marina and treated her well— or at least better than the Tabascans had. She was eager to repay their comparative kindness, and when Cortez needed a Nahuatl speaker to convince certain tribes to follow him, Marina volunteered her services as a translator. She quickly became indispensable to him, and her eloquence won the loyalty of many Indians. She became so important, in fact, that the Indians knew her and Cortez by one name —Malintzin—which in time was corrupted and became Malinche.

Malinche offered the ultimate proof of her loyalty to the Spaniards when she discovered a plot to destroy their forces. The plotters offered her wealth and marriage to a *cacique*—in short, a chance to recover the life she should have led. She went to Cortez, informed him of the plot, and ruined the Aztecs' last chance of victory. Cortez and Malinche became lovers; they had a three-year affair, and in 1522 Malinche bore Cortez's son, one of the first *mestizos*. Unfortunately for Malinche, the conquerors had little more appreciation for her than the conquered. When she became a political liability, Cortez discarded her, and in his dispatches to Spain, he mentioned her only twice, and then only as "a native Indian girl." He gave her gold, servants, land, and a Spanish husband, Lieutenant Juan Jaramillo; she and Jaramillo had one daughter. Malinche died soon afterward, probably in 1528. Jaramillo remarried a few weeks and later tried to disinherit their daughter, and even Malinche's name was tarnished and despised, becoming synonymous with "traitor" in Mexico.

# 18

**MARGARET BRENT.** *Born in Gloucester, England, in about 1601.* Brent was the daughter of an English lord, and she might never have been included in history books if she had been content with that position. But for some reason she was not content. Perhaps it was because she had twelve brothers and sisters and felt understandably crowded. Perhaps it was because she was a Catholic in a nation that hated and feared Catholicism. Perhaps she wanted an excuse to avoid marriage, or perhaps she was just excited by talk of emigration to the colonies. For whatever reason, in 1638 she set sail, with her sister Mary and two of their brothers, to Lord Baltimore's Catholic colony, Maryland.

At that time, the colonial government would give land grants to anyone wealthy enough to transport and employ male workers, but it was assumed that anyone with that much money would be a man. Brent was therefore something of a surprise to the residents of Maryland, and for many years she remained an anomaly. When she was granted, with her sister, the seventy-acre estate they called "Sisters Freehold," she became the first female freeholder in the colony. Furthermore, in a region where women were immeasurably precious because they were in such a minority, Brent and her sister were almost the only spinsters in seventeenth-century Maryland.

Brent appears to have had little desire to change her marital status. She was far too busy running her farm. Soon after she arrived, Lord Baltmore increased her grant, and she quickly acquired other large portions of land through shrewd business deals. In her spare time, she acted as an agent and attorney for her brothers and often brought matters to court in her own name. Her unusual stature in the community and the confusion of sex roles it caused led her to sign official documents "Margaret Brent, Gentleman."

Her proudest moments came between 1644 and 1647. During this period she became an increasingly important advisor to the colonial governor, Leonard Calvert, even raising troops for him on one occasion. The real proof of her worth to him came when a group of soldiers mutinied; she calmed them, quelled the rebellion, and satisfied the soldiers' demands by selling some of Lord Baltimore's property to pay them. Lord Baltimore objected after the fact, but the Maryland legislature defended her actions and Brent emerged as a heroine.

Unfortunately, the legislature was

fickle in its loyalties. In 1647, Governor Calvert died, naming Brent as his executor. Accordingly, she demanded two votes in the legislature, one as a lawful property holder and one as the ex-governor's executor. The assembly responded by refusing her the vote altogether and Brent in turn declared the assembly's actions illegal. She never got the vote, and in 1650 she left the colony and moved to Virginia, where she became almost as prominant as she had been in Maryland.

# 19

**ALEXANDRA KOLLONTAI,** *born Alexandra Mikhailovna in St. Petersburg (now Leningrad), Russia, 1872.* When Kollontai was a young woman, it appeared that she could have whatever she wanted. Her father was wealthy and aristocratic, a general in the Imperial Army. She had plenty of servants and plenty of money. What she wanted, however, was plenty of knowledge, and she asked permission to study in Europe. Her parents refused. They let her travel, but made it clear that she was not to enroll in school.

So in 1892 she took her first trip abroad, and it altered the entire course of her life. Her childhood had been shadowed by her country's political upheavals, and she was well aware that a rebellion was brewing. But it was not until she made this trip, during which she read the *Communist Manifesto* and joined a socialist discussion group, that she decided to devote her life to the revolution.

She returned to Russia in 1893 full of ambition, but it was temporarily stifled when she married her cousin, Vladimir Kollontai. She did some writing, but she felt awkward and hated domesticity. It took three years for her rage and frustration to explode, and even then it was in a distinctly political manner. In 1896, she and her husband went to inspect a textile plant. It was her first look at a large factory, and she was shocked at the working conditions and even more shocked by her husband's casual acceptance of the situation. She became an active Marxist and began organizing working women, distributing leaflets, speaking, publishing, and writing for the cause. She spent several years working in and out of Russia, depending on the current level of disfavor in which she was held by the police, and in 1917 she returned to Russia for some time.

Kollontai was a favorite of Lenin's, and she was the only woman in the first Bolshevik government. She was also one of the few high-ranking government officials to survive the Stalinist purges, although her blunt honesty, her vocal disagreements with other leaders, and her advocacy of free love made her controversial. Finally, to avoid execution, she accepted posts in other countries. Her accomplishments from 1917 until her death in 1952 are varied and many. In November, 1917, she was appointed the People's Commissar of Social Welfare, making her the world's first woman cabinet minister. When one hundred thousand soldiers' wives marched for more food after the revolution, only Kollontai had the courage to meet with them and solve their problems. In 1920, she joined a group which opposed the government's New Economic Policy. The group was subsequently banned, but Kollontai continued to criticize the government. From 1923 to 1925 she served

LIBRARY OF CONGRESS

ALEXANDRA KOLLONTAI: *Her affair with a seaman almost got her executed for dereliction of duty, but Lenin saved her.*

as a trade delegate to Mexico and Norway. From 1925 to 1927 she was minister to Mexico, and then she was stationed in Norway again. From 1930 to 1945 she was minister and then ambassador to Sweden, making her the world's first woman ambassador. In 1944 she negotiated an armistice which ended the Soviet-Finnish War, and later in her career she was an adviser to the Russian foreign minister. In addition, she wrote short stories, books on economics, and her autobiography; the last was banned in the Soviet Union.

# 20

**ADRIENNE LECOUVREUR,** *dies at 37 in Paris, France, 1730.* The daughter of a hatter, Lecouvreur began acting at the age of fourteen. With a little help from the actor and playwright Marc Antoine Legrand, she made her debut at the Comédie Française in 1717, and she remained there for thirteen years. A lover of authenticity, she insisted on historically accurate costumes and broke tradition by using realistic speech and gestures rather than the elaborate and formal manner which was then in

vogue. Famous for her skill in tragic roles as well as for her active love life, she was passionately admired by Marshal Saxe and Voltaire. Her death was a blow to many. Its suddenness led to rumors that she had been poisoned by her rival, the Duchesse de Bouillon, and the displays of grief that followed her death confirmed her popularity. Nonetheless, the Church was unmoved. Popular or not, she had been an actress and therefore immoral. She was refused Christian burial, a decision that drew fierce criticism from Voltaire, and friends buried her in secrecy at night near the rue de Bourgogne.

# 21

**BOUDICA,** *dies in Britain, in 62, exact date unknown.* This woman, whose name has been variously spelled as Boudica, Boudicia, or Boadicea, first emerged as a public figure when she married Prasutagus, king of the Iceni of eastern Britain. Prasutagus had been deeply impressed by the new Roman presence in Britain, and he hoped to achieve some sort of peaceful union with the Romans. So when he died he willed his kingdom to Rome. What he had not foreseen was that the Romans considered the Iceni a conquered people, will or no will, and they proceeded to ravage the countryside. They stripped Boudica naked and publicly beat her; her two daughters they raped repeatedly.

In the year 61, in response to her brutal treatment at the hands of the invaders, she organized an army of at least 230,000 and led them into battle, riding in a chariot and wielding a spear. Tall, broad, "with fierce eyes and a rasping voice," and letting her long fair hair fall loosely to her waist, she terrified the Roman soldiers. Her daughters fought beside her, sacking the three largest

LIBRARY OF CONGRESS

ADRIENNE LECOUVREUR: *Was she poisoned by her rival?*

Roman encampments in Britain, and according to legend, killing the women after the battles with particular brutality by cutting off their breasts, sewing the breasts to their mouths, and then impaling the women on stakes.

Boudica was finally stopped, however, in a disastrous battle for the Britons. Only four hundred Romans were killed, but eighty thousand of Boudica's people died, and she committed suicide rather than be captured. Tradition has it that her elder daughter married her rapist, a Roman soldier named Marius, while the younger daughter, Vodicia, led an army against York and burned the city, only to be captured and executed by the Romans shortly afterward. In later years, Boudica became a patriotic symbol to many, although some including the poet John Milton, thought she'd gone too far. Milton was convinved that the entire story was a Roman slander meant "to brand us with the rankest note of barbarism, as if in *Britain* women were men, and men women."

# 22

**APHRA BEHN,** *born Ayfara Amis near Canterbury, England, probably in 1640.* Aphra was a generous, attractive, witty, passionate, forgiving, intelligent woman who spent her whole life doing things that women weren't supposed to do. In her youth she traveled to Surinam with her family, but her father died en route, leaving her much freer than she might have been. She took advantage of her freedom to go hunting, to visit an Indian tribe who'd never seen Europeans, to have an affair with an ex-spy and political exile named William Scot, and to get involved in a slave rebellion led by an African prince named Oroonoko.

In 1664, she returned to England and Scot went to Holland. She then married a Mr. Behn, about whom almost nothing is known. He probably died in the plague that swept through London not long after their marriage. So the year 1666 left her without any means of support, and she found a most unusual way out of her problem. She volunteered as a spy to King Charles II, who was at war with the Dutch. She went to Holland and made contact with an English emigré who was providing information to the Dutch; the emigré, not so coincidentally, was William Scot, and through him Behn acquired a great deal of valuable information. Unfortunately, her superiors ignored her advice (thus allowing the Dutch to sail right up the Thames before they were stopped) and refused to pay her enough to cover her expenses. On her return to England, she was shipwrecked and landed in debtor's prison.

All seemed lost, but Behn was a resourceful woman, and she began to write. It was the final blow to her reputation, for while a few brave women of the upper classes wrote in her day, they did so under very strict conventions. They published anonymously for the most part, and they always had some excuse for publishing at all. Behn wrote to make a living, just as her male peers did. She signed her name to her productions, just as her male peers did. And she wrote in a witty, bawdy style, just as her male peers did.

She was extraordinarily successful, producing seventeen plays in seventeen years in a city that only had two theatres. She wrote thirteen novels, translated foreign works, and wrote verses whose eroticism shocked many of her contemporaries. One of her poems, "The Willing Mistress," ends with these lines:

"A many kisses he did give
   And I returned the same,
Which made me willing to receive
   That which I dare not name.
He did but kiss and clasp me round . . .
And laid me gently on the ground;
   Ah who can guess the rest?"
Such lines scandalized many readers, as did her celebration of lesbianism in "To the Fair Clarin-da" and her lampoon on impotence in "The Disappointment." Although Behn was the first woman in England to support herself by writing, in later years she was mostly forgotten, as were most of her literary contemporaries, whose rakish style was considered indecent in the later Victorian period.

When she wasn't forgotten, Behn was attacked. Even her defenders admitted that "a little too loosely she writ," and her enemies spared no venom. One commentator wrote in 1888 that "she was a mere harlot, who danced through uncleanness" and that "her pleasures were not those which became an honest woman." Elsewhere during the same period, it was said that "if Mrs. Behn is read at all, it can only be from a love of impurity for its own sake" and that "it is a pity her books did not rot with her bones." Only in the twentieth century has she begun to be appreciated as the very embodiment of her age.

# 23

**FLORENCE ELLINWOOD ALLEN,** *born in Salt Lake City, Utah, 1884.* Allen's father was Utah's first congressman and a classics professor who taught his children Greek and Latin. Her mother was an early graduate of Smith College who raised seven children while remaining active in local organizations. Her maternal grandfather advocated higher education for women, and her father's father was a justice of the peace who thought she could do no wrong. Given such encouraging surroundings, it's hardly surprising that she grew up full of ambition, determination, and confidence. But even her relatives, perhaps, could not have foreseen such an illustrious career.

Allen studied law at the University of Chicago and New York University, graduating second in her class in 1913. She was called to the Ohio bar in 1914. Allen worked for a few years defending impoverished clients and promoting the cause of woman suffrage, and in 1919 she was made assistant prosecutor for her county. In 1920 she became the first woman to be elected judge of a court of common pleas, and only two years later she was the first woman elected to the Ohio Supreme Court—making her the first woman in the world to sit on a court of last resort. Unsuccessful bids for House and Senate seats were offset by her reelection to the Ohio Supreme Court by a wide majority in 1928. During her terms as judge she acquired the support of labor, academic, business, religious, reform, and women's groups. The newspapers also joined the Florence Allen bandwagon, perhaps because she made such good copy—she campaigned in her Model T Ford, and by 1922 there were sixty-six Florence Allen Clubs in Ohio.

In March of 1934, Allen achieved another first when President Franklin D. Roosevelt named her to the U.S. Sixth Circuit Court of Appeals. She was now the first woman to serve as a federal judge. She remained on this bench for twenty-five years, and by the time she left it, she was its chief judge. Critics complained that she was a token, but Attorney General Homer Cummings said: "Florence Allen was not appointed because she was a woman. All we did was to see that she was not rejected because she was a woman."

During her service as a federal judge, Allen heard thousands of cases, ruled on the constitutionality of Roosevelt's Tennessee Valley Authority, and chaired committees of the International Bar Association and the International Federation of Women Lawyers. In her spare time, she gave lectures on the Constitution, spoke on behalf of peace, and called for international cooperation in space exploration. Before she retired in 1959, there was some talk of nominating her for a seat on the U.S. Supreme Court, but she'd seen too much resistance to women exercising authority to put much faith in the rumors. Quite correctly, she said, "That will never happen to a woman while I am living." She died in 1966.

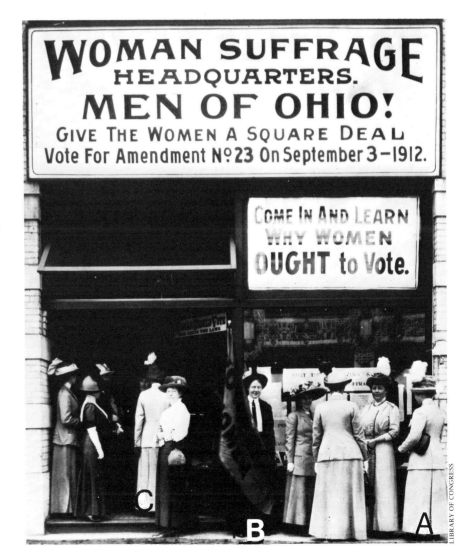

FLORENCE ELLINWOOD ALLEN: *"B" marks the spot.*

# 24

**ALICE GUY-BLACHÉ,** *dies at 95 in Mahwah, New Jersey, 1968.* Female movie directors are still relatively rare, yet one of film's true pioneers was a woman, Alice Guy-Blaché. Born in Paris, she began her career working as a secretary to an early filmmaker, Léon Gaumont. In 1896 she made a short film, *La Fée aux choux,* the first fictional film ever produced. By 1905 she was directing all of Gaumont's films, and a few years later she established her own production company, Solax. Operating on tight schedules, tight budgets, and a huge sign facing the actors that said "Be Natural," she churned out one-reelers at a breakneck pace.

Between 1896 and 1920 she worked on at least 200 films, often as director, producer, and screenwriter for the same movie. In 1920, however, she quit. She separated from her husband, Herbert Blaché-Bolton, for whom she had closed Solax a few years earlier, and moved back to France. Later in the 1920s she tried to return to the film industry, but no one would hire her, and she spent most of the rest of her life working as a translator in France, Belgium, and the United States. She was not entirely forgotten, though, and in 1955, she received the French Legion of Honor.

# 25

**FLANNERY O'CONNOR,** *born in Savannah, Georgia, 1925.* Flannery O'Connor spent her life fighting two battles. The easier to win was a battle against her audience. She was a devout Catholic whose faith was inseparable from her writing, and she lived in a secular age. "My subject in fiction," she wrote, "is the action of grace in territory held largely by the devil. I have also found that what I write is read by an audience which puts little stock in either grace or the devil." She overcame this disadvantage, however, by creating grand, extraordinary tales that demanded critical attention and earned critical acclaim. "To the hard of hearing you shout," she explained, "and for the almost blind you draw large and startling figures."

O'Connor's other battle, however, was one in which she just barely held her own for many years. In 1950, she was stricken with lupus, a debilitating, fatal disease which had killed her father thirteen years before. Steroids kept her alive for fourteen years, long enough to write her greatest works, *Wise Blood, A Good Man Is Hard to Find, The Violent Bear It Away,* and *Everything That Rises Must Converge,* but the same medication that kept the lupus at bay softened and eroded her bones. Often bedridden, she could eventually move only on cruches because her hip bones couldn't support her weight. Throughout it all, though, she retained her determination and her sense of humor. "Everywhere I go," she wrote, "I'm asked if I think the universities stifle writers. My opinion is that they don't stifle enough of them. There's many a bestseller that could have been prevented by a good teacher."

# 26

**SANDRA DAY O'CONNOR,** *born Sandra Day in El Paso, Texas, 1930.* Sandra O'Connor is a staunch Republican who, in 1981, after about twenty-five years of legal experience, became the first woman to serve as a U.S. Supreme Court justice. She got there in a sort of dress-for-success, 1980s-woman way, by not being too feminine, too masculine, too dangerous, or too anything. During her confirmation hearings, the *Christian Science Monitor* described her as displaying "an even balance of professionalism and femininity." And some people think sexism is dead! Who ever head of a male justice having to strike "an even balance of professionalism and masculinity?" The Washington *Post* saw her in the same light: "She is an achieving woman without an edge. She is good-looking without being alienatingly beautiful and bright without being alarmingly intellectual." And a good thing, too. We wouldn't want to have any justices who were ambitious, attractive, or, worst of all, "alarmingly intellectual." Predictably, O'Connor has managed to upset almost everyone who has very strong opinions. Members of the right think she's too liberal; members of the left think she's too conservative. At least she's convinced the public—at last—that women can handle the job. Next time around, maybe we'll get another woman on the Court. Maybe, if we're lucky, we could even get someone "alarmingly intellectual."

# 27

**"HACHETTE,"** *born Jean Laisné in France, in the fifteenth century.* This is the story of how any little girl with determination, drive, and a good axe can grow up to be famous and tax-exempt. Jeanne Laisné Fourquet was a citizen of

Beauvais, France, in the summer of 1472, when Charles the Bold, Duke of Burgundy, was rebelling against French authority and killing everyone in his way. He laid siege to Beauvais, and the townspeople fought fiercely, knowing they'd be slaughtered if they lost. Nonetheless, they were weakening, and the Burgundians had planted a flag on the town's battlements. Fourquet quickly organized a company of women who, waving axes or whatever other weapons were at hand, drove the Burgundians back. Fourquet herself pushed the flag-bearer into a moat and captured the Burgundian flag. The whole incident was a great boost to the townspeople's morale, and they repelled the attack, but the security of her town was not Fourquet's only reward. King Louis XI commended her bravery and exempted her descendants from taxation in perpetuity, and for centuries an annual parade was held in Beauvais in her honor. Its chief distinction was that the women marched in front of the men.

# 28

**DOROTHY HODGKIN,** *born Dorothy Mary Crowfoot, in Cairo, Egypt, in 1910.* Hodgkin did her undergraduate work at Oxford and got her doctorate from Cambridge. In 1937 she married Thomas Hodgkin; they had three children. During World War II she studied the structure of the new wonder drug, penicillin, and in 1948 she turned her attention to the structure of a complex vitamin, $B_{12}$. It took her eight years to analyze the $B_{12}$ molecule, using x-ray crystallography, but her work made her the first researcher to solve a biological puzzle by means of computer analysis. She also discovered the structure of insulin, and she was widely honored for her accomplishments. In 1947 she was elected to Britain's Royal Society; in 1960 she was made the Society's first Wolfson

Research Professor. In 1965, she became the first woman since Florence Nightingale to be awarded the British Order of Merit, and in 1964 she received the greatest honor of all, the Nobel Prize for Chemistry. She was only the third woman ever to win it. She used the Nobel money to sponsor a scholarship and to fund peace work and famine relief.

# 29

**HANNA REITSCH,** *born in Hirschberg, Silesia, Germany (now Poland), 1912.* One of the most famous German pilots in World War II never flew a combat mission, although she did practically everything else. Honorary Flug-

LIBRARY OF CONGRESS

HANNA REITSCH: *An* Übermensch *who preferred American men for their "lack of aggressive self-assertion."*

kapitän Hanna Reitsch ferried high-ranking officers to various cities throughout the Reich (including surrounded Berlin in April, 1945) and performed test flights dangerous enough to win her the Iron Cross, Second Class. Had she been less determined, however, she would never have gotten off the ground. Her parents wanted her to be a good little *hausfrau,* but at thirteen or fourteen she decided to become a flying missionary doctor. Her father made a deal with her: if she didn't mention flying again until she graduated from high school, he'd buy her lessons at a prominent glider pilots' school. She kept her part of the bargain, but he, hoping she'd forgotten all about it, bought her a gold watch as a graduation present. Politely, she returned the watch and reminded him of their agreement, and although he tried to talk her out of it, she would not be deterred.

Having conquered her father, Reitsch next had to conquer her peers. She was still a teenager when she became the only woman student at the Grunau glider school, and she was blonde, blue-eyed, 5'½" tall, and only ninety pounds in weight. Her fellow students found it impossible to take her seriously and ridiculed her mercilessly—until she outperformed them all. The head of the school took her on as his own pupil, and she was allowed to fly state-of-the-art gliders. On her first flight after she earned her license, she had such a good time that she stayed in the air for five hours, unwittingly setting a women's endurance record. In 1933,

while testing a new craft, an up-draft swept her to 9,750 feet and deposited her into a pocket of rain and hail. Her instruments froze, the glider stopped responding, and her hands turned blue. Then the glider plummeted, turning upside down. She righted it, and when she landed she found she'd set an unofficial gliding altitude record.

From 1934 to 1945 Reitsch was primarily a test pilot, although she did some racing as well. She tested new types of dive brakes for gliders, set a women's world record for long-distance soaring, learned to fly twin-engined planes, became the first woman in the world to fly a helicopter, and tested military craft for the Luftwaffe. Her serenity in the face of danger and pain was legendary. She was the test pilot for a notoriously unstable rocket plane which could fly up to six hundred miles per hour and reach thirty thousand feet in ninety seconds. On her fifth flight, she was forced to make a crash landing. When the plane stopped, she felt herself bleeding and raised her hand to her

face to find that "at the place where my nose had been [there] was now nothing but an open cleft." She reached for a pad and pencil, drew a sketch detailing the cause of the crash, and *then* lost consciousness. No one thought she would live, but she did. Plagued by headaches and dizzy spells, she climbed roofs and trees to regain her sense of balance, and within months she was flying experimental planes again.

Toward the end of the war, Reitsch proposed two plans to Hitler. One of them called for a group of women to train as suicide pilots of rockets aimed at targets in England. Hitler liked it—after all, women were expendable—and approved of it, although the plan was abandoned after D-Day. The other plan, an earlier proposal, was rejected outright, but it was Reitsch's most cherished dream: to organize a squadron of women fliers "to fight for the Fatherland, on the same terms as the men of the Luftwaffe—without any privileges or restrictions."

# 30

**JULIA JACKSON,** *exact dates unknown.* In nineteenth-century New Orleans, Catholicism was the most visible and respectable religion. Voodoo, more furtive and more disreputable, was acknowledged to have strong powers, though, and so, in consequence, were its practicioners—the voodoo women. Julia Jackson was one of the most prominent of the voodoo women in New Orleans' red-light district, Storyville. Six feet tall and cross-eyed, she was rumored to have incredible skills. It was said that she could cause pregnancy or abortion from a

distance, but these feats were not what made her universally feared by New Orleans prostitutes. It was her alleged power to use goat testicles or wasp blood to induce venereal disease that frightened them, and, worst of all, Jackson's dreaded "sealing power," which could "close up a whore so she couldn't do no business." In Storyville, when prostitutes fought (which they did often and fiercely), the worst threat that one could level at the other was a threat to hire Julia Jackson to "close up" the rival.

# 31

**AL-KHANSĀ,** *born Tumādir bint 'Amr into a nomadic tribe in Arabia in about 575.* Al-Khansā first demonstrated her rebelliousness and determination as a young woman. Her family found her a husband who should have been a catch—he was a great poet and warrior—but Al-Khansā refused to marry someone chosen for her and, after several affairs, she found a husband for herself. He was a kinsman of hers named Mirdās ben Abī 'Amir, and they had six children.

According to tradition, Al-Khansā took her pseudonym quite early, when she began writing poetry for special occasions. She soon became skilled at composition; even the prophet Mohammed was said to admire her work immensely. She converted to Islam, leading a delegation of would-be Muslims to Medina in 629. She is known as an Islamic poet, although her work owes more to the pagan, nomadic tradition than to Islam. Her finest work was in the elegy, a

very old form which she polished and imbued with her deep, personal sorrow. She had sorrow to spare—two of her brothers had died in battle, and she was present at the battle of al-Kādisiyyo, where four of her sons died. It was the elegies for these warriors with which she won male-dominated poetry contests, and it is the elegies for which she is duly famous. About a thousand of her verses survive today.

ANNE SULLIVAN (right), with Helen Keller: *"It was my teacher's genius,"* Keller wrote, *"her quick sympathy, her loving tact which made the first years of my education so beautiful."*

LIBRARY OF CONGRESS

# APRIL

## 1

**SOPHIE GERMAIN,** *born Marie-Sophie Germain in Paris, France, 1776.* Sophie Germain's father was a wealthy silk merchant who was interested in liberal reforms—but not interested enough to allow his daughter an education. When he discovered that she was teaching herself geometry and Latin, he ordered the light and heat cut off in her room. Germain simply wrapped herself in her quilts and read by the light of smuggled candles until her mother secretly began helping her. Finally even Germain's father, impressed by her dedication, surrendered and allowed her to study openly.

Isolated from the academic world because of her sex, Germain did the best she could under the circumstances. Eventually she grew bold enough to ask for an expert's opinion, and she submitted a paper, under the name "Monsieur LeBlanc" to a professor at the École Polytechnique. He encouraged her to continue her work. Germain corresponded with German mathematician Karl Friedrich Gauss for years, did important work on Fermat's Last Theorem, won a prize from the French Academy for a complex study of elasticity, taught herself differential calculus, and worked on philosophy and number theory. Gauss suggested that she receive an honorary doctorate from the University of Göttingen, but before it could be awarded, she died in 1831 of breast cancer. Her death certificate listed her not as a scientist or mathematician, but simply as a "property holder."

## 2

**PHRYNE,** *born in Tespiae, Greece, in the fourth century B.C., exact dates unknown.* One of the greatest heitarai or courtesans of ancient Greece, Phryne was born to a poor family. Phryne, by the way, is not her real name; it's a nickname meaning, oddly enough, "the toad." Her real name is unknown today. Despite that unflattering epithet, given perhaps ironically, she was renowned for her extraordinary beauty and grew quite rich in Athens—so rich, in fact, that she could pick her clients selectively.

In a competitive market like the one in Athens, it helped for a courtesan to have a gimmick, and Phryne chose hers with a shrewdness that served her well all her life. Although people hardly paraded naked through the streets of Athens, nudity, especially where prostitutes were concerned, was not a rare sight. But Phryne clothed herself more completely than her competitors. She never went to the public baths and entertained her lovers only in the dark. All of this secrecy did exactly what she had hoped—it aroused the curiosity of most Athenian men.

But Phryne took the game one step further and made it a triumph. Once a year, at the festival of Poseidon, she performed a special ritual, ostensibly to honor the god. She stood by the ocean and slowly removed all her clothing. Then she dived into the sea and reemerged as Aphrodite being born from the foam. She stood wet, naked, and beautiful on the shore for one long moment, and then she covered herself for another year.

The problem with Phryne's popularity was that it made her rivals jealous. Eventually, her striptease was denounced as blasphemous by a man named Euthias. His motives are unclear. Some believe he was pushed by a group of hetairai, others that he was encouraged by a jealous married woman. Still others believe that he had aspired to become one of Phryne's customers and been rejected. Whatever the reason, he placed her in a very bad situation. The penalty for profaning the sacred mysteries was death, and Euthias was an eloquent man. Just when all seemed lost, Phryne's attorney ripped off her clothing and displayed her naked body to the judges. It was an argument none of them could refute. Phryne was acquitted.

## 3

**JANE GOODALL,** *born in London, England, 1934.* In 1957, Jane Goodall was to all appearances a perfectly normal middle-class woman. Born to parents of moderate means, she had gone to secretarial school and marked time in various jobs, apparently waiting, like most of her peers, to marry and raise a family. But in 1957, she went to Kenya on vacation and fell in love with Africa. She took a job as secretary to anthropologist Louis Leakey and soon graduated to helping him with his field work. By 1960 she knew what she wanted to do. She wanted to study chimpanzees.

At that time, relatively little work had been done with primates in their natural habitats, largely because the researchers frightened the animals. Goodall took it slowly, settling near Lake Tanganyika and letting the chimps get used to her presence. Within a year she could get within thirty feet of them, and within two years, they were making stops at her camp for bananas. She gave the chimps names and made important discoveries about their behavior, including their habit of promiscuity, their ability to make tools, their complex social structure, and their occasional tendency to eat meat as well as vegetation.

# 4

**DOROTHEA LYNDE DIX,** *born in Hampden, Maine, 1802.* "She is a kind old soul," wrote Louisa May Alcott of Dorothea Dix, "but very queer, fussy and arbitrary, no one likes her and I don't wonder." Fortunately, Dix's main concern was helping people, not securing their affections. A teacher who had written elementary school textbooks, a hymn book, and some devotional works, Dix was teaching Sunday school in Boston when her life was irrevocably altered. A friend asked her one Sunday to teach the women in the East Cambridge House of Correction. Dix found when she got there that she was speaking not only to criminals, but also to the insane housed with them.

When she began a massive survey of asylums, prisons, and poorhouses, she found that mental hospitals were almost nonexistent and that placing the insane in prisons was the least of the barbarities committed against them. They were often confined in cages, cellars, and stalls, and bound with ropes and chains. In 1843, she submitted her research to the Massachusetts Legislature; by 1854, she had helped to establish dozens of mental hospitals and create laws mandating humane treatment of the insane in eleven states. She also founded mental hospitals in Scotland, Turkey, France, Russia, and the Channel Islands, and worked on behalf of the poor and the blind.

During the Civil War when the Union needed a supervisor of nurses, she won the post. She quickly and efficiently converted

buildings into temporary hospitals and mobilized thousands of "strong, matronly, sober, neat, and industrious" women between the ages of thirty-five and fifty. Her autocratic style made few friends, however, and after two years, in 1863, the secretary of war limited her powers. In 1866 she resigned and continued her prewar work. She died in 1887 in Trenton, New Jersey, in a hospital she had helped to establish.

# 5

**BETTE DAVIS,** *born Ruth Elizabeth Davis in Lowell, Massachusetts, 1908.* Like Dorothea Dix, Bette Davis has a style that can make enemies. The fiery, brazen, independent characters she's played on the screen are reflections of her own integrity, pride, and determination.

In the 1930s, despite having won

BETTE DAVIS: *The fifth recipient of the American Film Institute's Life Achievement Award, the first woman to be so honored.*

an Oscar for *Dangerous* and having delivered an exceptional performance in *Of Human Bondage,* Davis was on her way to becoming a victim of the Hollywood studio system, which placed actors' careers entirely in the hands of their employers. Warner Brothers continually cast Davis in bad films or in supporting roles when it was obvious that she deserved starring roles and good scripts. Finally, she did the unthinkable—she refused to play the roles the studio awarded her. A long battle resulted in a nominal victory for Warner Brothers and better roles and increased popularity for Davis. Films like *Jezebel* and *The Little Foxes* made her so important to the studio that

some called her "the fifth Warner brother."

Nonetheless, her strength and agressiveness frightened or irritated many of her colleagues. Once, while rehearsing a scene for *The Private Lives of Elizabeth and Essex,* she slapped Errol Flynn so hard that he nearly lost consciousness. Directors called her "a ball breaker," "a rebellious hellion," and "very, very difficult." Undoubtedly, some, if not most, of the resentment arose because Davis was a woman, but there's no denying that she had (and still has) a wicked tongue. She once said of a rival actress, "She's the original good time that was had by all."

# 7

**BILLIE HOLIDAY,** *born Eleonora Fagan in Baltimore, Maryland, probably in 1915.* If anyone had a right to sing the blues, it was Billie Holiday. Born in poverty, she worked as a maid before dancing in a Harlem nightclub. She took the name Billie from a movie star, Billie Dove; Holiday became her surname when, in 1918, her father married her mother.

One night in 1931, she was asked to sing at the club where she worked. She did, and "the whole joint quieted down. If someone had dropped a pin, it would have

# 6

**ROSE SCHNEIDERMAN,** *born Rachel Schneiderman in Saven, Poland, 1882.* In 1890, Rose Schneiderman's family emigrated to the United States to find a better life. What they found, like millions of immigrants before and after them, was that America was a land of mixed blessings. For Rose it meant formal education through the ninth grade, a vast improvement on what she would have received in the Orthodox Jewish community of her homeland. It also meant that when her father died in 1892, many of the ties that would have sustained her family had been severed. Her mother took in boarders, but it wasn't enough, and the children were scattered in orphanages for over a year until Rose was old enough to take care of them while her mother worked as a seamstress.

At thirteen, Rose, too, joined the work force. For three years she worked in a department store for as much as seventy hours a week at a salary of two dollars a week. Despite the long hours and low pay, being a cashier was considered genteel work, and it was over her mother's objections that Schneiderman quit her job and went to work in a cap factory for much higher wages.

LIBRARY OF CONGRESS

ROSE SCHNEIDERMAN: *She fought against a system which valued property above workers' safety.*

In 1903, Schneiderman organized the women in her shop into the first women's local of the Jewish Socialist United Cloth Hat and Cap Makers' Union. Thus began a remarkable career of speaking, organizing, and campaigning in which she worked for peace and woman suffrage, lobbied for the eight-hour work day and a minimum wage, and fought the sexism of male unionists who tried to lead strikes she'd organized. Shy and lonely as a young woman, she became a militant, professional speaker who electrified audiences. She organized workers and led strikes in a variety of trades; perhaps her most famous effort was her co-leadership of a three-month shirtwaist workers' strike in New York which became known as the "Uprising of the Twenty Thousand." She was president of the Women's Trade Union League for over twenty-five years.

sounded like a bomb." Slowly, she worked her way through the New York nightclubs, earning a few dollars a night, a loyal following, and the nickname "Lady." She made recordings that were largely ignored, but in the late '30s her recognition grew when she toured with Count Basie's and Artie Shaw's bands. Yet, everywhere she went, she encountered prejudice.

The 1940s and 1950s brought her increased fame and increased troubles: fights with managers, unsuccessful battles with drug and alcohol addiction, several narcotics arrests, and one conviction resulting in a nine-month jail term. And there was more: luckless affairs, marriages, and divorces. She repeatedly institutionalized herself to break her drug addictions, but she never stayed clean for long, and in 1959, while she lay dying in New York's Metropolitan Hospital, she was again arrested for narcotics possession. Warm, generous, and vital, she was often unhappy, but her audiences loved her. And she loved to sing. She had an unshakable reverence for music and the power of emotion. "I can't stand," she said, "to sing the same song the same way two nights in succession. If you can, then it ain't music, it's close order drill, or exercise or yodeling or something, not music."

# 8

**MARY PICKFORD,** *born Gladys Marie Smith in Toronto, Ontario, Canada, 1893.* In contrast to Billie Holiday's life, Mary Pickford's is a fairy tale. Let's face it; in contrast to almost *anyone*'s life, it's a fairy tale. Try this on for size: a beautiful little girl changes her name and makes money for her poor family by touring in vaudeville. At thirteen she decides to make her Broadway debut or become a seamstress. She gets an interview with a famous producer who puts her in a Broadway show. At sixteen she is discovered by Biograph studios' D. W. Griffith and turned into a film star. Within a few years, she is making $10,000 a week. She meets and marries a film prince, Douglas Fairbanks, moves into a palace calld Pickfair, and founds United Artists with Fairbanks and Charlie Chaplin.

It wasn't quite as perfect as it sounds. At that time, films, known as "the galloping tintypes," were considered disreputable by members of the "legitimate" theatre establishment, and it was a step down in status for her to act in them. She and Griffith didn't get along; both were always staging tantrums to get their way. When she married Fairbanks, she had already been married and divorced, and in 1935 she divorced Fairbanks as well. In 1937 she began a long and happy marriage to fellow actor Charles "Buddy" Rogers. Last but not least, she spent almost her entire career fighting the typecasting that kept her "the eternal image of girlhood" well into adulthood. Her long blonde curls and "winsome, expressive face" got her the nicknames "America's Sweetheart" and "Little Mary," and when she bobbed her hair in the late '20s it caused a national uproar. Still, there are worse fates than being wealthy, successful, and mostly happy.

# 9

**AMBAPALI,** *born in Vaisali, India, in the sixth century B.C., exact date unknown.* Ambapali lived during the time of Siddharta Guatana, or the Buddha. She was the greatest courtesan of her time, and by charging outlandish prices for her services, she amassed a huge personal fortune with which she bought a lavish home and some mango groves. When the Buddha passed through Vaisali, he visited Ambapali, and he apparently made quite an impression on her. She retired from her profession, gave her mango groves to the Buddha, and began to study his teachings. In time, she became an *arhat,* or holy one—quite a feat since few *men* ever achieved this state, which was

MARY PICKFORD: *As winsome as she was shrewd. The film mogul Adolph Zukor once told her: "Mary, sweetheart, I don't have to diet. Every time I talk over a new contract with you and your mother, I lose ten pounds."*

LIBRARY OF CONGRESS

as far as a human could go without actually *being* the Buddha or achieving nirvana. Her accomplishment was even more impressive than it would have been for a man, however, since the Buddha had suspicions about women. It was believed at the time that only men could attain nirvana.

# 10

**CLARE BOOTHE LUCE,** *born Clare Boothe in New York City, 1903.* Clare Boothe Luce was a woman of many talents and many careers. She began as an actress, serving as Mary Pickford's understudy until, deciding that Pickford was too healthy, she quit. (Pickford grew ill and gave up her part a month later.) Next, she tried wifehood as a career, marrying tycoon George Tuttle Brokaw in 1923. Unhappy, she divorced him in 1929, later telling a reporter, "It is ridiculous to think you can spend your whole life with one person. Three is about the right number. Yes, I think three husbands would do it."

After her divorce, she turned to journalism, beginning in 1930 as an editorial assistant for *Vogue* and becoming managing editor of *Vanity Fair* by 1933. She married again, this time choosing Henry Luce, millionnaire publisher of *Time* and *Fortune,* but she didn't stop writing. On the contrary, she traveled to Europe as a correspondent, eventually covering the war, and began a new, simultaneous career as a playwright and novelist. Her biggest Broadway success, *The Women* (1936), was made into a movie that today is a still-funny museum piece of outdated female stereotypes.

Next, she tried her hand at politics, winning a seat in Congress in 1943 and keeping it for a second term. In 1944, she delivered the keynote address at the Republican national convention. Some thought that if she had been a man, she could have campaigned successfully

LIBRARY OF CONGRESS

CLARE BOOTH LUCE: *Actress, journalist, editor, playwright, and diplomat.*

for president. However, she chose as her next career one she thought especially suited to women: diplomacy. Her appointment as ambassador to Italy made her the most powerful woman in the history of the United States diplomatic corps.

# 11

**LADY MARY BANKES,** *dies in Corfe Castle, England, 1661.* Lady Bankes and her husband, Sir John, owned Corfe Castle in the south of England, a fortress known to be "one of the impregnable forts of the kingdom." Advantageously situated and protected by walls ten feet thick, it was also luxuriously decorated with green leather, blue damask, silk, ebony and gold cabinets, tapestries, satin and crimson velvet cushions, and Turkish and Persian carpets. Lady Bankes stocked Corfe with plenty of maid-servants, but she never thought of repurchasing the "chiefest guns" of the castle, which had been sold by her predecessor.

This was rather unfortunate, since one day Sir John trotted off to London to confer with the king, leaving his wife with only five soldiers as a guard. While he was gone, the English Civil War began. As a Royalist, Lady Bankes was suspected and disliked by the near-by townspeople, who sympathized with the Parliamentarians. Quick to recognize the possibility of a siege, she stocked up on provisions, kept the gates of the castle locked, stalled when she was ordered to yield her last four cannon, and got a Royalist commander to lend her fifty extra soldiers. Eventually, she was forced to bow to local pressure and surrender her guns, but she did so only to buy time to obtain extra supplies and to create the impression that she was helpless.

The siege of her castle began on June 23, 1643. As many as six hundred heavily armed men bombarded the castle from a nearby church, preventing a counterattack. Lady Bankes organized raids for food, one of which resulted in the theft of eight cows and a bull; she herself, "to her eternal honor be it spoken," defended the upper ward of the castle with her maids and daughters, hurling stones and hot embers on the attackers, who "ran away crying."

Finally, though, in 1646, the "prudent and valiant" lady was defeated. She and her children were given safe conduct from the castle, which was ransacked and its lavish decorations seized as spoils of war. Lady Bankes died in 1661. Her gravestone praises her for "constancy and courage above her sex."

# 12

**JUANA LA LOCA,** *dies at 75 in Tordesillas, Spain, 1555.* Juana, daughter of Spain's King Ferdinand and Queen Isabella, was a strange little girl. Fluent in Latin and French, and skillful at playing the clavichord, organ, and guitar, she was unpleasantly melancholy, aloof, and silent, with a fondness for solitude and rebellion.

At the age of sixteen, the nervous Juana was sent off to Flanders to marry an Austrian prince, Philip the Handsome. All she knew of him was that the marriage was advantageous to her parents and the little that Philip's nickname implied. Although they were scheduled to be married on October 20, 1496, when they met on October 19 they grabbed the first priest they saw and demanded to be married that instant. Then they found a quiet

JUANA LA LOCA: *Sadness becomes her.*

UNIVERSITY ART MUSEUM, SANTA BARBARA, SEDGWICK COLLECTION

room and made love. The next day, their official marriage was celebrated.

Unfortunately, desire was the only thing they had in common. Juana was shy and intense; Philip was active, extroverted, and irresponsible. She fell passionately in love with him the moment she saw him; he saw her as a reasonably attractive brood mare and had no intention of remaining faithful to her. He quickly grew bored with her possessiveness and went back to his favorite pastime, seducing young women. He returned to Juana often enough though to make her pregnant six times.

Whether or not Juana was insane, and to what degree she was insane, has been a fascinating puzzle for historians for centuries. But there is no question that she and Philip had a bizarre, obsessive relationship that was insane in itself. She loved Philip, wanted him, hated him, sought revenge on him, and could not bear to be separated from him. When her older sister and brother died, leaving her the heir to the Spanish throne, she brought Philip to Spain with her. Simultaneously, she wanted to make him love her native country and withhold it from him; he wanted to be King of Spain, but he could only be so through her, and she wanted to deny him something.

Philip hated Spain and left it as soon as he could. Hoping to make him come back, Ferdinand and Isabella refused to let Juana accompany him. They had her locked in a castle, where she screamed, threatened executions, and hurled insults at her captors from the battlements, then stood silent and motionless at the gates for days, refusing to eat and staring toward Flanders and Philip. The scandal created by her behavior forced Ferdinand and Isabella to free her, but when she got back to Philip, he was unimpressed by her devotion.

Just when it seemed that her life couldn't get any stranger or less bearable, it did. Her mother died, leaving the crown to Juana. Ferdinand would act as a regent until Juana could return to Spain. He would also rule if Juana was unable to do so. Instantly, Juana became the center of a power struggle between Philip and Ferdinand, each of whom tried to use her to get control of Spain. In the ensuing conflict, Ferdinand fled to safety in Italy, but before Philip could enjoy his victory, he died of a fever.

Juana's grief was nearly uncontrollable. She dressed in black for the rest of her life and grew increasingly obsessed with Philip's body. She kept it with her whenever she could, frequently opened the coffin to look at him even after his face was a less than lovely sight.

She sent to Italy for her father; since he wanted Spain so badly, he could have it. After an emotional reunion, she made him king, but she failed to understand her own position. She could not simply retire and hope to become an ordinary person. She was still Queen of Spain, and if Ferdinand wanted to have absolute power, she had to be removed. He had his daughter imprisoned in the dark, gloomy castle of Tordesillas, and he told everyone she was insane.

Juana was imprisoned, first by her father, and later by her son, for the next forty-six years until her death.

# 13 _____

**JOSEPHINE BUTLER,** *born Josephine Elizabeth Grey in Milfield, Northumberland, England, 1828.* In 1857, an estimated six thousand London houses, or one in every sixty, was a brothel. Girls of eleven were offered for sale on English streets. Syphilis was rampant.

The government was determined to do something about these evils, but what it did wasn't exactly what you might expect. It passed three Contagious Diseases Acts, in 1864, 1866, and 1869, which said that in garrison towns, any woman suspected of prostitution was subject to police "inspection" for venereal disease. These inspections could be devastating—the doctors performing them (all male) had been rumored to rape their patients, and if the inspectors declared that a woman was diseased, she could be held and treated with mercury until she was considered cured. If she were menstruating, she could be detained until an examination was possible. A refusal to submit to the examination could result in imprisonment at hard labor.

Sometimes eager policemen would flirt with a woman, and if she seemed to like it, arrest her. Many women arrested under the new laws became prostitutes after they had been "examined."

There were murmurs against the Contagious Diseases Acts, but only murmurs. One of the few people to raise a loud and clear voice against the laws was Josephine Butler, the wife of a liberal Oxford professor. She asked her husband for permission to begin a "great crusade" in public. After much thought, he said, "Go, and God be with you."

Butler toured England, making speeches to large crowds, taking her case directly to the recently-enfranchised working men whose daughters were feeding the prostitution trade. She was serene in the face of danger, even when hostile crowds set one of her meeting-places on fire. She wrote newspaper articles which made their point (although facts were liberally mixed with hearsay and exaggeration), and she took her case to Parliament in 1882, announcing: "I am not here to represent virtuous women alone: I plead for the rights of the most virtuous and the most vicious equally, and I speak for the womanhood of the world."

"The moral character of a woman," she continued, "though it be of the lowest, does not alter the sacrilegious character of an indecent assault upon her person." In 1886 the Contagious Diseases Acts were repealed.

# 14

**ANNE SULLIVAN,** *born Joanna Mansfield Sullivan in Feeding Hills, Massachusetts, 1866.* Throughout their friendship, which lasted all their lives, Anne Sullivan and Helen Keller, her famous pupil, were consistently irritated by one thing: everyone marveled at Keller's brilliance and made much of her, while "Teacher" was ignored. Anne Sullivan was indeed a great woman and a great educator who deserved far more attention than she got.

Sullivan's childhood was far more miserable than Keller's. She was born to a family of poor Irish immigrants. Her mother died when she was eight; by the time she was ten, Sullivan was nearly blind, and one of her brothers was lame. Her father abandoned his three children, and they were sent to a

poorhouse where they were treated cruelly when they weren't entirely neglected. Sullivan's lame brother died there. Charles Dickens could hardly have written a sadder story.

But even Dickens wouldn't have let his tragic heroine languish forever; eventually she must die or get luckier. Sullivan got lucky. When she was fourteen years old, she was sent to Boston's Perkins Institution for the Blind, where she acquired a solid education. She also gradually regained her sight, although it always gave her trouble. In a few years she was offered a job teaching a spoiled little girl in Alabama—Helen Keller.

Some people claimed that Sullivan exploited and manipulated Keller, and it is true that she didn't want Keller to learn to speak, that

she was extraordinarily possessive of her pupil, and that she kept Keller in deliberate ignorance of the facts of life for some time. However, it's also clear that Sullivan loved Keller a great deal, and she sacrificed her marriage to Harvard professor John Albert Macy because her commitment to Keller always came first. Such devotion is all the more remarkable because, when she first met Keller, Sullivan had no particular interest in teaching. As she wrote in 1888, shortly after her arrival in Alabama, "I came here simply because circumstances made it necessary for me to earn my living, and I seized upon the first opportunity that offered itself, although I did not suspect . . . that I had any special fitness for the work."

# 15

**ISABELLA STEWART GARDNER,** *born Isabella Stewart in New York City, 1840.* Isabella *was* her name, but almost no one ever called her that. To friends, she was "Belle," or, after her marriage in 1860 to John Lowell Gardner, "Mrs. Jack." Both names seem a little informal for one of the wealthiest women in Boston, but Gardner was not formal. She was outrageous. Her dresses were too tight and low-cut; she wore too many pearls and drove around the city in her coach with a pair of footmen behind her and a pair of lion cubs on the seat beside her. She obviously had a mind of her own. Instead of waiting for her husband to come home from his club every night, she pursued her own hobby, collecting young men of artistic persuasion.

In the 1890s, though, two things happened that multiplied the rumors and curiosity about Mrs.

Jack. In 1891, her father died, and in 1898, Jack Gardner died at his club. Between them, they left Gardner over $5 million. She knew exactly what she wanted to do with the money; she'd known ever since she was sixteen. "If I ever have any money of my own," she had said then to a friend, "I am going to build a palace and fill it with beautiful things." In 1899, she began building Fenway Court, an Italianate palace which incorporated some of her treasures—an ancient mosaic floor from Rome, stone lions from Florence, and balconies from Venice. Her architect and the Boston building inspector complained that she was violating the rules of design and the state of Massachusetts, but she said, "it will be built as *I* wish and not as *you* wish." She had her way, and she appeared at the worksite every day for three years, eating with the work-

men, demonstrating painting techniques, and swinging a broadax to make ceiling beams.

Meanwhile, she set her artistic young men to work finding the exquisite works of art to fill her palace.

Everyone who was anyone came to the opening night at Fenway Court on New Year's Eve 1902, to marvel at the treasures, to hear the concert given by fifty musicians from the Boston Symphony Orchestra, and to see Mrs. Jack in her pearls, her diamonds, and her glory.

Upon her death in 1924, she left Fenway Court to the public—on one condition. Nothing, she stipulated, must be changed. And nothing has been; not one painting has been added, sold, borrowed, lent, or moved.

ISABELLA STEWART GARDNER: *Henry James likened her to "a figure on a wondrous cinquecento tapestry."*

**POLLY ADLER,** *born Pearl Adler in Yanow, Russia, probably in 1899.* "In the world of the Twenties," wrote Adler in her autobiography, *A House Is Not A Home,* "the only unforgivable sin was to be poor." By the time she was twenty-four, she knew how to avoid the sin of poverty: break the rules.

A factory worker, Adler was rooming with an actress on New York City's fashionable Upper West Side when she was introduced to celebrities and bootleggers, wealthy, and glamorous people. But she was frightened by the actress's growing drug addiction. She wanted to move out, but she didn't have enough money to escape until a gangster offered to pay her rent if he could use her apartment to meet his girl-friend occasionally. Adler agreed, and soon she was procuring women for him and his friends. Business boomed, but Adler wanted to run a legitimate business. The resultant lingerie shop was bankrupt within a year, and at twenty-four, she reopened her brothel, determined "to be the best goddam madam in America." She combined bribes to the police and sound business skills with highly visible excursions to nightclubs accompanied by her "girls." Writers, movie stars, busi-nessmen, and gangsters made "going to Polly's" a euphemism for the world's most popular indoor sport. Although she was arrested frequently and hounded by prose-cutors eager to prove that her house was really run by the mob, she spent only twenty-four days in jail—for possession of porno-graphic films. After World War II, plagued by poor health, she retired to Los Angeles, untroubled by ques-tions of legality or morality. Her business career, in her own words, was nothing more nor less than "an American success story."

ISABELLA STEWART GARDNER MUSEUM

# 17

**ISAK DINESEN,** *born Karen Christentze Dinesen in Rungsted-lund, Denmark, 1885.* When Karen Blixen, known to her readers as Isak Dinesen, died, she was buried in a Danish grave, but mixed into the soil was a handful of earth she had brought back from Africa. It was a fitting reflection of her life, which had been a curious blending of European and African influences. Born in Denmark, she was a stubborn, passionate, courageous woman who studied art in Copenhagen and "longed for wings to carry her away." She fell in love with the handsome Hans von Blixen-Finecke, famous as a horseman and an aviator. But he didn't love her, and she ended up marrying his brother, Bror, famous as a lover and a bad credit risk. It was Bror who taught her to shoot, took her to Africa, and gave her a particularly virulent case of syphilis that resulted in a long, embarrassing, and painful course of treatment.

Karen, or Tania, as she was known to her friends, had loves of her own, the two most powerful being her loves for Africa and for Denys Finch-Hatton. Musically gifted, athletic, and charming, he met her in 1919, and they had a long and passionate relationship.

As for Africa, she loved everything about it—the land, the animals, and the people, whom she did her best to protect from European exploitation. However, she was forced to leave Africa when her coffee plantation went bankrupt. Her life seemed to end. She was divorced, she no longer had her farm, her adopted country, or even her lover—Finch-Hatton had left her.

Back in Denmark she began a second life, as a writer. Her first book, *Seven Gothic Tales,* was accepted in 1934 by a publisher who said, "This won't sell but it is too good not to publish." To everyone's surprise, it *did* sell—very well—and she continued to write. Although she never returned to Africa, its moods and rhythms permeated her writing, and she drew on her experiences there for the stories in *Out of Africa* and *Shadows on the Grass.* She came close to winning a Nobel prize with her romantic, dramatic style.

# 18

**LUCREZIA BORGIA,** *born in the fortress of Subiaco, near Rome, Italy, 1480.* This illegitimate child of Cardinal Rodrigo Borgia and his long-time concubine grew into not one, but two, women. One was a poisoner and courtesan. The other was a virtuous mother, wife, and patron of the arts. Both of these

LUCREZIA BORGIA: *The dramatic Renaissance woodcut to the contrary, a dagger did not kill the notorious Borgia; she died in childbirth.*

LIBRARY OF CONGRESS

personae were the products of power.

In 1492, when Lucrezia was twelve, her father became Pope Alexander VI. The fact that he had several illegitimate children bothered no one; prominent churchmen of the day had mistresses as a matter of course. As soon as Alexander came to power, he began to use his position to strengthen the papal states and make advantageous marriages for his children. Inevitably, Lucrezia became a pawn in various political games, and the resentment that some felt for her father was transferred to her.

Before she entered puberty, she had been engaged to two Spanish noblemen, but she married neither of them. She ended up with an Italian nobleman. When this marriage became politically unsuitable, her father annulled it, and Borgia signaled her anger at being used by announcing her intention to become a nun. Her father cured her

of this notion with a marital prize, Alfonso of Bisceglie, a gentle, intelligent, honest, extraordinarily handsome man. It seemed to be a perfect match; Alfonso's good looks were an exquisite complement to Borgia's blond beauty, and his thorough education matched her good sense, her taste for poetry and the lute, her skill at drawing, and her knowledge of Latin, Greek, Italian, French, and Spanish. They were happy with each other, and together they offered their patronage to the poets they admired.

Then Borgia's father made an alliance with France, an alliance detrimental to Alfonso's interests. Borgia was trapped between her husband and her father, and in 1500 someone, probably her brother Cesare, had Alfonso attacked. He was wounded, and, when it appeared he would recover from his injuries, he was strangled. Borgia was furious and miserable, so her father gave her some papal lands to administer and found her a third

husband, Alfonso d'Este, Duke of Ferrara. This Alfonso was chronically unfaithful, and Borgia seems to have had affairs as well.

Her third marriage gave Borgia the ability to patronize the arts again, and the poets she hired praised her virtue, her beauty, and her wisdom. Gossips said that she was no better than a prostitute, a monstrous woman who had slept with her father and two of her brothers and who had poisoned countless people. So there are two Lucrezia Borgias—one the product of her own economic power, one the product of her father's political machinations and the envy they aroused. The real woman, as is usually the case, undoubtedly lay somewhere between the two images —probably, given the sources of the wilder rumors, quite close to the poets' image of her. *How* close will never be known. She died in childbirth in 1519.

# 19

**BRIGID,** *born in Leinster, Ireland, in about 450.* One of the most beloved of Irish saints, Brigid is surrounded by legends and rumors. One of these says that as a child, she was sold to a Druid whom she converted to Christianity. Another says that her father tried to marry her to the king of Ulster, who released her when he witnessed the depth of her piety. Still another says that she was so beautiful that she was constantly pestered by suitors, and that when she prayed to be disfigured and thus released from their attentions, she was stricken by smallpox in an unusual manner. Half of her face was scarred; half remained beautiful.

Very little is known for certain about her life. The year of her birth is uncertain, but her birthdate is known. It is certain that at an early

age she chose to become a nun, and she convinced seven of her friends to join her. Courageous, cheerful, and compassionate, she quickly became famous for her piety, good deeds, and knowledge, and prominent men came to visit her and to ask her for advice. Eventually she decided to establish a convent—the first in Ireland—and she chose a site near an oak sacred to the Druids. At this point, legends take over again; it is said that the local ruler told her she could have as much land for her abbey as she could cover with her shawl, so she wove one that expanded miraculously and covered a large piece of ground. The convent soon became almost as famous as its founder, mostly for a sacred fire tended by the nuns and associated with a number of miracles. Brigid died in

525, but for centuries after her death "the Mary of the Gael" was said to take her turn tending the fire at night.

# 20

**CLEOPATRA VII,** *born in Alexandria, Egypt, in about 69 B.C., exact date unknown.* Few women have captured the imaginations of more people than Cleopatra, who could be called the first international sex symbol. She is most famous, of course, for her relationships with powerful men, but she was a politician first and a lover second, and her story has an interesting epilogue that not many people know about.

At seventeen, Cleopatra married her brother and they co-ruled Egypt. But she soon grew tired of being a co-ruler, and about five years later, in 48 B.C., she took advantage of Julius Ceasar's visit to Egypt to solve her problem. She was smuggled into his camp wrapped in a bedroll, and won his support and his passion. By the time she was finished with him, she had a villa in Rome, a statue of herself in the temple of Venus Genetrix, a son named Caesarion, a dead brother, and a throne of her own.

When Caesar was assassinated in 44 B.C., Cleopatra went back to Egypt, but it wasn't long before she found a new protector—the now famous Mark Antony, who had assumed the rule of Egypt. He quickly fell prey to Cleopatra's magnetism and set up his court in Alexandria.

They had a symbiotic relationship. Cleopatra funded Antony's military expeditions, and he legitimized her political power. Not only did he confirm her claim to the Egyptian throne, but he also divided various territories among their three children.

Meanwhile, Antony had a political rival, Octavian, with whom he was sharing authority over the lands of the now-dead Caesar. Octavian was not pleased with Antony's infatuation with the Egyptian minx, and he coerced Antony to marry his own sister, Octavia. The marriage didn't work out, and Antony returned to Cleopatra. But Octavian now considered Antony a serious threat, and soon the two co-rulers were embroiled in a naval battle. In 31 B.C. Antony's fleet was crushed, and he committed suicide. Cleopatra followed him in suicide when she realized she couldn't charm Octavian into becoming her third husband. Cleopatra's son by Caesar was executed, but her three children by Antony were allowed to live—and in a fitting irony, the only person willing to care for them was her old rival, Octavia.

# 21

**CHARLOTTE BRONTË,** *born in Thornton, Bradford, Yorkshire, England, 1816.* Okay, let's see a show of hands: how many of you have read *Jane Eyre*? A lot of you. How about *Villette*? Not so many. How about *Shirley*? Almost no one. The fact is that to most people, Charlotte Brontë is just a misty figure lurking behind the figures of Jane and Mr. Rochester, and she's all too often confused with her sister Emily. It's a shame, because she was an extraordinary woman who accomplished what she did against staggering odds.

For starters, by the time she reached adulthood she'd witnessed the deaths of her mother and her two older sisters. She and the surviving Brontë children were yielded to the care of their stern, unloving Aunt Elizabeth.

Charlotte's next problem was one of social position. She was poor; therefore, she had to work. However, she was also technically a gentlewoman, which meant that there were very few occupations she could have and still be considered "respectable." Given her lack of money, there were only three: teacher, governess, and wife. Unfortunately, she hated teaching and found being a governess demeaning. She was also shy, awkward, and (in the opinion of her contemporaries) very plain, if not ugly. William Thackeray called her "a little bit of a creature without a penny worth of good looks." So it's something of a miracle, especially considering the social pressure for women to marry, that she turned down not one but three proposals.

And this brings us to Brontë's real problem, in her art and in her personal life: she had the misfortune to be born a woman. She had genius, fire, anger, and ambition in an age when women were supposed to be sweet, subservient, and placid.

In her work as a writer, as in her life, she was plagued by conflicts between her natural impulses and the world's expectations. As a

young woman she sent some samples of her poetry to Robert Southey, England's poet laureate, and asked his opinion of them. He wrote back, acknowledging that she was gifted but advising her to stop writing. "Literature cannot be the business of a woman's life," he wrote.

Faced with prejudice against women writers, Brontë disguised herself as a man. Under the name Currer Bell, she submitted a novel to a number of publishers. It was universally rejected, but she wrote another, *Jane Eyre,* which was published in 1847. It was an enormous success, and she began her next novel, *Shirley.* Unfortunately, at about this time people began to spread the word that "Currer" was in fact a woman. Critics shouted words like "trickery" and "artifice"; reviewers who had praised her work now found fault with it, and *Shirley* was a financial failure.

Brontë was criticized even by her friends for "want of womanly delicacy and propriety" and for "coarseness here and there in her works," and her enemies simply called her works "naughty books." *Jane Eyre*, however, has fascinated every generation of readers since its publication, and even the much-neglected *Shirley* makes good reading today.

# 22

**MARIE TAGLIONI,** *dies at 70 in Marseilles, France, 1884.* Marie Taglioni was the foremost ballerina of her day, although some preferred her only real rival, Fanny Elssler. She was also one of Europe's foremost romantic heroines in an era full of romantic heroines.

Her father was a dancer and choreographer, and as soon as she could possibly withstand the rigors

MARIE TAGLIONI: *With her brother, Paul, performing the principal roles in* La Sylphide, *a ballet choreographed by their father.*

of training, her father began to coach her, demanding all that she could give, and in 1822 she made her debut in Vienna. She had a unique style and a graceful, ethereal quality that drew attention from the press and public, and soon she began dancing to thunderous acclaim at the Paris Opéra.

Within a few years, Taglioni was not only a celebrated dancer but the standard by which all other ballerinas were judged. Her choreography was much admired, and she was a success wherever she went.

England, Poland, Austria, and Russia welcomed her as eagerly as France; in St. Petersburg she was praised by Tsar Nicholas I, and after her farewell performance "a pair of her ballet shoes was eaten 'cooked and served with a special sauce.'" Tasty. Legend even has it that she was kidnapped by bandits who laid furs down in the snowy road and, instead of taking her money, commanded her to dance for them.

In 1847 Taglioni retired to her home on Lake Como, but in the 1850s she returned to Paris to coach ballet at the Opéra. After her favorite pupil died in a fire during rehearsal, she moved to London and taught ballet there. Only in 1880 did she return to her native France, where she died.

# 23 _____

**HANNAH SNELL,** *born in Worcester, England, 1723.* The daughter of a hosier and the granddaughter of a professional soldier, Snell was orphaned at seventeen and went to live with her sister in London. There she met and married a sailor, James Summs. He deserted her after only a few months, leaving her pregnant and without a means of support. Snell was not a woman to take such treatment lying down. She left the baby with her sister, dressed herself in men's clothing, and went to find her husband. There she joined an infantry regiment and fought against the supporters of the

## 24

**ELEANOR of Aquitaine,** *born near Bordeaux, France, in 1122, exact date unknown.* In her day, Eleanor was the most powerful woman in the western world. She was heir to a collection of tremendously important lands comprising Aquitaine, a source of struggle between England and France for many years. At age sixteen she married Louis VII and became queen of France. Despite what seemed a harmonious relationship, the marriage was annulled after fifteen years, and Eleanor was back on the marriage market. Among her many suitors—all of whom wanted control of Aquitaine—she chose Henry II of Normandy, and within two years they were king and queen of England. The pair had five sons and three daughters. Eleanor already had two daughters from her marriage to Louis. All five girls married into various ruling houses of Europe, making Eleanor the "Grandmother of Europe" seven hundred years before Queen Victoria earned the same title. But it was the sons who gave her problems.

A battle over who should succeed Henry to the throne of England pitted the royal couple against each other. The concept of primogeniture had not yet taken hold. Eventually Henry had Eleanor imprisoned, and she wasn't released until his death fifteen years later. But all good things really do come to those who wait. Upon her release Eleanor staged a triumphal procession, gave amnesty to criminals, and generated popular support for her son Richard to succeed Henry as king. That her public relations campaign worked is evident in his nickname—the Lion Heart. Eleanor secured for herself a strong role in her son's government. She founded schools and religious establishments, patronized poets and scholars. She died in 1204, at the age of eighty-two, having outlived all but two of her children.

LIBRARY OF CONGRESS

HANNAH SNELL: *Soldiering was in her blood.*

pretender, Bonnie Prince Charlie.

At some point, she was involved in a dispute with her sergeant. She claimed that he was sexually assaulting a woman and that she prevented the attack, but whatever the reason, she was sentenced to be flogged. She also claimed to have been given five hundred lashes, although it's likely that the number was far smaller. At any rate, she was so incensed at being beaten that she deserted and headed south. In Portsmouth she signed onto the sloop *Swallow* as "James Gray" and headed for the East Indies. There she was badly wounded in the groin, but she got help from a woman who removed the bullet and kept Snell's sex a secret.

The fleet returned to Europe, and in Lisbon Snell discoverd that her husband had been executed some time before her arrival. Her mission was at an end, and it appeared that she had three choices. One was to continue her service in the navy. Another was to return to her old way of life in London. She chose the third: to return to female dress, but to milk her experiences for all they were worth. She published an autobiography, appeared on the stage in uniform, got a government pension, and opened an inn, the Female Warrior.

# 25

**RUBY DORIS SMITH ROBIN-SON,** *born Rubye Doris Smith in Atlanta, Georgia, 1942.* From 1960 until her death in 1967, Robinson was one of the most prominent and respected civil rights workers in the United States. A leader of the Student Non-Violent Coordinating Committee (SNCC), she headed many of the first lunch counter sit-ins. She was one of the "Rock Hill Four," the first four students to draw attention to their cause by serving jail sentences for violations of Jim Crow laws rather than being released on bail. She registered voters, was arrested for trying to use white-only bathrooms, and took part in the perilous Freedom Rides which challenged segregation in interstate travel. Friends recognized her as "one of the few genuine revolutionaries in the black liberation movement," and a colleague said: "Ruby was probably the nearest thing I ever met to a free person. I mean really free. . . . Ruby just stood up to *anybody.* That's just not the way blacks acted in the South. As a result, she made you stand taller."

She died at twenty-five in Atlanta, from lymphoma, but many in SNCC believed she'd been poisoned. A woman who worked with Robinson had her own theory. "She died of exhaustion. . . . I don't think it was necessary to assasinate her. What killed Ruby Doris was the constant outpouring of work, work, work, work with being married, having a child, the constant conflicts, the constant struggles that she was subjected to because she was a woman. . . . She was destroyed by the movement."

# 26

**EMMA HAMILTON,** *born Emily Lyon in Neston, Cheshire, England, 1765.* One of the most notorious women of her time was *probably* born on April 26, although it might have been the sixth, the sixteenth, or even May twelfth. Emily was a beautiful young woman with reddish-gold hair that fell to her heels, big blue-gray eyes, and a smooth, lovely complexion. Despite her beauty, however, she was still just a working-class girl with no real future, or at least none that satisfied her. She worked as a nursemaid and a shopgirl (her enemies later added "prostitute" to the list) until, for unknown reasons, she and her mother moved to London and changed their names. Mrs. Lyon became known as Mrs. Cadogan, and Emily became Emma Hart.

In London Emma's beauty was a marketable asset. She acted, sang, posed for sculptors, and sat for the painters Romney and Reynolds. She also quickly found herself a keeper, Sir Harry Fetherstonehaugh. He set her up in comfort at his Sussex estate, but she was not giving him in return the absolute faithfulness he demanded. She had fallen in love with one of his occasional guests, the Honorable Charles Francis Greville, who had a small income and could only afford another man's mistress.

Fetherstonehaugh tolerated this situation for a few months, but when Emma became pregnant, he suspected that Greville was the father and refused to support the

LIBRARY OF CONGRESS

EMMA HAMILTON: *Less faithful than man's best friend.*

child—or its mother. Greville found himself honor-bound to set Emma up in a modest London house, but he quickly sank into debt. He solved his problem in a rather unusual way by introducing Emma to his wealthy uncle, Sir William Hamilton. Hamilton, charmed by his nephew's beautiful mistress, offered to pay Greville's debts—in exchange for Emma.

So Emma was transferred to yet another male patron, this time in an outright purchase. She and her mother went to Naples with Hamilton, where she learned Italian, posed for another series of artists, and served as Hamilton's mistress. In 1791 she convinced him to marry her; she did not love him, but she was genuinely grateful for being made "respectable." She became a close friend of Queen Maria Caroline of Naples and was a social success until 1793, when she met Admiral Horatio Nelson and her life changed.

At least, her level of social acceptability changed, but it was really the same old story. She became Nelson's mistress and, in 1800, moved to England with him. Since Nelson was a national hero, Emma's relationship with him was considered disgraceful, and their daughter, Horatia, became a symbol of a "harlot's" corruption of the great man.

In 1803, Hamilton died, and Emma and Nelson had a couple of splendid years together, living on Hamilton's money. But in 1805, Nelson died in the Battle of Trafalgar, leaving his wealth to Emma. Unfortunately, his beneficiary proved incapable of handling her fortune, and by 1812 she was in debtor's prison. A friend helped her escape to Calais where she died in 1815.

# 27

**MARY WOLLSTONECRAFT,** *born in Hoxton, England 1759.* Wollstonecraft's life reads more like legend than fact. At twenty-one she left her unhappy home—a bold step, but soon she took bolder ones, traveling without a chaperone to Lisbon to nurse her best friend on her deathbed and kidnapping her own sister Eliza to rescue her from a miserable marriage. Meanwhile, Wollstonecraft worked as a teacher, a lady's companion, and a governess before settling in London and getting a job with a publisher. She wrote articles and a novel, did translations, and joined an intellectual circle which included radicals like William Godwin and Thomas Paine. When French revolutionists stormed the Bastille, this group went wild, and Paine published his *Rights of Man* in celebration. He was immediately attacked by the nation's most prominent philosopher at the time, Edmund Burke, who was terrified of a similar revolution on English soil. Wollstonecraft leapt to Paine's defense in 1790 with *A Vindication of the Rights of Man*, and she decided to write a history of the French Revolution as it unfolded.

So in 1792, again without a chaperone, she traveled to Paris. There she met a fascinating and thoroughly unscrupulous American, Gilbert Imlay. He registered her as his wife at the American embassy, thus granting her the protection of United States citizenship, but they never married. However, they both advocated free love and began an affair.

For a while they were quite happy together. Wollstonecraft gave birth to a daughter, Fanny, in 1794, and as the Reign of Terror mounted in Paris, Imlay sent her back to London with the child.

By the time they were reunited, she found Imlay living with another woman, and in despair she tried to

MARY WOLLSTONECRAFT: *A brilliant radical who died an untimely death.*

LIBRARY OF CONGRESS

commit suicide by throwing herself off a bridge. She emerged from the water very much alive and mostly cured of her obsession with Imlay. By August of 1796, she had begun an affair with her old friend William Godwin. They lived in separate homes in an effort to maintain independence; she wrote to him, "I wish you, from my soul, to be riveted in my heart, but I do not desire to have you always to my elbow." When she became pregnant, however, Godwin bowed to social pressure and convinced her to marry and live with him. Wollstonecraft worked on a novel, *Maria,* throughout her pregnancy, but it was never finished. She gave birth to a daughter on August 30, 1797. During eighteen hours of labor, she contracted peritonitis, caused by her doctor's efforts to remove the placenta. All they could do for Wollstonecraft was ease her pain, so they gave her wine and brought in puppies to suck at her swollen breasts. She died on September 10, but her baby lived to become Mary Shelley, author of *Frankenstein.*

Wollstonecraft's greatest accomplishment is *A Vindication of the Rights of Woman* (1792), one of the earliest surviving works of feminism and a historic treatise that attacked the forces that kept women the social, economic, political, and intellectual inferiors of men.

The *Vindication,* combined with the details of her personal life, made Wollstonecraft *persona non grata* for a century after her death. She was called "a hyena in petticoats" and a "philosophical wanton"; the *Vindication* was denounced as "a scripture archly framed for propagating whores." Her death was seen as a fitting punishment and a lesson to "strong-minded" women. For decades it was considered a serious blot on a woman's reputation to defend Wollstonecraft, to admit to having read a word of the *Vindication,* or, except in a warning never to be like her, even to mention her name.

# 28 _____

**SARA ADLER,** *dies at about 95 in New York City, 1953.* Sara Levitzky was born to a wealthy Jewish family in Russia, but by the time she was a young woman, it was clear that she would not simply marry into another wealthy family and bear children. She had a talent for performing, and after studying voice at the Odessa Conservatory, she joined Maurice Heine's Yiddish theatre company and married Heine. What her career in Russia would have been like is unknown. Fierce pogroms followed the assassination of Tsar Alexander II in 1881, and in 1883 the Yiddish theatre was banned.

So, early in 1884, Sara and the rest of the Heine company emigrated to the United States, and she became one of the biggest stars of New York's Yiddish theatre. She toned down the broad, exaggerated gestures then in vogue, relying on realism rather than histrionics for effect, and audiences loved it. Over the next several decades of her career, she played three hundred roles, although two characters in particular made her famous— Katusha Maslova in *Resurrection* and the abandoned, unstable wife in Jacob Gordin's *Homeless.*

Sara's personal and professional lives were eternally linked. She came to the United States with a man who was both her husband and manager, and when she divorced Heine in 1890, it was as much a career move as an emotional one. She married another popular actor, Jacob Adler, and together they revitalized the Yiddish theatre, replacing old-fashioned plots with new ones about immigrant life and contemporary problems. They staged these new plays at their equally new theatre in the Bowery. After her husband's death in 1926, Adler performed less frequently, but her five children all took to the stage, and two of them, Stella and Luther, became the great stars of their generation. In 1939 a New York theatre revived *Resurrection* as a tribute to Sara Adler, and to the end of her life she was known as "the mother" or "the dowager duchess" of the Yiddish theatre.

# 29 _____

**CATHERINE OF SIENA,** *dies at about 33 in Rome, 1380.* When she was six years old, this child of a Siena cloth dyer had a vision of Christ. It was the first of many, and from her youth she decided that she would vow her virginity to God. She announced to her family that she would not marry, but she was equally determined not to become a nun. Her parents were appalled, and her older sister tried to dissuade her. Everyone told her that even though she wasn't that pretty, she did have lovely hair; if she'd only take a little trouble with her appearance, they'd find her a nice husband so she could forget about this nonsense. Catherine's answer was to cut off her beautiful hair; then she fell ill with smallpox.

Forced to take her seriously, Catherine's family decided to help her. They approached the Third Order of St. Dominic, a secular group whose members led lives of prayer, charity, chastity, and asceticism. Normally the order did

not accept young women, but representatives were convinced of her sincerity, and her smallpox-scarred face seemed to pose no threat. She became an exemplary member of the group, wrote a spiritual treatise called the *Dialogo,* and won followers for her piety. Eventually, she became respected as an adviser, and she became increasingly involved in public affairs and church politics. It was she who convinced Pope Gregory XI to leave the new papal seat in Avignon and return to Rome. Deeply revered for her writings and her holiness, she was made a saint in 1461.

# 30 _____

**ALICE B. TOKLAS,** *born Alice Babette Toklas in San Francisco, California, 1877.* The image of Alice B. Toklas is often obscured by the imposing shadow of her lifelong lover, Gertrude Stein. But Toklas deserves as much recognition as Stein, and not just because she was the first cookbook author to publish a recipe for hashish brownies. Stein's illustrious career could not have existed without the help of Toklas, who served as the author's secretary, companion, friend, supporter, manager, social coordinator, and cook. For nearly forty years she provided invaluable encouragement and assistance, and many of the couple's friends believed Toklas to be the wiser and more mature.

Although the famous *Autobiography of Alice B. Toklas* was actually Stein's autobiography, Toklas was an author in her own right. After Stein's death in 1946, she wrote memoirs, articles, cookbooks, and gossipy, witty, shrewd letters. However, writing and lecturing were unsatisfying; what she really wanted was to be with Stein again, and she turned to religion, hoping for an afterlife and a reunion with Stein. In 1963, she wrote: "Gertrude Stein . . . held my complete attention, as she did for all the many years I knew her until her death, and all these empty ones since then." Toklas died in 1967.

PORTRAIT BY EDWARD BIBERMAN; THE NATIONAL PORTRAIT GALLERY

MARTHA GRAHAM: *An innovator who created a new language of dance movement.*

## 1

CALAMITY JANE: *Army scout chic, a century before Ralph Lauren.*

Furthermore, no one knows where the name "Calamity Jane" came from in the first place. She may have earned it through her kindness to the victims of an 1878 smallpox epidemic or through her reputation for brashness and drunken brawling. She was rumored to have been a muleskinner, a pony express rider, and a stagecoach driver, although she probably only the first.

We do know that she was orphaned in her teens and left to wander throughout the West, mainly in Wyoming. She worked on and off as a prostitute and lived with a succession of men she called her husbands, among them "Wild Bill" Hickok. She liked to wear men's clothes, worked as a scout for the U.S. cavalry, and, later in life, joined various traveling shows including the Buffalo Bill Wild West Show. In 1903, she died in poverty and was buried in Deadwood, South Dakota, next to Wild Bill Hickok. Everything else is a mist of legends and rumors, some of them created by the East Coast press in its fascination with her character, but most of them originating with the unreliable Jane herself.

**CALAMITY JANE,** *born Martha Jane Canary in Princeton, Missouri, 1852, exact date unknown.* Nobody's absolutely sure that Jane was born on this date, but nobody's absolutely sure about anything when it comes to her. She was *prob-* *ably* born in Princeton, *probably* on May 1, *probably* in 1852. Her birth name may have been spelled Canary or Cannary, and the name of her husband (who may not have been her husband) may have been Burk or Burke.

**HARRIET QUIMBY,** *born in Coldwater, Michigan, 1875.* Quimby was *probably* born in Michigan, but almost as much mystery surrounds her birth as Calamity Jane's. Depending on which reports you believe, she was born in Michigan, Massachusetts, or California, and her childhood is even more obscure than her birth. She first appeared in a public capacity as a drama critic in California in 1902, and in 1903 she moved to New York City to write for *Leslie's Weekly.* She might have had a long career as a writer,

LIBRARY OF CONGRESS

but in 1910 she happened to see an air show.

Quimby enjoyed the air show, but was surprised that there were no women flying in it. She asked one of the pilots for flying lessons, but before she could take them he was killed in a crash. Undeterred by what could have been interpreted as a bad omen, she asked his brother to become her teacher instead. He agreed, and soon Quimby passed her test by executing two almost perfect solo flights. She was the first woman in the United States, and only the second woman in the world, to earn a pilot's license.

She joined an exhibition team and toured with it, wearing a much-publicized suit "of wool-backed plum-colored satin with a monklike hood" and goggles. She also encouraged women to get involved in aviation, suggesting air courier service could be a pleasant and profitable occupation for them. But

Quimby, herself, was most interested in glory. She decided, in 1912, to be the first woman to fly the English Channel. With backing from the London *Daily Mirror,* she did so, becoming not only the first woman to make the flight, but also the third pilot of either sex to do it, and the second solo flier. A male friend had been so doubtful of her abilities that he had offered to make the flight for her, dressed in her distinctive purple suit.

Unfortunately, by the time she set her Channel record, Quimby's career was almost over. Three months later she died in a crash into shallow water in Boston's Dorchester Bay, as five thousand spectators watched. The Boston *Post* mourned her passing in a manner typical of its time, "Ambitious to be among the pathfinders, she took her chances like a man and died like one."

# 2 _____

**NANNIE HELEN BURROUGHS,** *born in Orange, Virginia, probably in 1878.* As a young woman, Nannie Burroughs tried and failed to get a job as a domestic science teacher in a Washington, D.C., school. She wasn't rejected because she wasn't qualified, or even because she was black, but because she was *too* black; the District wanted even its black teachers to be as white as possible. Angered and dismayed, Burroughs decided then that some day she would start a school that "would give all sorts of girls a chance."

Her dream took a long time to realize. First, she had to get a job. She worked on a Baptist newspaper for a year, then returned to Washington and took the civil service exam. Her high score didn't help her, though. She was simply told there were no jobs available for "a colored clerk," so she worked as a janitor and bookkeeper. Her free time was spent working for the National Baptist Woman's Convention as its energetic corresponding secretary and later as its president. She also organized the Woman's Industrial Club, which served lunches to office workers at low prices, and held night classes for members in domestic and clerical skills for ten cents a week. Soon the club was so successful that she quit her daytime job and gave it her full attention.

However, Burroughs's primary ambition had always been to found a school for black girls, and she first proposed such a school to the Baptist Woman's Convention in 1900. In 1906 the Convention agreed to help fund the project and donated a six-acre site in Washington; on October 19, 1909, the National Training School for Women and Girls opened with seven

LIBRARY OF CONGRESS

NANNIE HELEN BURROUGHS: *Purpose, determination, and pride.*

students and eight staff members. By the end of the year it had thirty-one students.

Burroughs's fund-raising efforts, sound business sense, and personal encouragement of students made the school a success. Taking as her motto, "We specialize in the wholly impossible," she offered practical courses in sewing, home economics, nursing, bookkeeping, shorthand, typing, gardening, laundering, interior decorating, printing, shoe repair, and barbering, but she stressed academic subjects as well and made each student pass at least one course in black history before graduation.

She died in 1961; in 1964 the school was renamed the Nannie Burroughs School, and in 1975, May 10 was designated Nannie Helen Burroughs Day in the District of Columbia.

# 3

**GOLDA MEIR,** *born Goldie Mabovitch in Kiev, Russia, 1898.* Golda Meir was never quite at ease with what she perceived as her divided loyalties. On the one hand, she was a woman—and for her that meant total dedication to her husband and her children. On the other hand, she was a political being, a deeply-committed Zionist, a diplomat, a legislator, a cabinet minister, and, from 1969 to 1974, the prime minister of Israel. Those roles demanded total dedication to her cause, her people, and her nation.

At first she was able to combine the two roles. She married Morris Myerson on the condition that they emigrate to Israel, and they spent their first two years together on a *kibbutz.* However, Myerson wasn't thrilled with life on the farm or with his wife's growing political involvement, and he and Meir gradually drifted apart. She also had less time to spend with her children than she would have liked. She blamed herself; working mothers,

she felt, were somehow unnatural and doomed to failure: "the mother . . . suffers in the very work she has taken up. Always she has the feeling that her work is not as productive as that of a man, or even of an unmarried woman. . . . And this eternal inner division, this double pull, this alternating feeling of unfulfilled duty . . . this is the burden of the working mother." At the same time, she felt unable to relinquish her political work. The working mother, she realized, "cannot let her children narrow down her horizon. And for such a woman there is no rest."

# 4

**AMINA,** *born in Nigeria, in about 1560, exact date unknown.* Amina was a royal heir in the Hausa state of Zaria. Refusing all suitors, she trained as a warrior, accompanied the chief in battle, and, when he died in 1576, succeeded him to the throne. For thirty years she reigned, conquering the cities around her and extending her empire. Tradition has it that whenever she conquered a city she exacted huge payments of tribute and took a lover also, beheading him the next morning. No male equivalent of Scheherezade charmed Amina enough to survive her embraces. Wherever she went she built a walled camp, and the ruins of Hausa fortifications were called "Amina's walls" centuries after her death. But not all Amina's achievements were on the battle-field. She opened new trade routes and encouraged merchants, and she was remembered as a good, if somewhat bloodthirsty, ruler. A song after her death ran: "Amina, daughter of Nikatau, a woman as capable as a man."

ELIZABETH COCHRANE SEAMAN: *Around the world in 72¼ days.*

# 5

**ELIZABETH COCHRANE SEAMAN,** *born Elizabeth Cochrane in Cochran Mills, Pennsylvania, 1867.* One afternoon, Elizabeth Cochrane was reading her local newspaper, the *Pittsburgh Dispatch,* when she came across an article entitled "What Girls Are Good For." The answer, according to the author, was nothing but home and family. Outraged, she wrote a stinging letter to the editor, who hired her to write a series of articles on working women. Since it was considered improper at the time for women journalists to use their real names on bylines, she chose a pseudonym: Nellie Bly.

Soon after her arrival at the *Dispatch,* she was promoted to society and arts editor, and not long afterward, she was offered a job on Joseph Pulitzer's *New York World.* In New York she became famous for her sensational articles on slum and labor conditions and

LIBRARY OF CONGRESS

her frequent use of undercover techniques. For example, she had herself committed to an insane asylum and published a scathing account of the conditions there, entitled *Ten Days in a Mad House*.

Her most widely publicized stunt, however, had nothing to do with the reform-minded hard news she loved to cover. She got the idea for the story in 1890 from the fuss being made over Jules Verne's latest novel, *Around the World in Eighty Days*.

## 6

**MARIA MONTESSORI,** *dies at 81 in Noordwijk, Holland, 1952*. There are certainly books that have changed the world more than *Metodo della pedagogia scientifica*, published in 1909. But the influence of this one book on education can not be underestimated. It was written by Maria Montessori, a thirty-nine-year-old teacher of slum children who was also Italy's first female doctor. At the turn of the century, she had become interested in helping slow learners, and she had been assigned to a group of eight-year-old "idiots." She found that it was not the children but the educational process that was defective, and soon her "idiots" were outscoring "normal" children on state-administered proficiency tests. She proposed a system of education which would stress use of the senses, especially the sense of touch, in which students would work at their own paces and in which grades, rewards, and punishments would have no place. She publicized this method not only in her books on the subject, but also through lectures around the world and at training centers for teachers. Today, Montessori schools can be found throughout the Western world, and Maria Montessori's theories still have a powerful influence on education.

She suggested that the paper finance an attempt to break Verne's "record." Under a hail of publicity, Bly began her voyage, riding boats, trains, and horses, and stopping briefly in France to interview Verne. She finished her trip in 72 days, 6 hours, and 11 minutes, welcomed to New York by such headlines as: "Even imagination's record pales before the performance of the World's Globe Circler."

## 7

**ANNE BAUCHENS,** *dies at about 86 in Woodland Hills, California, 1967*. It isn't fair to say that Cecil B. DeMille wouldn't have made it in Hollywood without Anne Bauchens, but it is fair to say that his films wouldn't have been the same. She was his film editor from 1918 until his death in 1959. Working sixteen to eighteen hours a day at first, Bauchens edited thirty-nine movies for him, and he refused to make a film without her. She was small and soft-spoken, but she had confidence in her skill and resisted compromise, even when her opponent was the great C. B. "Annie is stubborn," said an acquaintance, "and Mr. DeMille is three times as stubborn. If they disagree, one of them has to bring the other around, because neither of them will give in." In 1940 she became the first woman to win an Academy Award for film editing, but she didn't get the Oscar in 1956 for what was perhaps her greatest achievement: *The Ten Commandments*. Sixteen cameras had produced one hundred thousand feet of film, and DeMille wanted it reduced to twelve thousand. DeMille, always a lover of superlatives, called it "the most difficult operation of film editing in motion picture history." When he died, Anne Bauchens retired.

## 8

**EADBURGH,** *born in Mercia, England, in the eighth century, exact date unknown*. Eadburgh, or Eadburga as she is sometimes known, was one of Anglo-Saxon England's most notorious rulers, although she was only slightly more ruthless than her male counterparts. Her father was Offa II, king of Mercia, and in 789 he married off Eadburgh to Beorhtric, king of Wessex. Eadburgh had apparently paid attention to court business in Mercia; at any rate, by the time she moved to Wessex she was skilled at acquiring power, and Beorhtric proved no match for her. She involved herself in court intrigues and quickly removed every favored courtier, either by denouncing them to her husband or poisoning them herself.

Her downfall came about in 802, and it was entirely her own fault. She had poisoned a drink intended for one of the king's favorites, and Beorhtric drank it instead and died. With no one left to protect her, Eadburgh was driven out of the castle and for centuries the memory of her intrigues was invoked to deny the wives of British kings the title of "queen." Eadburgh fled to the court of Charlemagne, taking most of the movable cash in Wessex with her. According to legend, she gave Charlemagne beautiful gifts, and he offered himself or his son in marriage. Eadburgh said, "I choose your son, because he is the younger." Charlemagne replied, "If you had chosen me you should have had my son; but as you have chosen my son, you shall have neither him nor me."

Charlemagne, however, was not without pity for the exiled ruler. He generously accepted a portion of her wealth and in exchange made her the abbess of a powerful convent. Once again, though, Eadburgh ruined what she had. She broke her vow of chastity (which was, at the time, an acceptable sin for *priests*) and was driven from the convent. She is said to have died in poverty in Italy.

# 9

LIBRARY OF CONGRESS

**BELLE BOYD,** *born in Martinsburg, Virginia (now West Virginia), 1844.* A Washington debutante and a charismatic, if not a pretty, woman, Boyd became a diehard secessionist at the start of the Civil War. By the time the war was over, she had become one of its most flamboyant figures. She raised money for the Confederacy until July 4, 1861, when her career took a more active turn. Union soldiers looted the Boyd house and tried to raise the Stars and Stripes over it. Boyd, who had watched the vandalism silently and passively, said quietly, "Every member of my household will die before that flag shall be raised over us," and when the soldiers ignored her, she shot one of them. She was let off with a warning by the local federal commander, who was more amused than threatened by her daring.

Encouraged by her success, Boyd began gathering intelligence for the Confederate troops. She was discovered almost immediately, but again she was given a warning, and

she returned to her spying with a little more caution. Captured again and freed again, she must have begun to feel invulnerable. One day in 1862, she put this theory to a grueling test. She discovered a Union plan to burn the bridges of Front Royal, Virginia, as the army retreated. Clad in "a dark-blue dress, with a little fancy white apron over it," she was "far more conspicuous than was just then agreeable," but without thinking, she ran to the Confederate lines, dodging a hail of bullets. As she reported the incident in her autobiography, "the rifle-balls flew thick and fast about me, and more than one struck the ground so near my feet as to throw the dust in my eyes." She was unharmed and told the rebels what she'd learned, enabling them to switch tactics and take the bridges. However, Northern soldiers soon regained Front Royal, and Boyd was up to her old tricks again and arrested by the Union for the fourth time. This time she was imprisoned in Washington, where

BELLE BOYD: *A stereoscopic view of the daring Confederate spy.*

reporters came to see the famous spy. Some were utterly charmed by her; some thought her merely "an accomplished prostitute."

Boyd was exchanged for a Union prisoner, but she was soon back in a federal jail. This time she was released immediately, and she promptly boarded a blockade-running ship headed for England, with a plan to deliver messages to the English from Confederate leaders, but her ship was seized by the Union before it ever got to port, and she burned the papers and retired from the spy business.

Even this was not her last adventure. She married a Union officer, Samuel Hardinge and lived briefly with him in England until his death in 1866. By way of apology for this unpatriotic deed, she wrote: "His every movement was so much that of a refined gentleman that my 'Southern proclivities,' strong as they were, yielded . . . to the impulses of my heart." After his death, she became an actress and, upon building a successful stage career in Britain, Boyd returned to the United States. She married again, this time unhappily. By 1884 a ruined career, a weakened body, a nervous breakdown, a divorce, and a dead son. The only bright spots in her life were her two daughters. Boyd remarried—this time she chose an actor seventeen years her junior—and tried to revive her career, but she had been forgotten and ended up with only a few bookings in shabby theatres for almost no money. Boyd died on tour in Evansville, Wisconsin, on June 11, 1900.

# 10

ELLA GRASSO, *born Ella Rosa Giovanna Oliva Tambussi in Windsor Locks, Connecticut, 1919.* After graduating from college with honors, Ella Grasso married, had two children, and began working her way through the ranks of the Democratic party. In 1952, she won a seat in the Connecticut state assembly. By 1955, she was the assembly's floor leader, and from 1958 until 1970 she was Connecticut's secretary of state. She worked on the Democratic National Committee and helped to write a minority protest against involvement in Vietnam for the party's 1968 convention. In 1970, she ran for Congress, won, and compiled a liberal voting record, and in 1974, she won Connecticut's gubernatorial election by a large majority.

She wasn't the first woman to be elected governor of a state—that honor went to Nellie Taylor Ross of Wyoming in 1924, and Ross was closely followed by Miriam "Ma" Ferguson of Texas. But Grasso was the first woman governor who hadn't been preceded in the post by her husband.

Grasso was a good governor. She had promised to reduce the state's deficit, and she did, but she did it by means of unpopular measures that might have cost her the next election were it not for a fortuitous blizzard. Her quick organization of emergency relief restored her popularity, and she won re-election with a seventy-five percent majority. Cancer cut short her career; she was hospitalized in 1980, and although she ran the state from her bed for several weeks, she was soon forced to resign. She died two months later.

# 11

MARTHA GRAHAM, *born in Pittsburgh, Pennsylvania, 1893.* "No artist is ahead of his time," she once said. "He *is* his time . . . others are behind the times." Martha Graham has never been behind her times. She has created over one hundred and fifty dances of varying length and scope, and in 1932 she was the first dancer to receive a Guggenheim fellowship. As a young woman she experimented with primitive dance styles and new ways of moving to create almost tangible moods. Her use of staging, design, music, and patterns of "contraction and release" gave new depth and power to her art.

Always in exceptional physical condition, she was still performing in her sixties, although eventually failing strength and health forced her to turn her attention to teaching, lecturing, and running the Martha Graham Dance Company. Her dances generally tell stories— stories about famous women, including the Brontë sisters, Joan of Arc, Clytemnestra, Mary Queen of Scots, and Emily Dickinson; stories of protest in works such as *Revolt, Immigrant,* and *Heretic;* and stories from American history in *Salem Shores, Appalachian Spring,* and *American Document.* However, the tales themselves, she once said, are not the main point of her dances: "It is not important that you should know what a dance means. It is only important that you should be stirred."

# 12

FLORENCE NIGHTINGALE, *born in Florence, Italy, 1820.* "My present life is suicide," she wrote in her journal. "In my 31st year I see nothing desirable but death; What am I that life is not good enough for me? Oh God what am I?" The answer was simple; she was bored. She and her sister Parthenope, intelligent, energetic women who had been extraordinarily well educated for their time, were told to sit still and wait for marriage. Parthenope adjusted well to this sort of life and berated Florence for acting "like a man," while Florence treated her sister with contempt, writing, "The whole occupation of Parthe and Mama was to lie on two sofas and tell one another not to get tired."

At thirty-one, Nightingale was without a vocation, even though it was fourteen years since she had first felt called by God to a life of service. She was writing a feminist work entitled *Cassandra,* but it was not to be published until almost twenty years after her death. Otherwise, her only accomplishment, if it could be called that, was a negative one—she had avoided marriage. One year later, at thirty-two, Nightingale found her vocation. And it was one that horrified everyone who knew her. She decided to be a nurse.

In the mid-nineteenth century, nursing was held in the lowest esteem. It was menial, dirty work, reserved for the lower classes (who were thought to be drunken and immodest) or religious women (who were usually poorly trained). Nightingale's family, hearing that she wished to join the ranks of servants and celibates, exploded.

But Nightingale was determined. While working as a nurse in England, she heard about the high mortality rate in the Crimea and was shocked to discover that only one-eighth of the deaths were caused by wounds from the war then in progress. She volunteered her services, and within a few months, with the help of nuns and nurses, she vastly improved sanitary conditions and reduced the death rate by twenty percent. It was a doubly difficult task, since she was fighting not only battle wounds, gangrene, cholera, typhus, dysentery, and scurvy, but also the ignorance of the religious nurses, the poor discipline of the professional nurses, and the resistance of military officials who resented a woman's interference in their war.

When she returned to England, she discovered she was famous. The public had raised £44,000 for her, which she used to found the Nightingale School of Nursing, and Queen Victoria made her the first woman to receive the Order of Merit. But Nightingale was not one to seek the limelight. She did not see herself as she was often por-

FLORENCE NIGHTINGALE: *"The Lady with the Lamp."*

trayed, "the Lady with the Lamp," a saint with eyes brimful of compassionate tears. She acknowledged freely that she disliked women and declared herself "brutally indifferent to the wrongs or rights of my sex." Her view of nursing was utterly practical.

# 13 _____

**MARIA THERESA of Austria,** *born in Vienna, Austria, 1717.* In 1740, Charles VI, the Holy Roman Emperor, died. He was succeeded to the throne by his only child, Maria Theresa.

When she took the throne, Maria Theresa became the only woman ruler in the 650-year Hapsburg dynasty. Her sex was a great disadvantage, since many men would resent her authority or try to exploit

her supposed weakness, but she had several things in her favor. She was already married to the Duke of Lorraine, a man competent enough to advise her, but not powerful enough to pose a serious threat to the empire. Furthermore, she was happily married and thus likely to produce an heir. In fact, Maria Theresa had sixteen children, most of whom survived to adulthood. (One of them was the ill-fated Marie Antoinette.)

Other factors in Maria Theresa's success were her judicious choice of advisers, her distrust of dogmatists and extremists, her exceptionally good health, and her blonde-haired, blue-eyed good looks. She discovered quickly that she could make stereotypes about women work to her advantage. She emphasized charm and piety, made much of her weakness, and appealed to the chivalry of her subordinates.

When she began her reign, she still had a wide streak of frivolity

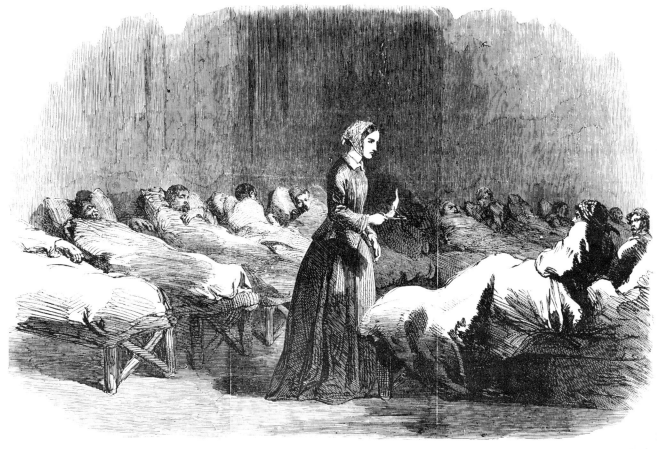

LIBRARY OF CONGRESS

MARIA THERESA, with her minister of state, Kaunitz: *Hers was the most moral court in eighteenth-century Europe.*

and impulsiveness and spent hours dancing and gambling. Soon, however, plagued by wars and tight finances, she grew tyrannical, austere, and suspicious. She lost much of the popularity she had won through charm, and later in her reign she suffered from conflicts with her son, co-ruler, and heir, Joseph. Nonetheless, her achievements were considerable. She secularized the University of Vien-

na, partitioned Poland, reduced the power of the nobility, centralized the government, and instituted educational, bureaucratic, and economic reforms. Even her enemies admired her. When she died, her lifelong opponent, Frederick the Great of Prussia, said: "She did honor to her throne and to her sex: I fought with her but never was I her enemy."

# 14 _____

**RITA HAYWORTH,** *dies at 68 in New York City, 1987.* It seems appropriate in a strange, tragic way that Rita Hayworth, "the Love Goddess," should have died of the debilitating disease called Alzheimer's. From the time that she was a child, she was almost never in control of her life. She was born Margarita Carmen Cansino in 1918 to a famous Spanish dancer and a former Ziegfeld girl, and her parents, she said later, "had me dancing almost as soon as I could walk." Her two brothers were al-

lowed to choose their own hobbies and professions, but not she.

Hayworth's plight was all the more poignant because although beautiful, graceful, and naturally gifted when it came to dancing, she was also painfully shy. But it didn't matter. When she was too young to dance in American nightclubs, her father took her to Mexico to perform there. Forced to work like an adult, she was allowed none of the freedoms of adulthood; in an effort to preserve her chastity and innocence, her father allowed her

only a few carefully planned and chaperoned dates, and between shows he kept her confined to her dressing room. To make her even more convincing as a Spanish dancer, her hair was dyed jet black. In short, she was treated like a beautiful, mobile doll, although by this point she was her family's main source of income.

Once she made it to the movies, things looked better, but they were basically the same. True, she was making more money. True, she got to work with Cary Grant, Glenn Ford, and Fred Astaire. True, she got to go out on dates with Tony Martin, David Niven, Errol Flynn, Howard Hughes, Orson Welles (whom she later married), and Kirk Douglas. But gossip columnists Hedda Hopper and Louella Parsons were even more effective chaperones than her parents had been, and Columbia Studios governed almost every aspect of her life. The studio chose her roles, her clothes, and most of her escorts to public places. It had her hair dyed red and thinned by electrolysis. It created the Love Goddess. Rumor had it that her dressing room was bugged.

Her first husband, Eddie Judson, was twenty-two years her senior, and he ran her life completely for five years before she divorced him. Next she married Orson Welles, and the newspapers pounced on what was called the union of "the Beauty and the Brain." That marriage lasted four years, during which time Welles manipulated her career and, for *The Lady From Shanghai,* cut and—you guessed it—dyed her hair. This time she was a blonde, but it didn't last for long, and Columbia hid her for a few months and dyed her hair red again. Hayworth's third husband, Prince Aly Khan, courted her lavishly but basically forgot about her as soon as they were married. His habit of sleeping with up to six women a day quickly angered her, and she divorced him as well. Her fourth and fifth marriages also ended in divorce. In the end, very little was under her control. Her personal life, her career, and her popular image were largely in the hands of others.

LIBRARY OF CONGRESS

# 15

**DOROTHY HANSINE ANDER-SEN,** *born in Asheville, North Carolina, 1901.* In the late 1920s, a young doctor named Dorothy Andersen was trying to find a job. She had been trained as a surgeon, but she found it impossible to get a residency in surgery because of her sex. She did find an assistantship in the department of pathology at Columbia University in New York City, and she took that job.

Andersen was interested in embryology and had published two papers on the subject, so when Babies Hospital at New York's Columbia-Presbyterian medical center offered her a job in 1935, she jumped at the chance. Working as an assistant pathologist, she began collecting infants' hearts with congenital defects. Ten years later, when the pioneers of open-heart surgery realized that they knew little about children's hearts, they came to Dorothy Andersen for help. By 1950, no surgeon was allowed to open a child's chest at Babies Hospital without having passed a course on the subject taught by Andersen.

But that wasn't her only noteworthy accomplishment. In 1938, she detailed her findings on a previously unrecognized disease, which she called cystic fibrosis, and she spent most of the rest of her life searching for its cure. She developed a method of diagnosing CF in living patients, researched treatments, and described the genetics of the disease. Her last paper on the subject was published in 1959, four years before her death; it suggested guidelines for the care of young adults with cystic fibrosis—an entirely new field, since prior to her research, no one born with the disease lived beyond infancy.

# 16

**ADRIENNE RICH,** *born in Baltimore, Maryland, 1929.* Adrienne Rich's story is one of movement from conservatism to radicalism. She came from an extremely traditional family. Her father was strict and authoritarian, and her mother had sacrificed a career in music to devote herself to her family. Rich was sent to Radcliffe, where the English classes featured only the work of male poets, and where, she said, "I did not see a woman teacher for four years."

Her first collection of poetry, *A Change of World,* was conventional in form, with tight, highly structured verses, and it won praise from many prominent poets and critics, including W.H. Auden. However,

Rich was going through a number of changes. In 1953 she married, and by 1959 she had three sons. She and her husband became involved in the civil rights movement and antiwar activities, and she taught in a program for disadvantaged children. By the late '60s, her writing was increasingly political in subject and decreasingly structured in form. She left her husband, embraced lesbianism, and accepted her 1974 National Book Award not as an individual but on behalf of all women. More recently, she has joined the movement against pornography. "Pornography," she writes, "is relentless in its message, which is the message of the master to the slave: *This is what you are; this is what I can do to you.*"

# 17

**LADY NANCY ASTOR,** *born Nancy Witcher Langhorne in Danville, Virginia, 1879.* Once upon a time, a beautiful Virginia girl who loved to ride horses and attend parties traveled to Europe to console herself about her divorce.

In England, she was pursued by a number of men, but the one who caught her was Waldorf Astor—as in John Jacob, as in rich as Croesus—and Nancy Langhorne became Lady Astor. When they married in 1906, her husband was elected a Conservative Member of Parliament, Lady Astor developed a passion for politics that never left her. When, in 1919, Astor succeeded to his father's title, Lady Astor ran for her husband's seat in the House of Commons. Claiming to represent "the working classes" rather than "the shirking classes," she won, becoming the first female Member of Parliament, keeping her seat until 1945.

There were those who deeply resented her election, among them

LADY NANCY ASTOR: *As one member of her sex put it, "Nancy kept confusing herself with God. She didn't know when to step aside and give God a chance."*

Winston Churchill, who said, "When you come into the Debating Chamber, Nancy, I feel as though you had come into my bathroom and I had only a sponge to cover myself with." There were also many who resented her politics. She was known for her intolerance on a number of issues and her steadfast opposition to both Communism and anti-Communist witch hunts. She had a disarming lack of respect for propriety. She had been known to "fan herself with a dinner plate and push her tiara back like an old hat," and her sense of humor was famous. In a speech in 1951, she admitted: "I married beneath me—all women do."

# 18

**JEANETTE RANKIN,** *dies at 92 in Carmel, California, 1973.* What's wrong with this picture: Franklin Delano Roosevelt stands before a joint session of Congress and solemnly intones the words, "December 7, 1941, a date which will live in infamy." He calls for a declaration of war, and Congress, moved by his words and the aforementioned infamy, votes unanimously for war. Give up? The answer is that the vote wasn't unanimous. One person—Republican Congresswoman Jeanette Rankin of Montana—voted against a declaration of war. "America has the war habit," she said. "It is a habit we must break before we are broken by it."

Rankin spent most of her life working for peace. She served only two terms in Congress, from 1916 to 1918 and from 1940 to 1942. Both times she had run as a pacifist, both times had voted against entering the world wars, and both times had been refused reelection by her constituents, who were furious that she'd done exactly what she'd promised to do. Between terms and after World War II, she joined and led pacifist organizations, and worked against the Cold War and American involvement in Korea.

JEANETTE RANKIN: *A pacifist—and a Republican.*

# 19

**LORRAINE HANSBERRY,** *born in Chicago, Illinois, 1930.* If you've seen or read *A Raisin in the Sun,* you already know something about Lorraine Hansberry's life. One of the central conflicts in her brilliant play, the conflict between a white neighborhood and a black family moving into it, was a critical episode in her childhood. When she was eight years old, her father, a wealthy real estate broker, moved his family into an all-white neighborhood. Mobs gathered on the Hansberry porch. A brick thrown through one of their windows barely missed Lorraine. Her father went to court to fight for the family's right to live where it wanted; for eight months he was in Washington, DC, while his wife sustained their children's strength and courage. The

LIBRARY OF CONGRESS

Supreme Court ruled in favor of the Hansberrys, but their neighbors' anger did not subside. Crushed by the apparent hollowness of his victory, Lorraine's father died in 1945. It was believed by all who knew him that the court battle and its repercussions killed him. His daughter maintained for the rest of her life that "American racism helped kill him."

After graduating from college, Hansberry moved to New York City, where she eventually took a job as a reporter for Paul Robeson's newspaper, *Freedom*. Suddenly she was meeting American civil rights leaders and prominents Africans, and she was "on fire with black liberation."

Meanwhile, she married Robert Nemiroff, a white graduate student and playwright she'd met at a National Association for the Advancement of Colored People (NAACP)

protest. She was also writing for the stage, and on March 11, 1959, her first play opened on Broadway. *A Raisin in the Sun* created realistic, not stereotypical, black characters, and audiences loved it. Critically and financially, it was an enormous success, yielding 530 Broadway performances, a tour, and a movie. It also put Hansberry in the record books, making her the first black woman to have a play produced on Broadway and the youngest American, the fifth woman, and the first black to win the New York Drama Critics' Circle Award for the Best Play of the Year.

Hansberry used her new popularity to promote the civil rights movement. In the few years between the opening of *Raisin* and her early death from cancer, she worked to dispel two widespread myths: that "women are idiots" and that "people are white."

# 20

**ANTOINETTE BROWN BLACKWELL,** *born Antoinette Louisa Brown in Henrietta, New York, 1825.* "I did wish God had not made me a woman," wrote Antoinette Blackwell in a moment of despair. She had been fighting a long and tiresome battle against Oberlin College and the world around it.

Oberlin was fairly liberal for its times. Admitting women was a radical step the college took in the 1830s, and she was grateful. But Blackwell didn't give Oberlin any more gratitude than it deserved. While the school admitted women, it pushed them into the "literary" or non-degree course instead of the more rigorous theological course, which granted degrees. Blackwell finished the literary course in 1847 and then, over the objections of all who knew her, including suffragist Lucy Stone, she entered the theological course. For three years Oberlin authorities tried to drive her from

the program and discourage her from preaching. They failed, but they retaliated by not awarding her a license or a degree.

Blackwell served as a pastor for two years, becoming the first woman minister in the United States (although not the first woman to be officially ordained). She then resigned, converted to Unitarianism, and married. She worked as a suffragist, had six children, wrote a novel, a collection of poems, and books on philosophy and science. Nevertheless, she faced all her life the kind of reactions she'd encountered in Oberlin townspeople: "Sometimes they warn me not to be [too masculine], sometimes believe I am joking, sometimes stare at me with amazement and sometimes seem to start back with a kind of horror."

# 21

**ELIZABETH FRY,** *born Elizabeth Gurney in Norfolk, England, 1780.* The mother of ten children, Elizabeth Fry was a Quaker minister known for her work with prisoners. In 1813, Fry made her first visit to Newgate Prison, the jail that was known as "hell above ground." She was horrified at what she saw. Prisoners gambled, fought, and drank the liquor that was readily available, although bedding was not. The prison held three hundred women and their children, and those who had been condemned to death were housed together with those awaiting trial.

Immediately, Fry took matters in hand, establishing a school, a chapel, a system of supervision administerd by matrons and monitors, compulsory sewing duties, and Bible readings. She brought clothes which were plain but warm, and made frequent visits. Although she indirectly helped the authorities by keeping the women docile and orderly, her first interest was in the women themselves. She founded a prisoners' aid society, mobilized other women, inspected other prisons, testified before a royal commission, and eventually forced the government to make improvements in its prison system.

# 22

**MARY CASSATT,** *born Mary Stevenson Cassatt in Allegheny City (now part of Pittsburgh), Pennsylvania, 1844.* In 1898, Mary Cassatt, one of the foremost American-born painters of her time, best friend of Edgar Degas, and influential member of the Impressionist movement, made one of her few trips away from France. She went home briefly to visit some relatives and was greeted by this announcement in the Philadelphia *Ledger*: "Mary Cassatt, sister of Mr. Cassatt president of the Pennsylvania Railroad, returned from Europe recently. She has been studying painting in France and owns the smallest Pekingese dog in the world." No wonder she rarely came back to America.

She had wanted to be an artist ever since she was a little girl and had convinced her reluctant father to let her study art in Paris. However, she was soon disillusioned with the standard method of instruction there; the goal was to paint as much like one's teacher as possible. Still, she did her best, and in 1872 one of her paintings was accepted by the Paris Salon, *the* annual art show of the conventional painters. Her brother, writing of this success to a relative, said condescendingly, "I suppose she expects to become famous, poor child."

In 1873, Cassatt saw a pastel by Degas in an art shop window. Later, she wrote, "I used to go and flatten my nose against the window and absorb all I could of his art. It changed my life. I saw art then as I wanted to see it." She began adopting some of his principles in her own work, painting diligently from

eight in the morning until nightfall. Her paintings began to sell for as much as $100 each, quite a good price at the time, and in 1877 Degas met her and asked her to join his group of colleagues. She accepted without hesitation.

Initially labeled "five or six lunatics, one of them a woman," by the press, the Impressionists gradually achieved recognition and respect. In 1904, Cassatt was awarded the Legion of Honor. Her later work was strongly influenced by Japanese art and by the advice of Degas; she, in turn, shaped his style. Whether or not they were sexually involved remains unknown, but they were very close, and neither married. After Degas's death in 1917, Cassatt mourned deeply for him and attacked the French press for its scant appreciation of his work.

In old age, her eyesight failed. Despite her inability to paint, she continued to influence her world. She supported woman suffrage and continued her lifelong attempt to save artists from starvation and art dealers from bankruptcy.

# 23

**MARGARET FULLER,** *born in Cambridgeport (now part of Cambridge), Massachusetts, 1810.* Margaret Fuller stirred deep emotions and strong reactions in the people who knew her. Elizabeth Barrett Browning praised Fuller's "truth and courage," and Ralph Waldo Emerson called her "my audience," while to Thomas Carlyle she was a "strange, lilting, lean old maid." Nathaniel Hawthorne thought she was nothing but "a great humbug," and Edgar Allan Poe said, "Humanity is divided into men, women, and Margaret Fuller." Men often found her too serious, too threatening, and ugly, although contemporary portraits show her to have been pretty, with thick, blonde hair and bright, lively eyes.

Her own opinion is conveyed in

her diaries. "'Tis an evil lot," she wrote, "to have a man's ambition and woman's heart." However, recognizing that she was different didn't mean she wanted to change: "I am 'too fiery'. . . yet I wish to be seen as I am, and would lose all rather than soften away anything."

Fuller was used to being different. The eldest of nine children, she was given a rigorous education by her domineering father that turned her into a prodigy, but left her with nightmares and headaches for the rest of her life. She read Latin fluently at six and later learned Italian, French, German, and a little Greek; one of her first published efforts was a translation of Johann Peter Eckermann's *Conversations with Goethe.* Her adolescence was no easier than her

childhood; she had passionate crushes not only on men but on her girlfriends as well.

Fuller became involved with Transcendentalism, a philosophical movement led by Emerson, and from 1840 to 1842, she edited and contributed to the Transcendentalists' journal, *The Dial,* making her the first woman to edit a prominent intellectual magazine.

In 1844, she published her first original book, *Summer on the Lakes.* It described a trip she'd taken through the West, during which she'd slept in a barroom and ridden down a river in an Indian canoe. In it she voiced strong disapproval of the white man's treatment of the Indian. *Summer on the Lakes* gave her three more "firsts." She became the first woman to write about the American West, and the book got her a job on Horace Greeley's *New York Tribune,* making her the first professional literary critic of either sex and the first woman journalist in the United States.

Her next book caused almost as much fuss as Mary Wollstonecraft's *Vindication of the Rights of Woman.* Entitled *Woman in the Nineteenth Century,* it appeared in 1845 and was met with horror, ridicule, and phenomenal sales. The uproar over her radical book was so great that in 1846 Fuller decided to travel to Europe, where she was well-received. She continued to send articles back to the *Tribune,* making her the first American woman to work as a foreign correspondent.

From Paris, Fuller went to Rome, intending to write a history of the political upheavals taking place there. It was in Rome that she met Giovanni d'Ossoli, a radical aristocrat ten years her junior. They fell in love and began an affair that got her fired from the *Tribune.* When she found she was pregnant, she and Ossoli married secretly, and their son, Angelo, was born in 1849. The family fled to Florence when the political tide turned against them, and in 1850, they sailed for the United States. Just off Fire Island, New York, the ship sank, and all three drowned.

# 24

## LAURA DEWEY BRIDGMAN,

*dies at 59 in Boston, Massachusets, 1889.* Laura Bridgman suffered from scarlet fever at the age of two and lost her sight, her hearing, and most of her senses of smell and taste. She soon grew unruly, and by the time she was seven she could only be controlled by someone stamping on the floor near her. Her parents decided to institutionalize her; at that time it was believed that deaf-and-blind children could not be educated, and when they grew uncontrollabe they were sent to special homes where, if they were lucky, they were fed and housed in comfort.

Bridgman was very lucky. She was sent to the Perkins Institution in Boston. Its founder, Samuel Gridley Howe, had been a pioneer in the teaching of the blind, and now he wanted to help the deaf-blind. He taught Bridgman the alphabet and the names of objects by means of raised letters. After she experienced a breakthrough similar to Helen Keller's "water" experience, she learned rapidly, acquiring a love of geography, a passion for politics, and a fascination with colors. She had a temporary hatred of anything red, and she wrote poetry full of images of dark and light, black and white. She lived at Perkins for the rest of her life, knitting, crocheting, making beds, cleaning, writing letters, and entertaining the hundreds of visitors who came to see the first deaf-blind person to be educated. Her admirers included Thomas Carlyle, who called her "the good little girl" and said "one loves her to the very heart," and Charles Dickens, who came to see her in 1842 and later wrote, "Her face was radiant with intelligence and pleasure." When she died of pneumonia, her teacher Samuel Gridley Howe said: "It has been better for her generation that she lived in it."

# 25

LIBRARY OF CONGRESS

WINIFRED BLACK: *As Annie Laurie, she was one of William Randolph Hearst's best investments.*

**WINIFRED BLACK,** *dies at 72 in San Francisco, California, 1936.* When Nellie Bly emerged as Joseph Pulitzer's star reporter, William Randolph Hearst decided that he, too, had to have a woman reporter. He chose a failed actress from Chicago who had come to San Francisco with her family. She took the pseudonym "Annie Laurie" and began a career of Nellie Bly-influenced exposé-writing for the *San Francisco Examiner.* She staged a fainting spell on a downtown street in order to investigate emergency medical procedures; she was carried to the hospital in a cart, and her article on the trip resulted in the city purchasing its first ambulance.

The ambulance story was only one of her many famous articles based on tricks or sensational gimmicks. She hid under a table on President Benjamin Harrison's campaign train and thus got an exclusive interview with him. She visited the leper colony on Molokai in the Hawaiian Islands, became the first woman to cover a prize fight, and organized various charitable events for the paper, including a children's excursion to the World's Columbian Exposition in Chicago in 1893. When a flood ravaged Galveston, Texas, in 1900, killing seven thousand people, she disguised herself as a boy to get into the city, making her the first reporter and the only female journalist to cover the disaster. Other famous stories by Annie Laurie dealt with the Versailles peace conference, Mormon polygamy, the San Francisco earthquake, and the St. Louis cyclone.

# 26 _____

# 27 _____

**LADY MARY WORTLEY MON-TAGU,** *born Mary Pierrepont in London, England, 1689.* Today, Mary Wortley Montagu is known as a minor literary figure, the author of some brilliant letters, a play entitled *Simplicity,* and some poetry which was admired by Alexander Pope and which brims with defiance, sexual frankness, and humor. At her birth, she was simply the daughter of the fifth Earl of Kingston and the niece of novelist Henry Fielding. At her height she was known as one of England's wittiest, brashest women, with "a tongue like a viper and a pen like a razor." She was a woman who taught herself Latin in secret and defied her parents by marrying for love. She followed her ambassador husband to Turkey, and when the love disappeared, she began an affair with a young Italian named Francesco Algarotti. When Algarotti, too, proved disappointing, she took another lover in his place. She witnessed the use of smallpox inoculation in Turkey, and it was she who introduced the treatment to England, submitting her son and daughter to inoculation to encourage confidence in it. Lady Montagu was also a woman of surpassing brilliance who, since she was a woman, was not supposed to be brilliant. She advised her daughter, "Hide your learning . . . as if it were a physical defect," and of her own conflict merely wrote, "To my extreme mortification I grow wiser every day."

**AMELIA BLOOMER,** *born Amelia Jenks in Homer, New York, 1818.* Contrary to popular belief, Amelia Bloomer did not invent bloomers. She wasn't even the first to wear them. But she was a proponent of woman's dress reform. She was the wife of a lawyer-abolitionist-journalist, D. C. Bloomer, who lived in Seneca Falls, New York, Elizabeth Cady Stanton's hometown. She wrote occasionally for her husband's paper, the *Seneca Falls County Courier,* and eventually started her own journal, *The Lily.* Employing only female typesetters, she published the magazine from 1849 to 1855, promoting the causes of suffrage, temperance, marriage law reform, and higher education for women.

Bloomer advocated an outfit for women of baggy pants flared at the ankles covered with a loosely-belted tunic that ended at mid-calf. She wore this rather than the twenty-five-to-forty-pound outfits in vogue at the time. But she was ridiculed in the streets and in mainstream publications, and finally gave up her bloomers and returned to more conventional attire.

JULIA WARD HOWE: *"Mine eyes hath seen the glory. . . ."*

LIBRARY OF CONGRESS

# 29

**LOUISE MICHEL,** *born in Vroncourt, France, 1830.* Louise Michel was the illegitimate daughter of the mayor's servant and the mayor's son, and she spent half her life as a schoolteacher and half her life as a revolutionary. As Louis Napoleon's Second Empire declined, Michel's radicalism grew, and she first came to prominence in 1870 during the Franco-Prussian War. She emerged as a dynamic leader of the dispossessed in Montmartre, a charismatic figure and would-be martyr.

By 1871, Michel was popular enough to lead an armed march against the government, and when the Commune of Paris took control to protect the republic from tyranny, she became one of its most important leaders. Heading the Women's Vigilance Committee, she helped defend Paris, but when the Commune fell, she was captured, tried, and sentenced to exile. She spent four months on the *Virginie,* a prison ship headed for New Caledonia, locked in a cage with anarchist Natalie Lemel. During the journey, Lemel converted Michel to anarchism, and she continued to agitate for anarchism for the rest of her life.

Michel returned to France in 1880 under a general amnesty. Known as "the red virgin" and "la grande citoyenne," she organized followers in the hope of sparking rebellion and again posed a threat to the authorities.

After learning of a plot to commit her to an insane asylum in 1890, Michel fled to England, and she died there some fifteen years later while on a lecture tour. A symbol of decades of radical struggle, she was unlike other leaders in her vision of anarchism without terrorism.

**JULIA WARD HOWE,** *born Julia Ward in New York City, 1819.* Most people know Julia Ward Howe, if they know her at all, as the author of "The Battle Hymn of the Republic." In fact, she was a multifaceted woman who wrote poetry, plays, travel literature, biographies, and abolitionist and feminist articles. She edited three different journals, one for twenty years, and was the first woman elected to the American Academy of Arts and Letters. Her marriage to Samuel Gridley Howe, pioneering teacher of the blind, was not a happy one; she summarized the difficulties by saying, "I have never known my husband to approve of any act of mine which I myself valued." However, he allowed her a certain measure of independence, and after his death in the 1870s she was free to devote the next forty years entirely to activism and travel.

# 28

**ANNE BRONTË,** *dies at 29 in Scarborough, England, 1849.* Most people know of Anne's sisters, Charlotte and Emily, and have either loved or endured their works as school reading assignments. But you may not have heard of Anne's novels, *Agnes Grey* and *The Tenant of Wildfell Hall,* both of which are quite good.

Like the rest of the Brontës, Anne was sober, intense, and plagued by bad luck. Before she was two years old, her mother died, and the Brontë children were raised by a stern, somber aunt. Like her brother and sisters, she seemed to grow old before her time; asked as a child what she most wanted, she said, "Age and experience."

Anne had little formal education, but she read widely and began writing stories at an early age. At twenty-six, she published a few poems under the name Acton Bell, and a year later she published *Agnes Grey.*

Unfortunately, the novel didn't make much money, and Anne's troubles were multiplying. She was working as a governess and her brother, Branwell, as a drawing teacher for a family named Robinson. Branwell fell in love with Mrs. Robinson, who swore she loved him, too, but, with Mr. Robinson alive and well, their romance was hopeless. When Mr. Robinson died unexpectedly, Branwell waited for the call to join the widow, but it never came. She married someone else, and Branwell fell into depression, drug abuse, and alcoholism, dying at age thirty-one. Convinced the whole episode was her fault, as it was she who'd recommended her brother for the job, Anne wrote *The Tenant of Wildfell Hall* to make amends. The novel laments the practice of sending young, innocent men into the world to be corrupted, and dramatizes the power a vicious husband can wield over a good wife. Although the book was praised when it was first published in 1848, it was shunned when readers began suspecting the author was a woman—women were not to touch upon such subjects.

Anne's story goes downhill from there. Bad reviews piled up, her publisher cheated her, her sister Emily died in 1848, and Anne died of tuberculosis just five months later.

# 30

**JOAN OF ARC,** *dies at about 19 in Rouen, France, 1431.* Most people are familiar with the basic events of Joan's life. A poor farm girl from the town of Domrémy, she began hearing voices when she was about thirteen years old. Visions of saints followed, and she became convinced she was destined to lead France to victory over the English and ensure the coronation of the French heir. Charismatic and courageous, she won a few influential followers, equipped herself with a horse and a suit of armor, and quickly became so successful in battle, the English began to loathe her. In 1430 she was captured by the English, tried for heresy, and eventually burned at the stake.

What's missing from that quick sketch are the details, the instances of her wit and compassion that make Joan seem more like a mortal woman than a medieval saint. For instance, not many people know that she never killed a single foe in battle, or that she wept when English soliders were slain. The transcripts of her trial reveal her courage and spirit in the face of harrassment. Asked if she would like to have some female clothing, she replied, "Give me some. I will take them and go away from here." When told she ignored "the duties natural to a woman," she responded, "There are enough women to do the work you speak of."

Ultimately her cleverness and bravery were not enough; her enemies condemned her to death as a heretic. At her execution, a placard was posted, calling Joan "a liar and pernicious evil-doer, a misleader of the people, a soothsayer, a monster of superstition, a blasphemer of God, presumptuous in all her ways, a sinner against the Faith of Jesus Christ, boaster, idolater, cruel, one who invoked devils, apostate, schismatic, and heretic." The heretic's paper mitre was placed on her head, and a kind-hearted Englishman gave her a cross made of two sticks. As she burned, she screamed, calling on God, the Virgin, the archangels, the saints, and Christ. In 1456 her conviction was reversed, and in 1920 she was made a saint.

JOAN OF ARC: *Onward, Christian soldiers. . . .*

LIBRARY OF CONGRESS

# 31

**ELIZABETH BLACKWELL,** *dies at 89, in Hastings, Sussex, England, 1910.* One morning in 1847, a medical school class at Geneva College in New York heard what it thought was a very funny joke. A young woman named Elizabeth Blackwell, who had applied to several medical schools and had been rejected by all because of her sex, had applied to Geneva. The faculty, not wanting to accept her but afraid to take upon itself the sole burden of rejecting her, decided to put it to a vote. If one student objected to her presence, they announced, her admission would be denied. Howling with laughter, the students voted unanimously to welcome her. Two weeks later, when they had forgotten all about it, she arrived, entered the lecture hall quietly, and took her seat. She was the only person in the class to take notes.

Two years later, she became the first woman in America to be awarded a medical degree, and Geneva College, far from becoming enlightened, shut the doors behind her and refused to accept any more women. But Blackwell had made it through the system, and she spent the rest of her life making a place in it for her sex.

She established the New York Infirmary for Women and Children, and founded a medical college, which she subsequently closed when Cornell's medical school began accepting women. Her task was difficult at first; hospitals refused her permission to practice, local medical societies wouldn't accept her as a member, and male colleagues didn't refer patients to her. Eventually she became respected, if not as an equal, at least as an expert on "women's matters." She spoke against the legalization of prostitution and advocated training women as doctors in order to preserve the modesty of female patients. Her primary importance, however, was as a symbol: To the women of her time she represented all things made possible. She was inspiration, patron, teacher, employer, and pioneer, bringing distant worlds within reach.

LIBRARY OF CONGRESS

LILLIAN HELLMAN: *She didn't mince words.*

# JUNE

## 1

**MARY DYER,** *dies in Boston, Massachusetts, 1660.* Dyer was every good Puritan's two worst nightmares come true—she was a heretic and a woman who wouldn't be quiet. Governor John Winthrop of Massachusetts, who had enough trouble with rebel preacher Anne Hutchinson, found Dyer "notoriously infected with error" and "very censorious and troublesome," and he didn't want to have anything to do with her. Unfortunately for the authorities, Mary Dyer was determined to change the world or die trying. She began as a follower of Anne Hutchinson, and when Hutchinson was excommunicated and banished as a heretic, Dyer followed her into exile.

Boston saw nothing of the "troublesome" woman for almost twenty years, and it probably thought it had gotten rid of her, but in 1657 she came back, this time as a Quaker proselytizer. She was immediately jailed and, upon release, expelled from Boston, but she returned in 1659. She was again imprisoned and, upon release, banished from Massachusetts. If she returned, the penalty would be death. Of course, she returned immediately, determined to change the law, and she brought two male friends with her. All three were apprehended and sentenced to death, but the colonial authorities were nervous. After all, they reasoned, it was one thing to hang a man, but a woman was weak, so weak she couldn't really be held responsible for her own actions.

The authorities decided to teach Dyer a lesson by frightening her. They led her and her male companions to the gallows. All three were blindfolded. The nooses were placed around their necks. Then a reprieve came for Dyer, and her two friends were hanged. Dyer was escorted out of town and told that the next time the execution would

be completed. One guess as to what she did. She came back to Boston, and this time the hangman finished his job. Her last words were, "In His faith I abide faithful to the death."

## 2

**MARY READ,** *born near Plymouth, England, in about 1690, exact date unknown.* It was in the beginning of the eighteenth century when a resourceful young boy enlisted on a warship as a "powder-monkey." He stayed on the ship for six years, during which time no one discovered that the boy was in fact a girl named Mary Read. Read was probably illegitimate, and in order to strengthen a claim to an inheritance, her mother had dressed her and raised her as a boy. Apparently the inheritance was never awarded or didn't amount to much, since Read worked as a manservant at an inn and then as a footboy to a French noblewoman. Then, as a contemporary account of her adventures had it, "growing bold and strong, and having also a roving Mind, she entered herself on Board a Man of War."

After a while, Read deserted her ship and enlisted with an infantry regiment in Flanders. She fought the French, transferred to the cavalry, and fell in love with a Flemish soldier. She decided that love was more important than the army, married the soldier, and revealed her sex to the public at large—to the surprise of her comrades-in-arms. Unfortunately, her husband died suddenly, and after a brief return to warfare as a way of life, Read traveled to the West Indies, seeking a new life.

On its way to the West Indies, her ship was attacked by pirates and she was taken prisoner. She took the new situation in stride and joined

the pirates, and for some time she led a life of danger and excitement. She continued to dress in men's clothes, and her battle-seasoned swordsmanship proved an asset in her new career. She also devoted herself to romances of various kinds; she very probably had affairs with both the captain, Jack Rackham, and his lover, Anne Bonny, and on one occasion she fought a duel to save a male lover.

Her career ended in 1720, when her ship was captured near Jamaica. Because she was pregnant, she was jailed rather than hanged, but she died in childbirth in a Jamaican prison.

## 3

**JOSEPHINE BAKER,** *born Freda Josephine McDonald in St. Louis, Missouri, 1906.* In 1925, a show called "La Revue Nègre" opened at the Théâtre des Champs-Élysées. It might have been forgotten if it had not introduced Josephine Baker to Paris, and Paris to Josephine Baker. Moderately successful but far from famous in the United States, Baker made her first Paris appearance in a manner designed to endear her to that permissive city. *New Yorker* correspondent Janet Flanner remembered: "She made her entry entirely nude except for a pink flamingo feather between her limbs; she was being carried upside down

JOSEPHINE BAKER: *Sitting in the catbird seat.*

and doing the split on the shoulder of a black giant. Midstage he paused, and . . . swung her in a slow cartwheel to the floor, where she stood . . . in an instant of complete silence. She was an unforgettable female ebony statue. A scream of salutation spread through the theatre."

"La Revue Nègre" closed quickly, but Baker and some other members of the cast were hired by the Folies Bergère. She was an instant sensation; when Parisians talked of "going to see Josephine," no one needed to ask, "Josephine who?"

In 1937, she married a French industrialist and became a French

citizen, and even though she was divorced soon afterward, she stayed loyal to her adopted country. At the beginning of World War II, when most expatriates fled from Paris, she remained, working for the Red Cross and gathering information for the Resistance.

She spent her wealth on a chateau and adopted twelve children, planning to create a World Village, a "showplace for brotherhood" in which orphans of different races and religions would be raised. The experiment failed, and she went bankrupt in 1969.

Aging, penniless, no longer the toast of Paris, Baker might simply have given up and faded away, but she didn't. In 1973, she made a comeback at New York's Carnegie Hall and then went on to Paris once again.

**4** _____

**DOROTHY GISH,** *dies at 70 in Rapallo, Italy, 1968.* In 1905, a six-year-old girl named Dorothy Gish was appearing in a play called *Her First False Steps.* One of the scenes required her to be in close proximity to two live lions, but she wasn't afraid; she was too busy having fun. She was interviewed by a reporter at the time and told him proudly that "she had been on the stage for three years, that she just loves the stage, and that she is going to be an actress all her life." As it turned out, she was not an actress "all her life." By the time she was thirty-two, her long-suffering career was pretty much over.

Gish had two big problems as an actress. One was that her real talent was for comedy, but as a woman, she felt insecure about playing for laughs. (Most of her comic films, unfortunately, have been lost.) Her other problem was that her older sister, Lillian, was more popular than she. Lillian was one of the most gifted performers of her time. Dorothy was always compared with Lillian, first by their director, D. W. Griffith, next by the public, and finally by film historians. Almost every time, Dorothy's acting suffered by the comparison, and at some points she only got work through Lillian's intervention. She made sixty-one films for Biograph Studios before she finally got a star-level contract in 1915, and she only had five years of real fame between 1918 and 1923 before she began a slow decline into obscurity.

**5** _____

**MIRIAM LESLIE,** *born Miriam Florence Follin in New Orleans, Louisiana, 1836.* How has Miriam Leslie's life story evaded the clutches of miniseries producers all these years? Hers is the stuff of

DOROTHY GISH, with portrait artist Leon Gordon: *A more down-to-earth heroine than her ethereal sister.*

which prime time is made. It began in New Orleans, where the charming, imprudent, and beautiful Miriam grew up. Her family then moved to New York, where Miriam was briefly married. Next she hooked up with the noted dancer Lola Montez, who took Miriam on as a partner. Men fell for Miriam at every stop on their dancing tour, but it was Ephraim G. Squier, an archeologist and railroad president, who married her. Through him she traveled in the highest social circles, and even attended Abraham Lincoln's first inaugural ball. It was there she met Frank Leslie, a self-made businessman, and one of the most successful publishers in the nation. Despite his nineteen-year marriage, he fell for Miriam, and began scheming to win her. He employed the financially-troubled Squier as editor of *Leslie's Illustrated Newspaper*, and gave Miriam a job as editor of his *Lady's Magazine.*

Meanwhile, Leslie separated from his wife and moved in with the Squiers. For the next ten years, the three of them lived, traveled, and worked together. Finally Leslie and Miriam divorced their respective spouses and married each other. Within a month, Squier was committed to an insane asylum, and the press had a field day when it found that Miriam's first husband had also gone mad.

The Leslies made a fortune during the Civil War, and Miriam became a celebrated writer, but it wasn't to last. Their extravagence led to financial ruin, then suddenly Leslie died. Miriam worked ceaselessly to keep afloat, upgrading the newspaper, and legally changing her name to Frank Leslie to keep a firm hold on her husband's trademark.

There was more—more famous affairs, more marriages, and a devotion to the cause of suffrage. When she died in 1914 she left her entire estate of almost two million dollars to Carrie Chapman Catt, the American suffrage leader. So her story has a dash of politics along with the glamor, wealth, sex, scandal, war, and madness. What more could a producer want?

# 6

**META VAUX WARRICK FULLER,** *born Meta Vaux Warrick in Philadelphia, Pennsylvania, 1877.* No one could ever truthfully deny that Meta Fuller was a talented sculptor. Over and over again she proved her skill, winning a scholarship to art school, and graduating with the school's prize for metal sculpture for her "Crucifixion of Christ in Agony." There was just one problem with Fuller as far as the art establishment was concerned. She was black.

In Paris, where she achieved her first popular successes, Fuller also encountered prejudice. When she arrived in the city in 1899 to study at the École des Beaux Arts, she was refused a room at the American Girls Club because of her race. Fortunately, Auguste Rodin was not narrow-minded. When Fuller showed him a plaster model of one of her works, he was so impressed that he helped to get her statues exhibited in Paris.

In 1902, Fuller returned to Philadelphia, but discrimination kept her from achieving as much as she had in France. She received an award in 1907 for a series of "150 figures illustrating the progress of the Negro in America," but on the whole her career lay dormant for several years. In 1910 a fire raged through the warehouse where Fuller stored her work, destroying nearly sixteen years worth of statues. It was a crushing blow, and one might guess her career was thereby erased in one day.

But it wasn't over. Her greatest works were still to come. W. E. B. DuBois asked her to create a statue commemorating the fiftieth anniversary of the Emancipation Proclamation, and the result marked the beginning of a new phase for Fuller. For the next fifty years, she used black models increasingly in her work, and she was more prolific than ever.

# 7

**VIRGINIA APGAR,** *born in West-field, New Jersey, 1909.* You may never have heard of the Apgar Score, but if you were born after 1952 you probably were rated for one. Its developer, Virginia Apgar, was an energetic surgeon who quit her specialty in the face of over-whelming prejudice against women surgeons and decided instead to pioneer in the relatively new field of anaesthesiology. She quickly rose to a position of leadership at Colum-bia-Presbyterian Medical Center in New York City, where she served as the first female department head. After eleven years she left this prestigious job to do research on the use of anaesthesia in childbirth.

It was then that she invented the Apgar Score, a quick, easy checklist for evaluating the health of new-borns. Nurses rate on a scale of zero to two a baby's appearance (color), pulse, grimace (reflexes), activity (muscle tone), and respira-tion at one minute and at five minutes after birth. The score of these vital-sign checks indicates a baby's health and points clearly to possible areas of concern.

In 1959, Apgar made another career change, becoming a research-er and fund raiser for the March of Dimes. Later, she also taught at Cornell and Johns Hopkins. A gifted, witty teacher and an eternal optimist, she insisted that "women are liberated from the time they leave the womb," and when asked why she had never married, she replied, "It's just that I haven't found a man who can cook." She took up flying at fifty and hoped to fly under the George Washington Bridge in New York, but her sense of adventure was less celebrated than her devotion to her patients and the bizarre contents of her purse. Among the objects she always carried were an odd teaching aid—a fetus in a bottle—and equip-ment for resuscitation and emergen-cy tracheotomies. "Nobody, but nobody," she vowed, "is going to stop breathing on me."

# 8

**MARGUERITE YOURCENAR,** *born Marguerite de Crayencour in Brussels, Belgium, 1903.* In 1980, 345 years of tradition were broken in France. The oldest, most presti-gious, and most powerful of the world's literary academies, the Académie Français, admitted a woman to its ranks.

She certainly deserved the honor. Marguerite Yourcenar, whose pseudonym was a rough anagram of her last name, had been writing books for fifty-nine years. At first she had been well-received only by critics, but by 1980 she had devel-oped a popular following as well, and her works had been translated into nineteen languages. She wrote essays, poetry, short fiction, novels, autobiography, and translations of Virginia Woolf, Henry James, American black spirituals, and an-cient Greek poetry. Although she moved to Mount Desert Island, Maine, and became an American citizen, she continued to write only in French.

# 9

**ELIZABETH GARRETT AN-DERSON,** *born Elizabeth Garrett in Whitechapel, London, England, 1836.* Anderson was the first British woman to become an M.D. without posing as a man, although she was not the first to earn her degree *in Great Britain.* She tried diligently for acceptance at a medical school in her own country, but none would take her. So she could watch dissec-tions, she became a nurse at Mid-dlesex Hospital. She was allowed to study there for a while, but when she did too well in exams the male students complained and she was thrown out of the lecture halls. In 1865 she managed to get licensed by the Society of Apothecaries, which didn't specify that its licentiates had to be male. As soon as she accomp-lished this, however, the loophole which had allowed her certification was closed.

For a while, Anderson gave up her dream of becoming a doctor and turned her attention to prac-tical matters. In 1866 she delivered a suffrage petition to Parliament and opened the New Hospital for Women and Children (later the Elizabeth Garrett Anderson Hospital). The hospital kept her busy unitl 1870, when she decided that it was time to get her degree.

She learned French, went to the University of Paris, and at long last got what she'd wanted. The British Medical Register, in its supreme wisdom, refused to recognize her degree.

Once she was back in England, Anderson continued to engage in professional and political work, sometimes managing to combine the two, as she did in 1874. One Dr. Maudsley wrote a paper warning of "the dangers of continuous mental work" or physical exertion during menstruation. Anderson responded with "Sex and Mind in Education: A Reply." She pointed out that no rest during menstruation seemed to be required for working-class women and proposed that the ner-vousness of middle-class women was not due to hormonal fluctua-tions but rather to "days . . . filled with make-believe occupations and dreary sham amusements."

# 10

**JUDY GARLAND,** *born Frances Ethel Gumm in Grand Rapids, Minnesota, 1922.* Vaudeville's singing Gumm Sisters didn't last long, but Judy Garland lives forever. Her personal life—the financial struggles, the four marriages and three divorces, the drug addictions, the inevitable death after an overdose—has become a tragic show-business legend. The fresh-faced, apple-pie, girl-next-door image of Garland's child-star days lives on in *The Wizard of Oz,* the "Andy Hardy" movies, and the "Let's put on a show in the barn" movies like *Babes in Arms* and *Strike up the Band.* The flourishing, confident Garland of 1944's *Meet Me in St. Louis,* and the older, vital Garland of 1954's *A Star is Born,* appear on television in the wee hours of the morning. And for those of you who were there in 1961 or who own *Judy at Carnegie Hall,* the first double album to sell a million copies, her haunting, powerful, soul-shivering voice sings on.

JUDY GARLAND: *Over the rainbow.*

# 11

**JULIA MARGARET CAMERON,** *born Julia Margaret Pattle in Calcutta, India, 1815.* Cameron's life did not begin auspiciously, as her father was an East India Company official reputed to be "the biggest liar in India" and one of its heaviest drinkers. Nor did her early life indicate that she would be one of the world's most famous and talented photographers. She was educated in Paris and England and married Charles Hay Cameron in 1838, at which point she settled into a quite ordinary life in England. In 1863, when she was forty-five, she suddenly became interested in photography. A year later, she recorded "my first success," a portrait of a little girl.

Cameron became the most notable photographer in Britain. She rarely charged for her work. On occasion she accepted fees, as she did from Charles Darwin. (After the naturalist left her studio, Cameron ran to her husband, calling, "Look, Charles, what a lot of money!") Her photographs fell into two groups. One consisted of "story" pictures—allegorical, religious, or sentimental scenes; the other, of portraits of notable persons, among them Henry Wadsworth Longfellow, Alfred Tennyson, Robert Browning, Thomas Carlyle, Ellen Terry, and Alice Liddell (the Alice of Lewis Carroll's books).

Within a year of her "first success," Cameron had a one-woman exhibition in London. Another followed, and although she was quite tyrannical with her sitters, she never lacked for models. After a career of only fifteen years, she died in Ceylon. Her work has been featured in a number of posthumous shows, and in 1974, at a London auction, a Julia Cameron portrait of Mrs. Herbert Duckworth (Virginia Woolf's mother), brought the highest price ever for a photograph—£1,200.

# 12

**HARRIET MARTINEAU,** *born in Norwich, Norfolk, England, 1802.* The well-educated daughter of a strict father and an emotionally distant mother, Martineau was a sickly, nervous child who grew increasingly deaf and increasingly unhappy the older she got. Her sister, Rachel, who was feminine and domestic, was the family favorite, and Martineau felt rejected and lonely. In 1821, however, she finally found a path to acceptance. She wrote an anonymous essay which was published in a magazine called the *Monthly Repository.* Her brother, James, read it, praised it, and then discovered that his sister was the author. "Now, dear," he said to her, "leave it to the other women to make shirts and darn stockings, and do you devote yourself to this."

So Martineau threw herself into her literary career, sometimes selling her clothes to make ends meet. Her mother disapproved of the whole endeavor and insisted that Harriet stop writing and take up needlework, but her demands were ignored. Martineau continued to write, and soon she was signing her articles instead of publishing them anonymously. She was widely read and became highly respected for her novels, stories, essays, religious works, travel literature, and social criticism; by the middle of the nineteenth century she was considered one of the most gifted women of her time. Her strong political influence helped reform laws regarding prostitution and married women's property rights.

As she got older, Martineau grew more radical. She had begun her career with demure, crisp essays; she ended it with impassioned, eloquent pleas on behalf of women in the work force. Her well-written *Harriet Martineau's Autobiography* (1877), makes interesting reading and speaks clearly about the woman and her world.

# 13

**FRANCES BURNEY,** *born in King's Lynn, England, 1752.* On her fifteenth birthday, Frances Burney threw the novel she was writing into the fire. It was, in effect, a sacrifice to the god of propriety; at that time, novels were considered immoral and dangerous, and women who wrote novels were considered of questionable character and certainly not likely to marry. The quiet, unassuming career of Jane Austen was decades away.

However, Burney couldn't stop writing for long. She began a secret diary which she addressed to "A Certain Miss Nobody," since "to Nobody can I be wholly unreserved." In her diary, she left the modest, decorous young woman behind and became "the ingenious, learned, and most profound Fanny Burney." Eventually even the journal was not enough. She must write a novel. Taking her brother and sisters, and later her father, into her confidence, she began a story she called *Evelina.* Published anonymously, it was called "sprightly, entertaining, and agreeable" by critics, and it sold well, although she received only £30 for it.

Soon the secret of her identity leaked out, and she began to enjoy some of the perquisites of fame, such as fan mail, introductions to famous writers, artists, and thinkers, and an offer from a rival publisher of £250 for her next novel, *Cecilia.* Singlehandedly, she invented a new type of novel, the novel of manners, which combined a plausible story with sound advice on matters of etiquette.

She also wrote comedy, blank-verse tragedies, and two more popular works, *Camilla* and *The Wanderer.* And despite all the predictions of her relatives and readers, she *did* marry—quite happily.

# 14

**HARRIET BEECHER STOWE,** *born Harriet Elizabeth Beecher in Litchfield, Connecticut, 1811.* The seventh of nine children, Stowe grew up surrounded by exemplars. Her father was Lyman Beecher, a prominent Congregationalist minister. One of her brothers was Henry Ward Beecher, another well-known clergyman. One of her sisters was Catharine Beecher, a renowned educator and an exemplary, self-sacrificing Victorian woman. Harriet, too, was anxious to serve.

In 1836, she married the Reverend Calvin Ellis Stowe. The couple had seven children, but little income, and what Stowe made, he generally squandered. Harriet had a knack for sentimental prose, and her business sense was infinitely superior to her husband's, so she hired a servant to free her from "domestic slavery," took over the family finances, and began to write.

Her career was solid but undistinguished. She wrote syrupy tales for women's magazines, school geography texts, children's stories, a number of novels, and almost two dozen biographies. In the early 1850s, she had a "vision" of a scene in a novel, and, almost as if possessed, she quickly wrote *Uncle Tom's Cabin: or Life among the Lowly*. Published in 1852, it was a powerful statement against slavery. Although it made use of stereotypes, it moved and captivated readers and made its point—that the goodness or worth of a person has nothing to do with the color of his or her skin.

Within three months, she had made $10,000 from the book. By the end of 1853, over three hundred thousand copies had been sold, an astronomical figure in those days, when even popular novels sold only a few thousand copies. Over one million pirated copies were sold in England, and within three years, Southerners had written thirty anti-*Tom* novels in an attempt to reverse public sympathies. Stowe had established her literary reputation, ensured the financial security of her family, and—best of all—been of service.

HARRIET BEECHER STOWE: *Far more than a one-book author.*

# 15

**VERA NIKOLAEVNA FIGNER,** *dies in Moscow, Russia, at 90, 1942.* Born to a wealthy family, Figner studied medicine in Switzerland, but returned to Russia at the urgence of her radical friends. She joined the People's Will movement (*Narodnaya Volya*), and wrote propaganda, organized a resistance movement within the army and navy, and plotted in 1879 and 1880 to blow up the tsar's train. Figner's plot failed, but when the tsar was assassinated in 1881, the leadership of the People's Will was arrested, and she took over the group.

Figner was arrested in 1883 and condemned to death, but her sentence was never carried out. Instead she spent a year in prison, and twenty years in solitary confinement in another prison—the notorious Schlusselburg on an island in the River Neva. During this period she achieved her greatest fame by writing exquisite poetry and her memoirs, *How the Clock of Life Stopped.* She was released from prison in 1904 and sent into exile in Siberia, but remained there only two years. Ten years later, with the Bolsheviks in power, Figner was made chairman of the amnesty committee and became a national heroine.

# 16

**SARAH STICKNEY ELLIS,** *dies in London, 1872.* If you had been born a middle-class woman in Victorian England, you would have worshipped not one deity but three —God, the Queen, and Sarah Ellis. Of the twenty-six books Ellis wrote, four of them were particularly influential: *The Women of England, The Daughters of England, The Wives of England,* and *The Mothers of England.*

Ellis was, in her heyday, the most

SARAH ELLIS: *She not only played by the rules, but helped codify them.*

popular etiquette writer in England. Whatever she said was law, and what she said was that man was the master, woman the servant. Men in Sarah Ellis's world were rational, authoritative, and aggressive, while women were beautiful, gentle, submissive, pure, and attentive. She admitted "that there are men occasionally found who are not, strictly speaking, noble, nor highly enlightened, nor altogether good," but even these men were to be treated with deference and respect. Fortunately, she rejoiced, by the time a woman married, she had years of training in passivity. "From their early childhood, girls are accustomed to fill an inferior place, to

give up, to fall back, and to be as nothing in comparison with their brothers." If you sense a little bitterness in this passage, you're not imagining it. Ellis, even while she lauds men's natural superiority, betrays resentment and condescension. While advising the young wife to indulge her husband, she says giving him the best place to sit and whatever he likes to eat is "something which man can understand without an effort."

# 17

**ARTEMISIA OF HALICARNASSUS,** *born in the sixth century, B.C., exact date unknown.* The educated may have heard of the war that the Persian emperor Xerxes waged against the Greeks, and some have even heard of Salamis, the decisive sea battle of 480 B.C. that destroyed most of the Persian fleet and saved Athens from invasion. But almost no one knows about one of the greatest commanders in the battle— the only one who advised against engaging the Greeks at sea, and one of the few who survived the battle. She was Artemisia, Queen of Halicarnassus.

Not just a capable ruler, Artemisia also was a successful sea captain, distinguishing herself in battle against the Greeks, who were so outraged that a woman should take arms against them that they offered ten thousand drachmas for her capture.

But she was too clever for the Greeks, and in the decisive battle of Salamis she outwitted them and proved herself to the Persians on whose side she was fighting. Persian emperor Xerxes watched from a cliff as Artemisia fought bravely; legend has it that as he watched, he murmured, "My men have behaved like women and my women like men."

LIBRARY OF CONGRESS

# 18

**DJUNA BARNES,** *dies at 90 in New York City, 1982.* "I was rather gay and silly and bright and all that sort of stuff, and wasted a lot of time," said Barnes of her youth in Paris among the American ex-patriates. Few who knew her then or who know her works now could call her career there a waste of time. She produced poems, drawings, and plays and wrote explicitly about lesbianism. Her 1928 novel *Ryder* was called "explosive" by contemporary critics, and her dark, strange, claustrophobic *Nightwood* would probably be considered a classic if homophobic prejudice hadn't kept

her out of the literary canon. Only recently has it received the attention it deserves. Barnes had a wicked sense of humor, too, and nowhere is it more evident than in her *Ladies' Almanack,* a thinly veiled description of Natalie Barney's circle of Parisian lesbians. One character is described as having "developed in the Womb of her most gentle Mother to be a Boy," but having come "forth an Inch or so less that this." Undeterred, the little girl grows up resolving to seduce women anyway and to "do it without the Tools of the Trade."

# 19

**ETHEL ROSENBERG,** *executed at 37 in Sing Sing Prison, 1953.* Until 1950, Ethel Rosenberg led a fairly normal life. The daughter of Jewish immigrants, she wanted to be an actress or a singer, but had to settle for a job as a stenographer. She became involved in unionization and met and married a fellow activist, Julius Rosenberg. He took a job as an engineer in the U.S. Signal Corps, and she worked as a typist, did volunteer work, and raised their two sons.

Then, in 1945, Julius lost his job on political grounds. He went into business with Ethel's younger brother, David Greenglass, but was unsuccessful. In 1950 Greenglass was arrested for allegedly smuggling atomic secrets to a Soviet spy. He claimed that he had been recruited for these activities by Julius Rosenberg. At first, only Julius was arrested, but in August, 1950, Ethel was taken into custody as well. For eight months she was held without specific charges against her while authorities tried to get her to confess to complicity in espionage.

Meanwhile, no one could decide

what to do with her. The prosecuting attorney, Myles Lane, admitted, "the case is not too strong against Mrs. Rosenberg. But for the purpose of acting as a deterrent, I think it is very important that she is convicted, too, and given a stiff sentence." Federal Bureau of Investigation Director J. Edgar Hoover recommended a mere thirty-year sentence, since she was "the mother of two small children" and "would, in a sense, be presumed to be acting under the influence of her husband." The assistant prosecutor, Roy Cohn, not a man to take half measures, wanted the death penalty.

In the end, she was sentenced to death for having (possibly) typed some of the reports sent to the (alleged) Soviet spy. She spent two years as the only woman prisoner in Sing Sing and was allowed weekly visits with her husband, separated from him by a wire fence, while her pleas for clemency and her lawyers' pleas for the admission of new evidence went unheeded. Her last letter to her children before her execution read in part, "Always remember that we were innocent."

# 20

**LILLIAN HELLMAN,** *born Lillian Florence Hellman in New Orleans, Louisiana, 1907.* That Hellman's plays reflected the course of her own life is hardly surprising. It's not odd at all that Hellman, a staunch feminist and socialist, wrote a number of plays that feature strong women and strong anti-fascist messages. What is a little unusual is that in 1934 she wrote a play that would reflect the state of her life in 1952.

*The Children's Hour* was her first play, and in many ways, her most successful. Banned in Britain and in Chicago, Boston, and other American cities, it told the story of a girls' school run by two women. A rumor that the women are lesbians, and the repercussions of that rumor make up the drama of the play. Whether or not rumors are true, they can shatter lives. This was the theme of the play, and a theme in Hellman's own life during the communist witch hunts of the 1950s.

Other successful plays led to lucrative screenwriting contracts for Hellman. In 1947, however, a change in one of her contracts hinted of things to come. If she wanted the job, she was told, she'd have to disclaim in writing any connection with communism and apologize for any former involvement in radical causes. Hellman had for seventeen years been the lover of Dashiell Hammett, who was certainly a radical and practically a "radical cause" himself. In 1947, she was still his lover, and she continued to be until his death in 1961. She refused the job, saying, "You know, I live with Dashiell Hammett. I don't think he is going to stay in the attic and be taken out on a chain at night."

In 1951 Hammett was called before the House Committee on Un-American Activities and then imprisoned for his communist connections. In 1952 Hellman received her subpoena. Until then, those called to testify before the committee had either incriminated others to save themselves or invoked the Fifth Amendment, refusing to speak. Hellman did neither. Nearly bursting with suppressed rage, she offered to tell the committee anything it wanted to know about herself, but she refused to give evidence about anyone else. "I cannot and will not cut my conscience to suit this year's fashions." From the press box, she heard a voice say, "Thank God somebody finally had the guts to do it."

The committee, which technically could have charged her with contempt, was so flabbergasted by this challenge to its authority that it simply let her go after only one hour and seven minutes of questioning. Although Hellman was blacklisted for her defiance, her hearing set an important precedent. The committee gradually lost its image of moral superiority, was instead placed on the defensive, and eventually fell from political grace.

# 22

**MARY FRITH,** *born in London, England, 1584, exact date unknown.* Also known as Mary Markham, and as Mary Thrift, Frith became most famous under a third sobriquet—Moll Cutpurse. According to her autobiography, *The Life and Death of Mistress Mary Frith,* published in 1662, "She

# 21

**JUDY HOLLIDAY,** *born Judith Tuvim in New York City, 1921.* Judy Holliday's performance before the Senate Internal Security Subcommittee wasn't as defiant as Lillian Hellman's before the House committee, but it was supremely effective. She was called to testify because she had associated with suspected communists. Holliday, who was a shrewd, intelligent woman, had made a career of playing scatterbrained blondes. Her characters in *It Should Happen To You, Adam's Rib,* and *Born Yesterday* were all endearing, dizzy creatures with a tenuous grasp on reality.

Holliday knew that people confused her with her stage and film persona, so when she was summoned before the Senate subcommittee, she put on a show. She pretended to be a lovable scatterbrain and led her questioners in circles of illogic and forgetfulness. Finally, convinced she was really an idiot, they let her go without getting a single piece of usable information from her—never realizing that they'd been the victims of a masterful joke.

JUDY HOLLIDAY: *A comedienne of great intelligence and intuitive precision.*

could not endure the sedentary life of sewing or stitching, a sampler was as grievous to her as a winding-sheet [shroud]." She tried taking a service job, but she hated it, so she dressed herself as a man, acquired a sword, and began her life as a thief. But Moll was no ordinary robber; she was a "bully, pickpurse, fortune teller, receiver, and forger" with a sharp wit, an active brain, and a

healthy measure of gall. She did everything women weren't supposed to do—she wore men's clothes all her life, spoke bawdily, smoked, and drank heavily—and she got away with it. She organized a gang of thieves and established a pawnshop at which she sold stolen items back to their original owners. She also used some of her considerable profits to visit the jails each Sunday

and feed the inmates. In short, she quickly became a living legend.

The extraordinary thing was that while everyone knew how Moll made her money, no one could touch her. She quickly acquired powerful patrons, giving them in exchange lifetime freedom from pickpockets. Moll died in 1659, a very rich old woman.

# 23

**WILMA RUDOLPH,** *born Wilma Glodean Rudolph in St. Bethlehem, Tennessee, 1940.* By all rights, Wilma Rudolph never should have been a runner. A childhood illness left her with a crippled leg, and it was considered doubtful she would ever walk normally, much less run. Nevertheless, with the help of therapy and her family's encouragement, she learned to walk again and became not only a great runner but a good basketball player as well. In fact, in high school she set a state record for the most points scored in one basketball season. Still, luck seemed to continue to work against her as she trained for the 1960 Olympics. In 1958, she was ill. In 1959, she was injured. In 1960, she underwent surgery, and there were postoperative complications. Nonetheless, she went to Rome for the Olympics, anchoring the winning 400-meter relay team, setting a record of 23.2 seconds in the 200-meter dash, and running the 100-meter dash in an astonishing 11 seconds. Her time for the last event was disqualified as a world record because the wind was so much in her favor. But it didn't matter. Her long, graceful stride had made her the first American runner to win three gold medals in one Olympics.

# 24

**SARAH ORNE JEWETT,** *dies at 59 in South Berwick, Maine, 1909.* Sarah Orne Jewett once told her staunch admirer Willa Cather that her "head was full of dear old houses and dear old women, and that when an old house and an old woman came together in her mind with a click, she knew that a story was under way." Jewett, who was one of America's greatest local colorists and is now one of its most underrated authors, was born in South Berwick, Maine, in 1849. She suffered from arthritis as a child, and her father, a doctor, often excused her from school because of the affliction and took her with him on his rounds. It was on these trips through her neighbors' fields and homes and in the general store owned by her grandfather, a former sea captain, that Jewett gathered material for her later work.

Her father encouraged her to read, and when she decided she wanted to be a writer, he offered support and some valuable advice: "Don't try to write *about* things: write the things themselves just as they are." When she was eighteen her first story, "Jenny Garrow's Lovers," was published in *The Flag of Our Union,* a rather splashy periodical. Next she set her sights on the more respectable *Atlantic Monthly*; her third submission, "Mr. Bruce," was published in 1869. This boosted her career considerably, and she turned out more stories for magazines, as well as children's tales and poems under

the names "Alice Eliot" and "A.C. Eliot."

In 1873 she wrote the first of her many stories about Maine, upon which her small fame rests. Willa Cather called Jewett's *The Country of the Pointed Firs* one of the three great masterpieces of American literature. (The other two, according to Cather, were Nathaniel Hawthorne's *The Scarlet Letter* and Mark Twain's *Huckleberry Finn.)*

In her own time Jewett enjoyed modest popularity and some serious critical attention, and she was fortunate in having a happy life. She lived with Annie Fields, the widow of her publisher, in what was euphemistically knows as a "Boston marriage"—a polite way of saying that they were lesbians.

# 25

**"MA" FERGUSON,** *dies at 76 in Austin, Texas, 1961.* Ma Ferguson suffered for most of her life from a not-uncommon curse; she was known far and wide by a nickname she detested. Born Miriam Amanda Wallace in Bell County, Texas, in 1875, she left her well-to-do-family to attend a prep school and a women's college. In 1899 she married James Edward Ferguson, an aggressive young lawyer who was also involved in real estate and banking. Until 1914 he took care of

LIBRARY OF CONGRESS

"MA" FERGUSON: *She didn't shy from controversy.*

Amanda" to "Ma," much to her dismay.

Ma's first term as governor can be described by this joke circulating in Texas at the time: "How does it feel to have a woman governor?" "I don't know; we haven't got one." She fought the Klan, rescinded the ban on her husband's political involvement (although this move was later overturned by the Texas Supreme Court), and made her husband the highway commissioner. Almost immediately, she was plagued by charges of corruption.

When she ran for re-election in 1926, Ma was defeated. She was also defeated in 1930. But she was elected in 1932. She reduced spending at the beginning of the Depression, and, foreseeing bank runs, declared a Texas bank holiday two days before President Roosevelt did the same nationwide. Ma did not seek re-election in 1934; she ran unsuccessfully in 1940. She lived until 1961 as the "grand old lady" of Texas politics.

business, and she took care of the kids.

In 1914, however, James Ferguson, who had no experience at all in politics, ran for governor. On the basis of his opposition to both woman suffrage and prohibition, he won, and Miriam became the First Lady of Texas. Ferguson won re-election in 1916, but in 1917 all hell broke loose. Ferguson was accused of financial improprieties, among them illegal campaign funding. He was impeached and banned from holding political office again in Texas.

He was not the type to take his banishment without a fight. In 1918 he lost the gubernatorial primary. In 1920 he ran for president as the candidate from his own independent American Party, garnering 47,000 votes but no real power. In 1922 he lost a race for the Senate. In 1924 he tried again for governor of Texas, but the state supreme court upheld the ban on his holding office.

So Ferguson announced that his wife would run for governor. They staged a flamboyant campaign on the slogan, "Two Governors for the Price of One." It was at this point that reporters shortened "Miriam

PEARL S. BUCK FOUNDATION

# 26 _____

**PEARL S. BUCK,** *born Pearl Comfort Sydenstricker in Hillsboro, West Virginia, 1892.* The daughter of Presbyterian missionaries, Pearl Buck was raised in China and grew up "mentally bifocal." Chinese legends were as much a part of her education as American history, Biblical studies, and Victorian novels. Throughout her life, she felt the pull of both East and West. She taught American students about Chinese life, established the East-West Association to bring Asian cultural figures to the United States, edited *Asia Magazine,* wrote essays and novels meant to foster mutual understanding, and organized two foundations for the benefit of Asian and Amerasian children—one in the United States and one in Asia.

She is remembered today primarily for her books about China, although she was an extraordinarily prolific writer who published over a hundred books, including works about racism, sexism, imperialism, retarded children, life in early Kansas, and her own life. Nonetheless, only a few people can name more than one of her books, *The Good Earth.* Perhaps that's not surprising. *The Good Earth* was on best seller lists for months, sold two million copies, was translated into thirty languages, was adapted for the stage and for film, won her the Pulitzer Prize for fiction in 1932, and strongly influenced her selection as 1938's Nobelist in literature. She is still the only American woman to have received a Nobel Prize in literature.

PEARL S. BUCK: *"I feel no need for any other faith than my faith in human beings."*

# 27 _____

LIBRARY OF CONGRESS

**HELEN KELLER,** *born in Tuscumbia, Alabama, 1880.* Some of us learned who Helen Keller was through brutal little grade-school jokes. Others of us met her through one of the innumerable stage, film, and television productions of "The Miracle Worker." We all know that she was a blind, deaf, spoiled, ill-behaved little girl who was tamed and taught to speak, read, and finger-spell by Anne Sullivan, a woman Keller knew simply as "Teacher." We're all familiar with the image of water running over the little girl's hand as she realizes that *"everything has a name."*

What we often forget is that

HELEN KELLER: *"Literature is my Utopia. Here I am not disfranchised. No barrier of the senses shuts me out from the sweet gracious discourse of my book friends."*

that's where the story *begins,* not ends. Keller continued to grow, to communicate, and to have perfectly normal human feelings.

Keller's education did not stop at home. She graduated *cum laude* from Radcliffe College in 1904. Always conscious of herself as a symbol and an inspiration, she mastered five languages; lectured, wrote, and lobbied on behalf of the handicapped; and advised blind children, "Never bend your head. Always hold it high. Look the world straight in the face." She had a natural sympathy for underdogs and identified herself as a "Socialist and a Bolshevik," a militant suffragist, an opponent of child labor and capital punishment, and a supporter of birth control and unionization.

In 1918, Keller starred in an autobiographical film, *Deliverance,* in an attempt to spread "a message of courage, a message of a brighter, happier future for all men." She continued throughout her life to support just causes and to serve as a symbol of hope to the handicapped.

# 28

**MARY ASTELL,** *born in England in 1666, exact date unknown.* Little is known of Astell's early life. The daughter of a merchant, she was educated by her uncle, a clergyman. The two-part book, written in 1692, for which she is known, *A Serious Proposal to the Ladies for the Advancement of their Time and Greatest Interest,* outlined a course of education for women and argued that their minds should be trained, just as men's were. "Since God has given women as well as men intelligent souls," she wrote, "why should they be forbidden to improve them?" She proposed a sort of academic, Protestant convent for women who could not or would not marry, and she reviled the women who were frivolous and therefore "most acceptable to all sorts of men" while exalting the "good devout women" who read books and did charitable work.

It was a bold proposal, although she felt the need to temper it in many ways. She published the book anonymously, addressed it only to "poor fatherless maids and widows," lauded marriage as "the institution of heaven, the only honourable way of continuing mankind," and cautioned: "We pretend not that women should teach in the church, or usurp authority where it is not allowed them; permit us only to understand our own duty, and not be forced to take it upon trust from others." Nevertheless she was universally attacked. Some felt that the academic convent smacked too much of Catholicism. Some felt she exceeded her little authority as a woman by writing the book. And Bishop Gilbert Burnet, an influential churchman and historian, who might have been able to assist her in realizing her plans, attacked her and her idea. Astell was hurt and angered, but she lived long enough to witness the ultimate irony. Not long before his death in 1715, Burnet proposed an idea for the Protestant convent which looked suspiciously like Astell's concept without, of course, giving her any credit for it.

# 29

**ELIZABETH BARRETT BROWNING,** *dies at 55 in Florence, Italy, 1861.* There was considerably more to Elizabeth Barrett Browning than "How do I love thee? Let me count the ways." Although those words to Robert Browning are her best-known, she was a lifelong writer. Elizabeth Barrett Browning probably wrote her first poem at the age of four. A precocious child, she wrote an epic of sorts at fourteen, and at sixteen she studied Greek and wrote a long philosophical poem, *An Essay on the Mind.* Although she had always been frail, at fifteen her life of invalidism and drug addiction began, but she continued to study, to write, and to establish a literary reputation. She translated Aeschylus's *Prometheus Bound,* published a collection of poems, and composed an *Account of the Greek Christian Poets.*

When she was thirty-nine she received a fan letter from a struggling young poet named Robert Browning. He begged to be allowed to meet her and said of her works, "I do . . . love these books with all my heart—and I love you too." She agreed to an interview, and they began a long friendship and correspondence. Soon afterward, she defied her father (who had forbidden all of his children to marry) and eloped to Europe. Mr. Barrett never forgave her and never saw her again.

Meanwhile, the Brownings fell in love with each other and with Europe. The story of their love affair is a classic. Living mostly in Florence, where they formed the center of an English expatriate circle, they became involved in Italian politics and had a son. Elizabeth Barrett Browning's poems and her epic-novel, *Aurora Leigh,* attracted particular attention because they were so powerful and so blatantly political. She was an ardent feminist, still a rare and deeply feared creature, yet she achieved great success in her field and was admired by the likes of William

# 30

**E.D.E.N. SOUTHWORTH,** *dies at 79 in Washington, D.C., 1899.* Born Emma Dorothy Eliza Nevitte, Southworth worked as a teacher until she was about thirty. She had married when she was twenty, but she contravened tradition by continuing to teach. It was well that she held on to her job, since the marriage failed. She and her husband separated in 1844, and she moved to Georgetown, where she taught and began to write short stories. In 1849, she wrote her first novel, *Retribution,* and began fifty years of financial success.

Southworth had the ability to churn out pulp Gothic romances by the cartload. She wrote more than sixty of them, quite a lot in the days before typewriters and word processors, serializing them in popular periodicals and making more than ten thousand dollars in her first year as a writer. Although there were many authors of Gothic melodramas in Southworth's time, she was the best, the most popular, and the most prolific of them all. Her most successful novel, *The Hidden Hand,* featured an independent, aggressive heroine named Capitola. It was in print for sixty-two years and adapted four times for the stage. Her books were quite forgettable. After her death her reputation declined, and her books began to gather dust on library shelves. However, she was enshrined for all time in a lefthanded way: she was ridiculed, as Mrs. S.L.A.N.G. Northbury, in Louisa May Alcott's *Little Women.*

LIBRARY OF CONGRESS

ELIZABETH BARRETT BROWNING: *Tyrannized by one man and freed to be herself by another.*

Thackeray, Edgar Allan Poe, and Margaret Fuller. When Wordsworth died, Elizabeth Barrett Browning was quite seriously considered for the post of England's poet laureate. Even her *Sonnets from the Portuguese,* today thought rather drippy and sentimental by some readers, was revolutionary in its time, because she took a "masculine" form—the sonnet cycle used by Petrarch, Shakespeare, and

Spenser—and rewrote it from a woman's point of view. Her downfall, as always, was her fragile health. She died in 1861 from complications of bronchitis.

LIBRARY OF CONGRESS

CHARLOTTE PERKINS GILMAN: *Still worth reading are her humorous novels about a female Utopia called "Herland," where everything is "beauty, order, and perfect cleanness."*

# JULY

## 1

**AMY JOHNSON,** *born in Kingston-upon-Hull, England, 1903.* In 1928, a young secretary named Amy Johnson was working near a small airport, and she kept hearing the sounds of aircraft flying overhead. Far from annoying her, the sounds intrigued her, and she decided to learn to fly. It was a rather tall order, but somehow she made her £5-a-week salary stretch far enough to pay for lessons, and in 1929 she became the first Englishwoman to get an aircraft ground engineer's license.

It was only a few weeks later that she decided to be the first woman to fly solo from England to Australia and to break the existing record set by a man. It was madness. She had logged only eighty-five hours of solo flying time; her longest flight

had been 147 miles. And she now planned to fly 10,000 miles, over some of the most treacherous land and water in the world.

After much difficulty, she made the trip in nineteen days. She didn't break the record (fifteen and a half days), but she did become a celebrity. Even the plane she used was purchased as a memento by the London *Daily Mail.* Eventually, she

did break a record—in 1931, the London-to-Tokyo record.

Like so many aviators, she died in a crash. Johnson had come out of retirement during World War II to fly for Britain's Air Transport Auxiliary, and in 1941, her plane crashed over water. Entangled in her parachute, she called out, "Hurry, please hurry!" but before she could be rescued, she drowned.

## 2

**ANNA HOWARD SHAW,** *dies at 72, in Moylan, Pennsylvania, 1919.* Although she was a teacher,

preacher, and almost a doctor, Shaw's true devotion was to the cause of woman suffrage. From the

**GEORGE SAND,** *born Amandine Aurore Lucie Dupin in Paris, France, 1804.* In 1834, George Sand wrote in her journal, "Liszt said to me today that God alone deserves to be loved. It may be true, but when one has loved a man it is very difficult to love God." Sand loved not only one man, but many. Her affairs with writer Jules Sandeau, poet Alfred de Musset, and pianist-composer Frédéric Chopin were passions of legendary proportions and were as notorious and scandalous as her preferences for men's clothes and her dislike of her dull, lecherous husband, Baron Casimir Dudevant. One day in 1831, she simply left him, took a lover, and began writing. Between amorous adventures and Dudevant's threats, lawsuits, and abduction of their daughter, she managed to write eighty novels celebrating eroticism, pantheism, and the working class, and attacking conventional marriage and the clergy.

LIBRARY OF CONGRESS

ANNA HOWARD SHAW: *As solid and firm as the column behind her.*

moment she met Susan B. Anthony, the two became close. Anthony appreciated Shaw's dedication to the cause, and Shaw was "Aunt Susan's" right hand. Eventually Shaw became vice president of the National American Woman Suffrage Association in 1892. Shaw wanted dearly to succeed Anthony as president of the organization, but stepped aside for Anthony's own choice, Carrie Chapman Catt. A chance at the coveted job came in 1904, though, and Shaw won election. She held the position until 1915, during which time she did a terrible job. Although she was a woman of great principle and many talents, leadership was not among them. Factionalism hurt the group, and when Catt ran again for president, she was welcomed with open arms.

tions. Women taking the rest cure were not to work under any circumstances. They were not allowed paper, writing implements, or paintbrushes, and they were fed large, frequent meals to keep them fat and presumably happy. Many women did go thoroughly mad. Somehow, Charlotte survived.

Ultimately she left her husband. She began writing and lecturing on women's rights, social policy, and labor. In 1892, she wrote what is perhaps her best-known story, "The Yellow Wallpaper," a terrifying account of the rest cure based on her own experiences. Her 1898 book, *Women and Economics,* made her famous—or perhaps notorious—as an expert on feminist issues. The book attacked women's financial dependence on men, sexism in the workplace, and domestic drudgery

that kept women bound to the home. Probing deeper, it exposed myths about the sexes and mistaken assumptions about women's capabilities.

Charlotte married New York lawyer George Gilman in 1902, thereby acquiring the surname by which is is now known. In 1932, she discovered she had breast cancer and by 1935 knew it was fatal. Calmly, she finished her autobiography, *The Living of Charlotte Perkins Gilman,* and then committed suicide. Her final note read, in part, "when all usefulness is over, when one is assured of unavoidable and imminent death, it is the simplest of human rights to choose a quick and easy death in place of a slow and horrible one. . . . I have preferred chloroform to cancer."

SARAH SIDDONS: *The greatest actress of her day.*

# 3

**CHARLOTTE PERKINS GIL-MAN,** *born Charlotte Anna Perkins in Hartford, Connecticut, 1860.* Here's a nineteenth-century recipe for mental illness: take a busy, intelligent woman named Charlotte Perkins who has worked as a governess, an art teacher, and a commercial artist. Marry her to a self-satisfied painter named Charles Stetson, and tell her to stop working for pay. When she sinks into a deep depression after giving birth to her only child, call a "specialist" to prescribe "the rest cure."

The recipe's not foolproof. Charlotte came within a hair's breadth of madness, but she escaped from the rest cure with her sanity intact—not a small feat, given the nature of the treatment. It was usually used on women just like her—active, healthy women who had suddenly and inexplicably fallen into depression. No one seemed to notice the fact that their depression often coincided with disruptions in their professional lives. Instead of restoring them to their former occupations, these women were deprived of *all* occupa-

LIBRARY OF CONGRESS

# 4

**EDMONDIA LEWIS,** *born Mary Edmondia Lewis in Greenbush, New York, 1845.* Lewis was triply handicapped at birth; she was female, black on her father's side, and Indian on her mother's. Orphaned as a child, she was adopted by her mother's tribe, the Chippewas, who called her "Wildfire." In 1859 her brother's success in the California Gold Rush allowed her to attend Oberlin College. There she developed an interest in art, but in her senior year, she suffered in a particularly virulent outbreak of racial prejudice. Two of her classmates died and Lewis was accused of poisoning them. There was no evidence to implicate her; and she was acquitted.

After college she trained as a sculptor and became one of the most popular American artists of her day, famous for her sympathetic portraits of women, slaves, and Indians. By 1870 one of her pieces could command as much as several thousand dollars, and her friends included sculptor Harriet Hosmer, actress and art patron Charlotte Cushman, and poets Robert and Elizabeth Barrett Browning.

# 5

**SARAH SIDDONS,** *born Sarah Kemble in Brecon, Wales, 1755.* Like many another fine actress, Siddons was the daughter of actors, and she was born while her parents were on tour. Her father was noted performer Roger Kemble, and Sarah was groomed for the stage almost from birth. She made her debut at eighteen, however, playing opposite an actor named William Siddons. She married Siddons six years later, despite strong objections from her parents. Sarah and William had seven children, two of whom died in infancy, but the care of babies didn't put a stop to her career.

After a failed London debut, she polished her technique and returned to London a smashing success at the Drury Lane Theatre. Until her retirement in 1812, she reigned supreme in London, drawing lavish praise from her contemporaries for her dignity, her majesty, and her round, resonant voice. She was most noted for her portrayal of Lady Macbeth. By the time of her retirement, she and the Scottish noblewoman were almost identical in the public mind.

# 6

**MADELEINE SOPHIE BLANCHARD,** *dies over Paris, France, 1819.* Blanchard's prominence was the indirect result of her marriage to the famous balloonist, Jean-Pierre Blanchard. He suffered from a lingering illness, and he worried that she would starve when she became a widow. So he taught her to fly balloons, and in 1805 she made her first solo flight. Mme.

MADELEINE BLANCHARD: *A balloon explosion claimed her life.*

LIBRARY OF CONGRESS

Blanchard quickly achieved fame and developed a repertoire of stunts which drew large crowds. Napoleon appointed her his Chief of Air Services, a mostly honorary post, in which she piloted beautiful balloons at state festivals and toured Europe on behalf of France. It was during one of these performances that she died. Fireworks she was setting off from her balloon ignited the hydrogen used to keep it aloft, and the craft exploded, making Blanchard the first woman to die in an aviation accident.

CHRISTIAN DAVIES: *Intrepid soldier, innkeeper, and autobiographer.*

## 7

**CHRISTIAN DAVIES,** *dies at about 72 in London, England, 1739.* As a girl, said Christian Davies, who was born Christian Cavanagh in Dublin, she liked "manly Employments, such as handling a rake, flail, pitchfork, and riding horses bareback." Her taste for the outdoor life would serve her well, for when her husband, Richard Welsh, was drafted in 1692, she decided to follow and find him. In 1693, she dressed in men's clothing, enlisted in an infantry regiment as Christopher Welsh and fought against the French in Holland.

Ten years later, she found her husband. She convinced him to keep her secret, and he pretended that she was his brother, but the ruse didn't work long. "Christopher" was badly wounded in battle, "his" skull fractured. During an operation to repair the wound, her sex was discovered, and she was discharged. She remained with the army, however, working as a cook.

Unfortunately, her husband was killed, and it was she who found his body. For a week, she refused to eat, and her grief stirred the pity of a captain named Ross. The nature of their relationship is not known, but she soon acquired the nickname "Mother Ross." Whatever their arrangement, it could not have been binding, since within three months she married a grenadier, Hugh Jones, who was killed in battle shortly afterward. In 1712, she returned to England, got a lifetime pension of a shilling a day from Queen Anne, married a soldier named Davies, and opened an inn. Her autobiography, *The Life and Adventures of Mrs. Christian Davies, commonly call'd Mother Ross,* appeared in the year after her death. Some, without any real proof, believe it to have been written by Daniel Defoe.

## 8

**KÄTHE KOLLWITZ,** *born Käthe Ida Schmidt in Königsberg, Germany, 1867.* Kollwitz was a woman who prized life, beauty, and love so fiercely and proudly that they became her creed, her trinity, her religion. It seemed sometimes that if she stopped defending them her very soul might perish. Yet she was also a woman who lived through two world wars and who saw all the things she valued most trampled by the feet of soldiers. If she had had no gifts besides her dignity, her torment might have gone unheard, but she was a talented artist who por-

LIBRARY OF CONGRESS

trayed her pain in drawings, prints, and sculpture.

She was born to a liberal family, and she was fortunate in having a father who recognized and encouraged her artistic skills. The Berlin Academy was not quite so open-minded and rejected her on the basis of sex, but she took private drawing lessons anyway.

As the old century closed and the new one began, Kollwitz had developed a solid artistic reputation. As tensions mounted in Europe before World War I, her work became more pacifist in content, and the trend was accelerated in 1914, when her much-loved son, Peter, died in the war.

Kollwitz spent the rest of her life coping with this tragedy. Always skeptical of "the joy of sacrificing," she now dedicated herself to fighting the image of the noble wartime mother who willingly offers her sons for the cause. Her art was filled with images of mothers mourning over dead children or shielding their children from death; so powerful were her anti-war messages that in 1936 Hitler banned her work.

# 9

**ANN RADCLIFFE,** *born Ann Ward in London, England, 1764.* When Christina Rossetti, the nineteenth-century poet, wanted to write a biography of Ann Radcliffe, she couldn't find enough material to complete the project. Radcliffe lived an ordinary life. She knew no famous, fascinating people, and in 1823 she died of a severe attack of asthma.

For about seven years, however, Radcliffe was one of the most popular authors in England. Her style was widely imitated, and at least eighteen forgeries appeared under her name, which became synonymous with the genre she had shaped—the Gothic romance. She didn't invent this type of novel; she perfected it. While most Gothic

novels were popular, they were eminently forgettable. Radcliffe's, on the other hand, were well-written and durable. Two of her best-loved books are *Mysteries of Udolpho* and *A Sicilian Romance.* Generations after her death, her books were being read in English, French, and Italian, and her trademarks—

# 10

**MARY McLEOD BETHUNE,** *born Mary McLeod in Mayesville, South Carolina, 1875.* She helped found a hospital and a college for blacks; she organized Franklin Roosevelt's "black cabinet" to push for an equitable New Deal; she worked for racial pride and against discrimination in every aspect of American life. Mary McLeod Bethune was a driven activist, an eloquent, impassioned speaker, and

crumbling castles, bandits, a brave young hero, a middle-aged villain, picturesque scenery, seemingly supernatural events, and a beautiful, talented, sentimental heroine—became such standard elements of the Gothic novel that today they are cliché.

a woman of integrity. "I have unselfishly given my best," she wrote, "and I thank God I have lived long enough to see the fruits of from it."

MARY McLEOD BETHUNE: *With $1.50 in assets, she built a college on a dump site.*

LIBRARY OF CONGRESS

# 11

**JEAN GARDNER BATTEN,** *born in Rotorua, New Zealand, in 1909, exact date unknown.* Jean Batten spent most of her youth preparing for one flight—from England to her native New Zealand. She was obsessed with planes from age ten. Unfortunately, her father had other ideas. He wanted her to be a concert pianist, insisting flying was too dangerous and too expensive. She answered his objections by selling her piano to finance her flying lessons.

Driven by her goal, Batten learned to fly, studied aircraft maintenance, meteorology, and navigation, and sought financial backing for her flight. Her first two attempts failed, and she was ridiculed in the press. On her third try, Batten was able to go only as far as Australia, where she learned she'd broken the women's record for that trip by four days. An instant celebrity, Batten was welcomed grandly at home and had no trouble financing her later expeditions, many of which broke records, too.

She did make the England-to-New Zealand trip in 1935, in a record eleven days. She reveled in the "greatest and most lasting of joys: the joy of achievement," which can be infinitely shared without being diminished. Batten proved how strongly she believed this in 1980, when her record was at last broken by another female aviator and Batten was on hand to congratulate her when she landed.

# 12

**KIRSTEN FLAGSTAD,** *born Kirsten Malfrid Flagstad in Hamar, Norway, 1895.* There was a time in this country when German opera was sort of the bastard of the family. A German work never, never began an opera season, and it was generally assumed that Wagner was less popular than Verdi. Then, in 1935, Kirsten Flagstad came to the Metropolitan Opera in New York and changed everything.

Until that year, Flagstad had performed mostly in Scandinavia, and mostly in musical comedies and operettas. It was thought that her light, rather small soprano voice would not be suitable for Wagner, but it was Wagner that she loved. At eleven she had memorized the role of Elsa in *Lohengrin,* and although she sang more than seventy different roles in her career, it was Wagner's characters she most enjoyed.

A Metropolitan employee heard Flagstad sing one evening and arranged an audition for her. For some reason, the room used for the audition had poor acoustics, and her voice sounded smaller than ever. The Met hired her for one year only, on a trial basis, and only because a fine soprano had just quit. Flagstad's first role was Sieglinde, in *Die Walküre,* and at her first rehearsal it became clear that her voice was extraordinary. Her co-star was so surprised that he missed his cue, and the conductor laid down his baton in shock. Audiences reacted with similar pleasure and shock, and Flagstad returned later that season as Isolde in *Tristan and Isolde* and Brünnhilde in *Die Walküre* to critical acclaim and public adulation. By the end of the season, she was a sensation, Wagner was suddenly profitable, and Flagstad's international career was launched.

# 13

**CATALINA DE ERAUZO,** *born in Spain, in 1592, exact date unknown.* Locked in a convent for most of her youth, and trained as a nun, at fifteen Eurazo decided she'd had enough and escaped in a set of hand-made boys' clothes. As Antonio Ramírez de Guzmán, she led a life of adventure, crime, and amorous affairs. She, as he, had a reputation for gambling, dueling, purse-snatching, and wooing, winning, and abandoning several ladies. Garbed in a flashy costume of a silver-trimmed black suit, knee-high red leather boots, and a red hat with a black ostrich feather, she fought innumerable duels and street battles, winning all, wounding several opponents and killing at least seven. In one fight alone she stabbed three men to death because one had denounced her latest love by claiming the lady "had the smile of a toad."

But luck didn't remain with her. Still dressed as a man, she accidentally killed her brother during a nighttime fight. She took refuge in a church for eight months before slipping past guards. Pursued by a reputation for violence, she was finally convicted in about 1623 for another murder. On the day of her execution, she confessed all her crimes and also her sex to a clergyman, who brought her to a nearby convent for examination by the nuns. Astonishingly, when the brazen Erauzo was revealed to be a woman, a nun, *and* a virgin, she was freed, given permission to wear men's clothing, and absolved of her sins by the Pope.

# 14

**EMMELINE PANKHURST,** *born Emmeline Goulden in Manchester, England, 1858.* From her early childhood, Pankhurst felt that there was something wrong with the world. It was an absence, or an error, or an imbalance; she couldn't quite put her finger on it, but it surfaced everywhere.

By the age of fourteen, Pankhurst was convinced she had identi-

LIBRARY OF CONGRESS

EMMELINE PANKHURST: *The British suffragist who inspired generations.*

Christabel and a few other women, she formed a group called the Women's Social and Political Union (WSPU). They were destined to achieve in fifteen years what polite delegations had been unable to do in fifty. From the beginning, Pankhurst advocated radical tactics.

WSPU members invaded political meetings, carrying banners that read "Votes for Women." They questioned candidates for office about their attitudes toward suffrage, demanded audiences with important officials, held public lectures, rioted, and went to jail. There they went on hunger and thirst strikes and were forcibly fed. They started their own newspaper, *Votes for Women,* and held parades. And they got what they wanted, dispensing with gentility and operating on Pankhurst's sacred principle—that "the argument of the broken pane of glass is the most valuable argument in modern politics."

# 15

**FRANCES CABRINI,** *born Maria Francesca Xavier Cabrini in Sant' Angelo Lodigiano, Italy, 1850.* It is said that when Frances Cabrini was born a flock of white doves was seen flying around her parents' house. Whether or not there were doves, it seems certain she was destined for a gentle, peaceful life. By age seven she was determined to be a missionary. From twelve to eighteen she made annual vows of virginity, and at eighteen she swore herself to lifelong chastity. She tried to join the Daughters of the Sacred Heart, a religious order, but was rejected because she had been seriously weakened by smallpox.

Undaunted, Cabrini operated an orphanage, and in 1877 she took religious vows to become superior of the orphanage. Three years later she established her own order, the Missionary Sisters of the Sacred Heart. Still, she longed to go abroad, and she asked Pope Leo XIII for permission to open a mis-

fied the source of imbalance in the world and its cure. She began attending suffrage meetings, and at twenty-one she married a fellow suffragist, Dr. Richard Marsden Pankhurst. Twenty years her senior, Dr. Pankhurst was a progressive lawyer whose support of socialism and women's rights frightened po-

tential clients. Emmeline ran a store to supplement his income.

The marriage was a happy one, and she called her husband's death in 1898 "an irreparable loss," but she couldn't afford to grieve for long. She had four children to support, so she took a job as the registrar of births and deaths in Manchester. Here, she was horrified every day with tales of infanticide, incest, and thirteen-year-old mothers. She was more firmly convinced than ever that women needed the vote.

So, in 1903, with her daughter

sion in China. He advised her to go west rather than east, and in 1889 she landed in the United States. There she worked with Italian immigrants, and although the local archbishop resented her interference, she was allowed to establish her mission because she had papal support. In 1909 she became an American citizen, and in 1910 she was named Superior General for life. She died in 1917, was beatified in 1938, and was canonized in 1946, becoming the first U.S. citizen named a Roman Catholic saint.

LIBRARY OF CONGRESS

FRANCES CABRINI: *Sainthood was her ultimate reward.*

# 17

**MAUDE ADAMS,** *dies at 80 in Tannersville, New York, 1953.* If the name "Peter Pan" is mentioned, what actress comes to mind? A number of women have played the boy who wouldn't grow up, but for American audiences at the beginning of the twentieth century, Maude Adams *was* Peter Pan. She was her generation's queen of comedy, and she played the role more than fifteen hundred times.

She had begun in the theatre as "Little Maude," playing children's roles. A break in career to attend school eased her transition to adult parts, and by 1892, at nineteen, she was the leading lady of Charles Frohman's company. Audiences loved her, and critics praised her "simple sincerity" and "charming intelligence and restraint." One reviewer wrote in 1895, "Miss Maude Adams is a delicious young actress."

In 1896, Adams was appearing in *Rosemary*. During one perform-

# 16

**MARGUERITE HARRISON,** *dies at 87, 1967.* A truly remarkable woman, Marguerite Harrison was a most unlikely candidate for distinction. Born to a wealthy shipping magnate and his socially-conscious wife, Harrison grew up in the lap of luxury, but had a spirit beyond her comfortable circumstances.

Faced, as a young widow, with sudden financial trouble, she took a job on the *Baltimore Sun*, where she eventually had her own weekly column in which she lauded work done by women in World War I. Early in 1918 she decided to go to Europe to write about the progress of the war. To do so, she took the best route available; she volunteered as a spy. Deemed by the government as someone who could "readily deceive the average person," she was approved for a mission in Germany, but before she left, peace was declared. Harrison went anyway to gather nonmilitary information, beginning a spying career that later took her to post-revolutionary Russia, where she worked for a time as a double agent—or so the Russians thought—and where she was twice imprisoned. An adventuress

at heart, she spent most of her life traveling the globe, by ship, horse-drawn wagon, train, mule, car, camel, and goatskin barge.

**IDA WELLS-BARNETT,** *born Ida Bell Wells in Holly Springs, Mississippi, 1862.* Ida Wells-Barnett spent all her life fighting for her beliefs. An early black challenger of the South's Jim Crow segregation laws, she sued a railroad company for forcing her to leave an all-white car. She won, too, but the decision was overturned.

At twenty-six Wells-Barnett was a rather successful columnist for a Memphis, Tennessee, newspaper, with a small syndication of her columns in black newspapers around the country. An exposé of the prejudice permeating the Memphis school system got her fired from one job, but she didn't slacken her crusade. Next she tackled lynchings which were rampant in the South,

exploding the myths surrounding that crime. She encouraged blacks to leave Memphis, and their obedient flight crippled white businesses. Death threats followed, and Wells-Barnett moved to New York just in time to avoid the fire which destroyed her office.

But it wasn't only whites who were angered by Wells-Barnett's aggressive character. Black men accused her of overshadowing them. She didn't cave in to this, either. She continued fighting for justice. She organized a black woman suffrage club, and protested segregation in that movement; she was also a co-founder of the National Association for the Advancement of Colored People.

ance, her audience included James M. Barrie, who was having trouble with a stage adaptation of his novel *The Little Minister*. Adams's performance charmed and inspired him, and when he finished the play, he insisted that she take the leading role, Lady Babbie. *The Little Minister* was immensely successful. Adams played Babbie almost as many times as she did Peter Pan, and with her profits she was able to start her own company. Her collaboration with Barrie lasted until his death in 1937, and it had advantages for both of them. Barrie found in Adams the perfect embodiment of his favorite creations, and her popularity meant financial success for him. Adams, on the other hand, got roles designed especially for her. She was not a tragedian and had been, by her own admission, "very bad as Juliet," but Barrie's light comedies brought out all her strengths. In fact, she and Barrie's plays were so suited to each other that even when the playwright wasn't in the audience, Adams said she could feel him watching her.

MAUDE ADAMS as Peter Pan: *She avoided all roles that did not feature youthful, good, and optimistic characters, and she excelled in the realm of the sweetly sentimental.*

# 18

**LADY JANE FRANKLIN,** *dies at 83 in London, England, 1875.* Men did much of the initial mapping of the Arctic, but much of what they accomplished couldn't have been done without Jane Franklin. Her husband, Sir John Franklin, was among these early explorers. She married him in 1828, and for seventeen years, they traveled together and established a scientific society, a botanical garden, a natural history museum, a state school, and a prison reform society in Tasmania, where Sir John was the provincial governor. Lady Franklin, an adventurer herself, was the first woman to climb Mount Wellington and the first woman to travel overland from Melbourne to Sydney, Australia. In 1845 her husband went off to the Arctic, hoping to chart a northwest passage.

By 1848, with no word from her husband's expedition, Lady Franklin offered a £2,000 reward for information. When that bore no fruit, she talked the English government into sending three ships after him. The British Admiralty offered a reward of its own, and throughout the 1850s the Arctic was crowded with ships looking for Sir John Franklin, all of them sent in one way or another by Lady Franklin. She personally funded several expeditions, pressured various governments into sending more, and even convinced American whalers to look for him. In 1857, evidence was found of Sir John's death, and Lady Franklin eventually found consolation in other interests, traveling to Japan, India, the United States and the Hawaiian Islands. In 1860, Britain's Royal Geographical Society offered her its Patron's Medal in recognition of the knowledge her expeditions had made available. However, she was not allowed to receive the medal in person. She was, after all, a woman, and the Geographical Society was for men only.

# 19

**LIZZIE BORDEN,** *born Lisabeth Andrew Borden in Fall River, Massachusetts, 1860.* Everybody knows the rhyme: "Lizzie Borden took an axe, / Gave her mother forty whacks. / When she saw what she had done, / She gave her father forty-one."

But did she or didn't she? No one really knows for sure, although some people *think* they do. Inconsistencies in her initial testimony,

LIZZIE BORDEN: *An enigma.*

her well-known dislike of her stepmother, the assumption that she was the only one with an opportunity to commit both murders, and her alleged burning of a dress shortly after the crimes led to Borden's arrest. However, some now argue that the family maid also had opportunity and was allowed to leave the house with a large, uninspected package on the night of the murders. There is also the possibility that Borden and the maid acted in collusion. No one knows. Borden didn't appear at her trial, and after her acquittal in June, 1893, she didn't give away any secrets. She lived quietly in Fall River until her death in 1927, taunted by children and shunned by adults.

# 20

**THEDA BARA,** *born Theodosia Burr Goodman in Cincinnati, Ohio, probably in 1885.* Theda Bara's stardom lasted only about five years, but in those five years she made thirty-nine films and was the subject of thousands of legends. From the moment in 1915 that she mouthed the line, "Kiss me, my fool!" she was the recipient of both hate mail and ardent admiration. Studio publicists fed the fire by pointing out that her name was an anagram for "Arab Death." Fan magazines said that she'd been born in the shadow of the Sphinx and that she had been a star in Paris as well. Clergymen denounced her, but theatregoers loved her. Fox's Hollywood studios were built on the proceeds from her films. Under all the hype, however, she was just Theodosia Goodman, the daughter of a Jewish tailor from Ohio. The only difference between Theda Bara

THEDA BARA: *"Kiss me, my fool!"*

THE FALL RIVER HISTORICAL SOCIETY

and the girl who'd tried unsuccessfully to make it on the Broadway stage a few years before, was that Theodosia had been broke and Theda Bara made $4,000 a week. As Cleopatra, Carmen, and Sa-

lome, she was a voluptuous, exotic, deadly beauty who made her fortune by personifying what she called the "little bit of vampire instinct in every woman."

# 21

**POPE JOAN,** *born in the ninth century, place and date unknown.* Some church fathers and historians have been claiming for centuries that Joan never existed, while some say she was very real and that all the claims to the contrary are simply a whitewash. Even if she did exist, not much is known about her, but here are the best guesses. Her birthplace is given variously as England, Germany, and Ireland, and her original name as Agnes or Gilberta. She masqueraded as a priest and went to Rome, either to study or to follow her lover, a monk. She was a brilliant scholar and apparently also an adept politician, and she rose rapidly in the ranks; Pope Leo IV made her a cardinal, and when Leo died in 855, she was elected Pope and took the name John.

Joan was supposedly Pope for three years, but unfortunately she fell in love with her chamberlain,

seduced him, and became pregnant. She managed to hide her condition for nine months under her robes, and perhaps she hoped to slip away in time to deliver the child, but according to tradition she misjudged the timing a bit. She was marching in a procession through the streets of Rome when she went into labor and a child emerged from her robes. At first the crowd thought it was a miracle, but when they examined her and discovered her sex, they dragged her away and stoned her to death. In 1601 the whole story was declared a myth by Pope Clement VIII, and a great deal of ink was spilled in an attempt to destroy the story's credibility. But there have always been those who believed it, and it is a fact that since the time when Joan supposedly died, no papal procession has been held in the street where she allegedly gave birth.

# 22

**HELOISE,** *born in France in about 1100, exact date and place unknown.* The story of Abelard and Heloise is one of the greatest love stories of the Western world—as passionate as that of Romeo and Juliet or Pyramus and Thisbe, but entirely true, not a legend. Heloise was a supremely intelligent and beautiful woman, wealthy enough to receive a superior education. Fortunately, or unfortunately, depending on your perspective, her tutor was the renowned scholar Peter Abelard. As he wrote in his auto-

biography *Historia calamitatum,* "A gift for letters is so rare in women that it added greatly to [Heloise's] charm . . . I considered all the usual attractions for a lover and decided she was the one to bring to my bed, confident that I should have an easy success."

And so it was. But the two fell in love, and they shared an extraordinary passion as well as a common philosophy. The justified their affair on the grounds of the purity of their passion; they felt marriage was nothing more than legalized prosti-

tution. However, after Heloise gave birth to Abelard's son, her family sought retribution against Abelard and arranged for him to be castrated.

He became a monk, and he pressured Heloise to join him in his new life by becoming a nun. Both rose to positions of power within their orders, but Heloise had not lost her powerful love for Abelard. Despite her numerous letters to him in which she beautifully and urgently expressed her feelings, Abelard did not respond. "The pleasures of lovers which we have shared have been too sweet," she wrote. "I should be groaning over the sins I have committed, but I can only sigh for what I have lost." With no response from Abelard, Heloise eventually gave up trying for his attentions. She died in 1164.

# 23

**CHARLOTTE CUSHMAN,** *born Charlotte Saunders Cushman in Boston, Massachusetts, 1816.* Cushman originally trained as an opera singer, but she chose the wrong teacher. A New Orleans voice trainer tried to change the girl from a contralto into a soprano, with the result that her voice failed utterly. Determined to get on the stage in one way or another, Cushman took drama lessons and made her New York debut in 1837. Light comedy was an anathema to Cushman; tragedy was her element. She was magnificent as Lady Macbeth and as Nancy Sykes in *Oliver Twist,* but she was also applauded for her performances as Hamlet, Romeo, and *Henry VIII*'s Cardinal Wolsey. Financially successful, she became as well known for her generosity to artists of all kinds as for her "farewell performances," which began in the 1850s. Although she claimed to be leaving the theater after each of these, she returned to the stage again and again, until her death from cancer in 1876.

CHARLOTTE CUSHMAN: *As Romeo, with her sister, Susan, as Juliet.*

# 24

**AMELIA EARHART,** *born Amelia Mary Earhart in Atchison, Kansas, 1897.* On May 20, 1932, an Irish farmer standing in his field watched in astonishment as a plane landed among his cows. A woman jumped from the plane, smiled, and said cheerfully, "I've come from America."

Amelia Earhart hadn't made it to her intended destination, Paris, because of mechanical problems; she was, nevertheless, the first woman to fly solo across the Atlantic, and she had beaten the record time.

As much notice as the transatlantic trip brought her, Earhart is probably most famous for the trip she didn't make: the 1937 flight around the world. Her disappearance near Howland Island in the Pacific Ocean has been the subject of myths since the day it happened —among them that (1) she landed safely on another island and re-mained stranded there, (2) she was shot down by the Japanese because she was secretly spying for the United Stated Navy, and (3) she was kidnapped by aliens.

The speculation over Earhart's death sometimes obscures her accomplishments. She was a pioneer in a dangerous field who prized her skill and independence, and had married only on her own terms. She had contempt for women who used their sex to get special treatment. From the time that, as a child, she received a football and a rifle from her father, to the time her plane went down near Howland Island, she fought against the system of "dividing people according to their sex, and putting them in little feminine or masculine pigeonholes."

# 25

**JAMES BARRY,** *dies at about 70 in London, England, 1865.* In 1810, a "frail-looking young man" of about fifteen entered the medical school of Edinburgh College. In 1812 he got his degree, and a year later he entered the army. He served in South Africa, the West Indies, and the Crimea, quickly working his way through the ranks and becoming, ultimately, the inspector-general of Canadian hospitals. Colleagues thought him brilliant, but eccentric and effeminate; he was often teased for his short stature, his high voice, and his appearance, which was that of "a beardless lad." Barry had a quick temper, and such taunts often ended in duels. Otherwise he was a model officer and "the most skillful of physicians." It was only after his death in 1865 that people began to say that *he* had actually been a *she.* An autopsy was ordered, and Barry was found not only to be a woman, but also to have given birth sometime during her military career. Terribly embarrassed, the British army quickly denied that Barry was a woman, buried her as a man, and conveniently misplaced her records.

AMELIA EARHART, with pilot Wilmer Stutz (*left*) and mechanic Lou Gordon (*right*): *In 1928, as a passenger in their plane, she became the first woman to fly the Atlantic. Four years later, she made the flight* for *herself and* by *herself.*

# 26

**GRACIE ALLEN,** *born Grace Ethel Cecile Rosalie Allen in San Francisco, California, 1895.* Gracie Allen was an intelligent woman who made a career of acting dumb. She first appeared on the stage at the age of five, but she wasn't really successful until she was twenty-seven. She was then, to all appearances, a failed actress who had decided to become a secretary. But in 1922 she met a struggling song-and-dance man who, despite having changed his name from Nathan Birnbaum to George Burns, had come no closer to stardom. Allen and Burns decided to work together in vaudeville. She would deliver the straight lines, and he would tell the jokes.

When they got on stage, though, they found that she was getting more laughs than he, so they reworked the act and molded the characters which made them famous. Burns became the long-suffering boyfriend, and Allen a scatterbrained, illogical woman with a strange collection of relatives. The act was an instant hit despite Allen's chronic stage fright, and by 1926 they had enough money to get

married. Their London debut on the BBC was so popular that their show was extended for twenty weeks. Eddie Cantor asked Allen to appear on *his* radio show, and for two years she and Burns were guests on various programs.

In 1932, Burns and Allen got their own American show, "The Adventures of Gracie." By 1940, they had forty-five million listeners and were making nine thousand dollars a week. Gracie's trademarks,

"I don't get it," and "Oh, George, I'll bet you tell that to all the girls," had become nationally-known catch phrases. The show became famous not only for Allen's "illogical logic" but also for its adept use of gimmicks. In 1933 Allen made visits to other CBS shows in a search of a long-lost fictional brother that drove her real brother into hiding, and in 1940 she ran for president as the Surprise Party candidate and actually got a few hundred write-in

GRACIE ALLEN, with George Burns: *"Say goodnight, Gracie."*

votes. Burns and Allen had a popular TV show in the 1950s, still in reruns, and still funny. She finally retired in 1958, weighed down by what Burns called the "chronic strain of making like someone she isn't."

# 27

**DIANE ARBUS,** *dies at 48 in New York City, 1971.* One evening in 1957, fashion photographer Diane Arbus was describing her day to a guest. In the middle of her account, she burst into tears. She decided at that moment to quit the business. It was too competitive and time-consuming, and she was a shy person who needed to spend more time with her two daughters.

She left her husband and moved into her own apartment, taking her children with her, and she began to take photographs on the streets of New York. Losing her shyness, she sought "danger and excitement" and began what she called "collecting things," choosing as her subjects people on the fringes of society. Drawn by her own curiosity and rebelliousness, she photographed giants, midgets, drag queens, fat ladies, junkie hippies, nudists, twins married to twins, and the mentally retarded. Within just ten years, she earned an international reputation, two Guggenheim fellowships, a following of admirers and imitators, and her own exhibition at New York's Museum of Modern Art. And then, just as suddenly and unexpectedly as it had in 1957, something gave way, only this time with greater force, and on this day in 1971 she committed suicide.

# 28

**JUDITH LEYSTER,** *born in Haarlem, Holland, 1609.* Leyster, unlike many female artists of her time, was not the daughter of an

artist. Her father was a brewer. Nonetheless, when she showed an early gift for drawing, her father sent her to study with painter Frans Hals, and she quickly became his best pupil. By the time she was twenty, she was considered an extraordinarily gifted artist, and by 1633 she was sufficiently well-established enough to open her own studio and take pupils.

Leyster was not only famous for her brushwork, her deft use of color, and the simple beauty of her genre scenes and portraits. She also achieved a certain degree of notoriety for a legal battle in which she was involved. It seems that one of her apprentices was stolen by her old teacher, Frans Hals. Leyster was thereby cheated of the fee for the apprentice's training. In an unexpected move for a woman at that time, she sued Hals for the lost money. Even more unexpectedly, she won her case.

In 1636, Leyster married a fellow artist, Jan Miense Molenaer. The three children that followed kept her very busy, and she did much less painting after her marriage. Her reputation lapsed, and after her death in 1660 many of her paintings were attributed to male artists. Almost no one knew who she was until 1893, when the Louvre acquired a Frans Hals and discovered that it was instead a signed Judith Leyster. Since then, she has become increasingly well known, especially for *The Proposition,* which turns a male artistic tradition on its head by portraying a man's sexual overtures as harrassment.

# 29

**CLARA BOW,** *born Clara Gordon Bow in Brooklyn, New York, 1905.* Like Theda Bara, Clara Bow enjoyed only a short period of stardom. Like Bara, she was typecast—not as a vamp, but as a flapper. She was the personification of the new college girl, who had a boyish figure and a pixie-like face and ex-

uded both innocence and sensuality. She drank, bobbed her hair, wore short skirts, smoked, rolled her stockings below her knees, played the ukelele and the kazoo, chewed gum, and fooled around in rumble seats. Bow was the "It" girl—"It" stood for sex appeal—and soon after her arrival in Hollywood she was receiving more fan mail than any other actress in town. Her lovers included actors Gary Cooper and Gilbert Roland, director Victor Fleming, and (allegedly) the entire University of California football team.

Bow longed to escape the flapper role, but never did. In the early 1930s, when she was already overworked and depressed, she suffered a number of setbacks. She sued her secretary and companion, Daisy DeVoe, for embezzlement, and for spite DeVoe released details of Bow's love life to the press. Bow's 1933 film *Hoopla* was a dismal failure. She had trouble sleeping, and her mental condition deteriorated steadily. She married millionaire rancher Rex Bell, a fellow silent-movie star, who later became lieutenant governor of Nevada. Bow retired, spending the remaining thirty years of her life swimming, watching television, playing poker with her servants, and growing increasingly dependent on psychiatrists and drugs. She died in 1965 of a heart attack precipitated by acute drug intoxication.

# 30

**EMILY BRONTË,** *born Emily Jane Brontë in Thornton, Bradford, Yorkshire, England, 1818.* Of all the Brontës—and they were considered quite odd in their time—Emily was perhaps the most displaced and least understood. She fulfilled all her "womanly duties," caring for the house and her ailing father when her sisters could not, but she made no other concessions to anyone's expectations. Even while she kneaded bread, she kept pen

CLARA BOW: *Daughter of a Coney Island waiter and a mentally unstable mother, she moved from poverty to movie stardom . . . and thirty years of mental institutions.*

and paper handy and composed as she worked.

She could play the piano "with precision and brilliancy," but she preferred to spend her time in less ornamental ways. She trained a hawk, roamed the Yorkshire moors with her dogs, whistled (*very* unfeminine of her), taught herself German and French, and learned to shoot a pistol with great accuracy. She was utterly without fear; she tamed her half-bulldog, half-mastiff companion, Keeper, by the use of her bare fists. She once extricated Keeper from a fight with another dog by simply wading into the thick of the snarling and biting, grabbing the dogs by their necks, and separating them, while a crowd of men stood by, afraid to intervene.

No one understood this woman. She refused to compromise; when chided for her inattention to dress, her unfeminine habits, and her silence and impassiveness before strangers, she merely replied, "I wish to be as God made me." Her father, a clergyman, did his best. Her sisters came closer, but even they didn't understand Emily's in-

tense need for privacy. One of her teachers appreciated Emily's "powerful reason," her genius, and "her strong, imperious will," but the only conclusion he could draw from his observations was that "she should have been a man."

Predictably, the people who appreciated her least of all were the critics. When *Wuthering Heights* appeared in 1847 under the name "Ellis Bell," reviewers rushed to condemn it. One called the author "a man of uncommon talents," but "dogged, brutal, and morose."

Emily was already ill when the reviews appeared, but during the following year her condition worsened and she began to die. Although she was suffering from tuberculosis, she refused to see a doctor, insisted that she felt no pain, and continued to do the heaviest housework, keeping busy from seven in the morning until ten at night. Her last words were, "If you'll send for a doctor, I'll see him now." She was so emaciated that her coffin was only sixteen inches wide. The funeral procession was led by Keeper, who for the rest of his life slept outside the door to her bedroom, and who was perhaps the only creature who really accepted her "as God made her."

# 31

**HELENA BLAVATSKY,** *born Helena Petrovna Hahn in Ekaterinoslav (now Dnepropetrovsk), Russian Ukraine, 1831.* Helena Blavatsky lived a fairly ordinary life as a child, until at sixteen she married a forty-four-year-old bureaucrat. Within three months, she was so revolted by him, she ran away and joined the circus. She met a Hungarian opera singer and toured Europe with him, trying to work as a medium, but she met with little success. While en route by sea to Cairo, their ship exploded, and Blavatsky was one of only seventeen

HELENA BLAVATSKY: *Philosopher or fraud?*

passengers who survived. Again, she tried her hand at spiritualism, but failed to arouse interest. In 1873 she made her way, via steerage, to New York City, where she eventually met Colonel Henry Steel Olcott, who was gullible, literate, and wealthy. He became Blavatsky's chief pupil, an ardent spiritualist, who abandoned his family to devote all his time—and money—to his studies.

In 1875, Blavatsky founded the Theosophical Society, with Olcott as chairman. Its purposes were to encourage the "universal Brotherhood of Humanity" and to reveal "unexplained laws of Nature and the psychical powers latent in man." Blavatsky claimed to have received her knowledge from certain unidentified "masters" on an alleged visit to Tibet.

Blavatsky was charismatic, despite a lack of physical beauty, fits of rage and cursing, and various obsessions. But in 1884 she was called to England to face challenges against her authority. She was labeled a fraud in a report which described her as "one of the most accomplished, ingenious, and interesting imposters in history." Despite this, in 1891, when she died, she had one hundred thousand followers.

LIBRARY OF CONGRESS

ANNIE OAKLEY: *Anything you can do, I can do better.*

# AUGUST

## 1

**MARIA MITCHELL,** *born in Nantucket, Massachusetts, 1818.* In October of 1847, a Massachusetts librarian made a lot of men very angry. Most of the world's notable astronomers were hoping to win a gold medal offered by the king of Denmark to the first person who discovered a new comet with a telescope. Mitchell had beaten them all by spotting one on October 1. How humiliating! The mighty astronomers with their university educations and their expensive observatories had been defeated by a woman without any substantial formal education, who used only a two-inch telescope that she kept on her roof.

As revolting as this turn of events was for the male scientific establishment, it was the focus of pride and jubilation for women. A group of women banded together to make sure Mitchell got plenty of attention in the press and to buy her a larger, more suitable telescope. She was offered a job with the United States Nautical Almanac Office, sited satellites, nebulae, and sunspots, and became the first woman elected to the American Academy of Arts and Sciences. In 1865, with the opening of Vassar College, she became the nation's first female professor of astronomy and director of the then all-female college's observatory.

## 2

**MARGERY KEMPE,** *born Margery Burnham in Lynn, England, in about 1373, exact date unknown.* Kempe achieved only moderate notoriety in life. She was not rich, powerful, or beautiful, or even especially famous. Her real claim to fame is that between 1431 and 1438 she wrote *The Book of Margery Kempe,* the first extant autobiography in English. Through the book we know something of her life, which was quite eventful, and of her personality, which was lively and intriguing. At twenty, she married a tax collector-brewer-miller named John Kempe, with whom she had fourteen children.

The story would very likely have ended there had she not been a passionate religious enthusiast. She began to have visions in which Jesus urged her to leave her husband and wed God instead, but she was unsure and afraid. Kempe finally struck a compromise and convinced her husband to release her from her sexual obligations. She visited the famous anchoress and visionary Juliana of Norwich, who confirmed her as having grace and warned her not only to welcome disapproval, but also to be actively suspicious of praise. After this visit, Kempe began to wear only white clothing and a ring engraved with the words "Jesus Christ is my love." She fasted, burst into tears frequently, wore a suit of haircloth under her dresses, and woke at two or three every morning so she could spend about twelve hours in church. Writing of herself in the third person, Kempe wrote that "she was slandered and reproved by many people, because she kept so strict a life," and, because of her zealousness, the church threatened to burn her as a heretic. But she also found many followers and became a minor celebrity in Europe. She traveled throughout England and to Jerusalem, Rome, Germany, and the Baltic states, preaching and reproving the local church officials for negligence and immorality.

## 3

**REBECCA COX JACKSON,** *born Rebecca Cox near Philadelphia, Pennsylvania, in 1795, exact date unknown.* Like Margery Kempe, Rebecca Cox Jackson was a mystic whose visions led her to renounce the pleasures of the flesh. But the two women were separated by an ocean and by about four centuries, and Jackson's religious rebellion took a somewhat different form from Kempe's. She was born a free black, and, once married, she lived with her husband and her brother's family.

As a young woman Jackson began to "receive gifts and visions." She was mourning her illiteracy, a deficiency that she said "pierced my soul like a sword." But then "these words were spoken in my heart, 'Be faithful, and the time shall come when you can write.'" Later she heard another voice which said that God, "who learned the first man to read . . . can learn you." Her reaction was instantaneous: "I picked up my Bible, ran upstairs, opened it, and kneeled down with it pressed to my heart, prayed earnestly to the Almighty God if it was consisting to His holy will, to learn me to read His holy word. And when I looked on the word, I began to read."

She began to dream of miraculous powers which enabled her to fly, to talk with angels, to walk through walls, to heal the sick, and to make the sinful holy. She believed she could foretell the future. She felt she knew other people's thoughts. Her initial reaction was identical to Margery Kempe's: she refused to have sex with her husband. He was convinced that she was holy, but it didn't stop him from being angry, and he even tried to kill her.

So in 1830 Jackson left home "to travel some and speak to the people," and, like Kempe, she experienced some success as an itinerant preacher. She eventually joined the Shakers, a sect which practiced chastity and plainness and emphasized the motherhood as well as the fatherhood of God. From then on, Jackson lived and traveled with a younger Shaker, Rebecca Perot, and in the 1870s she founded her own Shaker settlement in Philadelphia. She also wrote her memoirs, *Gifts of Power,* which remains a moving description of her spiritual experiences.

# 4

**MARY ROWLANDSON,** *born Mary White in Somersetshire, England, in about 1635, exact date unknown.* Mary Rowlandson was one woman whose life was altered by a war between American Indians and the Puritan settlers of Massachusetts during the 1670s. The story of her captivity and what she perceived as her miraculous deliverance by God became one of the most famous tales of early America. Held captive by the Narragansett Indians for eleven weeks, Rowlandson traded knitting and sewing lessons for food and eventually resorted to eating almost anything to stay alive, including horses' hooves, raw liver, frogs, dogs, skunks, and even tree bark.

The proud, intelligent Rowlandson was held by the family of the Narragansett chief; she was beaten and threatened, but ultimately ransomed for £20, to be reunited with the remaining members of her family. Her fame rests on her published account of her ordeal, a book that went through several editions, despite its typically unwieldy title: *A Narrative of the Captivity, Sufferings, and Removes, of Mrs. Mary Rowlandson, Who was taken Prisoner by the Indians, with several others, and treated in the most barbarous and cruel manner by those vile Savages. With many other remarkable events during her travels. Written by her own Hand, for her private use, and now made public, at the earnest Desire of some friends, for the benefit of the afflicted.*

# 5

**MARILYN MONROE,** *dies at 36 in Los Angeles, California, 1962.* Everything about Monroe was larger than life—her innocence, her sexiness, her wretched childhood, her vulnerability, her flair for comedy, her strength, her weakness, and her death. Everyone has his or her own theory about Monroe—that she was a feminist, an idiot, a child in a woman's body, or simply an ordinary woman who was twisted and ravaged and finally broken by a demented industry and a demented society. Norman Mailer called her "a very Stradivarius of sex, so gorgeous, forgiving, humorous, compliant, and tender." Gloria Steinem praised "her energy and terrible openness to life." But Billy Wilder, who directed her in *Some Like It Hot* and *The Seven Year Itch,* said: "The question is whether Marilyn is a person at all or one of the greatest Du Pont products ever invented. She had breasts like

MARILYN MONROE: *Always posing.*

granite and a brain like Swiss cheese, full of holes."

There are a thousand legends and stories about her, attesting to her many real and imagined qualities. This story illustrates her kindness. It concerns Ella Fitzgerald, who was having trouble getting a booking in a Los Angeles nightclub. Monroe went to the nightclub's owner and promised that if he gave Fitzgerald a job, Monroe would come to every performance and sit in the front row. Fitzgerald got the job, Monroe kept her promise, and the club was packed every night.

# 6

**LOUELLA PARSONS,** *born Louella Oettinger in Freeport, Illinois, 1881.* Louella Parsons had been a reporter and movie scenario writer before she found her niche in 1914 when she began one of America's first film columns. She quickly became a recognized authority on the industry, and as movies—and stars—grew more popular and powerful, so did Parsons. In 1919, working for William Randolph Hearst's *New York American,* Parsons climbed up the ranks in her field. By 1925 she was movie editor for Hearst's Universal News Syndicate. The following year she went to Hollywood, and for nearly four decades, Parsons was as much a part of that town as cameras and exploitation. Using the power of print to make or break celebrities by creating or shattering myths about them, she exercised the rule of a not entirely benevolent monarch over the motion picture industry. Studios sent her expensive gifts at Christmas and no rising (or even established) star could afford to sneer at the gossip queen and the hundreds of publications which ran her column. Her influence was undeniable, partly because of her merciless pen and partly because of the variety of her informants, chief of whom was her third husband, Harry Martin, a Hollywood doctor with contacts in many offices and

labs. Through him Parsons was privy to a lot of private information —often before the stars themselves.

Martin died in 1951, and Parsons' career began to lose its luster. Her rival, Hedda Hopper, had attracted many readers who had tired of Parsons' poor grammar, factual errors, and ruthless manipulation of actors and studios. Parsons finally retired in 1964, a woman who had loved her work. "Hollywood is and has been my life," she said. She died in 1972, in Santa Monica, California.

# 7

**ELIZABETH GURLEY FLYNN,** *born in Concord, New Hampshire, 1890.* Flynn had one of the most extraordinary careers in the history of American political activism. It spanned nearly sixty years, three ideologies, and two continents. It began in 1906, when a friend introduced her to anarchists Emma Goldman and Alexander Berkman. To the horror of her socialist parents, she began to embrace anarchism, and they hurriedly brought her back into the socialist fold. She started speaking in public, and with her black hair, blue eyes, and natural eloquence, she was a popular orator. She soon drew such large crowds that she was arrested for blocking traffic.

From 1907 to 1926, Flynn devoted her life to socialism. She organized strikes and workers' defense groups, spoke throughout the country, publicized cases of injustice, and was arrested for conspiracy and espionage. She also helped to found the American Civil Liberties Union (ACLU). In 1908 she married John Archibald Jones, a miner and labor organizer, but the marriage was unhappy. By the time they were divorced in 1920, Flynn had taken a lover, Italian

anarchist Carlo Tresca; she lived with Tresca for twelve years, but this too was a stormy relationship and ended after Flynn's sister bore Tresca's child.

In 1926, heart trouble forced Flynn to retire. She remained impatiently confined for ten years, finally deciding to return to public life even if it killed her. She became a national organizer for the Communist party, worked for attention to women's issues, and wrote a feminist column for the *Daily Worker.* Widely respected within the party, she was elected to the national committee in 1938. In 1961 she became the first woman to serve as its national chairman. However, not all of her associates were taken with her conversion to Communism. In 1940 the ACLU asked her to resign from its executive board. She refused, and the organization expelled her, an action which was not reversed until 1976, long after her death on a visit to Moscow in 1964.

LIBRARY OF CONGRESS

ELIZABETH FLYNN: *She agitated for just about every radical cause.*

# 8

**ALICE KYTELER,** *born in Ireland in the thirteenth century, exact date unknown.* Also known as Dame Alice or Dame Kettle, Kyteler came to public attention in 1324, when she was accused of witchcraft. She had been married four times, and her first three husbands had died in supposedly mysterious circumstances. Her fourth husband, John le Poer, was still alive at the time, but he was "afflicted with a wasting disease," exactly the sort of ailment often attributed to witchcraft. The real issue seems to have been money; all of her husbands had left their estates to her and to her son, William Outlawe, and the rest of the potential heirs were furious.

Kyteler seems also to have had a powerful enemy, the Bishop of Ossory. For a long time she defied him and even tried to make counter-accusations against him. But local jealousy of her riches and the fact that she was an aging woman (and thus automatically a potential witch) worked against her. She was believed to have had a familiar, Filius Artis, who appeared to her as a cat, a dog, or a black man, and who was an incubus and her lover. She was said to have used sorcery to tell fortunes, to have renounced Christ, to have sacrificed cocks at crossroads, and to have prepared various charms and potions from such ingredients as chicken entrails, plants, spiders, worms, snakes, the brains of unbaptized babies, and various parts of corpses "all boiled in the skull of a beheaded robber over a fire of dark wood." One of her servants swore that Kyteler was a witch and admitted to participation in satanic rites at her direction. Kyteler was excommunicated and fled to England. The servant, who had no powerful friends and no wealth, was burned at the stake.

# 9

**CONCHITA CINTRÓN,** *born in Antofagasta, Chile, 1922.* The daughter of an Irish-American mother and a Puerto Rican father, Cintrón was raised in Peru. As a child she learned to ride horses for *rejoneo,* the Portuguese style of bullfighting, and at twelve she first appeared in the ring as a *rejoneadora.* Women fighting bulls on horseback were not unknown in the arena, but fighting on foot was less common, and in Spain women were forbidden to do so until 1973. Cintrón wanted to fight on foot.

She went to Mexico at seventeen, where women were allowed to be *toreras.* By 1943, she had fought in 211 bullfights and killed 401 bulls on foot, and by 1944 she had fought throughout South America. But in Europe her record was unimportant; only her sex mattered, and in Portugal, Spain, and France she encountered continued resistance to her determination to fight on foot.

By 1949, Cintrón had killed 800 bulls on horseback and 400 on foot. In that year, she married a Portuguese nobleman who appreciated her beauty, intelligence, and daring, and she said farewell to the arena. But first she gave a final performance, in Spain. She rode in on her horse as the law demanded, then suddenly broke the rules. She dismounted, proved she could fight on foot by executing a perfect set of passes, and then dropped her sword, allowing the bull to live. She was immediately arrested, but the crowd was so stirred by her performance and so determined to riot if she were penalized that she was freed. She retired to Lisbon where she has raised several children and worked as a writer, a diplomatic attaché, and a dog breeder.

# 10

**ELLA BLOOR,** *dies at 89 in Richlandtown, Pennsylvania, 1951.* Ella Bloor was arrested more than thirty times during her life. At seventy-two she was charged with assault and inciting to riot. She had eight children and was married three times, to a lawyer named Lucien Ware, a socialist named Louis Cohen, and a farmer and Communist politician named Andrew Omholt. Her last name, Bloor, came from a man she never married and hardly knew.

The year was 1906, a year of transition for Bloor. In the past lay her work for women's rights and temperance and her recent conversion to socialism. In the future lay twelve years of work for socialism and labor unions, efforts on behalf of coal miners, campaigns for public office in New York and Connecticut, persecution by her government after World War I, disenchantment with socialism and adoption of communism, efforts to free Sacco and Vanzetti, a cross-country hitch-hiking tour for the *Daily Worker* at age sixty-three, and a visit to the Soviet Union as an honored guest on the twentieth anniversary of the October Revolution. And all this was made possible by the events of 1906.

Her friend Upton Sinclair had recently published *The Jungle,* a novel which exposed the shocking conditions in Chicago's meat-packing industry. The book had sparked a government investigation, but Sinclair wanted someone he trusted to help the officials with their inquiry. He asked Bloor to go into the meat-packing plants, verify his claims, and publish her findings. She agreed, even though the assignment was potentially dangerous. A potter, Richard Bloor, was sent along as a bodyguard. This measure, while securing Ella's safety, endangered her reputation, and Sinclair advised her to use the name Bloor and so make it look as if she and Bloor were married. Her report on the working conditions in meat-packing plants became famous, and she became famous as well—not as Ella Reeve (her birth name), Ella Ware, Ella Cohen, or Ella Omholt, but as Ella Bloor.

# 11

**LAVINIA FONTANA,** *dies at about 62 in Rome, Italy, 1614.* Born in Bologna in 1552, Fontana was the daughter of an artist, but she was destined to be a far better painter than her father. She quickly learned all that he could teach her and burst onto the Italian art scene in the 1570s. Noblemen were eager to have her paint their portraits, partly because her use of color and detail were exquisite, and partly because a woman artist was something of a novelty.

Some of these noblemen even proposed marriage, but Fontana universally refused them, not because she disliked them, but because she felt it unfitting that a woman of common birth should marry so well. Needless to say, such

LAVINIA FONTANA: *Famous for her humility and her deft brushwork.*

class-conscious views won her many admirers among the nobility, as did her famous humility. In the end, Fontana did marry, and it seems that she was wise to refuse her wealthy suitors. She married a fellow painter, Gian Paolo Zappi, who was quick to realize his wife was more talented and better known than he. He abandoned his own career to care for their eleven children (only three of whom survived to adulthood), leaving Fontana as the sole breadwinner.

It was a sound decision. Fontana acquired not only private commissions but public ones as well. Her portraits fetched higher prices than Van Dyck's, and three popes were among her patrons. By the time she died, she had studios in Rome and Bologna, was something of an art collector herself, and had been elected to the Roman Academy, a very unusual honor for a woman.

# 12

**RADCLYFFE HALL,** *born Margaret Radclyffe Hall in Bournemouth, England, 1880.* Hall wrote short stories, several volumes of poetry, and several novels, but she is primarily remembered for her lifestyle and for *The Well of Loneliness,* a novel she wrote in 1928. *The Well* made her notorious, since it was one of the first works of fiction to deal explicitly (if rather misleadingly) wth lesbianism. When it was published, there was an instant outcry from self-righteous public officials, who tried her for obscenity and suppressed the book. Testimonials from several authors, including E. M. Forster and Virginia Woolf, did no good; the book was regarded as having no literary merit and banned. One suspects that the apoplectic public officials were delighted to have an excuse to punish Hall, who wore short hair, called herself "John," lived with women all her life, and had plenty of money of her own—who, in short, was both unfeminine and utterly independent of men.

# 13

**ANNIE OAKLEY,** *born Phoebe Anne Moses in Darke County, Ohio, 1860.* When Oakley was a little girl, her father died, leaving behind a hungry family and a mortgaged farm. Oakley, legend has it, remedied both ills by shooting game. Her family ate what it could and paid off the mortgage by selling the rest.

By her teens, she was a good enough shot to enter a shooting contest in Cincinnati. There she defeated a marksman of some renown, Frank Butler. Far from feeling humiliated by his loss, Butler was thrilled to meet his match. Within a year, he married Oakley and took her on tour with him. It was about then she adopted the stage name "Annie Oakley." She was quite a shot. It seemed she could hit anything, including moving glass balls, cigarettes held in Butler's lips, dimes thrown into the air, and the thin edges of playing cards. Before long, it became obvious that she was not only a better shot than Butler, but a more popular performer as well, so he bowed out of the act and became his wife's manager.

Oakley's career was a fairly long one, although it might have been

RADCLYFFE HALL: *A cris de coeur for acceptance of lesbianism.*

longer. In 1885, after some work in a circus, she joined the Buffalo Bill Wild West Show. It was her home for sixteen years, and it took her throughout the United States and to Canada and Europe. She was presented to Queen Victoria, and she shot a cigarette from the mouth of a German prince who later became Kaiser Wilhelm II. In 1901, however, her career came to a sudden stop. Injuries sustained in a train crash left her temporarily paralyzed, and she left the show. As soon as she recovered, she began touring again, but it wasn't the same. She joined Buffalo Bill once more for his last tour in 1917, taught trapshooting, and gave marksmanship demonstrations to American troops, then retired in 1922.

# 14

**ADELAÏDE LABILLE-GUIARD,** *born Adélaïde Labille, in France, 1749, exact date unknown.* Labille-Guiard's talent for drawing surfaced early, so she was given lessons in painting by a miniaturist. In 1769 she married a clerk, Louis Guiard, but she did not interrupt her training. In fact, when the marriage quickly turned sour, her work became all the more important. She studied hard, taking more lessons in oils from the son of her old tutor, and in 1774, she exhibited at the Académie de San Luc in Paris. Soon she was well known and admired, especially for her excellent series of portraits of academicians.

Labille-Guiard was never as famous as her chief rival, Marie Elizabeth Vigée-Lebrun, but many think she was a better artist. At any rate, she did achieve official recognition for her skill; she and Vigée-Lebrun became members of the Académie Royale on the same day, May 31, 1783. And she was admirable for reasons other than her deftness with a brush. Her dedication to the causes of women was deep, passionate, and unswerving. She took a number of female pupils, organized a strong network of women artists in Paris, and lobbied for state-subsidized art education for women. In 1785, she led a protest against the Académie's refusal to allow more than four women to be members at any one time, and, when that failed, she held her own exhibition with a group of women, only to be scourged by the critics. She also broke a long-standing tradition when, in 1795, she secured an apartment in the previously all-male Louvre.

# 15

**EDNA FERBER,** *born in Kalamazoo, Michigan, 1885.* Ferber was one of the most popular authors of the twentieth century. Her books sold hundreds of thousands of copies in the days before book clubs, and her plays, written in collaboration with George S. Kaufman, were equally succesful. Her 1926 novel, *Show Boat,* was adapted for the musical stage in 1927 and is probably still playing somewhere right now. And several of her novels, including *So Big, Cimmaron, Saratoga Trunk* and *Giant,* were made into profitable movies.

Unfortunately, Ferber got little respect from critics, partly because she didn't write about the "right" things. Socialism and attacks on American society were all the rage in literary circles, but Ferber was content simply to write about people who interested her, and she was able to do so even when her charac-ters' environments were completely alien to her.

She was also overlooked because she wrote primarily about female protagonists. When her first collection of stories, *Buttered Side Down,* was published, critics thought that it had been written by a man using a woman's name. Even more importantly, no one realized that Ferber simply liked women and liked to write about them.

The critics' opinions didn't really matter, though. Ferber loved what she did for a living, she made a lot of money at it, and she was assertive, ambitious, strong, and unconventional enough to have been one of her own heroines. She had a quick pride, a deep pride in herself and her Jewish heritage, and absolutely no interest in marriage. "Being an old maid is like death by drowning," she wrote in 1939, "a really delightful sensation after you cease to struggle."

# 16

**ETHEL BARRYMORE,** *born in Philadelphia, Pennsylvania, 1879.* Like many great actresses, Ethel Barrymore came from a theatrical family. However, she did not begin in children's roles as many actors' children did; her childhood was spent with her grandmother and at Catholic boarding schools. In 1894, in need of money, she made her stage debut in Montreal as Julia in Richard Brinsley Sheridan's *The Rivals.* From that moment on, she belonged heart and soul to the profession. In a way, acting owned her, and it wouldn't let her go—not when she married, not when she had three children (she simply took them on tour with her), not when her career slumped after her separation and divorce, and not when she nearly died of pneumonia in 1944. She tried to quit acting in 1936, but NBC offered her a radio series, and she couldn't resist. She gave her last theatrical performance in 1950.

American entertainment industry, eqully capable of playing a nun or a black woman and able to age believably from nineteen to seventy over the course of two hours.

## 17

**MAE WEST,** *born in Brooklyn, New York, 1892.* She was known as "the Queen of Sex." Conservative publisher William Randolph Hearst wanted Congress to legislate against her. In 1935, she was the highest-paid woman in the United States and the second-highest-paid person—ironically, only Hearst made more money. (With characteristic foresight, she used her money to invest in Los Angeles real estate.) Her Broadway shows *Sex, The Pleasure Man,* and *The Constant Sinner* were stopped by the police, panned by critics, and loved by audiences; *Sex* earned her a five hundred dollar fine and a ten-day prison sentence for "corrupt[ing] the morals of youth and others." *The New York Times* said of *The Constant Sinner:* "Seldom has fouler talk been heard on the Broadway stage, even in these frank and forward times." West's movies were outstanding until the censors began chopping them to pieces, and it was she who discovered the young Gary Grant walking along a studio street. "If he can talk," she said, "I'll take him." She was, without a doubt, one of the most quotable people of the twentieth century:

"Too much of a good thing can be wonderful."

'Between two evils I always choose the one I have never tried before."

"When women go wrong, men go right after them."

"I'm a girl who lost her reputation and never missed it."

"I used to be snow white, but I drifted."

ETHEL BARRYMORE: *The theater was her life.*

Her career then moved to film and television; she made more than twenty movies, won an Academy Award for best supporting actress, and appeared on both dramatic and comedy-variety shows on TV. She seemed a permanent fixture of the

MAE WEST: *The common
denominator of her original scripts was
not sex, not comedy, but the reality that
she, and not her leading man, always
had the upper hand.*

to the United Nations. Within a
span of fifteen years, she served as
ambassador to six countries: Ireland, Spain, Mexico, Great Britain,
the Soviet Union (where she was
treated as any other ambassador
would have been), and the United
States (where she was always seated
with the ambassadors' wives). She
was the first person in the world to
hold three ambassadorial posts
simultaneously. She worked to find
a solution to the conflict in Korea,
and in 1953 she became the first
woman to serve as president of the
United Nations General Assembly.
A complete list of Pandit's accomplishments would impinge on
the space needed for the remaining
August celebrants.

# 18

**VIJAYA PANDIT,** *born Vijaya
Lakshmi Nehru in Allahabad, Uttar
Pradesh, India, 1900.* Pandit's list
of achievements calls for a lot of
ink and humility. The following is
just an abbreviated list to suggest
how important this woman was,
and how dedicated she was to her
nation. She began her political
career working in Mahatma Gandhi's independence movement, for
which she was repeatedly arrested
and imprisoned. She was active in
local and provincial government,
was a member of the national
assembly, and eventually served as
the governor of Maharashtra, the
largest state in India. From 1946 to
1951 she led the Indian delegation

# 19

**JEHENNA DE BRIGUE and
MACETTE DE RUILLY,** *die in
Paris, France, 1391.* Most of the
witch trials in Europe began
because someone, or many people,
suffered misfortunes and looked for
a witch as the cause. But in this
case the trouble started because an
alleged witch *helped* her accuser.
The trial was also significant
because it was the first witchcraft
trial in Europe to be conducted in a
secular, rather than an ecclesiastical, court.

It began in 1390, when one Jean
de Ruilly accused his thirty-four-
year-old neighbor, Jehenne de
Brigue, of witchcraft. How did he
know? Because he had been ill and
had gone to her for help. She performed a ritual to protect him from
witchcraft and reportedly allowed
two toads to suck from her breasts.
The ceremony apparently worked,
but Ruilly, for reasons unknown,
accused his savior of sorcery.

When she was arrested, Brigue
claimed only that she was acquainted with a witch named
Marion who had taught her a few
charms. She later made a fuller
confession, saying her aunt had
taught her to summon the devil,
whom she called Haussibut. Brigue

was sentenced to be burned, but since she appeared to be pregnant, the execution was delayed.

After it was discovered she was not pregnant, Brigue appealed her case and the trial was reopened. She was stripped and tortured, at which point she made an interesting confession. She said she had been hired by Ruilly's wife, Macette, to bewitch him and poison him so that Macette could run away with her lover. Macette was duly arrested, and, after being tortured on the rack, she confessed to the charges. Sentence was soon passed—they were both "to be led to the Châtelet aux Halles, mitered as sorcerers, put in the pillory; then led to the Pig Market to be burned alive."

# 20

**ANNE HUTCHINSON,** *dies at 52 in Pelham Bay, New York, 1643.* When Anne Hutchinson was massacred by Indians in 1643, few people grieved. Instead, her death was regarded as a sign of divine justice and proof that God punished wicked, noisy, uppity women. What had she done to deserve such rejoicing at her demise? She had said salvation came only through the grace of God and not by means of good works. And she had said this to men as well as women.

She had come to Massachusetts in 1634. Her work as a midwife had brought her many contacts in the community, and soon she was holding religious meetings for the women of Boston, discussing sermons and offering her own interpretations of biblical passages. She became so popular and influential that eventually men began to attend the meetings as well, and within a few years she was addressing mixed groups of sixty to eighty Puritans per week. The local ministers felt deeply threatened by her, and they had her arrested in 1637 for heresy.

At her trial, under enormous pressure, Hutchinson proved calm, intelligent, and courageous, while at one point she enraged her judge, Governor John Winthrop, so badly that he shouted, "We do not mean to discourse with one of your sex." Although pregnant with her fourteenth child, she continued to foil her examiners' attempts to trap her in heretical or seditious statements.

Eventually, after months of imprisonment, questioning, and public pressure, Hutchinson broke down. She admitted her guilt, then suddenly retracted her confession and, in a violent outburst, cursed her judges and claimed that she'd spoken with God. That was all that was needed to condemn her.

Hutchinson was censured for her actions, which were "not tolerable nor comely in the sight of God nor fitting for your sex," and for her "eighty opinions, some blasphemous, some erroneous, and all unsafe." She was excommunicated and banished, but she took her dismissal with equanimity. She and her family left for Rhode Island, taking thirty-five families of followers with them. After her husband's death, Hutchinson moved to New York, where she met her end at the hands of the Indians.

# 21

**ELIZABETH BATHORY,** *dies at about 54 in Castle Cjesthe (now Cachtice), Transylvania, Hungary (now Rumania), in about 1614.* No matter how you look at it, Countess Elizabeth Bathory was a monster. Born in about 1560 to one of the richest, most powerful, and most thoroughly inbred families in Hungary, she was a bright child who was well educated even by male standards of the day. Although she was a noblewoman, married, and a mother of four, Bathory had enough idle time to murder more than six hundred female peasants—all of whom had been procured for her ostensibly as household help by other full-time servants. She chose her victims for their voluptuousness, and even in a society which condoned torture and considered peasants animals to be used or destroyed at the nobility's pleasure, Bathory was in a class by herself. It is said that rumors of her evil deeds influenced the Irish writer Bram Stoker in his creation of Dracula.

After selecting her victim, the countess would find an excuse for discipline, then murder the woman by any of several methods—bludgeoning, dragging her naked into the snow and pouring cold water on her until she froze, lighting pieces of paper stuck between her toes, ripping her flesh with her teeth, or torturing her by means even more horrible.

Because of her noble position, the few who knew of her inhuman behavior did nothing. But she made three fatal mistakes. She ran afoul of the Hungarian king over money, she began killing noblewomen, and she kept a diary of her killings. She was arrested and escaped execution, but was walled into a tower of her castle where she was fed through a crack in the wall for four years until she died.

# 22

**DOROTHY PARKER,** *born Dorothy Rothschild Parker in West End, New Jersey, 1893.* When George Bernard Shaw met actress Ruth Gordon in England, he questioned her about only one American—Dorothy Parker. Gordon replied that "Dorothy was pretty, small, dark-haired, loved fellers, fellers loved her, said memorable things, said cruel things, drank a lot, went to parties." "He was amazed," Gordon said, "and had imagined she looked like a schoolteacher." That's a pretty good summary of what Dorothy Parker was or seemed to be, although it leaves out most of the bitterness and pain. She tried more than once to kill herself, spent money carelessly, and drank far too much. Parker did indeed love "fellers," but she always seemed to pick the wrong ones. Her first marriage ended in divorce, her affairs with young men all ended in misery for her, and she had an on-and-off relationship with

DOROTHY PARKER: *A witty conversationalist, an unforgettable writer.*

her second husband, Alan Campbell. She married him in 1933, divorced him in 1947, remarried him in 1950, separated from him in 1953, and was reunited with him in 1956.

Despite the hectic, up-and-down lifestyle, Parker did say and write such wonderful things. She wrote marvelous stories and screenplays, but it was her snatches of doggerel and her one-liners that made her famous. In fact, if Mae West had a rival for quotability, it was Dorothy Parker. When asked by a stranger if she was Dorothy Parker, she said "Yes, do you mind?"

# 23

**CLARA GEISSLER,** *burned at 69 in Gelnhausen, Germany, 1597.* It wasn't easy being an old woman during the witch-hunting crazes in Europe. Old women were automatically suspect. Rumors and suspicion were grounds for arrest, and arrest was grounds for torture. Technically, a person could only be tortured three times without the introduction of new evidence, but in practice the limit was meaningless.

Clara Geissler was one woman who got trapped in the merciless system. In 1597 she was arrested on suspicion of witchcraft and subjected to the preliminary torture which usually consisted of threats, drawing on the rack or the ladder, whipping, and use of thumbscrews. The prisoner was stripped before torture, partly for purposes of humilation and partly to prevent the use of concealed talismans. At this point, many female prisoners were raped.

Next came the really important part—getting the witch to name her accomplices. The thumbscrews were applied again, but Geissler refused to implicate anyone. So her torturers moved to strappado, in which the accused was lifted on a rope and dropped, and squassation, the same procedure with weights tied to the victim's feet. Geissler broke under the torture. She screamed and confessed to whatever her inquisitors demanded. Geissler then named twenty other women who had been with her at her alleged witches' sabbats.

As soon as the torture was over, Geissler recanted and swore she had no knowledge of the women's involvement in any such activity, but the women she had accused were arrested and tortured as well, and when one of them confessed, Geissler was tortured again. Another confession and recantation was followed by yet another round of torture, during which Geissler died. Her judges took no responsibility for her death, claiming the devil had wrung her neck.

# 24

**BASUA MAKIN,** *born Basua Pell, in Sussex, England, possibly in 1608, exact date unknown.* Basua Makin was one of the first Western feminists, yet very little is known about her. Her date of birth is variously given as 1608 and 1612, and her name is often spelled "Bathshua." Makin received a fairly thorough education and at age nine she understood Latin, Greek, French, Hebrew, and Italian. In the 1640s she was hired as a tutor to the daughters of King Charles I, but the English Civil War interrupted her career.

She later ran a school for girls. Half of her students' time was devoted to the traditional feminine accomplishments—dancing, music, singing, writing and keeping ac-counts. The other half was spent on more radical pursuits—Latin, French, Greek, Hebrew, Italian, Spanish, and philosophy. This curriculum required some apologies, and Makin hurried to make them, insisting her goal was not "female preeminence." On the contrary, she assured worried parents, a well educated woman would merely be able to achieve a better understanding of her divinely ordained inferiority.

As Makin grew older, however, she grew less apologetic. In 1663 she called for an inclusive academic course of studies for girls, and in 1675 she published her official statement on the subject, the document for which she is remembered. It has, as most pamphlets did at the time, a rather unwieldy title: *Essay to Revive the Antient Education of Gentlewomen In Religion, Manners, Arts, and Tongues—With an Answer to the Objections against* *this Way of Education.* (Note that the essay is addressed to "Gentlewomen." The education of the lower classes was still considered unthinkable.)

# 25

**ALTHEA GIBSON,** *born in Silver, South Carolina, 1927.* When she was thirteen years old, Althea Gibson began playing tennis. She had only one goal, but it was a big one: to be "the best woman tennis player who ever lived." She began by winning the New York Negro Girls' Singles Championships in 1943. Five years later, she won the national title for black women, and she continued to win it for the next ten years. But segregated play wasn't the route to fame.

In 1950 Gibson entered the American Lawn Tennis Association championships. She was the first black player to do so. In 1951 she became the first black American to play at Wimbledon. Still, breaking ground was not the same thing as winning, and she kept trying. Throughout the 1950s, her game improved, but in 1956 she truly blossomed. Everything came together, and she began to win important titles, including the French and Italian singles championships and the Wimbledon doubles. In both 1957 and 1958 she won the U.S. singles title and the Wimbledon singles and doubles titles, making her the first black to win the singles championship at Wimbledon. She wrote an autobiography called *I Always Wanted to Be Somebody*, played twice on the U.S. Wightman Cup team, played for a few more years, and then explored several other careers. She sang, played professional golf, worked with a tennis program for inner-city children, ran for public office, and served as New Jersey's state athletic commissioner. In 1971, she was inducted into the National Lawn Tennis Hall of Fame.

# 26

**ELIZABETH CHUDLEIGH,** *dies at about 68 in Paris, France, 1788.* Chudleigh is often described as an "adventuress" by profession. No other name suits her better. Born near London in 1720, she was a beautiful girl who, at twenty-three, became a lady-in-waiting in the royal court, where she was pursued by a number of men.

After one ill-fated love affair, Chudleigh turned to a naval lieutenant, the Honorable Augustus John Hervey. As a royal-lady-in-waiting, she was supposed to be chaste, so she married Hervey secretly. She also managed to hide her subsequent pregnancy and the birth of her child, who was quickly sent away to a nurse and died shortly thereafter. The marriage soured and the couple separated.

Meanwhile she became the talk of the Court, because of her shockingly revealing dresses, her fashionable parties, and King George II's infatuation with her. The crowning glory was her affair with Evelyn Pierrepont, the 2nd duke of Kingston.

Chudleigh wanted to marry Pierrepoint, and he wanted to marry her, but Hervey was still most inconveniently alive. She dragged Hervey into court, got him to swear that they'd never been married, and got a legal declaration to that effect. Then she married the duke of Kingston. All went well until he died, and what should have been a blessing—his will bequeathing his fortune to her—turned out to be her downfall. She was traveling in Italy when she heard that Pierrepont's would-be heirs had discovered the marriage to Hervey and were suing for bigamy. Unfortunately, she didn't have enough cash on hand to get back to England for her trial, so she robbed a banker at gunpoint and fled.

The return to England didn't help her. She was found guilty of bigamy and stripped of the property she'd inherited. Ironically, at about this time Hervey inherited a title, making her countess of Bristol. Chudleigh had had enough of England, enough of Pierrepoint's heirs, and enough of Hervey. She left for France and lived there, in Italy, and most often in Russia, where she was courted by a prince, became a favorite of Catherine the Great, and opened her own brandy distillery.

# 27

**KATHARINE DEXTER McCOR-MICK,** *born Katharine Dexter in Dexter, Michigan, 1875.* This little known, but influential, philanthropist was the daughter of a wealthy Chicago lawyer who died in 1889, leaving her in possession of a fortune. She pursued her education, graduating from M.I.T. in 1904, with a B.S. in biology, and becoming the second woman ever to graduate from that school. In that same year she married a childhood friend, Stanley McCormick, a son of Cyrus McCormick, founder of International Harvester.

Her brief happiness was soon shattered, however, when it was learned her husband was a schizophrenic, and within two years he needed to be hospitalized. In 1909 he was declared legally incompetent, which left Katharine, again, with a lot of money and no one to tell her how to spend it. She chose to give it to worthy, but unpopular, causes—supporting the recently imprisoned Margaret Sanger, and helping smuggle diaphragms into the United States. McCormick donated heavily to Sanger's American Birth Control League (later Planned Parenthood), and it was through this association that she helped finance research which led to the creation of the first oral hormonal contraceptive—the pill.

Curiously enough, researchers she'd hired to help control her husband's illness noticed the relationships between hormone treatments and fertility. McCormick gave almost two million dollars to the contraceptive project, and, upon her death in 1967, left a five-million-dollar-endowment to Planned Parenthood.

# 28

**MOTHER SETON,** *born Elizabeth Ann Bayley in New York City, 1774.* It's not every New Yorker who can grow up to be a saint. Frances Cabrini was the first American citizen to become a saint, but Elizabeth Seton was the first native-born American to achieve that honor. She was born to a prominent colonial family—a Protestant family—and spent her youth dispensing charity and writing about spiritual matters. In 1794, she was married, apparently advantageously, to a merchant named William Seton, but he suffered a financial and physical collapse and took his family to Italy, where he hoped to recover. There, in 1803, he died, leaving his wife alone and in poverty.

Somehow, she made her way back to New York, and two years later she converted to Catholicism. Her family and friends shunned her, and she found herself unable to get a job because of her conversion. She applied for help to a priest, who found her work as the head of a Baltimore parochial school. Seton quickly proved herself to be an able

administrator. She was appointed superior, trained new teachers, shaped a new teaching order of nuns, wrote textbooks, wrote and translated spiritual works, continued her charitable efforts, and built the foundations of the American parochial school system. She died in 1821 and was canonized in 1975.

# 29

**INGRID BERGMAN,** *born in Stockholm, Sweden, 1915.* Toward the end of her life, Ingrid Bergman told *The New York Times:* "I have never regretted what I did. I regret things I didn't do. All my life I've done things at a moment's notice. Those are the things I remember. I was given courage, a sense of adventure and a little bit of humor." She needed all three. Her mother died when Bergman was three, and her father when she was

thirteen. She was transferred to the care of a maiden aunt who also died, six months later. Her next guardian was an uncle who disapproved of his niece's predilection for the theatre, and it was only with much pleading that she obtained his permission to study at the Royal Dramatic Theatre School.

Soon Bergman was playing leading roles, and in 1936 she appeared in the movie *Intermezzo,* which led to a Hollywood contract. Arriving in America with her husband, Peter Lindstrom, she immediately began to break the rules. The studio let her keep her own name, very unusual considering the times and the German sound of the name "Bergman." Cameramen found that her extraordinary beauty allowed them to shoot her from almost any angle and without makeup. Publicized as a fresh, wholesome, innocent girl, she won a huge popular following with *Casablanca, For*

INGRID BERGMAN: *No regrets.*

*Whom the Bell Tolls, Gaslight* (for which she won her first Oscar), *Notorious,* and *Joan of Arc.*

In 1949, everything changed. She went to Italy to make *Stromboli* with director Roberto Rossellini, leaving her husband and ten-year-old daughter, Pia, behind. While in Italy, she began an affair with Rossellini; when she discovered she was pregnant, she wrote Lindstrom that she wouldn't be coming back to the United States.

Bergman's pregnancy got more press than the hydrogen bomb. In March, 1950, she was denounced on the Senate floor as "a powerful influence for evil," and a short-lived motion called for the licensing of actresses to prevent them from behaving immorally. Raising a question on her radio show that was more hilarious than hysterical, gossip columnist Louella Parsons cried, "Ingrid, Ingrid! Whatever got into you?"

Things reversed themselves in the late 1950s, when she ended her marriage to Rosselini and found herself "forgiven" by the public. *The Inn of the Sixth Happiness* brought an upsurge in her popularity, *Anastasia* won her a second Oscar, and *Murder On the Orient Express* won her a third. In 1981, just a year before her death, she portrayed Golda Meir in the television film, *A Woman Called Golda,* for which she received a posthumous Emmy Award.

# 30

**MARY SHELLEY,** *born Mary Wollstonecraft Godwin in London, England, 1797.* Mary Shelley got off to a bad start. Her mother died after giving birth; for her entire life Mary Shelley mourned her motherlessness. At age eight, she began reading the works of her radical, outspoken mother, Mary Wollstonecraft, taking the books to the St. Pancras graveyard, and sitting on her mother's grave while she read. She often took her meals there and spoke to the dead mother she missed so much. She had already

done some writing of her own, based partly on the works of her mother, and partly on the sound education given her by her well-known father, the radical William Godwin.

In 1812, Mary met a student of her father's—Percy Bysshe Shelley. She was fourteen and he was twenty. Although he was married, he was drawn to Mary and they eloped together in 1814 to the Continent, without his getting a divorce. They led an active life, studying, writing, avoiding creditors and their reputation. In 1816 Shelley's wife committed suicide, allowing him to marry Mary. They had become close with Lord Byron, with whom they'd begun a game of inventing ghost stories. Mary's creation—*Frankenstein*—was well received by the public and it hasn't gone out of print since.

For most of the rest of her life, it was she who was famous and her husband who was considered a rather obscure scribbler, although in time their positions would change. In part, this was due to Mary's own efforts, after his untimely death by drowning in 1822, to glorify his reputation, and to publicize his poetry.

MARY PUTNAM JACOBI: *When she enrolled in medical school, her father advised, "Be a lady from the dotting of your i's to the color of your ribbons— and if you must be a doctor and a philosopher, be an attractive and agreeable one."*

# 31

**MARY PUTNAM JACOBI,** *born Mary Corinna Putnam in London, England, 1842.* Against their better judgment, Jacobi's parents allowed her to pursue her dream of a medical career, and she graduated from the New York College of Pharmacy in 1863 and the Women's Medical College of Pennsylvania in 1864. She was generous, helpful, and compassionate, and by American standards she was also well educated, but she didn't feel qualified to practice medicine yet. Instead, she went to Paris, and after two years of trying for acceptance, enrolled in the École de Médécine, graduated with high honors and an award for her thesis.

In 1871, Jacobi returned to the United States and took a professorship at Elizabeth Blackwell's Women's Medical College of the New York Infirmary. For twenty-five years, she did volunteer work in poor areas, urged her students to scientific excellence, worked for birth control and woman suffrage, and helped to establish the Working Women's Society (later the New York Consumer League). Through her happy relationship with pediatrician Abraham Jacobi, whom she married in 1873, she disproved the myth that a woman could not be both a good doctor and a good wife. She also published more than one hundred articles, one of which, "The Question of Rest for Women during Menstruation," won Harvard's prestigious Boylston Prize for medical literature. In it she argued forcefully against the commonly held belief that women were incapacitated and irrational while menstruating (and therefore unfit for important and well-paid jobs).

Jacobi became a popular speaker and a symbolic figure. Previously all-male hospitals invited her to serve on their staffs, and she achieved her childhood dreams "to be spoken of with affection" and to do "great things and glorious deeds."

ELIZABETH I: *"I know I have the body of a weak and feeble woman, but I have the heart and stomach of a king. . . ."*

LIBRARY OF CONGRESS

# SEPTEMBER

## 1

**LILY TOMLIN,** *born Mary Jean Tomlin in Detroit, Michigan, 1937.* Tomlin began doing stand-up comedy at a Manhattan nightclub and performing at off-Broadway clubs while working as a secretary. These appearances led to a spot on "The Merv Griffin Show," which in turn got her a job on "Laugh-In" in 1969.

For four years, Tomlin created crazy, lovable characters for "Laugh-In," including the two for which she is most famous, Edith Ann, the sassy kid, and Ernestine, the 1940s-style telephone operator. (Bell Telephone offered her $500,000 for a series of Ernestine commercials, which she flatly refused.) By the time Tomlin left the show, she was a celebrity, and she turned with ease to film and Broadway. Unfortunately, some of her films, especially *The Incredible Shrinking Woman* and *Moment by Moment*, were unimpressive, but she more than made up for them in *All Of Me* and *Nine to Five,* and in her one-woman Broadway hits, *Appearing Nightly* and *The Search for Signs of Intelligent Life in the Universe.* A committed, eloquent feminist and an admirable woman, Tomlin relies for her humor on the strength and warmth of her characterizations rather than self-deprecation or insult.

## 2

**BRYHER,** *born Annie Winifred Ellerman in Margate, Kent, England, 1894.* Bryher was the soul of contradiction. Twice married, she was a lesbian. Plain in appearance and shy, she was also charismatic and physically compelling. A central figure in the expatriate society of Paris between the world wars and a writer in her own right, she is remembered, when she is remembered at all, as the literary patron of poets Hilda Doolittle (known as H.D.) and Marianne Moore and as a player in a complex set of relationships.

And those relationships do make *awfully* good copy. Here's a relatively simplified version: Bryher's father was the richest man in England. As a result, she lived under nearly constant supervision and faced enormous pressure to be a good girl and help pass on the accumulated wealth to future generations. Unfortulately, Bryher hated supervision with a vengeance and wasn't particularly fond of men—at least not the way daddy would have liked. She did, however, have a strong interest in H.D., a poet and the wife of poet and translator Richard Aldington. In 1918, after memorizing all of H.D.'s book, *Sea Garden,* Bryher approached her, and they began a relationship that lasted forty-three years—far longer than H.D.'s marriage.

Bryher felt constrained by her family's expectations, but on a trip to the United Stated, she found a potential answer to her problems. There she met Robert McAlmon, a gay man who needed Bryher's money as badly as she needed a cover for her affair with H.D. So, in 1921, she married McAlmon. Things worked fairly smoothly, but after six years Bryher divorced McAlmon and instituted another marriage of convenience with Kenneth MacPherson, a writer. Now things get a little complicated. Bryher, H.D., and MacPherson all worked together in various ways; H.D. sometimes wrote for MacPherson's film magazine, *Close-Up,* and the three often wrote and directed movies together. They were also personally involved—not only was H.D. Bryher's lover, but MacPherson's as well. Furthermore, when H.D. divorced her husband in 1938, Bryher and MacPherson adopted H.D.'s daughter.

Throughout all this spectacular juggling of relationships, Bryher deliberately made herself appear as unremarkable as possible. She was already slim, short, and shy; to this she added a nondescript wardrobe and an absolute refusal to wear makeup or to curl her hair. Nonetheless, she emerges even in offhand accounts as a woman one would like to know more about, and despite her attempts to seem plain, she did not always succeed. One of her friends, Sylvia Beach, said: "I couldn't keep my eyes off Bryher's: they were so blue—bluer than the sea or sky or even the Blue Grotto in Capri. More beautiful still was the expression in Bryher's eyes."

## 3

**PRUDENCE CRANDALL,** *born in Hopkinton, Rhode Island, 1803.* Prudence Crandall learned the hard way just how liberal her Connecticut neighbors were. Crandall was a white Quaker who established a successful school for girls in Canterbury, Connecticut. Early in 1833, she allowed a black student to join her class. Horrified, the white families withdrew their daughters from the school in an attempt to punish Crandall for her odd notions. They hadn't counted on her determination. She revamped her school, announcing she'd be teaching only "young ladies and little misses of color." Since there weren't many black girls of suitable age and means in Canterbury—or in Connecticut, for that matter—most of the pupils came from out of state. Next the city government passed the "Black Law," which prohibited the teaching of black children from other states.

Crandall was arrested, convicted, and imprisoned, but the funds of abolitionists from New York and Boston bought her some publicity, and ultimately she was acquitted on a technicality. Crandall continued to run her school, but vandalism and threats to her life finally defeated her, and she finally closed it and moved to Illinois. Not until 1886 did the state of Connecticut see fit to award her a small pension.

# 4

**MARY RENAULT,** *born Mary Challans in London, England, 1905.* Renault is one of the literary world's great secrets. Her historical novels are popular, highly entertaining, and glowing with authenticity. They also happen to be the private passion of many an academician. So why have they received almost no critical attention? It may be because the novels have no glaring, incomprehensible symbolism or central trauma for critics to elucidate. It may be because they deal explicitly, positively, and sensitively with homosexuality. Or it may be because she hasn't been dead long enough to be taken seriously.

None of these explanations by itself is enough to disqualify Renault from serious critical attention, but taken together they seem to have excluded her books from the ranks of "real" literature. It's a great pity; they deserve far more respect than they've gotten. The novels about Greece in particular, which include *The Last of the Wine, The King Must Die, The Bull from the Sea, Fire from Heaven,* and *The Persian Boy,* are well-researched, thoroughly convincing narratives about the ancient world. Renault had a tremendous gift for bringing poets, warriors, Olympians, musicians, dancers, courtesans, philosophers, landowners, wanderers, and kings to life, and for making the reader feel as if he or she had been raised in ancient Greece and was as well acquainted with its gods and heroes as any orator or fisherman.

# 5

**SARAH EDMONDS,** *dies at about 56 in La Porte, Texas, 1898.* Little is known of Edmonds' early life, but it is said that to escape an arranged marriage she ran away from home at fifteen disguised as a boy. When the Civil War began, she was in Flint, Michigan, calling herself Frank Thompson and selling Bibles. "Frank" joined Company F of the 2nd Michigan Infantry and fought in several battles, including Blackburn's Ford and the first Bull Run. At the Battle of Fredericksburg she served as an aide to Colonel Orlando M. Poe, and she did occasional intelligence work in Confederate territory "disguised" as a woman. In April 1863, for some unknown reason, she left the army, took the name Sarah Edmonds, and worked as a nurse. Two years later, she wrote a fictionalized account of her adventures, *Nurse and Spy in the Union Army,* which became extremely popular because of its astute mixture of violence and sentimentality.

# 6

**JANE ADDAMS,** *born in Cedarville, Illinois, 1860.* If Jane Addams had succeeded in becoming a doctor, she probably would not have been famous, but fortunately for Chicago's Nineteenth Ward, she never made it through medical school. She fell ill with a spinal complaint within a year of beginning medical studies and was forced to withdraw. At home she was made to rest, and she sank into invalidism, spending two years in a straight jacket made of whalebone, leather, and steel, enduring endless treatments and an operation.

Her family fussed and fussed over Jane's body, but her own accounts of this period reveal that the ailment was largely one of the mind. She had just finished a busy, energetic, blissfully happy college education and gone on to medical school, only to realize that it didn't make any difference. She was still a woman, and no matter what she did, she didn't feel anyone would take her seriously. She felt "purposeless and without ambition," and "a failure in every sense." In 1886 she wrote, "I am filled with shame that with all my apparent leisure I have nothing at all to do."

Then, on a trip to Europe, Addams had an inspiration. She returned to the United States filled with exuberance and health, and in 1889, on the corner of Polk and Halstead Streets in Chicago, she and a friend opened Hull House. It was meant to provide social and political services for the district's varied immigrant populations. To counteract the influence of the saloons and the powers of political bosses, she established classes, social events, and clubs. She ran a boarding house, a nursery, a meeting room for women's trade unions, a gymnasium, Chicago's first public playground, and an information network that linked the community to doctors, clergymen, hospitals, charitable organizations, and summer programs for children.

By the early 1890s, a thousand

JANE ADDAMS: *Champion of the "homeless, friendless, and penniless."*

people participated in Hull House programs every week, and there were ninety volunteers. By 1910, buildings belonging to the project covered an entire block, and some of the most notable women of the time had served their apprenticeships there. Addams won the 1931 Nobel Peace Prize for her efforts on behalf of humanity.

# 7

**ELIZABETH I of England,** *born in Greenwich, England, 1538.* Henry VIII had three children when he died in 1547. The eldest two, Catholic Mary and Protestant Elizabeth, were barred fom the throne by tradition because of their sex. The youngest, Edward, was male, but in poor health. Henry left his kingdom to Edward with the stipulation that if Edward died without heirs, Mary would take the throne, and if she died without heirs, Elizabeth would follow.

Henry had hoped with all his heart his daughters would never be queens, not because he disliked them, but because he loved England. The little island nation was barely keeping itself indepen-dent. A woman on the throne would make England seem easy prey for powerful Spain or France.

In 1553, Edward died, and Mary took the throne. Elizabeth, who had been surrounded all her life by intrigue and suspicion, found her troubles were just beginning. Throughout Mary's five-year reign, Elizabeth was always under suspicion, partly because she was a focus for Protestant rebellions, and partly because Mary expected her to convert to Catholicism. Elizabeth spent a substantial portion of Mary's reign imprisoned in the Tower of London, and she narrowly escaped execution, but Mary died in 1558, and Elizabeth was proclaimed queen.

At her accession, Elizabeth had much to recommend her as a monarch. She was twenty-five, in the prime of youth and health, yet old enough not to be manipulated by her council as Edward had been. She was beautiful, charismatic, and canny, and her shows of temper could intimidate the bravest of men. She was good at choosing able advisers without regard to rank. She was intelligent, experienced in matters of intrigue, and fluent in Spanish, German, French, Italian, Greek, and Latin. Nonetheless, not everyone took her seriously at first.

While all England, and a host of royal foreign suitors waited to see who Elizabeth would marry, she kept them at bay. Meanwhile she suppressed rebellions in Ireland and the north of England, instituted currency reform and poor relief, stimulated trade, encouraged national pride, and supported Protestants in other countries. She made grand tours throughout England which increased her subjects' loyalty and cost the Crown nothing, since the expenses were paid by the lucky nobles at whose homes she stayed. She created an environment in which the arts flourished, and she sent adventurers to raid Spanish ships and to explore the New World. Most importantly, she maintained peace with both France and Spain for thirty years.

By the time she died in 1603,

UNIVERSITY OF ILLINOIS AT CHICAGO, THE UNIVERSITY LIBRARY, JANE ADDAMS MEMORIAL COLLECTION

Elizabeth was the living symbol of her nation. Her stubbornness, her vanity, her eighty wigs, and the cloth she stuffed in her lips to make it appear she still had teeth were all trifles. Her greatness, her dignity, and her courage were all that mattered. Her people loved her, and even Catholic rulers admired her. Henri IV of France said, "She only is a king! She only knows how to rule!" To the very end, she kept the majesty and wit that had kept her queen for forty-five years.

# 9

**REBECCA LEMP,** *dies in Nördlingen, Swabia, Germany, 1590.* In March, 1590, Rebecca Lemp was the respected wife of an accountant, Peter Lemp. She was the mother of six affectionate, intelligent children.

# 8

**LADY BRILLIANA HARLEY,** *born in Brill, the Netherlands, in 1600, exact date unknown.* Lady Harley might have lived a perfectly ordinary, happy life had the English Civil War not intervened. In 1623 she became the third wife of Sir Robert Harley, owner of Brampton Bryan Castle near Hereford, England. Here they raised a large family (they had seven children; Harley had nine others from his previous marriage) and were very content. Pious, well-educated, and affectionate, Lady Harley lavished love on her husband and children.

The Harleys sympathized with the Parliamentarians, and when the war broke out Harley went to London to take part in the brewing political disputes, leaving his wife in care of the castle. She followed the political developments closely, and took precautions to safeguard her family possessions. In December, 1642, Royalist troops ordered Lady Harley to surrender to them, but she refused. For six months, chivalry forbade them from attacking the lady, but on July 26, 1643, they began their siege, with a total of seven hundred men facing her tiny garrison. Lady Harley withstood three months of thrice-daily attacks, but finally in October she died from complications of a cold. Early in 1644, the defenders of her home capitulated, and although her family was unharmed, the castle was destroyed, and £13,000 worth of property she had worked so hard to save was seized.

LADY BRILLIANA HARLEY: *She defended her castle as bravely as any soldier.*

In April, because of the ambition of two local lawyers and a burgomaster, she was one of dozens of women arrested for witchcraft.

Her husband was away when Lemp was arrested, but at first she and her children were relatively untroubled and certain that justice and reason would prevail. Her children sent her food, money, and news, and assured her: "do not be worried about the housekeeping." Lemp sent a letter to her husband, pleading, "Don't hide thy face from me, thou knowest my innocence. In God's name, do not leave me in this anguish which is choking me." She believed she would not be tortured, "since I am not guilty of anything."

Peter Lemp believed his wife and stood by her during the months she was held in jail. However, her sanguine expectations of fair treatment were soon destroyed. She was tortured five times, and she finally confessed. Complaining of a heart "nearly broken," she tried to smuggle a note to her husband in which she marveled that God seemed not to hear her prayers and pleaded with her husband to send her some poison so she could commit suicide and escape another session of torture.

Her plea went unheard. The note was intercepted, and the lawyers merely added another charge to that of witchcraft—attempted suicide. They forced her to write a confession to her husband, but he didn't believe it. He wrote the court an eloquent defense of his wife's piety and innocence, but it was ignored. She was tortured again, and she was burned at the stake. Rebecca Lemp was not alone; in 1590, thirty-two highly respected women were burned as witches in Nördlingen.

# 10

**HILDA DOOLITTLE,** *born in Bethlehem, Pennsylvania, 1886.* Critical opinion is divided on Doolittle, or, as she called herself, H.D., but her poetry, with its classical and matriarchal elements, is certainly interesting, and her life is a perfect example of the expatriate artist in Europe. At fifteen, she met the sixteen-year-old Ezra Pound. He in turn introduced her to William Carlos Williams, who was struck by H.D.'s "bizarre" beauty and her "provocative indifference to rule and order." After a short stint at Bryn Mawr, during which she suffered a nervous breakdown, H.D. ignored her family's objections and became engaged to Ezra Pound.

She began writing and in 1911 sailed to Europe to join Pound and begin her career in earnest. Living primarily in England and Switzerland, she became a proponent of Pound's Imagist movement and signed a 1913 poem "H.D. Imagiste" at his suggestion. It was then she picked up "H.D." as a nickname. She met D. H. Lawrence, Havelock Ellis, William Butler Yeats, and poet and translator Richard Aldington, with whom she translated some Greek poetry. She decided not to marry Pound and to marry Aldington instead, and everyone, including Pound and her parents, seemed happy with this arrangement.

The World War I years proved particularly traumatic for H.D.; she had a miscarriage, Aldington was drafted, her marriage fell apart, her older brother was killed in the war, her father died, and she was stricken with double pneumonia. She gave birth to a daughter, Perdita, and left Aldington, although she was not divorced until 1938. It was at this point that she met the woman who she said "saved" her—Winifred Ellerman, who called herself Bryher, and whose friendship with H.D. is outlined in the entry for September 2. In her busy lifetime, H.D. was psychoanalyzed by Freud, wrote books about almost everyone she knew, suffered another nervous breakdown, and fell in love with an R.A.F. commander and a Haitian journalist.

# 11

**JOANNA BAILLIE,** *born in Lanarkshire, Scotland, 1762.* The daughter of a Presbyterian minister, Baillie led a confined life as a child, both because her father was strict and because she was physically delicate. Nevertheless, she was intelligent and brave, and she developed talents for music, drawing, mathematics, debating, and acting. She was especially good at extemporaneous speaking. In 1790, she became a minor celebrity when her collection of poems, *Fugitive Verses,* was publised, but it wasn't until 1798 that she achieved real fame. In that year, she began to publish her *Plays on the Passions.* Each of these blank verse plays focused on a particular emotion, and they instantly became the subject of a literary controversy. Some said it was wrong to isolate one emotion and devote a play to it. Others, including the great actress Sarah Siddons, enjoyed Baillie's works and begged for more.

Baillie was happy to oblige, and she wrote more plays and headed a literary circle in Hampstead. However, despite her fame, she suffered throughout her career from condescension and lefthanded compliments. At first, her works were attributed to her friend Sir Walter Scott. Even after she was firmly established as the writer, she had to endure such faint praise from critics, who admitted that, "with all their deficiencies," the dramas were undoubtedly "the best ever written by a woman."

# 12

**MARIA AGNESI,** *born in Milan, Italy, 1718, exact date unknown.* Agnesi was the eldest of twenty-one children. By the time she was nine it was clear she was a prodigy. She spoke Latin, Greek, French, and other languages and delivered a one-hour oration in Latin to an assembly of scholars. In her teens she studied math, which she enjoyed; tutored her brothers, which she didn't mind; and hosted her father's parties, which she hated. By nature she was shy, and only the demands of her father kept her from joining a convent.

Nevertheless, she was allowed to stop giving public demonstrations of her knowledge when her mother died. As the eldest daughter, Agnesi was duty-bound to care for the children left behind, and that she managed to continue her career at the same time is little short of astonishing. She turned to writing instead of speaking, and the two books she produced established her as one of the great thinkers of her time. The first, published in 1738, and entitled *Propositions of Philosophy,* contained 190 essays on philosophy, logic, mechanics, elasticity, celestial mechanics, and Newton's theory of universal gravitation. It also contained a plea for higher education for women.

The second of her works took her ten years to write. Entitled *Analytical Institutions,* it made use of her skill with languages to correlate the works of many authors. It also proposed new methods for algebra, geometry, and differential and integral calculus. Published in 1748, it was the standard mathematical text for fifty years.

Agnesi was much admired by her male colleagues, but this admiration rarely translated itself into recognition. The Bologna Academy of Sciences accepted her into its ranks, but the French Academy of Sciences, though it praised her, would not admit her. Pope Benedict XIV appointed her Professor of Mathematics at the University of

LIBRARY OF CONGRESS

MARIA AGNESI: *The famous mathematician was known for many years as "the witch of Agnesi" because a poor English translation of her work misinterpreted "versiera", a type of sine curve, as "wife of the devil" rather than "curve."*

Bologna, but Agnesi never took the post. Her father died, and at last she could do as she had always wished and retreat from public life. She converted the family home into a hospital and spent the rest of her life caring for the sick and the poor. Near the time of her death in 1799, she was asked about mathematics. Her reply was, "such matters no longer occupy my mind."

# 13

**CLARA SCHUMANN,** *born Clara Josephine Wieck in Leipzig, Germany, 1819.* The daughter of a composer, Clara Wieck received a thorough musical education early in childhood. At nine she gave her first piano recital in Leipzig, and she began her first concert tour when she was only eleven. By the time she was sixteen, she was acclaimed throughout Europe as a

great prodigy; she was honored by various groups, appointed *Kammervirtuosin* to the Austrian court, and admired by Goethe, Mendelssohn, Chopin, Paganini, and (later) Liszt.

Wieck might have had a longer career had she not fallen in love with one of her father's pupils, Robert Schumann. She wanted to marry him, but her father objected, so she and Schumann went to court, sued for their right to marry, and won. They married in 1840, and from that point on her career was a fragmented one.

Although her husband never said she should abandon her career, they both agreed his work should not be interrupted, so that meant hers must suffer. She felt the need to minister to his wants, and then there were eight children to care for, as well. Clara Schumann made tours of Denmark, Russia, and England, taught piano later in life, and spent a few years composing before she convinced herself (falsely) she was no good at it. She was never as prominent as she had once been, and most of her life after her husband's death in 1856 was devoted to promoting his reputation and that of her close friend, Johannes Brahms. Within a few generations she was known only as "Robert Schumann's wife."

# 14

**MARGARET SANGER,** *born Margaret Louise Higgins in Corning, New York, 1879.* Every man and woman who's practiced contraception should pay a little homage now and then to Margaret Sanger. Before she began her birth control crusade, the world was a decidedly less attractive place. Abortions were available only for the most wealthy —and even then they weren't necessarily safe. Many women died of self-induced abortions or raised large families in misery. Doctors refused to provide contraceptive information, and sending such material through the mail was punishable under United States law.

LIBRARY OF CONGRESS

MARGARET SANGER: *Her "Family Limitation," once the most comprehensive publication on contraception available in English, was declared obscene and "contrary not only to the law of the state, but to the law of God."*

Margaret Sanger was determined to change all this. "No woman can call herself free who doesn't own and control her own body," she said. Sanger wrote a series of articles on female sexuality, which she convinced a socialist newspaper, *The Call*, to publish in 1912. Entitled "What Every Girl Should Know," the articles described and named parts of the genitalia and reproductive system and insisted that sex was natural and good. In 1913 an article on syphilis Sanger wrote for her column was declared obscene and unmailable by the Post Office, and for that issue, *The Call* simply printed the headline "What Every Girl Should Know." Below that was a box in which appeared the words "NOTHING, by order of the Post-Office Department." A month later, the article was allowed to be printed, and during World War I it was circulated among American troops by the government, without credit to Sanger.

Sanger took her crusade across the nation, determined to remove the stigma associated with birth control. She published information on contraception, faced highly publicized obscenity charges, and

opened the first birth control clinic in America in Brooklyn, New York. She established the organization which grew into Planned Parenthood, smuggled diaphragms into the country, and aided in the illegal manufacture of contraceptives. In 1936, the courts decided birth control information was not obscene, and soon afterward the American Medical Asociation called birth control a legitimate science and authorized its teaching in medical schools.

# 15

**SHIKIBU MURASAKI,** *born in Japan in about 978, exact date unknown.* So little is known of Murasaki's life that no one even knows her real name. Her father was a provincial governor and a member of the powerful Fujiwara family. Her personal name was not recorded because at the time it was considered impolite to write down the names of highborn women. "Shikibu" was a reference to her father's office.

Murasaki's father was an unusually enlightened man. He quickly recognized his daughter had an exceptional mind, and he regretted she hadn't been born a boy. He allowed her to study with her brother, and she became quite well educated. At twenty she married a distant cousin, a member of the Imperial Guard. They had one daughter, and the marriage was happy, so she must have felt particularly adrift when in 1001 her husband died and her father took a post far away from Kyoto and the imperial court.

Murasaki managed to get a position in the retinue of Empress Akiko, and by the time she left the court in about 1013, she had three great accomplishments to her name. She had become famous for her delicate, technically superb poetry. She had kept a diary for two years which later provided historians much information about her era. And, most importantly, she had

written *The Tale of Genji*. The world's first surviving long novel, *Genji* is a nostalgic romantic tale about the adventures of a prince and his son; it has been called the finest work of Japanese literature and one of the greatest novels of the world. Nothing is known of Murasaki's life after she left the court; she may have died as early as 1015.

# 16

**ANNE BRADSTREET,** *dies at about 60 in North Andover, Massachusetts, 1672.* In 1650, a collection of poetry entitled *The Tenth Muse Lately Sprung in America* was published in London. It was notable for a number of reasons: the poetry was quite good though rather imitative, the book was one of the most popular in London for the rest of the century, its author was the daughter of one governor of Massachusetts and the wife of another, and it was the first volume of poetry to come out of the American colonies. Perhaps even more remarkable is the fact that Anne Bradstreet managed to become the tenth muse while running a colonial household and raising eight children; in fact, she was still having children after some of her own were married. Her brother-in-law, who had taken the poems to England and published them without her knowledge, wrote a preface in which he assured the reader that Bradstreet's literary efforts had taken no time from "the duties of her place, and discreet managing of her family occasions," but only "from her sleep and other refreshments."

It is clear from the poems that she was deeply devoted to her husband and children, but it is equally clear that she chafed against her society's low opinion of women and their abilities. Two lines from a poem about Queen Elizabeth I proclaim: "Let such as say our sex is void of reason / Know 'tis a slander now but once was treason."

**LOUISE ARNER BOYD,** *born in San Rafael, California, 1887.* "I may have worn breeches and boots and even slept in them at times, but I have no use for masculine women . . . There is no reason why a woman can't rough it and still remain feminine." So spoke Louise Boyd, who took a maid on her Arctic expeditions, powdered her nose before coming on deck, and wore hats and flowers whenever possible. She was a society belle who raised prize camellias and who had been freed from social responsibilities by the death of her last immediate relative in 1920. She had traveled to France and Belgium and then, inspired by a distant view of pack ice, had decided to do a little northern exploration.

The hats and flowers were only one part of her personality. She was also a tough, determined woman who swore with a vengeance when angered. Her male colleagues on expeditions, while they sometimes treated her with disdain, admitted that she was "a hell of a gal." Between 1926 and 1955, she made nine trips to the Arctic, eight by sea and one by air. She battled polar bears, musk oxen, rough waters, fire on board her ships, illness, and ice in a region where waterways are frozen solid for most of the year and ice floes can be larger than most Caribbean islands. She photographed animals, plants, and ice formations, mapped new waterways and corrected old mapping errors, surveyed unexplored areas, collected botanical samples, and discovered a previously unknown ocean bank.

# 17

**"LITTLE MO" CONNOLLY,** *born Maureen Catherine Connolly in San Diego, California, 1934.* Connolly began playing tennis at age ten. Three years later, she won the division championship for her age

GRETA GARBO: *The public Garbo radiates grace and sophistication; the private Garbo writes, "I'm tired and nervous and I'm in America."*

group at the Southern California Invitational. At fifteen, she won almost every one of the fifty-four tournaments she entered and became the youngest girl ever to win the national junior championship. Clearly, she was going to accomplish great things.

In 1951, Connolly lost three tournaments and won eight, including the U.S. women's singles title. Pleasant and seemingly fragile off court, in competition she was emotionless, ruthlessly competitive, and powerful. In 1952 she won the U.S. title again and won for the first time at Wimbledon, and in 1953 she was the first woman to win the Grand Slam—consecutive victories at Wimbledon and the U.S., French, and Australian opens. 1954 brought another triumph at Wimbledon, a second win in France, her fourth year of Wightman Cup play without losing a match, and her third year as the Associated Press Woman Athlete of the Year. Then her leg was crushed in a riding accident, and tragically, prematurely, her career was over.

# 18

**GRETA GARBO,** *born Greta Louisa Gustafsson in Stockholm, Sweden, 1905.* At fourteen Greta Gustafsson dropped out of school. She worked at various jobs, attended the Royal Dramatic Theatre School, and became an overnight success throughout Europe in Mauritz Stiller's *The Story of Gosta Berling.* When in 1924, Stiller went to Hollywood to work for MGM, he did so under the stipulation that Greta, too, get a contract. It was Stiller who gave her the name Garbo, but while she became a success, he flopped. Garbo always resented the studio for its rude treatment of her benefactor, and she never partook of the glitzy Hollywood lifestyle.

Garbo, nevertheless, became one of Hollywood's most compelling figures. She made twenty-four films

for MGM, ten of them silent. Her fist talkie was *Anna Christie,* her first words "Gif me a visky, ginger ale on the side—and don't be stingy, baby." Her husky voice was the perfect accompaniment to her polished beauty. She continued to make films until 1941 when she suddenly retired, and dropped completely out of public life. Garbo was most associated with five words attributed to her: "I vant to be alone." Her actual words were, "I want to be *left* alone."

# 19

**MARY JEMISON,** *dies at about 90 on Buffalo Creek Reservation, near Buffalo, New York, 1833.* Mary Jemison was unusual for her time. Captured from her Pennsylvania settlement at age fifteen by Seneca Indians, Jemison found "captivity" far more enjoyable than "freedom." While sensational reports of the cruel treatment of Europeans at the hands of Indians abounded in the colonies and abroad, Jemison experienced nothing of the kind. She was adopted by a Seneca family that treated her with kindness and taught her Indian skills. She had many opportunities to return to "civilization," but always refused, much to the consternation of those who tried to rescue her. At twenty-two she married a Seneca warrior, and they had several children. Known as "the white woman of the Genesee," she followed Seneca ways to the end of her life.

# 20

**HARRIET E. ADAMS WILSON,** *born in the eastern United States in the early nineteenth century, exact date unknown.* The first novel published by a black American was *Our Nig* (1859); the author was a woman, Harriet E. Adams Wilson. Little is known of her. She was an

orphaned free black who somehow settled in Milford, New Hampshire, and in 1851 she married a sailor, Thomas Wilson. She bore a son in 1852—in a poorhouse, since by that time Wilson had deserted her. She named the baby George, and from that day he became the most important thing in her life. She set about trying to make enough money to feed him, but she had great difficulty doing so. She was momentarily encouraged when her husband returned, but he soon abandoned her again, and her health grew steadily worse. A business venture involving a hair dye supported her for a while, but when her health collapsed so did her finances. In 1859, in sheer desperation, she published a fictionalized account of her youth and pleaded with people to buy it. Not enough did, and in 1860 George died of "fever," undoubtedly aggravated by malnutrition. Of Wilson herself there are no further records, and her book was quickly forgotten. Most comprehensive anthologies of literature by black Americans continued to omit it until this decade.

Why was she so overlooked? The style of the book is a stilted, sentimental one, but no worse than that of most popular literature of the time. Moreover, the story itself is interesting, and the attitudes revealed throughout the book make it worthwhile as a social and historical study. As it happened, it was precisely this combination of the plot and the attitudes it revealed that ensured the book's obscurity. Some potential readers were shocked by the title, but most were put off byh the plot and purpose of the book. To begin with, Wilson depicted an interracial marriage, which horrified most of her readers. Furthermore, *Our Nig* was not the whole title. It was: *Our Nig; or, Sketches from the Life of a Free Black, In a Two-Story White House, North. Showing that Slavery's Shadows Fall Even There.*

That was the real problem with Wilson's book. Only two years after it was published, Linda Brent's *Incidents in the Life of a Slave Girl* would discuss many of the same instances of racism as *Our Nig*. But Brent's book was set in the South and edited by a prominent abolitionist, Lydia Maria Child. *Our Nig* did exactly what the abolitionist didn't want: it betrayed the racism displayed by "professed abolitionists" themselves, "who didn't want slaves at the South, nor niggers in their own houses, North. Faugh! To lodge one; to eat with one; to admit one through the front door; to sit next to one; awful!"

man "whom no other . . . could surpass in kindness, peacefulness, loyalty, and true love."

Unfortunately, Pisan had only a few years of happiness. In 1380, Charles V died, Pisan's father was demoted, and he died a few years later. In 1390, Pisan's husband died as well, leaving her with three children, a mother, and a niece to support. She began intensive studies in history, science, and poetry, and then she began to write lyric poetry

herself in the attempt to make a living. She did quite well and soon achieved a modest degree of fame. Eventually she started writing all sorts of things—critiques of misogynist literature, a book on etiquette for women, pacifist books, a biography of Charles V, books on the arts of government and war, the only contemporary tribute to Joan of Arc, and the first real feminist treatise, *The Book of the City of Ladies*.

# 21 _____

**CHRISTINE DE PISAN,** *born in Venice, Italy, 1365.* Pisan was unquestionably one of the most extraordinary women of her age, yet few people today, except for some feminist scholars and historians, have heard of her. She was one of the West's first feminists, its first professional female author, one of the only professional writers of her day, and one of the first vernacular authors to oversee the illustration of her books—all remarkable accomplishments, especially since at the time most women could neither read nor write. Although she was born in Venice, she did not live in Italy for long. When she was still quite young, her father, Tommaso di Benvenuto da Pizzano, became the court physician and astrologer of King Charles V of France.

In France, Pizzano made sure his daughter received a thorough education, and although her mother objected, Pisan learned to read and write Italian, French, and probably Latin. Perhaps her mother was worried that if her daughter were too well educated she'd have trouble finding a husband, but if so, her fears were unfounded. When she was fifteen, Pisan married Étienne de Castel, a courtier ten years her senior. Although the marriage was arranged by her parents, it was a happy and loving one; Castel encouraged her to continue her education, and she called him a

CHRISTABEL PANKHURST: *Having won the vote, she began an evangelical career and predicted that the millenium was imminent.*

LIBRARY OF CONGRESS

# 22

**CHRISTABEL PANKHURST,** *born in Manchester, England, 1880.* One day, British suffragist Emmeline Pankhurst was startled to hear her oldest daughter, Christabel, say, "How long you women have been trying for the vote. For my part, I mean to get it." And she did.

With her mother, she founded the Women's Social and Political Union and led it in the militant tactics that eventually forced the government to grant woman suffrage. Pankurst was an excellent student whose talent for the law won her some prestigious awards, and her wit, fire, and beauty made her a popular speaker. Her views were simple—anything that got women the vote was justifiable, and anything that attracted attention was likely to get women the vote.

She was one of the first militants to go to jail, stating proudly, "If it would get us the vote I should be ready to go to prison again at any time."

And she did go to prison, again and again and again. She encouraged prominent women to get themselves arrested, too, to embarrass the class-conscious authorities. She edited *The Suffragette,* attacking sexual double standards, prostitution, and political oppression. She ran for public office, advocated arson and vandalism, and at one point fled to France to avoid a particularly ruthless legal campaign against her. One of the many pieces of hate mail she received read: "You set of sickening fools—If you have no homes—no husbands—no children—no relations—why don't you drown yourselves out of the way?"

# 23

**VICTORIA WOODHULL,** *born Victoria Claflin in Homer, Ohio, 1838.* There's never been anyone quite like Victoria Woodhull. She was the eldest daughter of "Buck" Claflin, a shady fortune-teller and purveyor of something called the "elixir of life," who put Victoria and her sister Tennessee in his show as mesmerists and clairvoyants.

At fourteen, Victoria married Dr. Canning Woodhull, an alcoholic and morphine addict. They divorced after twelve years and two children; and Victoria married Colonel James Blood, who was not a real colonel. She moved to New York City with her sister, and they were joined not only by Blood, but also by Woodhull, the children, and a variety of relatives.

Victoria and Tennessee were enterprising young women, and they had no intention of doing factory work for starvation wages. They

went straight to the top, accosting Commodore Cornelius Vanderbilt himself. By means of seances, "magnetic healing," and a little sexual persuasion, they convinced him to set them up in business as Woodhull, Claflin & Co., Bankers and Brokers. To the delight of cartoonists and reporters, the first women on Wall Street made two-thirds of a million dollars in only three years.

And Victoria didn't stop there. From 1870 to 1876 she published *Woodhull & Claflin's Weekly,* which she promoted as an "organ of social regeneration and constructive reform." In its pages she advocated free love, liberalized divorce laws, communal parenting and property, currency reform, woman suffrage, legalized prostitution, and spiritualism—something for everyone. The *Weekly* serialized a George Sand novel and published the first

English translation of Karl Marx's *Communist Manifesto.*

Next Victoria got on the suffrage bandwagon, becoming a popular speaker, and she ran for president of the United States, conducting a campaign that landed her in jail on election day. A flamboyant, changeable woman, she continued to embrace new and controversial causes for the rest of her life.

# 24

**WETAMOO,** *born in the eastern United States in the seventeenth century, exact date unknown.* Wetamoo, unfortunately, is known largely through the accounts of English settlers, of whom she was often an enemy. Despite the prejudices against the "savage" Indians, a picture emerges from their accounts of a strong, decisive, angry, beautiful, and determined Indian woman known to the English as Queen Wetamoo and to her people as the Squaw Sachem ("woman chief") of Pocasset. She was a member of the Wampanoag tribe, whose thirty villages were scattered throughout what today is Rhode Island and Massachusetts. Both she and her sister married well; she married Wamsutta, the oldest son of Chief Massasoit, and her sister married Metacom, Wamsutta's brother.

It was this tribe and its royal family that assisted the Pilgrims with their first Thanksgiving dinner. So impressed were the English settlers that they established a forty-year treaty with the Wampanoags and vowed an unbreakable friendship. They named Wetamoo's husband "Alexander," and they called his brother "Philip." Soon, however, problems broke out over treaty violations on both sides, but Chief Massasoit refused to act against the Pilgrims; he trusted them implicitly. When he died, Wamsutta became chief, and he planned to overthrow the English, but he was arrested and died on the

LIBRARY OF CONGRESS

way to the English settlement. Wetamoo became convinced that the English had poisoned her husband. Metacom now became chief, and with Wetamoo organized twenty thousand warriors to fight against the fifty thousand settlers. The element of surprise was their only advantage. But their guerilla warfare tactics weren't enough, and soon they were driven back. In 1675 Wetamoo was cornered by the English and shot as she attempted to escape in a canoe. Her body was beheaded, and her head was placed on a pole and displayed in Plymouth. Within six days, Metacom received the same treatment, and the remaining members of the royal family were sold as slaves in the West Indies.

SARAH BERNHARDT: *When an admirer offered her anything she wanted, she chose a rosewood coffin as a reminder "that my body will soon be dust and that my glory will live forever."*

# 25

**SARAH BERNHARDT,** *born Henriette Rosine Bernard in Paris, France, 1844.* "I shall never be yielding or docile," wrote Sarah Bernhardt in 1908. Perhaps that was why she became an actress; it was the only profession in which she could be applauded for taking male roles. She herself believed acting was "the only art where women may sometimes prove superior to men."

At thirteen, Bernhardt began studying drama, but she did not make her stage debut until five years later. She served a long, hard apprenticeship before her first successes at the Comédie Française. Her grace, beauty, clear voice, and easily expressed emotion made her a favorite, and she became known as the "Divine Sarah." She followed her Paris successes with triumphal tours of the United States and London. From then on, her popularity never waned, not even when she was an old woman and had one leg amputated. Such celebrity gave her the freedom to become not only an actress, but a theatre manager, a playwright, a painter, and a sculptor as well.

Oddly enough, the roles which made Bernhardt famous were not her favorites. Her favorite character was not Phèdre or Cordelia or Andromaque, but Hamlet, and she played him several times. The female characters, she explained, seemed to be *entirely* composed of emotion and "the desire to please." They never seemed to think, only to feel. "It is not male parts," she wrote, "but male brains I prefer. . . . male parts are more intellectual than female parts."

# 26

**BESSIE SMITH,** *dies at 39 in Clarksdale, Mississippi, 1937.* During her career Bessie Smith reigned as "the Empress of the Blues." Born to a poor black family in Chattanooga, Tennessee, she began singing as a child and toured the South with "Ma" Rainey before starting her own group, the Liberty Belles. A trip to New York in 1923 led to a recording contract; in all she made 159 recordings with the help of such musicians as Louis Armstrong, Fletcher Henderson, and James P. Johnson. Her first record, *Downhearted Blues,* sold over two million copies. She became famous for the songs "St. Louis Blues," "Backwater Blues," and "Nobody Knows You When You're Down and Out," and she also made a film short called *St. Louis Blues* in 1929.

Smith lived the life of the blues. The specter of failure followed her constantly, threatening to overtake her. She was almost always broke and had trouble finding bookings; her marriage failed, and depression and alcoholism were constant companions. In 1937, while on tour in Mississippi, her truck crashed. She was rushed to the nearest hospital, but it was a hospital for whites only, and she was refused admittance. She was then taken to a hospital for blacks, and although efforts were made there to save her life, she did not survive.

# 27

**BABE DIDRIKSON ZAHARIAS,** *dies at 45 in Galveston, Texas, 1956.* As a child Mildred Didrikson earned the nickname "Babe" because she reminded playmates of Babe Ruth. She was destined to become as magnificent an athlete as her namesake. In high school she excelled in basketball, and was hired by an insurance company as a typist so she could play on the company team. Meanwhile she developed an interest in track and field events. By 1932 she held records in the eighty-meter hurdles, the javelin throw, the high jump, the broad jump, and the baseball throw. That year she won five out of the eight events she entered in the Amateur Athletic Union (AAU) Championships. At the 1932 Olympics, she won a gold medal in the javelin throw and a silver medal in the high jump, although she'd actually tied for the gold.

Her victories brought Didrikson a great deal of fame and very little money. She accepted a job promoting the Chrysler Corporation, but when the AAU learned of it, she was suspended. But Didrikson needed paying work. She toured with a vaudeville act, with a mixed-sex baseball team, and worked as a pitcher for minor league spring training games. Baseball was one of her favorite sports, but she was tired of being viewed as a freak in that male-dominated sport. Although she was accomplished at boxing, bowling, diving, tennis, billiards, swimming, marksmanship, and fencing, she chose golf as her career. After one year at the sport, she celebrated her first victory at the Texas Women's Amateur Championship in 1935, but the United States Golf Association invalidated it because of her past professional work. In 1938 she married wrestler and promoter George Zaharias and he helped her regain her amateur status, and she became famous all over again, winning tournament after tournament, proving herself the consummate athlete.

# 28

**FRANCES WILLARD,** *born Frances Elizabeth Candine Willard in Churchville, New York, 1834.* In 1874, Frances Willard appeared to be just another schoolmarm, albeit a very successful one. Her parents had both been schoolteachers, and she had followed in their footsteps in 1860. After some further education in the United States and an impressive stint abroad, she became president of a women's college, and when the college merged with Northwestern University in 1873, she became the dean of women and professor of athletics.

In 1874, however, this bespectacled woman quit her job to serve as president of the Chicago Women's Christian Temperance Union (WCTU). Eventually she would become president of the National WCTU and lead the fight for prohibition while teaching women throughout the country how to lobby for a cause. There were members of her immediate family who could perhaps have predicted this step. Even as a child, Willard had rebelled against the confinement of feminity, loving short hair and out-

American Woman and Her Political Peers.

FRANCES WILLARD (center): *This pro-suffrage postcard, in dubious taste by today's standards, makes the point that, by being denied the vote, women have been placed in the same class as idiots, convicts, lunatics, and Indians — all of them, save* women, *justly* disenfranchised.

LIBRARY OF CONGRESS

door games instead. When her brother marched off to vote, she pressed her nose against the window and longed to vote, too, but her sister warned, "don't you go ahead and say so, for then we would be called strong-minded."

Adolescence hit Willard hard. Suddenly, her tomboy games were no longer acceptable; her wildness must be tamed and made womanly. Feeling "choked with ribbons," she was forced into the appearance, at least, of propriety. Her first thought, which she recognized as impractical, was to steal her father's revolver and run away in a canoe. She gave up this idea, stayed, and suffered, writing in her diary: "This is my birthday and the date of my martyrdom. Mother insists that at last I must have my hair 'done up woman-fashion.' My 'back' hair is twisted up like a corkscrew; I carry eighteen hairpins; my head aches miserably; my feet are entangled in the skirt of my hateful new gown. I can never jump over a fence again, so long as I live."

# 29

**ELIZABETH GASKELL,** *born Elizabeth Cleghorn Stevenson in London, England, 1810.* Elizabeth Gaskell was, in many ways, a model Victorian matron. She was married happily to a minister who read all of her letters before she was allowed to send them; she did a great deal of charitable work, and she was the mother of six children. Despite having happily fulfilled the social obligations of her sex, Gaskell found she still needed an outlet for her creativity. She began writing to assuage her grief at the death of one of her children. Known formally to her readers as "Mrs. Gaskell," she was the author of six novels and two works of nonfiction.

Gaskell was a fine novelist whose works are now underrated because they are considered too moralistic, bland, and feminine, lacking in the violence which is presumably necessary to keep a modern reader's attention. Oddly enough, Gaskell was considered somewhat immoral in her own day because of the plot of her second novel, *Ruth.* Published in 1853, *Ruth* is the story of a dressmaker's apprentice who is seduced, abandoned, and cast into the streets with her illegitimate son. Gaskell obviously sympathized with the heroine, and the book was thought scandalous. A London library removed *Ruth* from its shelves, and reviewers panned it. Two members of her husband's congregation went so far as to burn it. Unaware that she would recover her good reputation with four more "respectable" novels, Gaskell trembled under public disapproval but refused to retract anything. "I shrink with more pain than I can tell you from what people are saying," she wrote, "though I would do every jot of it over again tomorrow."

# 30

**MMANTHATISI,** *born in what is now the Orange Free State of the Republic of South Africa in about 1780, exact date unknown.* Little is known of Mmanthatisi until she married the chief of a powerful tribe, the Tlokwa. In 1817 when her husband died, chieftanship fell to their oldest son, who was only thirteen and completely inexperienced. The Tlokwa were then just beginning to feel the reverberations of a great crisis. Known as the *mfecane,* or "the crushing," it was a constant displacement and destruction of tribes because of the southward movement of nomadic herders, the northward movement of Boer farmers, and the imperial ambitions of the great Zulu king, Shaka. Tribes were uprooted and spent years wandering, prey to famine, disease, and warrior raids.

Mmanthatisi became her son's regent and assumed all her tribe's troubles. She led the Tlowka in battles as tribes clashed over food and land. She didn't participate in the fighting, but generally planned the strategy. Her warriors were known as Mantatees, a corruption of her name, and legends of their bloodthirstiness spread. A missionary stationed nearby wrote: "It was said that a mighty woman, of the name of Mantatee, was at the head of an invincible army, numerous as locusts, marching onward among the interior nations, carrying destruction and ruin wherever she went; that she nourished the army with her own milk, sent out hornets before it, and in one word, was laying the world desolate." Mmanthatisi was the savior of her tribe and led them to safety in Lesotho, where she named her son chief of the Tlowka.

LIBRARY OF CONGRESS

GERTRUDE EDERLE: *Water was her metier, but ice was also nice.*

# OCTOBER

## 1

**ANNIE BESANT,** *born Anne Wood in London, England, 1847.* Annie Besant was born in 1847, but her life began in 1873. She had been married for six unhappy years to a clergyman, trying and failing to channel her passion for religion into a passion for a religious man. In 1873, while practicing at the church organ, she wondered what it felt like to speak from the pulpit. No one was around, so she stepped up to her husband's place and lectured to the empty church. Later she wrote: "I shall never forget the feeling of power and delight which came upon me as my voice rolled down the aisles . . . I felt that all I wanted was to see the church full of upturned faces."

Besant left her husband, taking their daughter with her. She threw herself into the birth control movement, co-writing a pamphlet called *The Fruits of Philosophy.* She was arrested, convicted, fined and sentenced to six months in jail, and although an appeal resulted in acquittal, Besant's child was taken from her. Heartbroken, she involved herself with new causes, declaring herself an atheist. Socialism was her next passion, and she joined the Fabian Society, helped to organize a match girls' strike in London, and wrote *The Legalization of Female Slavery in England,* in which she claimed: "women will cease to sell their bodies when they are able to sell their labor."

In 1889, Besant's life changed again when she was suddenly converted to Theosophy, a religious-philosophical movement founded by spiritualist Helena Blavatsky. Besant dropped everything and went to India to study religion. She learned Sanskrit, established the Hindu College in Benares, and translated the *Bhagavad Gita*; her religious writings are also heavily influenced by Indian literature. Her growing power in the Theosophical Society (she was elected its president in 1907) mirrored her growing prominence in Indian politics. An advocate of home rule, she began a daily newspaper, *New India,* was imprisoned by the British for her activism, and served for six years as the fifth president (and the first woman president) of the Indian National Congress.

## 2

**ELIZABETH THOMPSON BUTLER,** *dies at 86 in Gormanston Castle, County Meath, Ireland, 1933.* Butler and her sister were soundly educated by their parents, who encouraged academics and the arts. Her sister became the poet, Alice Meynell, and Butler became an accomplished painter.

Butler followed the same path as many other young artists. She learned foreign languages, studied at an art school, and traveled in Florence and Rome during her vacations, observing and copying the paintings there. But she was different from most other painters of her time; she was a woman, and she would become famous, not for paintings of flowers, scenes of motherhood, pictures of animals, or even portraits of notable people, but for military scenes. She achieved success almost overnight at the age of twenty-four, when her painting *Calling the Roll after an Engagement, Crimea* was displayed at the Royal Academy. The crowds were so large and so eager to see it, they had to be restrained, and the work was finally purchased by none other than Queen Victoria. It was the sort of success story artists dream of, but it had its drawbacks. As hard as Butler tried, she couldn't escape military subjects, and she was forced again and again to return to battle scenes for crowd-pleasing material.

## 3

**LUCY HOBBS,** *dies at 77 in Lawrence, Kansas, 1910.* Many people know of America's first woman doctor, Elizabeth Blackwell. But very few have heard of her equivalent in dentistry, Lucy Hobbs. Born Lucy Beaman Hobbs in New York in 1833, she began working as a teacher at sixteen. Her first dream was to be a doctor. She studied medicine privately for a while, but was rejected by a medical school on the basis of her sex. So she switched to dentistry, and, here, too, she found barriers. No one would consent to take her as an apprentice, and she ended up working for the dean of the Ohio Dental College. Finally, an open-minded dentist, Dr. Samuel Wardle, accepted her as a student; she began studying dentistry by day and supporting herself by sewing at night. In 1861, Hobbs applied to the Ohio Dental College. She was refused.

Undaunted, she opened a practice anyway in Cincinnati. During the Civil War she moved to Iowa. Her practice thrived, and in 1865 she became a member of the Iowa State Dental Society. She applied again to the Ohio Dental College, this time with the backing of her professional association, and this time she was accepted. She got her degree after only one term of study, since she already had a good deal of experience, and she received the highest score on the final exam. In 1867, Hobbs opened an office in Chicago and married James M. Taylor, whom she promptly instructed in dentistry. Together, they moved to Kansas, where they established a joint practice and, one assumes, lived happily ever after.

# 4

**SOPHIA ALEXEEVNA,** *baptised in Moscow, Russia, 1657.* When this seventeen-day-old infant was anointed and acccepted into the Russian Orthodox Church, her public life should have been over. She was a daughter of Tsar Alexis, prevented by religion from marrying a foreigner and prevented by birth from marrying below her rank. By tradition, she was doomed to the terem, a women's section in the palace, where she would have little to do, a few similarly trapped female relatives with whom to do it, and almost no visitors at all. Only close male relatives, a few priests, and her doctor would be allowed access to her, and even the doctor could only examine her through gauze.

But Sophia was too intelligent, restless, and ambitious to be kept in the terem. She demanded an education—a real education, not just perfunctory instruction in needlework and religion—and she received it. One of her teacher praised her "marvelous understanding and judgment"; another called her "a maiden of great intelligence and the most delicate understanding, with an accomplished masculine mind."

When she was nineteen, her father died, and her fifteen-year-old brother became Tsar Fedor II. She quickly took advantage of the situation, using her position as Fedor's friend and confidante to emerge from the terem and involve herself in politics. When Fedor died in 1682 without an heir, she dove headfirst into the struggle that followed. Although Sophia wanted supreme power for herself, she had to settle for being regent to the new co-tsars, her crippled brother, Ivan, and her young half-brother, Peter. Sophia ruled Russia for seven years, reveling in power and action, but when she tried once again to become an autocrat in name as well as fact, Peter staged a coup and became sole ruler.

Sophia herself was offered a fate worse than death; she was forced to live in the Novodevichy convent near Moscow. Despite the comfort of her apartments there and the fact that she was not made to become a nun, it was a living hell for her to be isolated from power and intrigue. In 1698, however, her life was made even worse. The Kremlin guards rebelled in Sophia's name, and even though she could not be implicated in the planning of the uprising, her head was shaved, she was made to take religious vows, and adopt the name Susanna. She was forbidden to have visitors, and one hundred soldiers guarded her until her death in 1704.

# 5

**SYLVIA BEACH,** *dies at 74 in Paris, 1962.* If you were a young aspiring writer during the period between the two world wars, and you had enough money to get to France, that's where you'd go. New York was an artistic wasteland compared with Paris. And when you reached the City of Lights, if you were wise, your first stop would be at a little bookshop called Shakespeare and Company. There, you could buy and borrow books, read the latest literary magazines, exchange money, and pick up mail. If you needed help of any kind, the woman behind the desk would lend you money or find you lodgings, a publisher, or a patron. And you would be in excellent company; her customers included James Joyce, T.S. Eliot, Ezra Pound, André Gide, Paul Valéry, Gertrude Stein, Samuel Beckett, Tom Wolfe, Thornton Wilder, Christopher Isherwood, Ford Madox Ford, E.M. Forster, Katherine Anne Porter, Elizabeth Bishop, Sherwood Anderson, Stephen Vincent Benét, and Ernest Hemingway (whom she called "really a very good boy, but primitive").

The woman behind the desk was Sylvia Beach, a charismatic American who used no makeup and wore loose, comfortable clothes. She once swam halfway across the Seine to rescue a parrot. She spent her summers, even when she was in her seventies, chopping wood in the countryside. Hemingway described her as having "a lively, sculptured face, brown eyes that were alive as a small animal's . . . she was kind, cheerful, and interested, and loved to make jokes and gossip. No one that I ever knew was nicer to me." Katherine Anne Porter said, "Her genius was for friendship; her besetting virtue, generosity." But Beach was more than attractive, vital, friendly, and kind. She was happy. She was one of those rare people who get exactly what they really want.

She fell deeply in love once in her life, and the woman she loved, Adrienne Monnier, loved her in return; Beach simply laughed at those who pitied her "single" state. "I have had a certain amount of luck in my life," she said, "and one piece of it is *not* being married." She was passionately fond of art and artists, so she opened a bookstore that was to become known as "the cradle of postwar American literature." She idolized James Joyce, and for years he grudgingly depended on her kindness and devotion. When publisher after publisher rejected *Ulysses* on the grounds of obscenity, Beach set up her own press and published it for him.

Beach fought a long, weary financial battle to keep Shakespeare and Company open, but war finally accomplished what lack of money couldn't. In 1941, the Nazis, angered by her persistent efforts on behalf of Jewish friends and her refusal to give a German officer her only copy of a rare first edition, informed her they would be confiscating all her books and closing the business. But Beach wouldn't let them. As quickly as she could, she found hiding places for most of her books, where they remained safe until after the war.

# 6

**JENNY LIND,** *born in Stockholm, Sweden, 1820.* The illegitimate daughter of a schoolteacher, the "Swedish Nightingale," Jenny Lind, found her profession by accident. One day when she was nine years old, she was singing to her cat when a ballerina's maid heard her. The maid told the ballerina, the ballerina told some influential friends, and before she know it Lind was a student at the Royal Theatre School. By the time she was twenty, she was a member of the Swedish Royal Academy and the court singer to the king of Sweden.

LIBRARY OF CONGRESS

Soon Lind was making trips to Germany and Austria, where her admirers unharnessed her horses and drew her carriage themselves. She sang in London, where she was honored for her exemplary piety and charity, where Queen Victoria threw her a bouquet, and where the House of Commons emptied and was unable to conduct any business during her performances. The composer Felix Mendelssohn claimed, "There will not be born in a whole century another being so gifted as she." Hans Christian Andersen was obsessed with her for years and wrote stories about his "vestal virgin."

In the United States, P. T. Barnum heard about her and brought her to America in a whirl of publicity, and although he sold everything he owned and borrowed more to pay for her services, he more than made up for his gamble. He ultimately made $712,161.34 from managing Lind's tour, a fortune in those days. Lind, too, found the arrangement profitable—Barnum had given her a thousand dollars per performance for ninety-five performances, a percentage of the profits, control over the hiring of her conductor and assistant singer, a secretary, a maid, a manservant, a sixty-piece orchestra at every performance, and a carriage in each city she visited.

A good deal of her success was because of Barnum's adept public relations work. In real life, Lind was a stocky, robust woman with a firm jaw, serious eyes, a two-and-a-half-octave range, and a lovely trill. By the time Barnum got through with her, she was perceived as an angelic, ethereal paragon of virtue. Tickets to her shows sold for as much as $625, and her image and

JENNY LIND: *On her American tour, she gave her $10,000 share of the first-night proceeds to charity.*

name appeared on bells, boxes, cigars, sewing stands, gloves, scarves, riding hats, perfume, fans, paper dolls, candelabra, and needle cases. Lind understandably grew a little tired of this, especially since she was not compensated for the use of her name on any of these products, but her biggest professional mistake was breaking with Barnum and trying to be her own manager. As soon as she dissolved her partnership with him, her popularity plummeted, and by 1852 her career was over.

# 7

**ISABELLA BIRD BISHOP,** *dies at 72 in Edinburgh, Scotland, 1904.* Bishop was a traveler. She made her first voyage in 1856. Twenty-five years old, sickly, and listless, she visited the United States, recovered her health somewhat, and wrote a book about her experiences called *The Englishwoman in America.* For the rest of her life, she traveled, and the books she wrote about her travels made her famous.

Bishop was particularly fond of the United States, perhaps because she was so fond of one American, a Rocky Mountain guide named Mountain Jim Nugent. She met him on a climbing trip and called him her "dear desperado," but when he asked her to live with him she found she couldn't give up her freedom. She returned to England to write *A Lady's Life in the Rockies,* but she grieved deeply when Nugent died in a gunfight in 1874.

She was never able to stay in England for long. While traveling, she always felt strong and healthy, but at home she invariably fell ill. So she wandered to Australia, New Zealand, Hawaii, Japan, Indonesia, and the Middle East, searching for health and excitement. There was a brief interruption in her travels when she married Dr. John Bishop in 1881, but when he died in 1886 she returned to her accustomed pace. She studied medicine in London, went to India as a medical missionary, traveled to Afghanistan and Persia, and became the first female fellow of the Royal Geographical Society. At sixty-three she made a three-year, three-thousand-mile tour of Canada, Japan, Korea, and China, and at sixty-eight she made a one-thousand mile trip on horseback through Morocco. She died while packing for another trip to China.

# 8

**CLAUDE KOGAN,** *dies at 40 on Cho Oyu, Nepal, 1959.* This is not, strictly speaking, the "real" date of death of Claude Kogan. Her specific date of death is not known, only that she died in this year, in this place, somewhere near the beginning of October. She was killed in a blizzard, along with a twenty-six-year-old Belgian woman and a Sherpa guide, at 23,000 feet, on the Himalayan peak known as the Turquoise Goddess. Had her climb succeeded, it would have been the culmination of her career; she was leading an all-female team of eleven climbers from five nations up a 26,867-foot mountain, the world's eighth highest and one of its most perilous. But instead, her team lost contact with the rest of the group. One hundred-mile-per-hour winds delayed a search, and when a party finally made it to Kogan's camp at 23,000 thousand feet, they found that it had been destroyed by the blizzard.

Before she embarked on the expedition, Kogan had explained her motivations, being careful not to associate herself with feminism. "I am not a suffragette," she said, "but I do not see why a group of women, animated by a love of climbing, should not try a great peak."

# 9

**AIMEE SEMPLE McPHERSON,** *born Aimee Elizabeth Kennedy near Ingersoll, Ontario, Canada, 1890.* "Don't ever tell me that a woman cannot be called to preach the Gospel," said Aimee Semple McPherson. "If any man ever went through one-hundredth the part of hell-on-earth that I lived in, they would never say that again." The "hell-on-earth" began with a childhood of misery and poverty on the farm where she was raised; perhaps as a means of escape, she went through a religious crisis as a teenager and was born again with the help of a Pentecostal preacher, Robert Semple. She burned her ragtime sheet music, novels, and dance shoes, and married Semple.

Life with Semple turned out to be another kind of hell. He took her to China, where they worked as missionaries, but within a year he was dead of dysentery, and she ended up alone in New York with no money and a baby to feed. In desperation, she married a man named Harold McPherson, but they divorced. She became a traveling evangelist, driving up and down the East Coast with her children and her mother.

She wasn't making enough money at small revivals, so she decided to work on a larger scale. She arrived in Los Angeles with nothing but a hundred dollars, a much-battered car, her charisma, and a talent for showmanship, but she quickly became popular—and wealthy. She built a huge, one-and-a-half-million-dollar church, the Angelus Temple, complete with its own radio station and a rotating neon cross. Soon she had 400 branch churches and 178 missions throughout the world. The poor little farm girl was a rich, famous woman who wore imported clothes and got periodic face lifts.

But success also brought serious problems. For one thing, she suffered from a loss of privacy. In 1926 she apparently faked her own kidnapping to escape the public eye. It seems she'd fallen in love with the Angelus Temple radio operator, Kenneth Ormiston. McPherson went swimming one day and disappeared. Although her body was not found, it was believed she'd drowned, and bereaved followers gave $34,000 to the temple in an outburst of grief. Shortly afterward, McPherson called from Arizona, saying she'd been kidnapped but had escaped. Her testimony was confused; the lack of evidence to corroborate her story furthered the suspicion that she was lying, and she was charged with conspiracy to obstruct justice. A few months later the charges were dropped, but the prevailing theory is that McPherson ran off with Ormiston and then changed her mind.

McPherson was also plagued by legal and financial worries. Her family squabbled over control of Angelus; at one point there were forty-five lawsuits pending. She died in 1944 from what was called an accidental overdose of barbiturates; fifty thousand mourners filed past her bronze coffin as it lay in state at Angelus. Her eulogy began: "Today, we are here to commemorate the stepping up of a country girl to God's Hall of Fame."

socialist, organizing female laborers, smuggling propaganda, throwing herself in front of the militia's horses, and longing to be arrested, although she never was. She followed her lover to Vienna in 1907, but as her love cooled, so did her radicalism. She entered medical school, married Dr. Felix Deutsch in 1912, and trained in the specialties of neurology and psychiatry, eventually becoming a prominent analyst. She was one of Sigmund Freud's most famous disciples, the first of his female pupils that Freud psychoanalyzed, and the second woman admitted to the Vienna Psychoanalytical Society.

Her two-volume *Psychology of Women,* an ambitious but ultimately destructive book, popularized Freud's theory that "normal" women were passive, self-sacrificing, and masochistic, a view which was heartily endorsed by the medical establishment. A well-adjusted woman, wrote the well-educated, ambitious Deutsch, does not devote herself to a career. Instead, she "leaves the initiative to the man and . . . renounces originality, experiences her own self through identification."

# 11

**ELEANOR ROOSEVELT,** *born Anna Eleanor Roosevelt in New York City, 1884.* Eleanor Roosevelt had a miserable childhood, one Dickens might have enjoyed portraying. Her mother neglected her; other relatives insulted her. The only person she could love without reserve was her father, and she called him "the love of my life" while he called her his "Little Nell." Unfortunately, he was an alcoholic, and usually absent. In 1892 Eleanor's mother died, and since her father was not considered competent to raise a child, she was sent to live with her grandmother, an unfeeling woman, who lost no time in letting her granddaughter know how unattractive she was.

When Eleanor married Franklin Roosevelt, her fifth cousin, in 1905, she was almost as naive about sex as it was possible to be. For the first several years of their marriage, Franklin tried to settle into a career, and Eleanor did her wifely duty by producing six children in ten years. She had no deep maternal instinct

# 10

**HELENE DEUTSCH,** *born Helene Rosenbach in Przemyśl, Galicia, Austria-Hungary (now Poland), 1884.* The youngest child of an intellectual family, Deutsch was ambitious all her life. Afraid of disapproval, she studied secretly at first, but when her conservative mother forbade her to prepare for a university education, she rebelled openly. She ran away from home at twelve, and when the police brought her back, she told her father she'd keep running away until he promised her an education. He did.

At sixteen, Helene fell in love with a married radical organizer. She became an active suffragist and

**GERTRUDIS BOCANEGRA,** *dies at 52, 1817.* Bocanegra's chief interest was founding schools for Indian children in her native Mexico, but the political climate of her day forced her to become a patriot and a martyr as well. She had already convinced her husband, a man of Spanish descent named Lazo de la Vega, to leave his post as a soldier for the Spanish royalists. But it was when Mexican nationalists rose against the Spanish government in 1810 in the War of Independence, that Bocanegra truly distinguished herself. She joined the group of insurgents led by Manuel Muñiz, taking her husband and their ten-year-old son with her. She organized an army of women, carried im-

portant messages between groups of rebels, got her daughters to join the fighting, and considerably aided the attack on Valladolid. Eventually she was sent to Pátzcuaro, her birthplace, to gather military information and to try to win royalist soldiers over to the insurgent cause, but she was discovered. She and her daughters were imprisoned; her husband and son had laready died in battle. Bocanegra was tried, sentenced to death, and executed on this day in 1817.

and felt inadequate and bored. In light of this predicament, World War I was a godsend. Suddenly, Eleanor had a noble, patriotic reason to escape from her dull social routine.

From the time she began rounding up volunteers to aid America's war effort, until her death forty-five years later, Eleanor never left public life. This was made possible not only because of her growing boredom, but also because her marriage to Franklin was increasingly one of convenience. When she discovered in 1918 that he was having an affair, she offered to divorce him but he declined, and they remained married but continued to grow apart, both personally and politically. Franklin saw other women, and Eleanor came to rely more and more on female companionship and political activism.

She joined the League of Women Voters and the Women's Trade Union League, worked for child labor laws and an eight-hour workday, organized female voters in New York, and tried to draw attention to women's issues in the Democratic party. When polio partially paralyzed her husband in 1921, she took an even larger role in politics, managing his campaigns and doing most of the actual campaigning.

Throughout Franklin's terms as governor of New York and president of the United States, Eleanor pushed him to support her favorite causes. She disagreed with her husband on many issues. She supported his New Deal, of course, but she envisioned a larger, broader, better New Deal that included programs for blacks and for women. She personally supervised efforts to clean up the Washington, D.C. slums, held press conferences at which only female reporters were welcome, worked to create jobs for women, and influenced the appointment of more women than ever before to government posts. She often dictated a hundred letters a day and answered fifty personally. She convinced the Postmaster General to appoint four thousand women to postmasterships, wrote recipes for inexpensive meals during the De-

LIBRARY OF CONGRESS

ELEANOR ROOSEVELT: *"No one,"* *she said, "can make you feel inferior* *without your consent."*

pression, wrote a syndicated column and children's books, and worked (unsuccessfully) for mandatory health insurance, a constitutional amendment banning child labor, and a national anti-lynching law. By 1936 she managed to get equal representation for women on the Democratic platform committee, and by 1940 Republicans were wearing buttons that said, "We Don't Want Eleanor Either." After Franklin's death, she served as a

delegate to the United Nations, taught at Brandeis University, and continued to support her favorite causes and politicians.

# 12

**EDITH CAVELL,** *dies at 49 in Brussels, Belgium, 1915.* Edith Cavell was an intelligent, attractive British woman whose family pronounced its name CA-vell; "We rhyme with travel and not with hell." She had artistic talent, but she was unable or unwilling to train as an artist; instead she became a governess and then a nurse. In 1907 she was made Matron of Belgium's first teaching hospital for nurses, and Cavell considered the post a great honor. She filled it with distinction, but it was not for her nursing or teaching skills that she became famous. It was for her activities after the Germans invaded Belgium during World War I.

Cavell found there were French and British soldiers trapped in Belgium who needed passage to the Netherlands and freedom. She began hiding these soldiers and helping them escape, sometimes keeping as many as thirty-five at once. In all, she managed to help about two hundred to escape, but word leaked out and thirty-five people, Cavell among them, were arrested by the Germans. Cavell was interrogated for less than four minutes and sentenced to death.

There are many accounts of Cavell's execution by firing squad. Some said the German soldiers refused to shoot a woman. *The London Times* reported her last words as: "I realize that patriotism is not enough. I must have no hatred or bitterness towards anyone." A friend merely said, "Miss Cavell would never make a scene." The simple fact is that on the eleventh of October, she wrote a few letters and that on the twelfth she was taken from her cell, bound, blindfolded, quite routinely shot, and buried. But she became a folk heroine and a source of national outrage for the British. When the war was over, her body was removed from its grave in Brussels and sent back to England to be buried near her home in Norfolk.

# 13

**MARGARET THATCHER,** *born Margaret Hilda Roberts in Grantham, Lincolnshire, England, 1925.* Whatever you may think of her politics, you have to admit this chemist-turned-lawyer-turned-politician has scored some pretty impressive victories. After all, in 1974, just one year before she became the leader of England's conservative party and five years before she became England's first female prime minister, even she was saying, "It will be years—and not in my time—before a woman will lead the party or become prime minister." It also seems rather obvious she's taken a lot of abuse, and been the subject of a lot of cutesy jokes, because of her sex. She's been called a "headmistress," "The Iron Lady," "Attila the Hen," and "Plunder Woman." Ronald Reagan called her "the best man in England," and a British commentator said, "She cannot see an institution without hitting it with her handbag." Fortunately, Thatcher has always had a sense of her own worth. Upon receiving a prize in school at the age of nine, she announced, "I wasn't lucky, I deserved it."

LILLIAN GISH: *Of "the First Lady of the Silent Screen," D. W. Griffith said: "She is not only the best actress in her profession, but she has the best mind of any woman I have ever met."*

LIBRARY OF CONGRESS

# 14

**LILLIAN GISH,** *born in Springfield, Ohio, 1896.* Lillian and her younger sister Dorothy were raised almost entirely by their mother, since their father, a grocer whose business had failed, abandoned his family in 1900. Mrs. Gish's efforts to support the family didn't bring in enough money, so her daughters had to go to work. Lillian and Dorothy went on the stage, and for years the children worked and traveled with acting troupes.

In 1911 the sisters, while watching a movie called *Lena and the Geese,* recognized the heroine as a childhood friend, Gladys Smith. They rushed to Biograph Studios, where they found Gladys, now calling herself Mary Pickford. Pickford got director D. W. Griffith to hire the girls as five-dollar-a-day extras, and soon they were starring in films of their own. Lillian had an air of innocence and vulnerability that Giffith found irresistible, but he wasn't too fond of Dorothy, and it was only through Lillian's insistence that Dorothy got parts at all.

In her first two years at Biograph, Lillian made twenty films, and soon she was appearing in Griffith's greatest productions: *Birth of a Nation, Intolerance,* and *Broken Blossoms.* Like all the great actresses of her day, she earned a host of nicknames, including "The World's Darling," "Queen of the Silent Drama," "Lillian the Incomparable," and "The First Lady of the Screen." Throughout her stage, film, and lecture careers, she was sustained by her famous beauty, which lasted well into old age, her ambition, and her absolute dedication to her art. In 1926 her realistic approach to acting endangered her life. For a death scene in *La Bohème* she researched lung diseases and starved herself. She was so weak and performed the scene so well the crew thought she had really died, and even director King Vidor was fooled and checked to make sure she was still alive.

# 15

**MATA HARI,** *dies at 41 in Vincennes, France, 1917.* Mata Hari, in true legendary fashion, was shot at dawn as a German spy. Ironically, although she herself claimed to be a double agent, she may not have been a spy at all, and even if she was, it's certain that she never gave anyone any valuable information. She was born Margaretha Geertruida Zelle in Leeuwarden, the Netherlands, and married an army captain named MacLeod when she was nineteen. With him, she traveled to Java where she picked up the rudiments of Balinese temple dancing. Returning to Europe, she left him and went to Paris, calling herself "Lady MacLeod," and later "Mata Hari," which meant "the sun" or "eye of the dawn" in Malay.

In Paris she became famous for "Indian" dances which were noted, not for their accuracy or difficulty, but for their nudity. Fame brought admirers and prominent lovers, but after a few years her notoriety and novelty began to fade, and she sought income from other sources. The other sources included German army officers, who gave her money in exchange for sex and any information she could elicit from her French lovers. Eventually, tired of spending money on her and getting little in return, her German friends allowed the French to discover her harmless attempts at espionage, and she was arrested and shot.

# 16

**MARIE ANTOINETTE,** *dies at 37 in Paris, France, in 1793.* Marie Antoinette and Mata Hari had a lot in common. They were both known and criticized for their sexuality; they were both executed by the French; and they were both assumed to be more powerful than they actually were. Marie Antoinette was nothing but the frivolous youngest daughter of Austrian Empress Maria Theresa, and the frivolous wife of Louis XVI. She had an irregular education and was taught to speak French only at the age of fifteen after her betrothal to Louis was concluded. Spoiled, lively, and easily bored, she was sent to France with a list of rules to live by and an exhortation to say her prayers regularly.

Her arrival in France was inauspicious. All of her Austrian clothes, possessions, and servants were sent back to Vienna and replaced with French equivalents. Nothing familiar remained. When she arrived in Paris, she was ignored by her young husband. Furthermore, although she was not expected to be intelligent or industrious, she *was* expected to be fertile. Her one duty was to bear an heir to the throne, but she failed to do so for several years through no fault of her own. Louis was impotent, and for years he refused to submit to the operation which would cure his problem. Once he overcame his fears and allowed the operation, Marie bore him two sons, but by this time most people were convinced his condition was permanent. Therefore, they assumed the boys were really bastards.

Thus began the rumors of Marie Antoinette's supposed debaucheries, rumors which grew rather than subsided with time and ended with accusations that she'd sexually abused her eight-year-old son. She became a focus of discontent, and when the republicans ousted Louis, Marie Antoinette was denounced as "the shame of humanity and of her sex." She wrote desperately to relatives in Austria, asking for help. When help didn't arrive, she and Louis tried to

MARIE ANTOINETTE, condemned by the revolutionary tribunal: *The next scene was the beheading.*

escape but were captured at Varennes and returned to Paris. In January, 1793, Louis was tried for treason, found guilty, and executed. Nine months later, Marie Antoinette followed him to the guillotine. Her hair was cut, her hands tied behind her, and her head cut off. Her body was placed with sixty others in a mass grave, and her clothes were sent to a charity hospital; a few years later, tourists in Paris could find no one who knew where she was buried.

# 17

## SOPHIA GREGORIA HAYDEN,
*born in Santiago, Chile, 1868.*
Hayden's story is the story of tokenism, of a woman attempting to find a niche in a profession which had no place for her. She was the first woman to enter M.I.T.'s school of architecture; by the time she graduated with honors in 1890, she was an exceptional artist and designer as well as a competent structural engineer. Unfortunately, there was simply no room for women in architecture. No one would give her commissions, and no firm would hire her, so she ended up teaching drawing at a Boston high school.

In 1891, a design competition was held for the World's Columbia Exposition in Chicago. Women's accomplishments would be segregated from men's at the exposition and a Woman's Building was therefore necessary. It was thought appropriate that a woman should design the structure. Hayden won the contest with a Renaissance Revival design and traveled to Chicago to complete a series of working drawings. She received only fifteen hundred dollars, while male architects for the Exposition received between forty-five hundred and fifteen thousand dollars.

Hayden was the first designer to begin construction on her building, and she was also, in 1892, the first to complete her project. The result was universally celebrated, and she received several awards for its "delicacy of style, artistic taste, and geniality and elegance of the interior hall." However, much of the praise was of dubious worth. One critic dismissed the building as "dainty but tasteful," and another said that its "graceful timidity or gentleness, combined however with evident technical knowledge, at once differentiate[s] it from its colossal neighbors, and reveal[s] the sex of its author." Despite its success, the Woman's Building was the only structure that Hayden built, she was offered no further commis-

LIBRARY OF CONGRESS

## 18

LIBRARY OF CONGRESS

SOPHIA GREGORIA HAYDEN: *A camel could pass through the eye of a needle before her name could be found in any history of American architecture.*

sions. She retired, tired of condescension and the lack of opportunities, and thoroughly exhausted from her work on the Woman's Building. Colleagues spread rumors of a nervous breakdown, and the *American Architect and Building News* concluded smugly that the alleged collapse presented "a much more telling argument against . . . women entering this especial profession than anything else could."

**MARGARET CAROLYN ANDERSON,** *dies at 82 in Le Cannet, France, 1973.* In the first decade of the twentieth century, Margaret Anderson wrote to a Chicago advice columnist, asking "how a perfectly nice but revolting girl could leave home." Evidently she found a way, for in 1908 she went to Chicago with her sister Lois and began writing book reviews. Beautiful, enthusiastic, and determined, she quickly drifted into a bohemian lifestyle, roaming from theatres to music recitals in search of inspiration and itching to start a project of her own.

In 1914, Anderson found her project and established the *Little Review,* a journal dedicated to modern literature and political thought. It survived for only a few years, but it was enormously influential. Operating on charisma, a shoestring budget, and the motto "Life For Art's Sake," Anderson managed to convince a host of authors to publish their work in the *Little Review* without pay. Contributors included Vachel Lindsay, Gertrude Stein, Ernest Hemingway, Hilda Doolittle, Carl Sandburg,

Maxwell Bodenheim, Ben Hecht, Sherwood Anderson, William Carlos Williams, Amy Lowell, Ford Madox Ford, Wallace Stevens, Malcolm Cowley, Ezra Pound, William Butler Yeats, T. S. Eliot, and Hart Crane. Psychoanalysis, feminism, and the philosophy of Nietzsche found their way onto the *Little Review*'s pages, although sometimes nothing at all did. Once, disgusted with current literary offerings, Anderson simply printed two covers separated by sixty-two blank pages. She was undaunted by political pressure. She published articles by anarchist Emma Goldman even though it cost her her biggest financial backer; she serialized James Joyce's *Ulysses* even though it resulted in a trial for obscenity and the seizure of four *Little Review* issues by the U.S. Post Office.

## 19

**ANNIE SMITH PECK,** *born in Providence, Rhode Island, 1850.* A classicist, archaeologist, and one of the first female college professors in the United States, Annie Smith Peck abandoned her academic career after a trip to Switzerland in 1885. She saw the Alps and fell in love; soon she was climbing mountains in Switzerland and Greece, tackling higher and higher peaks. Gifted with stamina and boundless energy, although she never exercised between climbs, she climbed Mount Shasta in the Sierra Nevadas in 1888. She called the 14,162-foot climb "delightful and invigorating."

She became famous in 1895 for her assault on the Matterhorn. The publicity was generated as much by the shocking fact that she wore pants while climbing as by the fact that she was only the third woman in the nineteenth century to scale the 14,690-foot peak. She was dubbed "the Queen of the Climbers" and lectured on her experiences, although she wasn't really impressed by the mountain and decided to find herself a real challenge. In 1897 Peck climbed North America's third and fifth highest peaks, calling the women's world altitude record she thereby set

an "easy goal" to achieve. She chafed at the lack of danger and difficulty.

"My next thought," she wrote later, "was to do a little genuine exploration to conquer a virgin peak, to attain some height where no *man* had previously stood." Her hope was to locate and climb the highest mountain in the Western Hemisphere, the "apex of America." In 1904 Peck found the mountain she had sought so long. She seems to have wanted a mountain as rugged, determined, and stubborn as herself, and she found it in Peru. Mount Huascarán was a double-peaked giant, and for five years it held her at bay. She made six attempts to climb it, and five times was driven back by bad weather, mutinous porters, funding problems, losses of equipment and fuel, injuries sustained in a fall, and treacherous, cowardly, lazy, or stupid male colleagues. With more than a little bitterness, she wrote: "One of the chief difficulties in a woman's undertaking an expedition of this nature is that every man believes he knows better . . . than she."

At last, on August 31, 1909, when she was sixty years old, she conquered Huascarán. *Harper's Magazine* called it "one of the most remarkable feats in the history of mountain climbing," although, typically, her guide's clumsiness prevented Peck from taking an altitude measurement. She was forced to guess at the mountain's height, and her guess was exaggerated by newspapers, leading later to claims that she'd lied. Nonetheless, she'd made an extraordinary climb of (as we now know) 22,205 feet. Two years later she climbed Peru's Nevada Coropuna (21,079 feet), planting a "Votes For Women" banner at the summit.

# 20

**LYDIA MARIA CHILD,** *dies at 72 in Wayland, Massachusetts, 1880.* Child wrote in almost every genre available to her in her time. She began with novels about New England called *Habanok* and *The Rebels,* then turned to juvenile literature and domestic works. Her *Mother's Book* encouraged educating women; her *Frugal Housewife,* which featured chapters like "How to Endure Poverty," went through thirty-three editions between 1829 and 1870.

Child knew all about poverty. Her husband, David Lee Child, was a lawyer, editor, reformer, and farmer who had the best intentions in the world but was completely in-

ept when it came to managing money. Most of the family income was derived from Child's literary career, which took another turn after she was exposed to her husband's abolitionist views. In 1833 she published an *Appeal in Favor of that Class of Americans Called Africans.* Sales of her other books plummeted, but she'd found a new audience and a lifelong crusade.

In 1836 she issued a pamphlet, the *Anti-Slavery Catechism;* apparently believing she needed a more continuous expression of ideas, she and her husband established a weekly newspaper, the *Anti-Slavery Standard.* But she didn't forget that others were oppressed. She wrote a pamphlet called *An Appeal for the Indians,* and she fought all her life (in a genteel way, of course) for the rights of her sex. Her *History of the Condition of Woman in Various Ages and Nations* went through twenty editions in seven years, and she was a popular speaker on the subject of women's rights.

# 21

**LADY JANE GREY,** *born in Bradgate, Leicestershire, England, 1537, exact date unknown.* Poor Jane. Nothing went right for her. You'd think if you were beautiful, elegant, born to the nobility, and knew Greek, Hebrew, Latin, Italian, and French by your early teens, life couldn't be too bad. But Jane was destined to lead a miserable life, and the final insult is that her actual date of birth is now unknown. Her troubles began with a pushy family who saw her as a means of securing the throne of England. First they tried to marry her to the child-king Edward VI, son of Henry VIII and brother of Bloody Mary and Elizabeth I. When that

LADY JANE GREY: *An upright young woman who valued religious loyalty above her own life.*

LIBRARY OF CONGRESS

failed, her family concentrated on the king's closest adviser, the Duke of Northumberland, who *really* ran the kingdom. The duke's fourth son, Guildford Dudley, was unmarried, and Jane's family arranged for her to marry him. She wasn't thrilled with the idea, but "with pinches, nips, and blows" they forced her to agree. No wonder she told her tutor that "whatever I do else but learning is full of great trouble, fear, and wholesome misliking unto me." Her husband's family mistreated her, and then, just when she must have thought it couldn't get worse, Edward VI died. Not only that, he'd been bullied by Jane's family's allies into leaving the throne to Jane instead of to Mary, the rightful heir, and there

was nothing in the world Jane wanted less than the throne. But, convinced it was her duty to rule, or perhaps persuaded with more "pinches, nips, and blows," she declared herself Queen Jane and ruled for nine miserable days before Mary rode into London to take back the crown. Mary wanted to spare Jane's life, but a rebellion on behalf of the nine days' queen made it too dangerous to leave her alive. So Jane and her allies were executed—first the Duke of Northumberland, then Guildford Dudley, and finally Jane herself. She was escorted to the block on February 12, 1554, dignified and calm to the last, "her countenance nothing abashed, neither her eyes anything moistened with tears."

## 22

**NADIA BOULANGER,** *dies at 92 in Paris, France, 1979.* At age twenty, Boulanger was a promising young composer who had written an opera and music for the cello and the piano. By the time she was thirty, she had stopped composing in deference to her sister, Lili, whom she believed to have superior talent. Instead, she became a teacher and a conductor, one of the most successful in modern times. By the time of her death she had won the Legion of Honor, received honorary doctorates from Harvard and Oxford, and taught at the Paris Conservatoire, the École Normale, Radcliffe, Wellesley, Juilliard, and the American Conservatory. She was the first woman to conduct a symphony orchestra in London, to conduct the Hallé Orchestra in Manchester, England, and to give regular subscription concerts with the Boston Symphony Orchestra and the New York Philharmonic. Her pupils were among the finest composers and teachers of their time. In fact, said *The New York Times* in 1985, "so influential was she that virtually every music department at major colleges in the

United States has at least one Boulanger student." One of her most notable pupils, Aaron Copland, remembered two things about that tyrannical, brilliant Frenchwoman—that she worked him "terribly hard" and that she knew "pre-Bach to post-Stravinsky . . . cold."

## 23

**GERTRUDE EDERLE,** *born in New York City, 1906.* By 1925 Gertrude Ederle was one of the world's best-known swimmers. She had set twenty-nine world and American amateur records, the first at age twelve, when she broke the 880-yard freestyle record and became the youngest person in the world to set a nonmechanical record. In 1922, she broke seven records in one day at Brighton Beach in New York, and at the 1924 Olympics she won a gold medal and two bronze medals although there were only five swimming events open to women. In

1925, however, she decided to set a special record; she wanted to be the first woman to swim the English Channel. Her first failed attempt garnered knowing remarks about the impossibility of a woman swimming the Channel. But Ederle refused to give up, and she tried again in 1926. She chose a bad day; rough seas and choppy water forced her to swim thirty-five miles to cover a twenty-one mile distance. Nevertheless, she finished the swim in fourteen hours and thirty-one minutes—nearly two hours faster than the men's world record.

## 24

**SARAH J. HALE,** *born Sarah Josepha Buell in Newport, New Hampshire, 1788.* "It is only in emergencies," wrote Sarah J. Hale, "in cases where duty demands the sacrifice of female sensitiveness, that a lady of sense and delicacy will come before the public, in a manner to make herself conspicuous." In Hale's case, the emergency that made her conspicuous was her husband's death. By her own admission, she despised a woman who was "arrogant in her pretensions." She believed women should limit themselves to "the chaste, disinterested circle of the fireside," but she had five children to support and found herself unable to do it through typical feminine occupations.

Instead, she made use of her knack for writing, producing a novel and several poems, including the famous "Mary Had a Little Lamb," and in 1828 she founded the *Ladies' Magazine.* Not only was she the magazine's editor, but she also wrote at least half of the copy (including, often, the letters to the editor), sometimes under her own name but more frequently under various pseudonyms.

In a time when most women's magazines were run by men and concentrated mostly on fashion, the *Ladies' Magazine* was run by a woman and touched discreetly on politics. Hale supported higher education, though only to make women into better wives and mothers, and she favored a cautious approach to the emancipation of her sex. "We should solicit education as a favor," she warned, "not exact it as a right." In Hale's perfect world, women were the dispensers of charity, the educators of the young, and the guardians of moral sanctity and "domestic felicity."

The *Ladies' Magazine* was always financially troubled, and eventually it merged with the most popular women's magazine of the day, *Godey's Lady's Book*. Hale was still allowed to advocate higher education, but politics and theology were now off limits. They were replaced by interior design hints, double-page fashion plates, recipes, etiquette tips, notes on housework, poetry, fiction, patriotic pieces, anti-suffrage arguments, and crochet, embroidery, and sewing patterns. Later, the advice column and the fiction sections were also trampled beneath the feet of the expanding fashion section.

Hale felt a twinge about sacrificing her principles, but she used her now-famous name to sell books on etiquette and housekeeping. She had begun writing ostensibly "not to win fame, but support for my little children." She stopped writing at eighty-nine, only two years before her death, but she maintained to the end that she had written only "to promote the reputation of my sex and my country," and that "the Mother, not the Author, has been successful."

SARAH J. HALE: *She advocated educating women to raise better men.*

# 25

**GRACE O'MALLEY,** *born in County Mayo, Ireland, in about 1530, exact date unknown.* Few women in this book have gone by so many variants of the same name as Grace O'Malley. She was also known as Graine Mhaol ("Grace of the Cropped Hair"), Graine ui Maille, Grany O'Mayly, Grainne O'Mailley, Grany ne Male, Grany ne Mayle, Grayn My Vayle, and Grany ne Malley. Her father, Dubhdara O'Malley, was a local chieftain. She married twice—the first time to Domhnall-an-Chogaidh O'Flaherty, with whom she had two sons, and the second time to Richard Mac Oileverius Burke, also known as "Richard of the Iron," with whom she had a daughter.

O'Malley came from a seafaring family, and she was raised around boats and water. So it seemed perfectly natural that she joined the fighting against the English by sea rather than by land. Leading rebellions and sea raids at the head of her fleet of ships, she made herself a general nuisance, and was finally captured and held briefly in Dublin in 1577. Once she was free, she continued to plot against English rule, and in 1586 she was arrested and sentenced to hang. The gallows were built, but her son-in-law pleaded eloquently for her life

and she was released into his custody. Eventually she was forced to relinquish her fleet, and in exchange she received a pardon from Queen Elizabeth I. O'Malley died in poverty and was immortalized by both sides of the conflict. The Irish remembered her as a great heroine, while in 1593 a pro-English writer called her "a notable traitress and nurse of all rebellions in the province for forty years."

# 26

**BERYL MARKHAM,** *born in Ashwell, Rutland, England, 1902.* Beryl Markham was one of those wonderful people whose life stories read more like those of mythical creatures than of actual beings. At age three, she accompanied her family to East Africa, but when her mother and brother returned to England in 1906, she stayed behind with her father, a horse breeder and farmer who was perpetually in debt. Hating formal education, she ran wild whenever she could, playing and wrestling with native children, learning to track animals and to hunt with a spear and a bow and arrow, half-domesticating a zebra foal, teaching herself to jump higher than her head, learning to shoot, and helping her father breed and train race horses. She survived tropical diseases, an attack from a baboon, and mauling by a lion. She grew up tall, tanned, strong, beautiful, and irresponsible.

After World War I Markham married a man sixteen years her senior and began to work on her own as a horse trainer. Her love of horses lasted longer than the marriage, which soon collapsed because of her numerous affairs. In 1927 she married the second son of a baronet, Mansfield Markham. This marriage was also a failure, but she liked the surface respectability of being married and refused to get divorced. Her husband lived in England, and she spent most of her time in Kenya having affairs with Denys Finch-Hatton (Karen Blixen's

lover), England's Prince Henry, and probably Karen Blixen's husband, Bror, as well. The romance with Henry caused quite a scandal and ended with the royal family buying Markham's silence for £15,000. Still, sex and scandal weren't sufficiently exciting to her. She needed to be doing something active, something dangerous. She decided to learn to fly.

With the help of another lover, flying instructor Tom Black, Markham quickly got her license, and from 1931 to 1936 she made a good living by ferrying mail, passengers, and supplies throughout East Africa. When she needed more money and greater challenges, she began scouting elephants for safaris, battling storms, dysentery, malaria, tsetse flies, and razorlike grass that could shred a plane's wings.

In 1936, she put her talents to a different use, becoming the first woman to fly the Atlantic from east to west. She made the 3,600-mile flight at the "wrong" time of the year—autumn—and under the "wrong" conditions—it was raining and dark. Nonetheless, despite engine trouble and a forced landing, she made it to Nova Scotia, Canada, in twenty-one hours and twenty-five minutes, breaking the men's record.

Widely celebrated for her feat, she worked as a film consultant, and wrote her autobiography, *West with the Night,* which Ernest Hemingway called "really a bloody wonderful book," and it is.

# 27

**MAXINE HONG KINGSTON,** *born Maxine Hong in Stockton, California, 1940.* To read *The Woman Warrior,* Kingston's autobiographical novel (or fictionalized autobiography, whichever you prefer), is to receive an instant and much-needed education. Kingston, whose Chinese-immigrant parents ran a Stockton, California, laundry, is well-versed in the myths and dreams of both American and Chinese culture. In *The Woman Warrior* and its companion, *China Men,* she weaves together and contrasts American and Chinese legends, ideals, and views of gender, language, and silence. She tells us about her Chinese ancestresses in American terms and translates American images into Chinese myths. She portrays heroes and heroines and the sexual and cultural clashes that threaten to break them. She catalogues injustices, discriminatory immigration procedures and local laws, misconceptions, and stereotypes. And she asks other Chinese-Americans, "how do you separate what is peculiar to childhood, to poverty, insanities, one family, your mother who marked your growing with stories, from what is Chinese? What is Chinese tradition and what is the movies?"

# 28

**NAWAL EL SAADAWI,** *born in Kafr Tahla, Egypt, 1931.* On Sunday, September 5, 1981, the police broke into Nawal El Saadawi's home. They searched her house, took some of her papers, and imprisoned her, along with 1,535 others, for "stirring up sectarian strife." The author of several novels, short story collections, important nonfiction books, and essays on gender, the woman who had been called "the Simone de Beauvoir of the Arab world," was

held for over eighty days and interrogated twice for "publishing articles critical of President Sadat's
policies." After Sadat's assassination on October 6, El Saadawi was
freed by Sadat's successor, Hosni
Mubarak. However, he did not end
the ban on her books, which are
censored in Egypt and other Arab
countries.

The daughter of a civil servant,
El Saadawi is a physician educated
in Egypt and the United States. She
served as Egypt's Director of Public
Health until her views got her fired;
among other things, she objects to
her culture's obsession with virginity and believes sex should be enjoyed by women as well as men.
She has been an especially fierce
enemy of the practice of clitoridectomy, still performed in many parts

of the world. The operation is
sometimes referred to as "female
circumcision," but in reality is better compared with the mutilation or
amputation of the penis. It varies in
degrees; sometimes only the tip of
the clitoris is removed, and
sometimes the whole clitoris and
even the labia are cut off. (A close
relative of clitoridectomy, infibula-
tion involves the closing of the
vagina, usually by sewing, to promote fidelity. Only a tiny opening is
left to allow urine and menstrual
blood to escape.) El Saadawi has
written a great deal about such
practices and exposes their ironies.
"Society looks at the woman as a
tool of love," she wrote in 1977,
"and deprives her of the one organ
which will make her be good at it."

phal, and there are at least two
reasons to be suspicious of it; first,
the story is not the only version of
how the poet died, and, second
Sappho simply wasn't the sort of
woman who would have jumped.

# 29

**FANNY BRICE,** *born Fanny
Borach in New York City, 1891.*
Born on Manhattan's Lower East
Side, Fanny Borach had a rather
unusual family. Her father was a
spendthrift and gambler whose
nickname was "Pinochle Charlie."
Her mother ran seven saloons at
once. As a child, Brice used to sing
in these saloons, dancing on tables
and bar tops.

Eventually, Mrs. Borach got tired
of having her profits spent reckless-
ly by Pinochle Charlie, and she left
him, sold the saloons, took the
children to Brooklyn, and went into
the real estate business. Fourteen-
year-old Fanny missed show business, however, and decided to go on
the stage as Fanny Brice. Easier said
than done. Within a year she
learned she was too tall and skinny
to be a chorus girl. So she tried the
vaudeville circuit, and soon she was
dancing and singing her way
through the northeast. She became
known for her clowning, and she
was chosen by Florenz Ziegfeld for
the *Follies of 1910.* Her first
number in the *Follies* earned her
twelve encores, and she soon became Ziegfeld's biggest female star
with her spoofs of Camille and
Theda Bara and her renditions of
"Second Hand Rose" and "My
Man."

Over the next thirty-five years,
Brice appeared in nine *Follies,*
several musicals, one dismal drama,
and six movies. Her biggest hit was
a character she'd created called
Baby Snooks, which got her several
theater appearances and a long-
running radio show. Brice was a
direct, forceful, earthy woman who
wouldn't trust anyone who didn't
say "shit." Apparently it wasn't a
good enough guideline, since none

**SAPPHO,** *born on Lesbos, in the
seventh century B.C., exact date
unknown.* She was one of the
greatest poets of ancient Greece,
revered by her contemporaries and
her students. Her work was so in-
ventive that she created her own
type of stanza, and, through the
centuries that followed, it bore her
name and eventually became a
favorite vehicle for the Roman poet
Catullus. Her name and the name
of her home, Lesbos, became
emblems of sexual love between
women. You'd think such a woman,
famous in her own time and in
ours, would have left behind a
better-documented life.

But most of what we know of
Sappho is from the fragments of
her poetry that remain to us. Her
date of birth may have been as early as 640 B.C. or as late as 613 B.C.,
and her date of death is equally
obscure, although she did live to
old age. She was the daughter of
Scamandronymus and his wife
Cleis, a wealthy, aristocratic couple
who lived on the island of Lesbos,
eight miles from the coast of
Turkey. When she was still quite
young, Sappho married a rich man

named Cercolas; they had one
daughter, Cleis, and were very happy, but Sappho unfortunately spent
most of her life as a widow.

Her poetry describes pastoral life,
religious festivals, weddings, love,
passion, anger, jealousy, and episodes in women's lives. She also
wrote a great deal of affectionate
poetry to her daughter and some
nostalgic pieces about her happiness in marriage. But it is for her
love poems to women that she is
best known. She ran a school for
girls on Lesbos at which she taught
poetry, singing, and dancing.
Several of her poems are addressed
to her students, and the love and
desire these verses express are
undeniable. Nevertheless, scholars
for centuries have tried to explain
away these poems and "restore"
Sappho to strict heterosexuality.
Ancient historians began this task,
claiming that in her old age Sappho
had an unrequited passion for a
youth named Phaon and that when
she realized he would never love her
she leaped off a cliff and fell to her
death. There's been a great deal of
quarreling among scholars as to
whether or not this story is apocry-

of her marriages was really happy. The first, to a barber, was hardly a marriage at all; she never lived with him. Her second husband, Jules W. "Nick" Arnstein, was a gambler, a fraud, and a thief who wasted most of her money and spent part of their marriage in jail. When he turned out to be unfaithful as well, Brice finally divorced him. Her third marriage, to producer Billy Rose, also ended in divorce. Brice died of a stroke in 1951.

# 30

**RUTH GORDON,** *born Ruth Gordon Jones in Quincy, Massachusetts, 1896.* Ruth Gordon always managed to combine sound advice to young actors with a good story and a dash of wit. "A career is hard to get going and hard to keep going," she once wrote. "Help it by choosing a good name. I chose Fentress Serene Kerlin, but my mother said if I was going to be that foolish I better stay home."

Gordon didn't stay home, didn't become a housewife, or a gym teacher, as her parents had wanted. She took to the stage, getting her start as Nibs in *Peter Pan.* And her stage career was long and satisfactory, highlighted by triumphs like *Seventeen* and *The Country Wife.* She wrote books and screenplays, and her friends included Thornton Wilder, Harpo Marx, Alexander Woollcott, Rosalind Russell, and Katharine Hepburn. She had a long and happy marriage with writer Garson Kanin, who was sixteen years her junior. And she continued to act. In her old age, Gordon was often tapped for movies, always playing the role of a spunky, upbeat woman who wouldn't deny life, love, or her own age. Her wit, ambition, joy, and obvious passion for living made her perfect for the characters she played in such movies as *Harold and Maude* and *My Bodyguard.* She died in September 1985.

RUTH GORDON: *An inspiration in the face of the inevitable.*

# 31

**NATALIE CLIFFORD BARNEY,** *born in Dayton, Ohio, 1876.* Wealthy, attractive, witty, charming, and well-educated, Natalie Barney left her native country for France as a young woman and never returned. Paris became her home, its notables her friends, and its expatriate circle her guests at her famous salon. In Paris she wrote about twelve books in various genres—memoirs, poetry, and fiction—but her life was her greatest work of art, and she became one of the most celebrated and notorious characters in the city.

Her salon contributed largely to her fame, as did the Parisian decor of her house, the fact that she always wore white, the cakes she served on Fridays which were reputed to be the best in Paris, her morning rides on horseback in the Bois de Boulogne, and her garden temple to Eros where, in the moonlight, pairs of lesbians danced. Barney was most famous for her sexual voracity; she made conquests whenever she had a spare moment. For more than fifty years she had an ongoing affair with painter Romaine Brooks, but while Brooks remained faithful, Barney did not—a fact which caused their breakup in 1969, only one year before Brooks died. Among those she seduced were a famous courtesan, Liane de Pougy, and an English poet, Renée Vivien. When Vivien died young, Barney grieved deeply and established a prize for female poets in Vivien's name. Barney frequently used her contacts and wealth to help women writers. Outraged by the Academie Française's steadfast refusal to admit women, she organized her own French Academy—the Académie des Femmes.

LIBRARY OF CONGRESS

NATALIE BARNEY: *A doe-eyed seductress of women.*

LIBRARY OF CONGRESS

FRANCES HODGSON BURNETT, creator of *Little Lord Fauntleroy,* modeled after one of her sons: *"The one perfect thing in my life was the childhood of my boys."*

# NOVEMBER

## 1

**SACAJAWEA,** *born about 1786, exact date and place unknown.* A common misconception is that Sacajawea was the chief guide of the Lewis and Clark expedition to the Pacific. She was not the chief guide; she did very little guiding at all, but she served other equally important functions and assured the success of the expedition. A member of the Shoshone Indian tribe, her name has many spellings and many meanings, including Bird Woman, Boat Woman, and Lost Woman. In 1800 she was captured by the Hidatsa tribe, which made her a slave and taught her its skills and customs.

When she was about eighteen, the Hidatsas sold her to Toussaint Charbonneau, a French-Canadian interpreter and guide with the Lewis and Clark expedition. She accompanied the explorers, and when she bore Charbonneau a son, Baptiste, in 1805, she took the baby along as well. She quickly endeared herself to the men, who called her "Janey," and no wonder—she was pretty and robust, she never complained, she cooked, cleaned, foraged, and translated for them, and she nursed them when they were ill. On one occasion she rescued some important papers and instruments from a swift river; on another occasion she convinced the Shoshones to lend the expedition some horses. She didn't get much for her trouble except a glimpse of the Pacific and the honor of being the first woman to cross the Rocky Mountains, but her son benefited greatly from her efforts. Captain Clark, who had always been fond of Sacajawea, took a great liking to Baptiste and made sure he got an education and some important introductions. Baptiste ended up spending six years in Europe as the guest of a German prince before beginning a varied and illustrious career.

## 2

**JESSIE DANIEL AMES,** *born Jessie Daniel in Palestine, Texas, 1883.* Shy and insecure, Jessie Daniel wanted one thing as a young woman: to get married. In 1905, when a friend of her father's, an army doctor thirteen years her senior, proposed to her, she jumped at the chance. However, once she was married she became less enthusiastic about wedded bliss. When her husband was stationed in Central America, she seems to have been almost relieved, and when he died of black water fever in Guatemala, she might have felt liberated had it not been for the fact that she had three children to feed.

It was a difficult time for Ames, but she began working and enjoyed it and her shyness and awkwardness gradually faded. She began campaigning for woman suffrage, and when that was achieved, she became the founding president of the Texas League of Women Voters. Then, troubled by racism within the women's movement, she joined the Atlanta-based Commission on International Cooperation and, in 1930, she established the Association of Southern Women for the Prevention of Lynching (ASWPL).

The ASWPL had limited effect, but it did form ties between existing women's groups, especially church groups, and through ASWPL women gained political experience. Most importantly, it challenged the excuse often used by lynch mobs— that they were protecting white women. Ames collected statistics on lynchings, proving that in only a minority of cases were the victims accused of crimes against white women. She maintained that chivalry was merely another way of stating that "white men hold that white women are their property [and] so are Negro women." By joining the ASWPL, she said, white women would reject complicity in the crime of lynching and rob racist

violence of its professed purpose.

In the 1940s, the ASWPL disbanded because lynchings were decreasing in frequency. Ames was by now an embittered woman, and although her organization had apparently succeeded, she wasn't fooled. In 1944 she wrote, "We have managed to reduce lynchings not because we've grown more law-abiding or respectable but because lynchings have become such bad advertising. The South is going after big industry at the moment, and a lawless, lynch-mob population isn't going to attract very much outside capital."

## 3

**HARRIET TAYLOR MILL,** *dies at 51 in Avignon, France, 1858.* At eighteen, Harriet Hardy married a manufacturer named John Taylor, who was eleven years her senior. By the time she was twenty-three, she had two children and a whopping case of intellectual boredom. It was then, most opportunely, that she met philosopher John Stuart Mill, and her life changed dramatically. For twenty-one years they met almost daily, exchanged essays they'd written, dined together in her husband's absence, and spent weekends together. Taylor didn't mind this, but he was livid when Mill suggested that his books, which were really "joint productions," bear Harriet's name as well as Mill's. Taylor thought that even a dedication to Harriet would be "a want of taste and tact which I could not have believed possible."

Harriet was drawn to Mill initially because they shared similar views about the equality of the sexes, but she soon discovered that Mill's ideas were somewhat less radical than her own. She favored abolition of marriage laws and supported the right and responsibility of a woman to control her own body, especially her own fertility. She also thought the perfect society would "let every occupation be open to all, without favor or discouragement to any." Mill thought women should be allowed to hold non-traditional jobs, but he always believed a woman's first duty was to marry and "adorn and beautify life."

Still, Harriet did her best, and Mill was undoubtedly one of the most open-minded men of his time on the subject of feminism. In 1851, two years after Taylor's death, Mill and Harriet married, but not before they drafted a formal protest against repressive marriage laws. They lived together only seven years before she died in Avignon; Mill set up house nearby and visited her grave every day until his death.

Today, Harriet Taylor Mill is best known for an essay she wrote in 1851 called "Enfranchisement of Women," in which she wrote what was then no less than a full-fledged battle cry: "We deny the right of any portion of the species to decide for another portion . . . what is and what is not their 'proper sphere.' The proper sphere for all human beings is the largest and highest which they are able to attain."

# 4 _____

**THEODORA,** *born in Constantinople about 497, exact date unknown.* If you were a Byzantine citizen in the year 501, wandering through some of the less fashionable streets in Constantinople, you might have seen a four-year-old orphan girl, Theodora, whose father had been the bear-tamer at the Hippodrome. Eleven years later, you might have seen her in the theatre, where she was a popular dancer, mime, and comedian. At neither time would you have suspected that she would become the Empress of Constantinople, and a far greater empress than her husband was an emperor.

When she grew up, Theodora

traveled to Egypt, had an affair with a minor bureaucrat, returned to Constantinople, and became a wool spinner. Then, through one of those marvelous tricks that history plays, the imperial heir, Justinian, fell in love with her. Justinian was not a particularly wise or strong man, but he had enough sense to recognize that Theodora had all the qualities he lacked. He enacted a special law that enabled him to marry a commoner, and in 525 he took advantage of it. When Justinian became emperor in 527, Theodora administerd the empire. She was involved in religious politics, sponsored the construction of new public buildings, and contributed vigorously to council discussions. She gave advice on legislation, encouraged religious tolerance, reformed the divorce and property laws, and prohibited fathers from selling their children as slaves. She outlawed pimps and madams, removed her enemies from office with ruthless efficiency, and bought girls from slavery and from brothels, caring for them at her own expense. When she died in 548, Justinian was incosolable, and the seventeen years he ruled without her were ineffectual and undistinguished.

# 5 _____

**JACQUELINE AURIOL,** *born Jacqueline Douet in Challans, France, 1917.* When she was thirty years old, Jacqueline Auriol learned to fly airplanes—because she was curious. Her curiosity then led her to learn stunt flying and to qualify as a tourist pilot, and after that it led her to the hospital. In 1949, while riding in a seaplane over the Seine, she crashed. Her jaw was broken and her skull fractured; she spent two years in hospitals and had fourteen operations to restore her facial structure. But she kept on flying. She qualified as a military pilot, became the world's first female test pilot, got a helicopter pilot's license, and learned how to fly jets. And in 1951, she broke the

world women's air speed record by traveling 507 miles per hour in one of the first Vampires. That feat earned her the Legion of Honor, and in 1952 she broke her own record in a Mistral jet, traveling 534.375 miles per hour. She became one of the first pilots in the world to break the sound barrier when she flew 687.5 miles per hour in 1953.

# 6 _____

**AGRIPPINA THE YOUNGER,** *born Julia Agrippina in Rome, Italy, 15 A.D., exact date unknown.* The fourth of six children and the sister of Caligula, Agrippina was married at the age of thirteen. In the year 37, when she was about twenty-two, two important things happened. Emperor Tiberius died and was replaced by Caligula, and Agrippina gave birth to Nero, the man who would have her murdered. She was highly ambitious on her son's behalf and anxiously consulted astrologers, who told her: "He will be emperor and will kill his mother." Her reply was stoic. "He is welcome to kill me, as long as he becomes emperor."

To assist her son, Agrippina associated with men of power and wealth. When Caligula's successor, Claudius, grew tired of the intrigues of his wife, Messalina, he had her executed. There was therefore a vacancy in the imperial bed, and Agrippina aspired to fill it. By 49 she was empress. Power-hungry, money-hungry, and authoritative, she exercised her new influence in various ways, but mostly to help Nero supplant Claudius's own son, Britannicus. In 50 Nero was adopted by Claudius and married the emperor's daughter Octavia; for herself Agrippina acquired the title "Augusta," a rare honor.

In 54, Claudius had an unfortunate accident and died after ingesting a dish of mushrooms. It was generally assumed, although without any proof, that Agrippina had poisoned him. Nero became emperor; it was time for the other half of the prophecy to be fulfilled. Nero grew tired of Agrippina's authority. He also grew tired of her overly affectionate kisses in public, which gave rise to rumors of incest. He decided to kill her but did not have the courage to have her executed; instead he had a ship specially designed to sink and lured her onto it with kind words and promises. The ship sank, but Agrippina was not killed. She watched as one of her ladies cried, "I am Agrippina. Help for the emperor's mother," only to be bludgeoned to death. Silently she watched, and silently she swam to safety.

She sent Nero news of her deliverance and waited to see what would happen. He panicked. Flustered and terrified of his mother, he finally managed to send assassins to find her. When they arrived, she faced them calmly. When they drew their swords to kill her, she pointed to her womb, saying, "Strike here."

---

AGRIPPINA: *Suetonius recounts how the Roman empress was seen leaving Nero's royal coach with her son's semen on her lips.*

LIBRARY OF CONGRESS

# 7

**MARIE CURIE,** *born Maria Sklodowska in Warsaw, Poland, 1867.* Whenever you get a little depressed, you can always turn to the story of Marie Curie. She had three strikes against her even before she started her career; she was a woman with an interest in science; she was a Pole living under Russian rule; and she was not wealthy. Nevertheless, she discovered radium and polonium, invented the term "radioactivity," and became the first female professor at the Sorbonne, the first female Nobelist in physics, and the first person of either sex to win two Nobel Prizes. The first step in this remarkable career, was a deal she made with her older sister, Bronia. Each of them wanted a career, and neither could achieve it on her own. So they decided that Marie would work to put Bronia through medical school, and then Bronia would send Marie to the Sorbonne.

All went as planned, although they struggled through years of poverty. Marie graduated with honors in physics and chemistry, and in Paris she met and married physicist Pierre Curie. Before he met Marie, he had decided he would never marry, since women were generally poorly educated, and he wanted an intellectual equal, not a housekeeper. He wanted an exceptional woman with whom he could share his work as well as his love, and he found her in Marie Sklodowska. They had two children, and hired babysitters while they worked in the laboratory. The scientific establishment was eager to celebrate Pierre and ignore Marie, but he insisted that his wife be given full credit for her share of their work, and he refused the Legion of Honor because at that time it was withheld from women.

Pierre died in 1906, but Marie's career did not end. She worked with radiation therapy, won the Nobel Prize for chemistry, and, during World War I, drove an ambulance to the front lines to x-ray wounded soldiers. She died in 1934 of leukemia caused by overexposure to radiation. Marie Curie's words, written in 1888 while Bronia was in medical school, are to some a source of comfort. "My plans for the future!" she wrote. "I have none . . . I mean to get through as well as I can, and when I can do no more, say farewell to this base world. The loss will be small, and regret for me will be short."

LIBRARY OF CONGRESS

MARIE CURIE: *"Nothing is to be feared. It is only to be understood."*

# 9

**ANNE SEXTON,** *born Anne Gray Harvey in Newton, Massachusetts, 1928.* Anne Sexton is often associated with Sylvia Plath for a number of reasons. Both Plath and Sexton were poets from Massachusetts. They were contemporaries—in fact, they were friends. They both wrote a good deal about their own lives. Both spent time in mental institutions, although Sexton was more frequently hospitalized and tried more frequently to kill herself. Both Plath and Sexton were unhappily married, had two children, and tried but failed to lead a life of conventional domesticity. Sexton lived longer than Plath—long enough to write several volumes of poetry, to receive the Pulitzer Prize and a nomination for the National Book Award, and to become a university professor. However, she grew increasingly dependent on alcohol and drugs, especially the tranquilizer Thorazine, and in 1974, she succeeded in committing suicide. Like Sylvia Plath, she gassed herself to death.

# 8

**KATHARINE HEPBURN,** *born in Hartford, Connecticut, 1909.* Let's face it. Ingrid Bergman was very, very beautiful in *Casablanca,* and Claudette Colbert was saucy and soulful in *It Happened One Night,* but if you could have been anyone in an old movie, wouldn't it be Katharine Hepburn in *Adam's Rib* or *The Philadelphia Story?* Hepburn always got her comeuppance —she had to, it was the movies— but it was always a *little* comeuppance, sort of a moral tacked on to the *real* story, the part with the spirited dialogue and the snappy repartee. Hepburn would never have let Clark Gable push her around. She never, never would have said, "You'll have to do the thinking for both of us." She was always glorious, strong, sexy *because* she was strong and beautiful in the way that any woman can be if she has enough pride.

Almost everything she touched turned into a classic—*Little Women, The African Queen, A Bill of Divorcement, The Lion in Winter, Woman of the Year, Bringing Up Baby, Guess Who's Coming to Dinner?* and *On Golden Pond.* Almost everything. In 1936 she made a dog called *Sylvia Scarlett.* Most of the sneak preview audience left halfway through. Some viewers actually ran out of the theatre. Hepburn sneaked away and went to the ladies' room, where a woman had fainted. "My God," Hepburn cried, "the picture's killed her!" However, the few failures are trifles in comparison to the successes. Hepburn has received more Oscars (four for best actress) than most actors have received nominations. It would seem she's done somewhat more than follow Spencer Tracy's advice on acting: "Know your lines and don't bump into the furniture."

# 10

**LULU WHITE,** *born in the nineteenth century, exact date unknown.* For a few legendary years around the turn of the century, New Orleans decided to kick its prostitutes out—almost. According to a statute initiated by a man named Story, prostitution was considered legal as long as it happened in a certain area outside the city limits.

KATHARINE HEPBURN: *A strong-willed individualist, she encouraged the independent woman by example.*

As a dubious honor, the red-light district was nicknamed Storyville. And Storyville became a place like no other, full of great musicians and rich men, cheap brothels and gaudy palaces, beautiful girls and voodoo women, street fights and expensive champagne, and, of course, madams.

The greatest and most famous of the madams was Lulu White. She appeared out of nowhere in the 1880s, proudly saying she was from the West Indies. All her life she was convinced she could have "passed for white," although no one who knew her agreed with her. Her conviction that she was better than others because her skin was light remained with her throughout her

career and irritated nearly everyone.

When the Storyville district was declared in 1898, White took advantage of the situation. Using forty thousand dollars and what contemporaries called her "atrocious taste," she built a four-story marble mansion at 235 Basin Street. Called Mahogany Hall and nicknamed "The Hall of Mirrors," it had five lavish parlors and fifteen bedrooms with mirrors installed at the head and foot of each bed.

White herself was one of Mahogany Hall's chief tourist attractions. Known, at least to herself, as "The Queen of the Demi-Monde," she had a passion for diamonds which went completely beyond reason. She put them everywhere—arms, head,

and neck. Gaudiest of all, she wore diamond rings on all her fingers, including the thumbs. She made her entrance every night smothered in jewels, wearing a red wig and an expensive, tacky gown, slowly descending a spiral staircase singing "Where the Moon Shines." It was a far cry from her early days in New Orleans, before legalization, when "bringing Lulu in" for prostitution and disorderly conduct was an almost weekly ritual. By the era of Mahogany Hall, she was so powerful that her mansion, with its thousands upon thousands of dollars worth of furnishings, was valued by the tax assessors in her favor at only $300.

Some people didn't like White at all. One acquaintance commented that "she had one of those masculine type voices that ring with authority and remove all traces of femininity." Some were jealous of her success, and some resented her airs. But no one—least of all White —was prepared to deny that her employees included some of the most popular women in Storyville. All of them were octoroons (a person with one black great-grandparent); the law forbade black and white prostitutes from working in the same brothel. Strict segregation was the rule in Storyville, and only white men had access to the more expensive houses. Black customers, therefore, no matter how wealthy, were banned from Mahogany Hall.

White did a tremendous business for a number of years, and she made a great deal of money, but by 1907 her luck began to change. She had lived by that time for about twenty-five years with a handsome, charming man named George Killishaw, whom she trusted completely. She was a shrewd businesswoman in most areas, and she was one of the first to see the potential of Hollywood. She gave Killishaw all her movable cash—about $150,000— and told him to invest it in Los Angeles real estate. He ran away with the money.

White recouped some of her losses by building a saloon next to Mahogany Hall, but as the years passed, Storyville's glamor faded. By 1915 the entire district had only seven hundred prostitutes, and Mahogany Hall had only eight regulars. In 1917, by Federal order, Storyville was shut down, and White's brothel, like the rest, was closed. She was last seen alive in 1941. No one known when or how she died.

# 11

**ABIGAIL ADAMS,** *born Abigail Smith in Weymouth, Massachusetts, 1744.* Abigail probably never would have been famous had she not been the wife of John Adams and the mother of John Quincy Adams. But she deserved more than reflected glory. A witty, honest woman who loved her husband and her five children, she was not only the first First Lady to live in the White House but a skillful farmer and business woman, an astute political adviser, and an articulate letter-writer as well. Her correspondence, first published by her grandson Charles, is full of gossip, affection, and political observations. She was an ardent abolitionist long before such views were even entertained as subjects of conversation. She expressed doubts as to Virginians' "passion for Liberty" since they "have been accustomed to deprive their fellow Creatures of theirs."

She was also a feminist, and she justly accused her husband of creating a republic for men only. In March, 1776, she wrote to John: "Remember the Ladies, and be more generous and favorable to them than your ancestors. Do not put such unlimited power into the hands of the Husbands. Remember all Men would be tyrants if they could. If particular care and attention is not paid to the Ladies we are determined to foment a Rebellion, and will not hold ourselves bound by any Laws in which we have no voice, or Representation." Adams, of course, thought the whole thing was a joke and advised her to forget all about it.

# 12

**ELIZABETH CADY STANTON,** *born Elizabeth Cady in Johnstown, New York, 1815.* Stanton has never been as widely admired as her protégée Susan B. Anthony, for two reasons. The first is a justifiable accusation: Stanton was a snob and very probably a racist, who believed that only the educated citizenry should be allowed to vote and who used almost any argument she thought would work to sway an audience. Anthony, while she condoned such tactics as necessary political realities, made a clear distinction between her personal beliefs and political behavior. Stanton did not make such a distinction.

This criticism of Stanton is a recent one. Previously she was ignored not because she was hypocritical but because she was radical. What the militant feminist is today, Stanton was in her own time; she was considered outrageous, horrifying, monstrous, unwomanly, depraved, ridiculous, and practically untouchable. Yet it was she who was feminism's most articulate proponent, and it was she who initiated reforms we take for granted today.

She began her career as an abolitionist, but soon she turned to feminism. At a London anti-slavery convention in 1840, she and several other women were rejected as delegates because of their sex. There she met Lucretia Mott, and these two women, angered by their exclusion, decided to do something. But first, Stanton raised her seven children, and it was not until 1848 that she and Mott organized a women's rights convention in Stanton's hometown of Seneca Falls, New York. The convention received a great deal of press coverage, most of it condescending, amused, or outraged, and the women present, to draw further attention to their cause, drew up a Declaration of Sentiments based on the Declaration of Independence. It listed women's grievances against men, and, at Stanton's suggestion, it included a demand for the vote. This provision was considered so appallingly radical that it almost didn't make it into the document, and many women refused to sign because it was included.

This was to be the story of Stanton's life. She would always support reforms long before they became popular. She urged laws which would allow married women to own property. She wanted divorce to be allowed on the same grounds for both men and women, and for a husband's alcoholism or the loss of love to be considered grounds for divorce. Most terrifying of all, she dared to claim that religion helped to oppress women, and she issued *The Woman's Bible,* a feminist commentary on all Biblical passages pertaining to women. Gradually, she was abandoned by almost everyone except Anthony, and she grew more and more bitter. Once, in a moment of irritation, she wrote to Anthony: "as anything from my pen is necessarily radical no one may wish to share with me the odium of what I may choose to say. If so, I am ready to stand alone. I never write to please any one."

# 13

**LAKSHMIBAI,** *born Manikarnika Tambe in Varanasi, India, 1835.* Nicknamed Manu, Lakshmibai was born to a Brahmin family, but even a Brahmin girl would not normally have received the sort of education she did. For some unspecified reason, she was allowed to do everything girls *didn't* do. She ran races, wrestled, fenced, jumped, flew kites, learned to read and write, and even studied horsemanship and martial arts. Absolutely fearless, she was charged at the age of seven by a panicked elephant rampaging through the city streets. She waited for it to draw closer, leaped onto its trunk, climbed onto a tusk, and calmed it.

When she was only eight years old she married the raja of Jhansi amid fireworks, pomp, and assurances from astrologers that she would be gifted with wealth, valor, and wisdom. It was at this time she took the name Lakshmibai. Although the marriage was not consummated for six years, the traditional confinement of purdah, in which women were secluded from the outside world, was imposed immediately. Her husband proved to be arbitrary, extravagant, and ill-tempered, and he had little patience with her wish to continue her riding and swordplay.

In 1853, her husband died, and by all rights Lakshmibai should have succeeded to the throne as rani and gained at last the freedom she wanted. But the reverse happened. The English seized Jhansi, and although they considered Lakshmibai intelligent, decisive, eloquent, and an exceptional judge of horses, they did not feel she could rule. She was enraged, and for four years she suffered one indignity after another at British hands. Finally she found an opportunity to avenge her wrongs. Indian soldiers working for the British had begun what the Indians called the Great Rebellion and what the British called the Sepoy Mutiny of 1857. Lakshmibai joined forces with the rebels, train-ing an army of women and defending the fortress of Jhansi against the English. Although, in April, 1858, she was forced to abandon Jhansi, she managed to escape with most of her troops.

She found herself praised but ignored by the male rebel leaders, and it was only with great difficulty that she got command of three hundred horsemen. Lakshmibai tried, but failed to impress on the rebel leaders the seriousness of their position; they reveled in recent victories, refusing to believe they were in danger, while she inspected the troops and braced herself for battle. It came soon, as she had feared, and she was killed. She has since become a national heroine in India and a patriotic symbol.

# 14

**FANNY MENDELSSOHN,** *born Fanny Cacilia Mendelssohn-Bartholdy in Hamburg, Germany, 1805.* Fanny, the sister of Felix Mendelssohn, received as thorough a musical education as did her brother. From their early childhood, both were made to practice piano regularly before their knowledgeable mother, who knitted and offered advice while they played. At thirteen Fanny gave her father an unusual birthday present; she played him twenty-four Bach preludes from memory. She sang beautifully and studied piano and composition in Berlin and Paris; Felix used to say when complimented on his playing, "But you should hear my sister Fanny!" Those who had the pleasure of hearing them both play agreed with Felix, and it seems certain she was at least equally as talented as her brother.

So why is she practically unknown except as Felix Mendelssohn's sister? Not necessarily because she was a woman, but certainly because she *believed* what she was told about women. All her life she sincerely believed that Felix was more important, more gifted, and more capable than she, and she sacrificed her own career to nurture his. As it was, Felix's music was less an individual accomplishment than the result of a collaboration; as Fanny wrote, "he never writes down a thought before submitting it to my judgment," and on occasion he left pieces incomplete and sent them to her to finish. She composed music on her own, but usually she left it unpublished. She only allowed a few of her songs to be printed—under Felix's name. Queen Victoria was especially surprised to find that her favorite Mendelssohn song was by Fanny, not Felix.

It's frustrating to read the story of Fanny Mendelssohn's life. Extraordinarily gifted, she could have given the world so much more than she did if she had had the courage. Still, it's impossible to blame her. She faced overwhelming pressure to conform, and even though her family loved her, rebellion would not have been tolerated. She did what she thought necessary to preserve the love of those she held dear, even when they asked her to hide her greatest gift, as her father did in a letter written on her twenty-fifth birthday. "You must become more steady and collected," he wrote, "and prepare more earnestly for your real calling, the *only* calling of a young woman—I mean the state of a housewife."

# 15

**GEORGIA O'KEEFFE,** *born in Sun Prarie, Wisconsin, 1887.* O'Keeffe is the one woman artist almost everyone knows, and although she shouldn't be praised to the exclusion of all others, she deserves her illustrious reputation. Her style, which has often been called a visual representation of female sexuality, is truly original. Her work is typified by distinctive use of color and images of mountains, flowers, skulls, black stones, bones, and the moon. O'Keeffe denied the critics' claims that her work is particularly sexual, but admitted that women feel especially drawn to it and said, "I am trying with all my skill to do a painting that is all of women, as well as all of me."

SOFONISBA ANGUISSOLA: *Few of her paintings have survived, but the best-known are self-portraits.*

LIBRARY OF CONGRESS

# 16

**SOFONISBA ANGUISSOLA,** *dies at about 90 in Palermo, Sicily, 1625.* Anguissola had the good fortune to be one of six daughters of an impoverished nobleman who could not provide a dowry for her. At the time, of course, it seemed a tragedy, but her father was an intelligent man. Perhaps, he reasoned, his daughters would never marry. If that were the case, then they should be able to support themselves.

As it happened, Anguissola was something of a prodigy when it came to drawing, so her father sent her to apprentice with two painters. She quickly became famous for her portraits, and two of her sisters, who were also her pupils, achieved some prominence as well. In 1559, she was called to the Spanish court by King Philip II, and she remained in Spain for some time—some say ten, others say twenty, years—with the rank of lady-in-waiting. When she left, Philip showered her with gifts, and she was thereby financially and socially able to marry a Sicilian nobleman and to move to Palermo with him. In 1584 her husband died and Anguissola returned to Italy, but the captain of her ship was so attentive that she married him and went back to Palermo. A skilled musician and scholar as well as an artist, she was the first Italian woman to achieve international fame for her paintings, which were so lifelike that, as one of her admirers said, they "lacked speech only."

# 17

**CATHERINE II OF RUSSIA,** *dies at 67 in St. Petersburg (now Leningrad), Russia, 1796.* One of Russia's two finest rulers, Catherine the Great was not a Russian at all. She was born Princess Sophie Auguste Friederike in Prussia, the daughter of an army officer. Although she was lively and had blonde hair, blue eyes, and an expressive face, she was not considered beautiful, and her mother was anxious to marry her off as soon as possible. So when Empress Elizabeth of Russia began pursuing Sophie on behalf of the Russian heir, Peter Ulrich, it was thought a godsend. Sophie thought so, too; ambitious and excited, she converted to Russian Orthodoxy, married Peter, and became Grand Duchess Ekaterina Alexeevna.

On the surface, Catherine's duties as a grand duchess were not that difficult. She was to dance, hunt, entertain, be pleasant to everyone, and try to conceive children. In fact, those duties were nearly impossible to perform. The dancing, hunting, and entertaining were all easy enough, but the last two duties were outrageously difficult. Her mother-in-law and husband had very different ideas about how Russia should be governed, and each was constantly trying to get Catherine to take sides. As for conceiving a child, Catherine couldn't do that alone, and her immature husband preferred to play with toy soldiers and execute rats for treason than to try to produce an heir. He showed no interest in her, no matter what she did, and then he blamed her for not getting pregnant.

In frustration and disappointment, and perhaps in an attempt to spark Peter's interest in her, Catherine began having affairs, and in 1754 one of these affairs produced a baby named Paul. Peter, as Catherine had guessed, was more afraid of confessing his inadequacy than of claiming a bastard as his heir, and he acknowledged the baby as his. He also finally consummated his marriage, and Catherine found that it hadn't been worth waiting for. He was a dreadful lover. But at about this time he let Catherine take over the administration of some provinces, and she loved it. She discovered her passion for ruling, began to study Russian history, and became involved in court intrigues.

Elizabeth died in 1761 and Peter became Tsar. He began his reign well by instituting some liberal reforms, but within months he had alienated nearly everyone. He insulted the Church, called the palace guards useless, and worshipped Russia's sworn enemy, Frederick the Great of Prussia. When Catherine tried to make suggestions, he threatened to arrest her. Fearing for

her life and encouraged by the grumblings of the people, she made her move in June 1762. While Peter was away, she rushed to the guards, telling them that Peter had threatened her life and that of her son. She begged for their loyalty and protection, won their support, and led a coup dressed in a guards uniform. Peter was captured, forced to abdicate, and imprisoned. Shortly thereafter he was murdered by his jailers, probably without Catherine's prior knowledge.

Crowned on September 23, 1762, Catherine proceeded to initiate reforms in nearly every aspect of Russian life. She encouraged agriculture, mining, industry, and foreign trade, especially with China. She restructured provincial governments and established a compre-

hensive system of free public education for all Russian children—girls as well as boys. She introduced smallpox inoculations, built the first hospitals for civilians, and established a special center for the treatment of sexually transmitted diseases at which it was forbidden to ask a patient's name. She also encouraged literary efforts and translations of the classics into Russian. She thought of freeing the serfs but was convinced that she would lose her throne if she tried it, so instead of being a great emancipator she became a great conqueror, crushing a Cossack rebellion, partitioning Poland in 1773 and 1793, strengthening the navy, and winning important battles against the Ottoman Empire.

CATHERINE II: *"I led a life which would have driven ten other women mad, and twenty others in my place would have died of a broken heart."*

LIBRARY OF CONGRESS

# 18

**MARGARET ATWOOD,** *born Margaret Eleanor Atwood in Ottawa, Ontario, Canada, 1939.* Margaret Atwood is not just one of the most talented women writing today; she's also Canada's foremost writer, and she's done a great deal to create a Canadian literature distinct from the literature of the United States. Her novels and poetry are full of conflicts, most of them politically charged—the conflicts between nature and culture, Canada and the United States, animals and humans, and men and women. Among her best works are *Surfacing, Life Before Man, The Edible Woman, Bluebeard's Egg, Bodily Harm,* and *Power Politics,* but her eeriest and most recent work is *The Handmaid's Tale,* published in 1986. It's the story of the Republic of Gilead, a nation created in North America when fundamentalist Christians stage a coup. Society is restructured around an Old Testament concept of patriarchy, and women are enslaved and become nothing more than baby-making machines. It is a thoroughly chilling story, one that should be required reading in this increasingly conservative age.

# 19

**INDIRA GANDHI,** *born Indira Priyadarshini Nehru in Allahabad, India, 1917.* It is hardly surprising that Indira Gandhi became a politician, or that she became a very powerful one, leading India's Congress Party and serving as India's prime minister from 1966 to 1977 and from 1980 until her assassination by Sikhs in 1984. After all, she came from a prominent Brahmin family. She came of age during India's turbulent fight for independence. Her aunt was Vijaya Pandit, one of the most powerful and respected women in the country.

Her father was Jawaharlal Nehru, the first prime minister of India, and she served as his hostess and adviser from 1947 to 1964; it would have been hard, under such circumstances, not to become politically experienced. But even had all of these things not been true, it would have been obvious to anyone watching the young Indira that she would

# 20

**WU CHAO,** *born in China, in 625, exact date unknown.* Wu Chao was of relatively humble birth, but she was legendary for her beauty, which won her a place in the emperor's harem when she was twelve. In 649, the emperor died, and, as tradition demanded, Wu Chao and the rest of the concubines were sent to a Buddhist convent. She would have died there had an interesting situation not developed in the palace.

The new emperor, Kao Tsung, had a customary marital arrangement. He had an official wife, an empress, and a huge collection of lesser wives and concubines of various ranks. For religious, traditional, and political reasons, the times when he could have sex with each of them were strictly circumscribed. However, a concubine named Hsiao Shu had caught the emperor's eye, and he was spending far too much time with her for the empress's happiness. So the empress recalled Wu Chao from the convent and ordered her to seduce Kao Tsung and bring him to his senses.

Wu Chao quickly replaced Hsiao Shu in the emperor's affections, but she had no intention of transferring her new power to the empress and then meekly returning to the convent. By 655, the old empress was out and Wu Chao was in.

She was not a particularly compassionate woman, and she quickly eliminated all her enemies. When she found out that Kao Tsung was still visiting the old empress, she had the old empress's hands and feet cut off. Kao Tsung stayed away

become a leader of some kind. As she herself once said, "My public life started at the age of three. I have no recollections of games, children's parties or playing with other children. My favorite occupation . . . was to deliver thunderous speeches to servants, standing on a high table."

after that. With her chief rival out of the way, Wu Chao consolidated her power, and soon she was attending all of Kao Tsung's council meetings, although she was discreetly shielded by a curtain. From then on her power increased geometrically. She had herself awarded the title "Divine Empress," and in 675 Kao Tsung abdicated in her favor. She ruled the country for nine years before he died and then installed puppet emperors until her retirement at the age of eighty. She was ruthless when it came to maintaining her power, but she ruled wisely and well overall, encouraging the arts, maintaining peace, stimulating trade, quelling revolts in border provinces, and basing government appointments on merit rather than on birth.

# 21

**PHOEBE FAIRGRAVE OMLIE,** *born Phoebe Jane Fairgrave in Des Moines, Iowa, 1902.* Phoebe Omlie devoted her entire life to aviation, and she was involved in almost every aspect of the industry's early days. She barnstormed, set records, did parachute jumps and wingwalks, spotted fires, raced, ran a flying school, trained ground personnel, and worked in the government on behalf of aviation. The daughter of a saloon keeper, Omlie was working as a secretary when

PHOEBE FAIRGRAVE OMLIE: *As if the term "aviatrix" weren't bad enough, women flyers had to prove that their femininity was still intact.*

she saw an air show and fell in love with flying. She bought four airplane rides and, at seventeen, took an inheritance from her grandfather and bought her own plane. Eager to make the venture seem practical to her parents, she went to the Fox Moving Picture Company and sold her services as a stunt pilot, even though she didn't have a pilot's license. "Dad thought I was crazy," she said. "Mother had more faith. She thought that if I was going to do it I was going to do it and that's all there was to it."

# 22

**BILLIE JEAN KING,** *born Billie Jean Moffitt in Long Beach, California, 1943.* Billie Jean King isn't famous just because she won her first Wimbledon tournament at seventeen and claimed a record twenty victories there between 1961 and 1979—six singles titles, ten doubles, and four mixed doubles— nor is she famous just because she continued to win after three knee operations and surgery on her heel or because she was the first female athlete to win $100,000 in one year. King's well-deserved fame comes only partly from her outstanding performance in her sport; the rest comes from her courageous discussion of her bisexuality, her complete devotion to tennis, and her uncompromising feminism. The day in 1973 when she beat male opponent Bobby Riggs before a crowd of thirty thousand spectators and a television audience of sixty million was a day of victory for all women and a day of defeat for those who claimed women were inferior. Her fierce battles for equal prize money and equal treatment for women in tennis have resulted in greater respect for women's sports and inspired countless girls to participate in athletics. Things aren't perfect yet by any means, but, thanks to Billie Jean King, it's unlikely a girl today would be told by her coach, as she once was, "You'll be good because you're ugly."

# 23

**XANTHIPPE,** *born in Athens, Greece, in the fifth century B.C., exact date unknown.* Xanthippe, the wife of Socrates, has been consistently abused ever since Plato first wrote about her, and the odds are that she didn't deserve her shrewish reputation. Let's look at the facts. She was probably married young, as most Athenian girls were. She almost certainly had nothing to say

LIBRARY OF CONGRESS

about the husband she was being given. She found herself married to a man who habitually ignored authority, who went around asking for trouble, and who made no money to speak of. There is every reason to believe she loved him; she spent the night in prison with him before his execution and had to be led away sobbing. She was as sympathetic as she knew how to be; she was thrifty; she was faithful. And, most importantly in Greek society, she was fertile.

So how did she get treated in exchange? Socrates sometimes defended her, but sometimes laughed at her and compared her scolding

to the noise of geese. And he could be brutally insensitive. When she heard he had been condemned to death, Xanthippe cried, "You will die unjustly." Socrates, perhaps trying to be amusing, replied. "Would you rather have me die justly?"

Socrates' disciples were even less tolerant than he was. They encouraged him to beat her. (To Socrates' credit, he refused.) Ancient Greek commentators called her affectionate but ill-tempered, and that's about the best treatment she's ever gotten. Most commentators have dismissed her as shallow, petulant, or just plain bitchy.

LIBRARY OF CONGRESS

## 24

**FRANCES HODGSON BURNETT,** *born Frances Hodgson in Cheetham Hill, Manchester, England, 1849.* Frances Hodgson Burnett was a mass of contradictions. She was, on the one hand, a perfect Victorian woman, a genteel writer of children's fiction who loved flowers and frilly clothes and was called "Fluffy" or "Fluffina" by her friends. Even the illnesses in her life were somehow appropriate; she often suffered from "nervous prostration," and her elder son, Lionel, died in 1890 of "galloping consumption." The stories she wrote for little girls, such as *The Little Princess* and *The Secret Garden,* were entertaining but antiseptic and thoroughly moral. Her most famous book about a boy, *Little Lord Fauntleroy,* was modeled after her younger son, Vivian, and it doomed generations of little boys to lovelocks and lace collars.

On the other hand, Burnett was a capable, shrewd businesswoman. When a plagiarist tried to produce an unauthorized stage version of *Little Lord Fauntleroy* before Burnett's own was finished, she did not accept it as a piece of bad luck, as was expected, but instead fought a landmark court battle and got his play forced off the stage.

Burnett also broke with convention in her relationships with men. Nice women were supposed to marry nice men, stay married, and enjoy sex as little as possible. But when Burnett's first husband showed disapproval of her literary activities (which were, incidentally, the family's chief means of support), she divorced him. Not only that, she married again and was

CARRY NATION: *Of her youth she wrote, "I was a great lover."*

divorced again. Her letters also betray a joyful discovery of eroticism that her public would have found shocking. One day she was on the beach and saw the local swimming instructor in a bathing suit. In a subsequent letter, Burnett gasped he was a "Greek God in bronze . . . I never noticed a man's body before. I was always so actively employed searching for their brains—but his—Mon dieu! Gott in Himmel! Santa Maria—and things! . . . I grow wild, and have to erase!"

# 25

**CARRY NATION,** *born Carry Amelia Moore in Garrard County, Kentucky, 1846.* "God forgive me for not strangling her with my bare hands," said a judge in whose court Carry Nation appeared. Nation was not a popular woman, but it wasn't really her fault. Her homely, bulldog-like face couldn't be helped, and syphilis-induced madness ran in her family. Her mother died believing she was Queen Victoria. Nation contracted it either directly from her husband or congenitally from her mother, who probably got it from *her* husband. By the time Nation began chopping up saloons in the name of temperance, she was in the advanced stages of the disease and thoroughly bonkers.

Nation began her saloon-bashing rather quietly. At first she would simply go into a bar and sing hymns and pray for the souls of the patrons. Eventually, when embarrassing the customers didn't work well enough, she stepped up to "hatchetiation" of the furniture, glassware, and mirrors. She lectured, wrote an autobiography, and sold souvenir hatchets to pay for her court costs, but in 1910 she retired, and not because of mounting legal fees. She took her axe to a Montana saloon, and the owner, a woman, beat her to a pulp.

# 26

**SOJOURNER TRUTH,** *dies at about 85 in Battle Creek, Michigan, 1883.* One day in 1851, a women's rights convention was taking place. Several speeches had been heard, including one by a man who had stressed women's need for protection and their divinely ordained inferiority. Suddenly, a six-foot-tall black woman stood and walked forward, demanding to speak. She was a former slave who called herself Sojourner Truth. She had given birth to at least eight children, won her freedom in 1827, and fought a successful court battle for the return of her son, who had been illegally sold into slavery in Alabama. She had been a preacher and had worked to reform prostitutes. She spent her entire life working for equal rights, but it is for this moment she is best remembered.

In a deep, hypnotic voice, she attacked the notion of man's divinely-ordained superiority. "Where did

SOJOURNER TRUTH: *In her stocking feet she was just a few inches shorter than Lincoln.*

LIBRARY OF CONGRESS

your Christ come from?" she demanded. "From God and a woman! Man had nothin' to do with Him." She also attacked the idea that women were always white, privileged, and pampered: "That man over there say that a woman needs to be helped into carriages, and lifted over ditches, and to have the best place everywhere. Nobody ever helped me into carriages, or over mud puddles, or gives me a best place . . . and ain't I a woman? Look at me. Look at my arm: I have plowed and planted and gathered into barns, and no man could head me . . . and ain't I a woman? I could work as much and eat as much as a man when I could get it, and bear the lash as well . . . and ain't I a woman?"

# 27

**SOR JUANA INÉS DE LA CRUZ,** *born in Mexico in 1651, exact date unkown.* The gifted daughter of Spaniards, Sor Juana pleaded with her parents to dress her and raise her as a boy so she could attend a university. They were perplexed but supportive, and in 1664 they took steps to see she got the education she deserved. They found her a pair of wealthy, powerful guardians—the viceroy of Mexico, the marqués of Mancera, and his wife—who raised her with affection.

Sor Juana quickly became famous for her beauty, her conversation, and her beautiful lyric poetry, much of which still survives. But her beauty and intelligence were problems as well as gifts, since as a woman she had no options but marriage or the convent. At age fifteen, she chose the convent and later explained, "I became a nun, because even though I realized my state was . . . repugnant to my temperament, given the total disinclination I felt toward marriage, it seemed the most fitting and decent thing I could do, especially since I wished to ensure my personal salvation."

It was not an arduous life; her guardians provided her with plenty of money, and her own talents provided her with plenty of visitors. She collected books and scientific instruments and continued to write her poems, which have been called some of the best ever written in Spanish. They included poems written for special occasions, love poems addressed to men and women, and poems defending the oppressed and criticizing the sexual double standard.

Her talents gave Sor Juana certain freedoms, in part because she had powerful admirers. For example, she hated her mother superior, whom she called stupid and talkative. At one point, she lost her temper and shouted, "Be quiet, Mother, you're such a fool!" The mother superior complained to the archbishop, who knew Sor Juana. He wrote: "If the mother superior can prove the contrary, justice will be done."

Unfortunately, her talents and her privileged status gave rise to secret doubts. Her love of knowledge made Sor Juana feel guilty, and many around her encouraged this. Criticized by more and more people, including her confessor, Sor Juana finally admitted defeat. She decided her work was impious, and she sold her books and scientific equipment. After giving the money to the poor, she became famous for the harsh penances she imposed on herself. She died tending plague victims in 1695.

# 28

**DONA BEATRICE,** *born Kimpa Vita in the Congo in the seventeenth century, exact date unknown.* Dona Beatrice came to power at the beginning of the eighteenth century, an era of apocalyptic visions in her country. The Congo, which had once been a mighty nation and which had dealt with Portuguese visitors on equal and friendly terms, had been reduced by the slave trade to a Portuguese conquest, a land of feuds and famine. Beatrice saw that the time was ripe for a great religious leader, and she decided to become that leader.

She claimed that while she lay ill she had had a vision of St. Anthony, but she said he had appeared as a black man, not a white man. She said he had told her to resurrect the Congo through a new doctrine, and she began spreading that doctrine with great vigor. It was a synthesis of European and African culture, a nationalistic religion that claimed Christ had been born in Congo and that celebrated black culture and permitted polygamy. Her followers abandoned European clothing and adopted a Christian symbolism that owed much to African influences. They believed Beatrice died and was resurrected every week. They cleared city streets so she could pass, and her table was set with lords' cloaks rather than odinary tablecloths. People came in droves to see her, and her presence in the capital city, São Salvador, stimulated a period of economic growth.

In short, her doctrine, known as Antonianism, had a tremendous popular appeal, and she became very powerful. The Portuguese felt distinctly threatened by her, and they were determined to destroy her. They got their chance in 1706, when she lost some followers after bearing a child and claiming that, like Mary, she was still a virgin. She was arrested, tried, and sentenced (along with her child) to death. Both were burned at the stake.

# 29

**TZ'U-HSI,** *born Lan Kuei (Little Orchid) in Peking, China, 1835.* Lan Kuei's father was a minor official of the ruling Manchu class, a fact which gave her several advantages. Chief among these were eligibility for the emperor's harem, but another was that the Manchurians, unlike the Chinese, did not bind their daughters' feet. To the advantages of birth Lan Kuei added another through her own initiative; she educated herself and became quite well-read and a fine calligrapher, unusual accomplishments in an age when few women were literate at all.

At sixteen, Lan Kuei was five feet tall, temperamental, broad of forehead, firm of chin, and considered a beauty by many. According to custom, her face was whitened by a thick layer of powder. Her cheeks were rouged, a round mark was painted on her lower lip, and her eyes were shaded with kohl. The nails on her third and little fingers were four inches long.

It was at this age that she was summoned to the emperor's palace to become a concubine of the fifth rank to Emperor Hsien-feng; she now took the new name of Concubine Yi. Always an adept politician, she made friends with a rising star named Niuhuru who eventually became the new empress, and in 1855, perhaps through Niuhuru, perhaps through the emperor, she was raised to the fourth rank. In 1856, she was raised another rank after she bore the emperor's only son.

Hsien-feng died in 1861, and two governments—an apparent one and a real one—came to power. The apparent government was complex and unwieldy; Lan Kuei's son was the new emperor, but because of his youth he was counseled by a group of advisers and by three regents— his mother (now calling herself Tz'u-Hsi), Niuhuru, and Hsien-feng's brother, Prince Kung. In actuality, however, Tz'u-Hsi was the sole ruler. She quickly eliminated or learned to manipulate her rivals, and she kept a stranglehold on the throne until her death in 1908—and afterward, if you believe the rumors that she had her successor poisoned as she lay dying.

Tz'u-Hsi was ruthless and greedy. She used funds earmarked for a new navy to rebuild her summer palace, and she sold offices and promotions and amassed a huge personal fortune. But she wasn't all bad. She kept the peace, established schools of foreign languages, and instituted adminstrative reforms. She ended foot binding, legalized intermarriage between Chinese and Manchurians, opened state schools to girls, built railroads, suppressed the opium trade, established a semi-constitutional government, and patronized the arts.

# 30

**SHIRLEY CHISHOLM,** *born Shirley Anita St. Hill in Brooklyn, New York, 1924.* Shirley Chisholm had an extraordinary political career, a lot of determination, and a strong sense of purpose. After earning an undergraduate degree in sociology at Brooklyn College and a masters in child education at Columbia, she worked in day care. In 1964 she won a seat in the New York State Assembly; in 1968, she was the first black woman elected to Congress; and in 1972 and 1976, she served on the Democratic National Committee. Throughout her political career, she worked on behalf of the underdogs—blacks, women, children, inner-city dwellers, and domestic workers. Education, day care, youth programs, and women's rights were her favorite issues.

By 1972, Shirley Chisholm was universally acknowledged to be talented, intelligent, honest, charismatic, and, as she put it, "unbought and unbossed." So she did what well-respected, skillful politicians often do—she ran for president. And then she experienced a series of betrayals that would have driven almost anyone out of politics. Feminists reacted coolly to her candidacy, dawdled, and endorsed her too late to help her. Local black politicians referred to her as "that little black matriarch who goes around messing things up." Most black organizations felt that "in this first serious effort of blacks for high political office, it would be better if it were a man," and only the Black Panthers gave her their support. Chisholm was furious: "I love a good fight and people know [it] . . . But what hurts me more than anything else . . . is the brothers in politics . . . they won't get off my back." In 1983, she announced that she would not run for Congress again.

LIBRARY OF CONGRESS

MAUDE GONNE: *Her spectacular beauty won her entrance to high society despite her scandalous past and lifelong commitment to radical causes.*

## 1

**BETTE MIDLER,** *born in Honolulu, Hawaii, 1945.* Bette Midler's mother, not knowing her daughter would grow up to be the self-proclaimed "last of the truly tacky women," named her after another great woman who didn't let anyone push her around, Bette Davis. Midler spent her youth feeling displaced. She was a poor, short, fat, homely Jewish girl in Hawaii. So she clowned around but dreamed of becoming a serious actress. She took her chance as soon as it came, headed for New York, and got a few off-Broadway roles, then landed the part of Tzeitel in the Broadway production of *Fiddler on the Roof.* After three years in that role, she'd had it, and she quit. She sang in a few nightclubs and got another off-Broadway part in a rock musical called *Salvation,* but her first real success came in an unexpected fashion.

She was offered fifty dollars a weekend to do two shows at New York's Continental Baths, a gay bathhouse. Initially shy, she started out with torch songs, but soon learned she could be outrageous, tell raunchy jokes, enjoy herself—and the more flamboyant she was, the more the audience loved her. "Ironically," she said later, "I was freed from fear by people who, at the time, were ruled by fear. And I will always be grateful."

At the baths she honed her remarkable act, and soon she was an underground sensation. As her popularity grew, she found her way into the mainstream, and it was her strong singing voice, not so much her off-beat comedy, which won her a recording contract with Atlantic Records. She played Las Vegas and Carnegie Hall, toured Europe, and wrote a book. Her film debut in *The Rose* (1981) won her an even wider audience and a Grammy for the title song. But a failed movie, *Jinxed,* left her film career in a slump until 1986 when she was

hired for *Down and Out in Beverly Hills.* In that film, Midler proved herself a comic genius, and her movie career was off and running again. Several hit films later, Midler continues to please audiences with her strong, vivacious, and continually outrageous characterizations.

---

BETTE MIDLER: *"My early years would have been much easier if only I'd known that one day the things that made me a 'social oddity' would be an asset."*

## 2

**RUTH DRAPER,** *born in New York City, 1884.* Like Bette Midler, Ruth Draper created a variety of characters on stage, but the resemblance between the two women ends there. Draper's fortes were not flamboyance and tackiness, but pathos, dialect, and improvisation. She tried for quite some time to act in traditional theater, but found it impossible to deliver other people's words. After 1917 she refused to appear in plays written by anyone but herself. Instead, she invented characters of all sorts, including a socie-

ty matron and an Irish charwoman, by observing real people and listening to their voices. Then she created stories around the characters, and took them to the stage. Her dramatic monologues won her admirers across the globe. In 1921 she performed at the White House.

Draper used only simple props—chairs, tables, and shawls. She didn't need anything else; with gestures she could create marvelous illusions and shift convincingly from one to another of her fifty-four characters. She was also a woman of great personal integrity who sheltered Italian refugees during Mussolini's regime and who missed only one performance in her entire fifty-three-year career. A month later, she returned to the town she'd missed and gave the performance.

One of her greatest successes, a sketch called "Three Women and Mr. Clifford," illustrates her exceptional skill. In this sketch, she played three characters: Clifford's wife, his secretary, and the woman he loved. Clifford himself never actually appeared on the stage, but people often thought he had. After seeing that sketch, a member of the audience was heard to say, "Wasn't Clifford the most long-suffering jackass?"—and only a moment later added, "My God, he wasn't there!"

## 3

**MARY BAKER EDDY,** *dies at 89 in Chesnut Hill, Massachusetts, 1910.* While Mary Baker Eddy was still in the womb, her mother told a friend that the child she was carrying was destined to be "holy and consecrated and set apart for wonderful achievements." For the first thirty or forty years of her life, though, Eddy appeared neither holy nor consecrated, but simply spoiled and chronically ill. She married, but her husband died within six months of their wedding. Her dreams of becoming famous as a writer were badly bruised by numerous rejections. She remarried, but she was miserable, and the marriage ended in divorce.

Her unhappiness was accompanied by an increase in physical problems. She sought the help of the mesmerist Phineas Parkhurst Quimby. He cured her, and she lauded his treatment to anyone who would listen, publishing dramatic testimonials in the local press and becoming his chief disciple. After his death in 1886, she reworked his ideas and promoted them as her own, founding a religion-cum-business. The religious part consisted of her concordance to the Scriptures and her belief that Jesus's true mission was to heal the sick. The business part was her school for mesmeric healers, a school noted for its steep tuition fees.

Eddy's business expanded and flourished. She wrote a text called *Science and Health,* held Sunday meetings, and established the first Christian Science church, a college, and a magazine. Her leadership of the movement was absolute; terrified of competition from within, she excommunicated anyone who seemed to threaten her power, and groups of followers often left because of her authoritarian manner. She permitted no sermons, commentary, or discussion and made her books the only source of church authority, allowing no changes in church procedure but

MARY BAKER EDDY: *She believed that healing came from God—but, when kidney stones afflicted her in old age, God took a back seat to morphine.*

LIBRARY OF CONGRESS

those she made personally. Thus, no changes have been made since her death. It might be expected that a group with such a powerful, charismatic leader would wither after the leader's death, but her religion continues to flourish today, as does the *Christian Science Monitor,* the journal she established in 1908.

# 4

**KAREN HORNEY,** *dies at 67 in New York City, 1952.* In the 1930s, when Sigmund Freud's theories were enjoying their greatest prominence in the United States, only a few psychoanalysts dared to challenge his views. Chief among the rebels was Karen Horney, who had left Germany when the Nazis came to power. (Although she was not Jewish, she was persecuted because she was a member of what was considered a "Jewish profession.") She had wanted to be a doctor since she was twelve, but her father had forbidden her to go to college. Only the determination of her mother enabled Horney to get her medical degree.

Horney became a successful psychiatrist, but she felt torn between her professional ambitions and her commitment to her family. She underwent analysis, but wasn't satisfied by it, and she began taking psychoanalytic patients herself to test her own theories about the mind. Her goal was to develop a model of women's psychoanalytic development; in Freud's view, women were simply castrated men who spent their lives looking for penises. Freud believed the only way a woman could find fulfillment was by producing a male baby—a sort of substitute for a penis.

Horney disagreed and turned Freud's theory upside-down. Men, she said, envied women's creative capacities. Since they couldn't bear children, she decided, men turned their frustration against women, developing hatred and fear of women and their sexuality. Horney's

theories caused her dismissal from the New York Psychoanalytic Institute, so she established her own anti-Freudian group, the Association for the Advancement of Psychoanalysis. As she grew older, Horney grew less convinced that there was an essential "female psychology" and more convinced that women's behavior was the result of their environments. A feminist, she stressed the positive aspects of both motherhood and wage-earning labor and attacked the social pressures that made women masochistic, insecure, and fearful.

# 5

**PHILLIS WHEATLEY,** *dies at about 30 in Boston, Massachusetts, 1784.* The story of Phillis Wheatley is one of the quiet tragedies of American history. Brought to this country as a slave in 1761, she was sold to John Wheatley, a tailor. Mrs. Wheatley taught Phillis Latin and English and allowed her to read widely, and at thirteen she began to write religious poetry. At seventeen she published her first poem, and in 1773 friends published a collection

PHILLIS WHEATLEY: *George Washington, to whom she had dedicated a poem, was among her greatest admirers.*

LIBRARY OF CONGRESS

of her works, *Poems on Various Subjects*. The work was often lacking in originality, but it was well done, and it made her the first black American to publish a book. In one of the most barbaric displays in literary history, one Englishman bound a copy of the book in the skin of a black man.

When the Wheatleys died, Phillis was set free, and she married a freedman named John Peters. When he was imprisoned for debt, she found work as a servant, literally on starvation wages. She and her three children died of malnutrition in the boarding house where she worked.

**DELIA J. AKELEY,** *born Delia Julia Denning near Beaver Dam, Wisconsin, probably in 1875.* A runaway tomboy who called herself "Micky," Akeley might never have become famous had she not married taxidermist Carl Akeley in 1902. He wanted to revolutionize the science of taxidermy, and Delia became his assistant. When they began their work, animal skins in museums were simply draped over crude frames, and the background was provided by milliners' flowers. The Akeleys mounted their displays carefully, paying attention to the animal's musculature and trying to pose it in a natural manner in an authentic surrounding.

The Akeleys also went on two safaris in Uganda and Kenya, once in 1906 and again in 1909. They shot and skinned elephants for museums, and a huge bull elephant shot by Delia is still on display at Chicago's Field Museum. They also fought meningitis, spirillum fever, black-water fever, and malaria. At one point, Carl was trampled by a wounded elephant, and only Delia's courage and decisiveness saved his life.

For most people, that would have been quite enough adventure and danger for one lifetime. But Delia, after divorcing Carl in 1923, went back to Africa to gather animal specimens, native crafts, and photographs for the Brooklyn Museum of Arts and Sciences—the first time a museum-sponsored safari was led by a woman. Furthermore, she was the first Western woman, perhaps the first woman at all, to travel from the Indian coast

of Africa to the Atlantic "alone." ("Alone," of course, in the terminology of the day, implied that her numerous native porters were not people.) Traveling by foot, litter, canoe, donkey, and camel, she braved crocodiles, disease, lice, snakes, and tsetse flies, and returned to the United States in 1925, triumphant and famous. She died in 1970.

# 6 _____

**CATHERINE CADIÈRE,** *born in Toulon, France, 1709, exact date unknown.* The trial of Marie Catherine Cadière and Father Jean-Baptist Girard, which began in 1731, involved one of the last formal accusations of witchcraft in France. It lasted for a year and remained one of the most sensational French trials for two centuries to come, rivaling the Dreyfus affair in public interest. Cadière wrote a book about her ordeal, a work which soon appeared in translation for an eager English audience. But in the end, the parliament at Aix concluded that nothing could be proven against either of the principals.

It began when Cadière aspired to become a saint. In so doing, she sought renown as a holy person, and she invented visions and ecstasies and brought herself to the attention of Father Girard, the fifty-year-old head of the Third Order of St. Theresa. He was im-

pressed with her at first, but after about a year of observing her decided she was not gifted with special holiness. She immediately exhibited signs of possession, and claimed she had been bewitched by Girard.

She further claimed that Girard had seduced her, and she blamed her acquiescence on his use of sorcery. Referring to herself in the third person, Cadière described how, "stooping down and putting his mouth close to hers, [Girard] breathed upon her, which had such a powerful effect on the young lady's mind that she was immediately transported with love and consented to give herself to him." Her lawyers also produced ten other secular devotees and nuns who claimed Girard had seduced them.

Girard denied the charges. He claimed that Cadière was a fraud and a liar. Beyond insisting upon his innocence, he charged her with faking her earlier visions. In the end, perhaps the judges were simply bewildered by the variety and vehemence of the charges and countercharges. Half the judges voted to burn Father Girard, the other half to hang Cadière, and the deciding vote sent the pair to other authorities—Girard to the ecclesiastical courts, Cadière to her mother. Both lived afterward in relative peace, but Cadière, poor woman, never did become a saint.

# 7 _____

**WILLA CATHER,** *born Wilella Sibert Cather near Winchester, Virginia, 1873.* In *O Pioneers!* Willa Cather told her readers "there are only two or three human stories, and they go on repeating themselves as fiercely as if they had never happened before." Cather herself spent her whole life acting out one of the oldest stories of them all—the tale of the proud, imaginative, strong, intelligent woman who is expected to subject herself to domesticity and a man's power. She couldn't do it.

Her first approach to the problem was to behave like a man. She called herself William, wore a crew cut, dressed in boy's clothes, and dreamed of becoming Billy Cather, M.D., but soon she moved toward a more socially acceptable role. She retained her natural assertiveness and preference for women as sexual partners, but now she began to play the role of the single career woman who had close female "companions." This role, unlike her former one, could be overlooked by the more circumspect members of society. It was a little strange for a woman to be so dedicated to her work, but single women were always a little odd, and anyone with a delicate "conscience" could choose to think Cather was asexual rather than lesbian.

After college, Cather was a journalist and a teacher, but she decided early that she wanted to write fiction. She published a collection of poems in 1903, a book of short stories in 1905, and her first novel, *Alexander's Bridge,* in 1912. Her works include some of the best books in American literature, among them *My Antonia* and *Death Comes for the Archbishop.* She was especially good at creating strong, likeable, believable, independent heroines whose romances were far less important than their pioneering spirits and wills to survive.

MARY STUART: *She told her executioner, "I forgive you with all my heart, for now I hope you shall make an end of all my troubles."*

# 8

**MARY STUART, queen of Scots,** *born in Linlithgow, West Lothian, Scotland, 1542.* Mary's birth was perhaps as inauspicious as possible. The two worst things a ruler could be in the sixteenth century were young and female, and Mary was both. Her father, James V, died when she was only six days old, leaving her queen. Things seemed to go well for a while. At age five, she was sent to the French court while her mother remained as regent in Scotland. Mary was immeasurably happy in France, and French remained her first language for the rest of her life, although she learned six other languages as well. She grew into a beautiful, pious young woman, fond of dancing, hunting, hawking, practical jokes, golf, croquet, fancy clothes, jewels, gambling, poetry, music, and lapdogs. She married the French heir, Francis, and when he succeeded to the throne in 1559, she reigned briefly as queen of France.

In 1560, Francis died, and Mary's troubles began. She returned to Scotland not only a virtual foreigner, but a heretic as well, for in her absence the country had largely converted to Presbyterianism. She also had trouble with her neighbor to the south, Elizabeth I of England. If the English queen died without heirs, Mary was theoretically next in line for her throne. But

LIBRARY OF CONGRESS

Mary was Catholic and Elizabeth Protestant. To succeed to the English throne with as little trouble as possible, Mary needed Elizabeth to name her as heir.

So there she stood—her own people on one side, grumbling at the supposed frivolity of their "French" queen; Elizabeth on the other, eager for an excuse to bar her from the throne of England, or worse, to seize control of Scotland. To make matters even worse, the Scottish nobility was treacherous, and her own council treated her like a child. Still, she might have overcome these difficulties if she hadn't had such appalling taste in men.

In 1564 Mary made a ghastly mistake by marrying Henry Stewart, earl of Darnley, another potential heir to the English throne. Both Elizabeth and the Scottish people were displeased. And Darnley himself, although attractive, turned out to be churlish and irresponsible. A group of noblemen had him murdered, and the murmurs against Mary became shouts when she married the chief plotter, James Hepburn, earl of Bothwell. The fact that she married him under duress made little difference to the Scots; they deposed her, put her infant son, James, on the throne, and imprisoned her.

Mary made a daring escape from Scotland, but instead of fleeing to France, where she had sure allies, she went to England, hoping to curry favor with Elizabeth. Elizabeth was trapped. If she helped Mary, she would be harming her own interests in Scotland. If she refused to help Mary, she would be setting a dangerous precedent by countenancing the overthrow of a rightful queen. Having nothing else to do with her, Elizabeth imprisoned Mary, holding her under tighter and tighter guard for nineteen years, and finally executing her in 1587.

# 9

**GRACE HOPPER,** *born Grace Brewster Murray in New York City, 1906.* Grace Hopper began life with two great blessings: intelligence and a liberal father who wanted his two daughters, as well as his son, to receive thorough educations. Hopper earned a bachelor's degree in mathematics from Vassar in 1928, a master's from Yale in 1930, and a doctorate from Yale in 1934. In 1943 she joined the Women Accepted for Voluntary Emergency Service (WAVES), the women's branch of the navy. Given the rank of lieutenant, she was assigned to the computer division. Thus began her long career as a software pioneer and a naval officer. Hopper co-wrote the computer language called COBOL, helped invent the term "bug" for a program flaw, became one of only two women in the Institute of Electrical and Electronic Engineers and one of only five women in the National Academy of Engineers. She was promoted to rear admiral, and in 1983 became the oldest naval officer of either sex on active duty.

# 10

**EMILY DICKINSON,** *born Emily Elizabeth Dickinson in Amherst, Massachusetts, 1830.* Even before she died and was discovered to have been a major American poet, Emily Dickinson was something of a legend. The daughter of an autocratic lawyer and his shadowlike wife, she left her home in Amherst only a few times. She attended Mount Holyoke for a year and then left, and she made brief visits to Boston, Washington, D. C., and Philadelphia. As she grew older, she retreated more and more from the outside world, and eventually, she stopped making and receiving social calls, hid from strangers, and fluttered around her house, dressed only in white.

Dickinson's Amherst neighbors were understandably curious about her. They speculated about why she hid from other people and wondered what she was really like. They probably knew or guessed that she read a great deal, for as Dickinson wrote of her father, "He buys me many Books—but begs me not to read them—because he fears they joggle the Mind." Today we know she read them all, despite her father's warnings—George Eliot, Thomas Carlyle, Elizabeth Barrett Browning, the Brontës, the Bible, the Transcendentalists, John Ruskin, and the Romantic poets. So although she was physically severed from the world, her intellect was active and adventurous; her neighbors knew this from rumors.

What the gossips of Amherst may not have known, and what those who have read only a few of her tamer poems still don't know, is that Dickinson was more than reclusive, eccentric, and intelligent. She was also angry, rebellious, mischievous, and bitter. Those who read her poetry today will find other glimpses of this most enigmatic writer's character in the more than seventeen hundred poems that were discovered by her family after Dickinson's death.

# 11

**ANNIE JUMP CANNON,** *born in Dover, Delaware, 1863.* Educated at Wellesley and Radcliffe, Cannon was a graduate student when the Harvard observatory hired her in 1896. She began working with the recently developed spectroscope, an instrument which enabled scientists to determine the chemical compositions of stars by looking at refracted light. This research led her to develop a system of classifications for stars and to classify and catalogue almost four hundred thousand. She also discovered about three hundred variable stars and five novae and doubled Harvard's collection of astronomical photographs, making it one of the best in the world.

Cannon did a great deal to turn astronomy into a systematized science, and her colleagues were quick to give her credit for her accomplishments. Harvard rewarded her with titled positions, including curator of astronomical photographs; she was honored by numerous professional societies, and in 1925, Oxford University awarded her the first honorary doctorate it had ever bestowed upon a woman. Perhaps the most inspiring part of Cannon's story is that she accomplished everything that she did in spite of a handicap—she was almost completely deaf.

# 12

**LINDA BRENT,** *born in 1818, exact date unknown.* Linda Brent's story is so sad, so painful, that sometimes it's easy to forget in the powerful retelling of her sufferings how many others experienced what she did and more without the ability to voice their anguish. Her real name was Harriet Brent Jacobs, and what we know of her comes from her autobiography, *Incidents in the Life of a Slave Girl,* published in 1861, and edited and introduced by abolitionist Lydia Maria Child.

Brent was born a slave; her first mistress taught her to read and write. Her parents died early, and she was raised by her grandmother. When she was fifteen, Brent began to be pursued by her master, Dr. Flint. She was beautiful, and he urged her constantly to give in to him. She wrote that he "met me at every turn . . . swearing . . . he could compel me to submit to him" and reminding her she was his property. Her mistress only made things worse; instead of being angry with her husband, she treated Brent with "jealousy and rage." Flint offered Brent wealth, but she refused, and in defiance she had an affair with another white man. "It seems less degrading," she reasoned, "to give one's self, than to submit to compulsion."

Others didn't see it that way. Flint was enraged, her lover abandoned her, and her grandmother told Brent she had disgraced her dead mother. Brent took a desperate chance and managed to escape to the North. But even there she was pursued by old ghosts. Flint continued to chase her, hoping to bring her back. Eventually, friends bought Brent's freedom, but she wrote that it felt a hollow victory. "The more my mind had become enlightened, the more difficult it was for me to consider myself an article of property; and to pay money to those who had so grievously oppressed me seemed like taking from my suffering the glory of triumph."

# 13

**GRANDMA MOSES,** *dies at 101 in Hoosick Falls, New York, 1961.* When Anna Mary Robertson Moses died she left behind two of her ten children, nine grandchildren, thirty great-grandchildren, and fifteen hundred paintings. She had begun drawing as a child, when her father bought her one-cent sheets of paper and encouraged her talent for making dyes out of grapes and berries. At twelve, however, her artistic career seemed prematurely finished. She went out to service as a hired girl, and in 1887 she married a farmer and moved to the Shenandoah Valley. There was little time for drawing; she was occupied with childbearing and farm chores, but eventually, as her children grew, she found a little leisure time.

Moses did what countless women have done with their free time—she used it to bring in extra money. She made and sold quilts, carpets, embroidered goods, dolls, cookies, canned goods, and potato chips—"a novelty in those days," she later recalled. But eventually arthritis prevented her from pursuing most of her favorite crafts and she returned, after more than fifty years, to painting. Creating simple scenes of the country life of her youth, she worked at a table under one light bulb, and sold her paintings at a local drugstore. In the late 1930s Louis Caldor, a respected art collector and dealer, stopped at the drugstore, saw some of Moses's paintings, and bought them all. He later visited her and bought another fifteen of her works. In 1939 he displayed three of them at New York's Museum of Modern Art, and a year later Moses had her own show at a New York gallery. Suddenly, at eighty-one, she was a celebrity. She was taken seriously by only a few critics; most thought her work merely "decorative" and said she had "faulty and awkward technique." But the public loved her, not only for her simple, pleasing paintings, but for her personal charm as well.

# 14

**CHARLOTTE STANLEY, countess of Derby,** *born Charlotte de la Tremoille in England in the seventeenth century, exact date unknown.* The wife of James Stanley, seventh earl of Derby, and mother of seven, Charlotte Stanley enjoyed a life of weath and power at her home, Lathom House. Aggressive, commanding, and seven years her husband's senior, she was said to have stolen "the Earl's breeches" because she was more competent than he.

In 1643 her husband was in the Isle of Man at the request of the queen, when a local parliamentary general tried to take Lathom House, thinking Charlotte would yield the house easily in her husband's absence. The general offered her a choice: surrender and receive safe-conduct, or fight and be damned. Charlotte stalled, but finally decid-ed to defend her Royalist senti-ments, and she refused to surrender.

And so the bombardment began. She stood fast, refused to negotiate, and bore the insults shouted by soldiers and her neighbors' pleas that she surrender. When Parlia-mentarians tried to cut off her water supply, Charlotte sent out a party to steal their biggest gun, which they did. Three months later, the siege was lifted by a Royalist force, and Charlotte went to the Isle of Man to join her husband. In December of 1645, the siege began again, and without her there to preserve morale, the garrison sur-rendered. Neglected by some historians, Charlotte Stanley was notorious in her time; a Parliamen-tarian saying had it that "Three women ruined the Kingdom: Eve, the Queen, and the countess of Derby."

# 15

**ELINOR SMITH,** *born Elinor Goulding Smith in New York City, 1917, exact date unknown.*
Although she now makes her living as a writer, Smith first achieved fame in the 1920s as a record-break-ing pilot. She began by setting women's altitude records with a determination that endangered her life; once at twenty-five thousand feet, her oxygen tube broke and she lost consciousness. She fell four miles before recovering at only two thousand feet. In 1929 she and California pilot Bobbi Trout made headlines when they battled for the women's solo endurance record. After months of competing, they coordinated their efforts, trying to break the men's endurance record of 420 hours in the sky. They failed, having logged only 42 hours be-cause of difficulties with their refueling plane, but they set a new women's record and it made them the first women aviators to refuel in midair.

"To some young women with dreams of a wider world," Smith once wrote, "there seemed to be two paths to follow, each with great romantic appeal. One led to Holly-wood, the other to a career in the sky. For me there was only one path: I knew from the age of six that I wanted to fly."

# 16

**JANE AUSTEN,** *born in Steven-ton, Hampshire, England, 1775.*
Poor Jane was one of Britain's best novelists—some rank her with Shakespeare as one of England's two greatest writers—yet she lived one of the most marginal lives in literary history. Lively, attractive, modest, forgiving, and witty, she was still condemned to the fringes of society for many reasons, of which her sex was only one. Had she been rich, she could have spent more time at the balls and gather-ings she loved, but she was not. She was a member of poor branch of a well-off family, and all her life she had to worry about money. Only three of her works were published in her lifetime: *Pride and Prejudice, Sense and Sensibility,* and *Mansfield Park.* She made only about £400 from these published novels, and she left almost all of that sum to relatives when she died.

Another factor in Austen's out-sider status was that she was that most dreaded figure, the horror of all good society, an old maid. Un-married women (but not unmarried men) were publicly chastised as un-productive, and at its best the role of an old maid was an awkward one.

Austen's last reason for isolation was her modesty. She refused to sign her name to any of her works. and none of her readers knew who she was until after her death. In her private circle, she deprecated both herself and her work; she called herself "the most unlearned and uninformed female who ever dared to be an authoress" and hid her work whenever anyone, including her own servants, walked near her desk.

# 17

**DEBORAH SAMPSON,** *born in Plympton, Massachusetts, 1760.* In 1782, a volunteer named Robert Shurtleff enlisted in the Revolu-tionary Army. Shurtleff was really an ex-teacher and indentured serv-ant named Deborah Sampson, but none of her fellow soldiers knew it. She served in a number of battles and was wounded twice, once by a saber and once by a musket ball. Both times, to avoid discovery, she cared for the wounds herself. She was undone, however, not by an in-jury but by a fever which landed her in an army hospital. There a surgeon discovered her secret and eventually informed the authorities, who gave her an honorable dis-charge. She married a man named Benjamin Gannett, settled down, and raised three children.

Toward the end of the eighteenth century, a biography of her life, *The Female Review or Memories of an American Young Lady,* was published. (Sampson may have written the book herself.) She occasionally appeared on stage in uniform to earn extra money. In 1792 she managed to get a pension from the state of Massachusetts, and in 1805 she was awarded a veteran's disability pension from Congress. She died in 1827, and a special act of Congress transferred her pension to her widower, as it might be transferred to a veteran's widow. The pension awarded to Gannett, however, was twice the size of that originally awarded to his wife.

# 18

**DESLE LA MANSENÉE,** *dies at 27 in Anjeux, France, 1529.* The case of Desle la Mansenée is a perfect example of how little it took to convict a woman for witchcraft in the sixteenth century. Mansenée didn't even fit the archetype of the witch—an old, ugly, woman, usually a widow, usually poor. Mansenée was married and young. Nevertheless, she was the subject of vague rumors, and when it came to prosecuting witches, rumor was everything. The claims against her were all unsubstantiated, of course. In some cases, the "testimony" was no more than that the speaker himself had heard rumors Mansenée was a witch.

Despite the weak evidence, however, Mansenée was interrogated several times. She proclaimed her innocence repeatedly, and no new evidence was uncovered. So she was tortured by squassation, in which a prisoner was tied with weights and dropped from a height. She confessed then to everything her accusers wanted to hear—that the devil had promised her riches if she turned from Jesus, that he gave her the power to alter the weather and poison cattle, that he made her attend sabbats, and that he made love to her. She was hanged—but oddly enough, not for being a witch. The official charges were murder, heresy, and renouncing the Catholic faith.

# 19

**MARY LIVERMORE,** *born Mary Ashton Rice in Boston, Massachusetts, 1820.* A biography of Mary Livermore would provide a wonderful cross-section of women's activities in the nineteenth century, since she was involved in almost every political cause open to a middle-class woman in her time, including abolition, woman suffrage, and temperance. She was briefly a schoolteacher—the only truly respectable paid employment available to women—before she married a Universalist minister, Daniel Livermore. After her marriage she wrote, lectured, edited two feminist publications, and led four major woman suffrage and temperance organizations. During the Civil War, she joined thousands of women and became a Union nurse. Throughout her life she maintained that woman should have access to higher education.

As a young woman, Livermore had taken a very interesting, though futile, step toward achieving full educational equality. She and five other young women had asked Harvard's president, Josiah Quincy,

MARY LIVERMORE: *American abolitionist, nurse, publisher, author, educator, temperance advocate, and feminist.*

LIBRARY OF CONGRESS

for acceptance to the university. They demonstrated their knowledge, and he admitted they were "very smart girls" and "unusually capable," but maintained that a woman's place was in the home. Enraged and frustrated, Livermore told Quincy: "I wish I were God, for the instant, that I might kill every woman from Eve down and let you have a masculine world all to yourselves and see how you would like that!"

# 20

**MAUD GONNE,** *born in London, England, 1865.* Maud Gonne was full of contradictions, and ironies, and she had an amazing ability to recover from strange situations. She spent her life agitating for radical causes, yet remained poular with conservatives. She was considered a scandalous woman, yet was the toast of Dublin society. And although she thought of herself as an activist and patriot, she is remembered today by many people primarily because a prominent poet fell in love with her. Her name will always be linked with that of William Butler Yeats, who loved her throughout his long life and immortalized her in his poetry.

Educated in France, Maud Gonne grew into a beautiful woman, six feet tall, slender, fair-complexioned, and bronze-haired. She learned quite early that she could be forgiven almost anything. She smoked cigarettes, had an affair with a French politician, and had two illegitimate children by him before returning to Dublin to become the object of every Irishman's fantasy and every reformer's admiration.

During her lifetime, Gonne did a little bit of everything. She was an actress, an activist, and a feminist who was often arrested and once spent six months in prison. She founded organizations, published suffrage newsletters, and worked on behalf of children, tenant farmers, political prisoners, and refugees. She was so dynamic and well known that "maudgonning" in Dublin slang meant to agitate flamboyantly for a cause.

Although Gonne was devoted to all of her causes, Irish nationalism meant the most to her. She spoke and lobbied on behlaf of Irish independence, edited a Parisian journal called *L'Irlande Libre,* and established a women's group, the Daughters of Ireland. In 1903 she went so far in her devotion to the movement as to marry a very conservative Irish patriot, John Mac-Bride. They were miserable together and soon separated, starting an avalanche of gossip. Gonne continued to fight for complete Irish independence, often with impromptu speeches. A tall, gaunt woman dressed in black, she haunted the city and spoke on street corners. She remained devoted to the cause until her death in 1953.

# 21

**ANZIA YEZIERSKA,** *dies at about 90 in Ontario, Canada, 1970.* When Yezierska died, she was just beginning to be famous—for the second time. For nearly forty years she had lived in obscurity, writing occasional essays, stories about aging, book reviews for *The New York Times,* and one autobiographical book, *Red Ribbon on a White Horse.* Yet in the 1920s she was very well known. She was the celebrated and successful author of novels and short stories about the lives of Jewish immigrants.

She came to the United States with her family in the early 1890s, and her name was changed to Hattie Mayer by immigration officials. Unlike many others, she did not submit passively to this treatment, and she legally changed her name back to the original Yezierska. Nor did she endure the tyranny of her autocratic father for long; she left home at seventeen and worked in sweatshops and laundries while she learned English. She went to night school and attended college lectures.

In 1916 she started writing short stories and then novels, most of them semi-autobiographical. Her topics were the difficulties of assimilation, the clash of old and new values, and, often, the special plight of Jewish women, which she described as follows in her best novel, *Bread Givers:* "Only if they cooked for men, and washed for men, and didn't nag and curse the men out of their homes; only if they let the men study the Torah in peace, then, maybe, they could push themselves into heaven with the men, to wait on them there."

Her writing brought Yezierska fame and financial success. Her new prosperity allowed her to move from New York's Lower East Side, but in leaving it she lost the source for her material. Starved for plots and new characters, her work deteriorated, and Yezierska began the long period of obscurity which would precede her rediscovery. As she wrote in *Red Ribbon on a White Horse,* she realized later that her move away from the immigrant community had left her "without a country, without a people . . . I could not write any more. I had gone too far away from life, and I did not know how to get back."

# 22

**TERESA CARREÑO,** *born in Caracas, Venezuela, 1853.* "The Valkyrie of the Piano" gave her first New York recital at age eight. At ten she gave a performance for Abraham Lincoln at the White House. By the turn of the century, she was famous throughout the Americas and Europe for her passionate, powerful, exaggerated style, her quick tempo, and her frequent pounding of the keys. "She was haughty, she was sloppy, she was incomparable," recalled one commentator.

Carreño's personal life was as flamboyant as her playing and as much discussed as her professional career. In fact, her personal and professional lives were inextricably linked, since she tended to marry fellow musicians, and since her marital problems were almost always caused by her husbands' demands that she sacrifice her career to nurture theirs. Her first husband, violinist Emile Sauret, encouraged her interest in string instruments, but soon their ego clashes led to a separation.

Before their divorce was final, Carreño began living with opera singer Giovanni Taglipietra. For years she managed an opera company which he had founded, and she dealt with his jealousy and financial irresponsibility until 1892, when she gave up and married her only professional rival, pianist and composer Eugène d'Albert. Their relationship was also stormy, and although d'Albert helped refine her technique, she left him in 1895. In 1902, she married Arturo Taglipietra, Giovanni's brother, and with him she was finally happy.

Carreño's career never suffered from her hectic personal life. She played piano on four continents to great acclaim. By the time she died in 1917, Carreño had achieved an immeasurable degree of fame and accomplishment. For generations after her death, performers were judged by the standards she had set.

# 23

**SARAH BREEDLOVE WALKER,** *born Sarah McWilliams in Delta, Louisiana, 1867.* Madame C. J. Walker, as she preferred to be called, rose from bitter poverty to become the world's first black woman millionaire. She accomplished this astounding feat after a dream in which a man told her "what to mix up for my hair." When she woke, she prepared the formula, which was intended to keep hair from falling out, and began a profitable mail-order business. Within a few years she had two thousand sales agents who toured the United States (and eventually the Caribbean and South America) for her, selling her oils,

TERESA CARREÑO: *The prodigy who performed for Abraham Lincoln and became the leading woman pianist, conductor, and composer of her day.*

LIBRARY OF CONGRESS

scalp treatments, hair thickeners, and hair straighteners to black women. Many have taken issue with the way she made her fortune, since the perceived need of hair straighteners contributed to black women's feelings of inadequacy, but the way she spent her money cannot be faulted. She supported the National Association for the Advancement of Colored People and endowed scholarships and old age homes for blacks. When she died in 1919 her will gave two-thirds of her estate to charity and mandated that her business always be run by a woman.

# 24 _____

**LORETA JANETA VELASQUEZ,** *born in Cuba in 1842, exact date unknown.* Velasquez seemed to carry a bizarre curse; almost everyone who married her died shortly thereafter. The daughter of a Spanish diplomat, she was educated at home and in a New Orleans convent, and in 1856, when she was fourteen, she married an American army officer. They had three children. In about 1860, the children died, and Velasquez went off to find her husband, who had joined the Confederate Army to fight in the Civil War. She enlisted, too, as Lieutenant Harry Buford, and she solved the problem of suspicious beardlessness by pasting on a beard and moustache.

She found her husband, but soon afterward he was killed in battle. She stayed with the army, serving as a scout and spy and fighting at the first Battle of Bull Run. After she was wounded, she left the army and married another army man, but he, too, was killed in action. She then went to Venezuela and married yet another military man, who died of a fever. Traveling to Nevada, she married again and was last seen heading west with her new husband to look for gold. Her autobiography, *The Woman in Battle*, was published in 1876, and it's an entertaining, if not thoroughly factual, account.

# 25 _____

LIBRARY OF CONGRESS

**CLARA BARTON,** *born Clarissa Harlowe Barton in North Oxford, Massachusetts, 1821.* Clara Barton began her remarkable career at fifteen, when she began teaching school for the starvation-level wages that women were then paid. Unlike most women in her position, however, she didn't consider her work a means of passing time until marriage; she educated herself beyond the levels of most of her peers and then started one of the first public schools in New Jersey.

CLARA BARTON: *A fitting birthday for this benevolent dispenser of charity.*

It was a tremendous success, but as soon as it was established, she was given a male superior. In protest, she resigned.

She worked briefly as a clerk in the United States Patent Office, making her one of the first women in the civil service, but when the Civil War broke out she left her position. The war provided Barton with the opportunity to be aggressive, assertive, and active, while still appearing feminine. She headed for the front and became a one-woman nursing operation, gathering and distributing supplies, nursing the wounded without pay, and establishing hospitals. She had power, authority, and plenty of work—and instead of being chastised for her behavior, she was made a national heroine, because she was simply doing what women were *supposed* to do by tending to the needs of men.

After the war, Barton traced missing soldiers, marked graves, and lectured. By 1868, however, she was bored, and she suffered a nervous breakdown. To cure herself, she took a trip to Europe and in

Switzerland she learned of the Red Cross. She worked for the organization during the Franco-Prussian War, and was so impressed with its operation that when she returned to the United States, she founded the American Red Cross. For the rest of her life, Barton served as its president. She continued to nurse the sick and wounded, and wrote many books and pamphlets. She also worked tirelessly for woman suffrage, making emotional appeals to Civil War veterans: "When you were weak and I was strong, I toiled for you. Now you are strong and I am weak. Because of my work for you I ask your aid. I ask the ballot for myself and my sex. As I stood by you, I pray you stand by me and mine."

# 26

**MARY SOMERVILLE,** *born Mary Fairfax in Jedburgh, Scotland, 1780.* Mary Somerville was raised to sew and keep household accounts, and she was destined for a life of housework. But one day in her youth she glimpsed some algebraic symbols on a page in a magazine and her interest in mathematics and science was begun. She bought geometry and algebra texts and taught herself at night by candlelight after she'd finished her housework. Her mother discovered her and took her candles away, but Somerville spent long hours working problems in her head. Eventually, her father was told of his daughter's eccentricities and Somerville overheard him say to her mother, "We must put a stop to this, or we shall have Mary in a straight jacket one of these days."

But her interest in science did not diminish. She married in 1804, and during her brief marriage her husband opposed the continuance of her education. He died in 1807 and then, as a widow, Somerville finally gained the independence she desired. She began to correspond

with the editor of a mathematical journal and, after she won a silver medal for solving one of the magazine's contest problems, he sent her a reading list.

Somerville immediately bought herself a library of texts and began on the work which secured her a sound reputation. She wrote countless treatises, became the first female member of the Royal Astronomical Society, and received a £300 government pension for her work. She later wrote: "I was considered eccentric and foolish, and my conduct was highly disapproved of by many, especially by some members of my own family. They expected me to entertain and keep a gay house for them, and in that they were disappointed."

She remarried, this time choosing William Somerville, who encouraged her studies. She had several children with him and was quite happy, and generations of feminsts pointed to her as proof that a woman could be both a good scientist and a good wife and mother.

# 27

**MARLENE DIETRICH,** *born Maria Magdalene Dietrich in Berlin, Germany, 1901.* Today, it's hard to imagine what it would take to get a movie poster banned. In Paris in the 1930s, all it took was Marlene Dietrich's legs. Apparently, rush-hour commuters took so long staring at her legs that traffic was severely impeded.

Maybe that's not really surprising. After all, Dietrich was for years the embodiment of cool cinematic sexuality. Her habit of wearing slacks shocked the American public, although the strong hints of bisexuality in her movies, especially in *Blonde Venus* and *Morocco,* eluded most viewers. Ernest Hemingway decided that "if she had nothing but her voice, she could break your heart with it." Maurice Chevalier, Fritz Lang, Josef von Sternberg, James Stewart, Douglas Fairbanks, Jr., John Wayne, Yul Brynner, and Adolf Hitler were all said to be in love with her. As she herself said, "Adolf Hitler wanted me to be his mistress. I turned him down. Maybe I should have gone to him. I might have saved the lives of six million Jews."

Dietrich had a double motivation to display her hatred of the Third Reich—the obvious ethical motive, and the need to save her career. As a German in Hollywood during World War II, she was especially subject to suspicion, even though there was no need for it, so she became an American citizen, performed for American troops, and refused to perform in Germany. As a result, her films were banned by Hitler, but she was not without influence in Germany and she used it to save her sister from the Bergen-Belsen concentration camp. She was decorated by the United States and France for her war work, but by that time her career was effectively over—not because she was a German, but because her "type," the blonde ice goddess, had gone out of style. And, by the standards that Hollywood set for its leading ladies, she was already over the hill.

MARLENE DIETRICH: *Kenneth Tynan wrote that "she has sex, but no particular gender. Her masculinity appeals to women, and her sexuality to men."*

# 28

**JOANNA SOUTHCOTT,** *dies at 64 in London, England, 1814.* Today's evangelists are amateurs compared with Joanna Southcott, who managed to convince her one hundred thousand followers that she was carrying the child of God. She was the daughter of a farming family, and for most of her life she was a servant. She took a number of

lovers but avoided marriage, and her insistence that she heard voices and had visions convinced some that she was a witch and others that she was a living talisman against witchcraft. Eventually she advanced to prophesying about crops and rainfall, and when her predictions came true, followers gathered.

A Methodist herself, Southcott hoped for authentication of her "miracles"' from a nearby convocation of her coreligionists, but she was met instead with hostility and suspicion. So she formed her own religion with herself as its leader; her followers were known as Southcottians. Over a ten-year period, Southcott wrote fifty-four books. She also began to issue seals—passages written, signed, and sealed by Southcott, ostensibly to guarantee an individual's entrance into heaven, although they were believed to have other, more worldly benefits as well. Among these were long life or eternal life and protection from Napoleon should England be invaded.

Southcott issued thousands of these seals, but that wasn't enough to meet the demand. Soon followers were buying the seals from each other for exorbitant sums, and the movement began to disintegrate in the wake of the resulting scandal. Desperate, Southcott announced that, at the age of sixty-three, she was pregnant with the child of God. Her voices, she said, had commanded her to call the child Shiloh and promised he would be a great king who would defeat the powers of darkness.

This announcement lost Southcott more followers, but she quickly gained ample replacements. When seventeen doctors verified her pregnancy, her books began selling wildly, newspapers provided updates on her condition, songs were written about her, and toy dolls of Shiloh were sold in miniature cradles. Despite all the excitement, nothing ever happened. Southcott died on this day in 1814, supposedly fourteen months pregnant. An autopsy revealed she had nothing more than an inflammation of the bowels.

# 29

**ELIZABETH of Russia,** *born Elizaveta Petrovna in the Palace of Kolomenskoe, Muscovy, Russia, 1709.* Elizabeth was an illegitimate child. Her father, Peter the Great, married her mother when Elizabeth was two. That fact alone made Elizabeth an unlikely candidate for the Russian throne. Her own disposition made her even less eligible. She was pefectly content to let others rule, and she sat quietly through the reigns of her father, her mother, and her cousin. Only after her cousin's reign, when the infant Ivan VI and his regent and mother Anna Leopoldovna took power, did Elizabeth claim her rights—and then she did so because her life was in jeopardy.

In 1741, Ivan VI was the nominal power in Russia. If Anna had had any strength, she would have been the most powerful figure in Russia. But she was ruled in turn by two German advisers who were hated by almost everyone but herself. In 1741 these advisers tried to have Elizabeth arrested. Someone warned her, and, after she prayed for guidance, she found some loyal guards, marched on the palace, and took the throne in one night without bloodshed. She swore on the spot never to condemn anyone to death and promised to put power back in the hands of Russians.

Unfortunately, she committed the same error as Anna. True, her advisers were Russians rather than Germans, and they were better

liked, but power really rested in their hands rather than Elizabeth's. She made a few reforms and encouraged the arts, but she was primarily concerned with maintaining the staus quo. Her chief strength was in foreign policy, and she conducted successful military campaigns and made valuable alliances, but after she died in 1769 her heir and nephew, Peter III, dissolved all of her alliances.

In the end, she became known not for her achievements but for her eccentricities. She gave weekly masquerade balls at which the men dressed as women and the women as men. She had a fear of the dark so great that she put off going to bed as long as possible and could only fall asleep with her female attendants gathered around her, stroking her legs to calm her.

Elizabeth was a passionate woman, but she never married—at least not publicly. In her youth she tried to marry for love, but her fiancé died before the wedding. As empress, she chose as her lover a poor singer, Alexis Razumovsky, who quickly earned the nickname "the night-time emperor." She may have married him secretly, and she always took care of him, but in later years she took another lover, poor and young as Alexis had been, but this time of noble birth. Such sexual behavior was stigmatized by her contemporaries because Elizabeth was an *empress,* not an *emperor.*

# 30

**ANGELA BURDETT-COUTTS,** *dies at 92 in London, England, 1906.* Burdett-Coutts had the extraordinary fortune to be the favorite grandchild of a very, very wealthy woman, and to inherit, at twenty-three, everything her grandmother owned. Normally, if a nice young Victorian Englishwoman inherited a lot of money, she'd place its management in the hands of a (male) financial expert and then set out to find a husband. Not so in Burdett-Coutts's case. She took care of her own money and did it very well, and although she was hounded by every fortune hunter in England, including the eighty-year-old Duke of Wellington, she married no one.

Instead, she gave her money away. She patronized the arts, built churches, endowed bishoprics, bought new bells for St. Paul's Cathedral, gave money to temperance organizations, and supported soup kitchens, schools, scientific work, vocational education, missionary work, and Henry Morton Stanley's expeditions to Africa. Nicknamed "the Queen of the Poor," she helped the needy find housing and work. She sent food to famine-ravaged Ireland. She sent aid to Turkish refugees during the Russo-Turkish War.

One of her favorite projects was a home for homeless young women and prostitutes, where no less a personage than Charles Dickens tried to make the young ladies "patient, gentle, perservering, and good-tempered." Dickens adored Burdett-Coutts and said, "She is a most excellent creature, and I have a most perfect affection and respect for her." She was, however, gifted with a rather distant breed of compassion. When Dickens left his wife for his mistress, he was immediately fired from his post. Burdett-Coutts never associated with the girls she tried to help; she was afraid of moral contamination if she came too near them.

Burdett-Coutts' efforts (and, no doubt, her strict morality) earned her the title of baroness. She was thus the first woman ever raised to the peerage for her own accomplishments. She kept enough of her money to become one of the most celebrated hostesses of her day. And at sixty-seven, she finally married. Her husband was her twenty-seven-year-old secretary, who, upon marriage, took the name Burdett-Coutts by special permission of Queen Victoria. He lived happily with Angela for many years, and together they worked on charitable projects in Turkey and Africa. By the time she died in 1906, Burdett-Coutts had given away nearly three million pounds.

LIBRARY OF CONGRESS

ANGELA BURDETT-COUTTS: *The generous but condescending "Queen of the Poor."*

# 31

**ELIZABETH ARDEN,** *born Florence Nightingale Graham in Woodbridge, Ontario, Canada, probably in 1878.* Whatever you may think of the *way* in which Elizabeth Arden made her fortune, there's no denying she was a skillful entrepreneur. She always dressed in pink and she combined a demure image with an aggressive business style, a ruthlessly competitive streak, a strong desire for power, and a shrewd knowledge of women's insecurities.

Between 1920 and 1940, she revolutionized the cosmetics industry. She was helped in this task by her chief rival, Helena Rubinstein, whose name she refused to speak. Arden simply called her "that woman."

When Arden entered the cosmetics business in the early 1900s, few women wore any makeup at all. By the time she died in 1966, she had created entirely new markets—for mascara, eye shadow, and lipstick—and taken a sizeable chunk of the

old markets for skin creams, clothing, and hairdressing. Her business grew even during the Depression, branching into salons, health resorts, and a radio show and pulling in six million dollars a year, and until the day she died she held every share of stock. Her insistence upon keeping full control of her company irritated her first husband, Thomas Jenkins Lewis, who divorced her in 1934 and avenged himself by going to work for Helena Rubinstein.

# BIBLIOGRAPHY

A complete listing of sources used in the preparation of this book would take several pages, so only the most important are listed below as suggestions for further reading.

Abir-am, Anna G., and Dorinda Outram, eds., *Uneasy Careers and Intimate Lives: Women and Science 1789-1979.* New Brunswick, N.J.: Rutgers University Press, 1987.

Alic, Margaret. *Hypatia's Heritage.* London: The Women's Press, 1986.

Balsdon, J. P. V. D. *Roman Women: Their History and Habits.* London: The Bodley Head, 1962.

Bingham, June. "Before the Colors Fade: Alice Roosevelt Longworth," *American Heritage.* February 1969 (Vol. 20, No. 2). pp. 42-43, 73-77.

Blackburne, E. Owens. *Illustrious Irishwomen.* London: Tinsley Brothers, 1877.

Blashfield, Jean F., *Hellraisers, Heroines and Holy Women: Women's Most Remarkable Contributions to History.* New York: St. Martin's Press, 1981.

Boase, Frederic. *Modern English Biography.* New York: Barnes & Noble, 1965.

Boller, Paul F., Jr., and Ronald L. Davis. *Hollywood Anecdotes.* New York: William Morrow and Company, Inc., 1987.

Boorman, Howard L., ed. *Biographical Dictionary of Republican China.* New York: Columbia University Press, 1968.

Boulding, Elise. *The Underside of History: A View of Women Through Time.* Boulder, Colorado: Westview Press, 1976.

Boyd, Nancy. *Three Victorian Women Who Changed Their World.* New York: Oxford University Press, 1982.

Brewer Annie. *Biography Almanac.* Detroit: Gale Research Co./Book Tower, 1981.

Cary, M., and H. H. Scullard. *A History of Rome Down to the Reign of Constantine.* 3rd ed. New York: St. Martin's Press, 1975.

Cheney, Lynne Vincent. "Mrs. Frank Leslie's Illustrated Newspaper." *American Heritage.* Oct. 1975 (Vol. 26, No. 6). pp. 42-48, 90-91.

Clark, Judith Freeman. *Almanac of American Women in the 20th Century.* New York: Prentice Hall Press, 1987.

Clark, Leta W. *Women Women Women: Quips, Quotes, and Commentary.* New York: Drake Publishers Inc., 1977.

Cohen-Stratyner, Barbara Naomi. *Biographical Dictionary of Dance.* New York: Schirmer Books, 1982.

Cott, Nancy F., and Elizabeth H. Pleck, eds. *A Heritage of Her Own.* New York: Simon and Schuster, 1979.

Crawford, Anne, ed., *et al. The Europa Biographical Dictionary of British Women.* Detroit: Gale Research Co./Book Tower, 1983.

Davis, Kenneth S. "The Story of the Pill." *American Heritage.* Aug/Sept 1978 (Vol. 29, No. 5). pp. 80-90.

Debus, Allen G., ed. *World Who's Who in Science.* Chicago: Marquis, 1968.

Deiss, Joseph Jay. "Men, Women, and Margaret Fuller." *American Heritage.* August 1972 (Vol. 23, No. 5). pp. 42-47, 94-97.

DuBois, Ellen Carol. *Feminism and Suffrage.* Ithaca, New York: Cornell University Press, 1978.

Evans, Hilary. *Harlots, Whores, and Hookers: A History of Prostitution.* New York: Taplinger Publishing Company, 1979.

Fuchs, Lawrence H. "The Senator and the Lady." *American Heritage.* Oct. 1974 (Vol. 25, No. 6). pp. 57-61, 81-83.

Gallagher, Robert S. "I Was Arrested, Of Course . . ." *American Heritage.* Feb. 1974 (Vol. 25, No. 2). pp. 16-24, 92-94.

Giddings, Paula. *When and Where I Enter.* New York: Bantam Books, 1984.

Gilbert, Sandra, and Susan Gubar, eds. *The Norton Anthology of Literature by Women.* New York: W. W. Norton & Company, 1985.

Gridley, Marion E. *American Indian Women.* New York: Hawthorn Books, Inc., 1974.

Harris, Ann Sutherland. *Women Artists: 1550-1950.* New York: Alfred A. Knopf, 1976.

Henderson, James D., and Linda Roddy Henderson. *Ten Notable Women of Latin America.* Chicago: Nelson-Hall, 1978.

Hudson, M. E., and Mary Clark. *Crown of a Thousand Years.* New York: Crown Publishers, Inc., 1978.

Hume, Ruth. "Selling the Swedish Nightingale: Jenny Lind and P. T. Barnum." *American Heritage.* Oct. 1977 (Vol. 28, No. 6). pp. 98-107.

James, Edward T. *Notable American Women.* Cambridge, Massachusets: The Belknap Press of the Harvard University Press, 1971.

Kendall, Elaine. "Founders Five." *American Heritage.* Feb. 1975 (Vol. 26, No. 2). pp. 33-48.

Kittredge, George Lyman. *Witchcraft in Old and New England.* New York: Russell & Russell, 1929.

Kort, Michelle. *"Ms., Conversation."* *Ms.* Feb. 1988, pp. 58-62.

Lewytzkyj, Boris, ed. *Who's Who in the Soviet Union.* Munich: K. G. Saur, 1984.

Lipschutz, Mark R., and R. Kent Rasmussen. *Dictionary of American Historical Biography.* Chicago: Aldine, 1978.

Lowe, David. "Mary Cassatt." *American Heritage.* Dec. 1973 (Vol. 25, No. 1). pp. 10-21, 96-100.

Mackenzie, Midge. *Shoulder to Shoulder.* New York: Alfred A. Knopf, 1975.

McHenry, Robert, ed. *Liberty's Women.* Springfield, Massachusetts: G. & C. Merriam Company, 1980.

Minai, Naila. *Women in Islam.* New York: Seaview Books, 1981.

Moffat, Mary Jane, and Charlotte Painter, eds. *Revelations: Diaries of Women.* New York: Vintage Books, 1975.

Moolman, Valerie. *Women Aloft.* Alexandria, Virginia: Time-Life Books, 1981.

Munsterberg, Hugo. *A History of Women Artists.* New York: Clarkson N. Potter, 1975.

Murray, Janet Horowitz. *Strong-Minded Women and Other Lost Voices from Nineteenth-Century England.* New York: Pantheon Books, 1982.

Olds, Elizabeth Fagg. *Women of the Four Winds.* Boston: Houghton Mifflin Company, 1985.

Pepper, Frank S. *The Wit and Wisdom of the 20th Century.* New York: Peter Bedrick Books, 1987.

Riemer, Eleanor S., and John C. Fort, eds. *European Women: A Documentary History 1789-1945.* New York: Schocken, 1980.

Robbins, Russell Hope. *The Enclcylopedia of Witchcraft and Demonology.* New York: Crown Publishers, Inc., 1959.

Rose, Al. *Storyville, New Orleans.* University of Alabama Press, 1974.

Sicherman, Barbara, *et al.,* eds. *Notable American Women: The Modern Period.* Cambridge, Massachusetts: The Belknap Press of the Harvard University Press, 1980.

Smith-Rosenberg, Carroll. *Disorderly Conduct.* New York: Oxford University Press, 1985.

Sweetman, David. *Women Leaders in African History.* London: Heinemann, 1984.

Uglo, Jennifer, ed. *The International Dictionary of Women's Biography.* New York: Continuum, 1985.

Van Donzel, E., *et al. The Encyclopedia of Islam.* Leiden; E. J. Brill, 1978.

Weiser, Marjorie P. K., and Jean S. Arbeiter. *Womanlist.* New York: Atheneum, 1981.

Wieczynski, Joseph L., ed. *The Modern Encyclopedia of Russian and Soviet History.* Gulf Breeze, Florida: Academic International Press, 1981.

Woloch, Nancy. *Women and the American Experience.* New York: Alfred A. Knopf, 1984.

# INDEX OF WOMEN PROFILED